Palgrave Studies in Urban Anthropology

Series editors
Italo Pardo
School of Anthropology and Conservation
University of Kent
Canterbury, Kent, United Kingdom

Giuliana B. Prato
School of Anthropology and Conservation
University of Kent
Canterbury, United Kingdom

Half of humanity lives in towns and cities and that proportion is expected to increase in the coming decades. Society, both Western and non-Western, is fast becoming urban and mega-urban as existing cities and a growing number of smaller towns are set on a path of demographic and spatial expansion. Given the disciplinary commitment to an empirically-based analysis, anthropology has a unique contribution to make to our understanding of our evolving urban world. It is in such a belief that we have established the Palgrave Studies in Urban Anthropology series. In the awareness of the unique contribution that ethnography offers for a better theoretical and practical grasp of our rapidly changing and increasingly complex cities, the series will seek high-quality contributions from anthropologists and other social scientists, such as geographers, political scientists, sociologists and others, engaged in empirical research in diverse ethnographic settings. Proposed topics should set the agenda concerning new debates and chart new theoretical directions, encouraging reflection on the significance of the anthropological paradigm in urban research and its centrality to mainstream academic debates and to society more broadly. The series aims to promote critical scholarship in international anthropology. Volumes published in the series should address theoretical and methodological issues, showing the relevance of ethnographic research in understanding the socio-cultural, demographic, economic and geopolitical changes of contemporary society.

More information about this series at
http://www.palgrave.com/series/14573

İlay Romain Örs

Diaspora of the City

Stories of Cosmopolitanism from
Istanbul and Athens

İlay Romain Örs
Istanbul Bilgi University
Istanbul, Turkey

Palgrave Studies in Urban Anthropology
ISBN 978-1-137-55485-7 (hardcover)   ISBN 978-1-137-55486-4 (eBook)
ISBN 978-1-349-71706-4 (softcover)
https://doi.org/10.1057/978-1-137-55486-4

Library of Congress Control Number: 2017955050

© The Editor(s) (if applicable) and The Author(s) 2018, First softcover printing 2021
This work is subject to copyright. All rights are solely and exclusively licensed by the Publisher, whether the whole or part of the material is concerned, specifically the rights of translation, reprinting, reuse of illustrations, recitation, broadcasting, reproduction on microfilms or in any other physical way, and transmission or information storage and retrieval, electronic adaptation, computer software, or by similar or dissimilar methodology now known or hereafter developed.
The use of general descriptive names, registered names, trademarks, service marks, etc. in this publication does not imply, even in the absence of a specific statement, that such names are exempt from the relevant protective laws and regulations and therefore free for general use.
The publisher, the authors and the editors are safe to assume that the advice and information in this book are believed to be true and accurate at the date of publication. Neither the publisher nor the authors or the editors give a warranty, express or implied, with respect to the material contained herein or for any errors or omissions that may have been made. The publisher remains neutral with regard to jurisdictional claims in published maps and institutional affiliations.

Cover design by Samantha Johnson

Printed on acid-free paper

This Palgrave Macmillan imprint is published by Springer Nature
The registered company is Nature America Inc.
The registered company address is: 1 New York Plaza, New York, NY 10004, U.S.A.

I dedicate this book to the two best stories in my life, Alex and Denis.

Prologue

Parallel Histories, Broken Pasts

Imagine the city through the eyes of its founder. Imagine your name to be Byzas: you are a Greek merchant looking for a convenient stop for your ships and caravans en route between Ionia and Thrace. You find a spot in the middle of the passage, taking the warm waters of the Mediterranean first to the Sea of Propontida, famous for the white marbles of its small islands, through a narrow but wide-enough strait leading to the Sea of Pontus. Wide enough for ships to pass, narrow enough to cross from land. You become amazed by its beauty: little hills surrounded with three different masses of water that mingle but not mix. You pick a lovely small peninsula for your colony overlooking that daily dance of land and sea, north and south, east and west, the sea and the Bosphorus. The Bosphorus—the name rings a bell: you remember it from mythology, as the passage of the cow, created when Hera turned herself into a fly to chase her husband Zeus' beautiful lover Io, whom she had made a cow. A story of beauty and jealousy. You know that, when you create your colony here in this beautiful place, the world will turn as jealous as the goddess and try to take it away from you. Knowing that your time there will end, but your city will be eternal, you call it by your own name, Byzantion.

> **680–658 BC**
> Foundation of Byzantium by Byzas as a Greek city-state
>
> **324–330 AD**
> Foundation of Constantinople "Nova Roma Constantino-politana" by Constantine the Great
>
> **356**
> Roman Empire splits; Constantinople becomes the capital of Eastern Rome
>
> **392**
> Christian Orthodoxy is accepted as the official religion

Imagine the city through the eyes of the beholder. Imagine your name to be Constantine, Emperor of the Roman Empire. Things are not going well in Rome; you are looking for another center from which you will rule the eastern wing of the empire. You consider revitalizing Troy, the once prominent ancient city along the western coast of Asia Minor, but you sacrifice the holy appeal of the mythological past for a new land where you can build your own glorious future. You pick the little but thriving colony called Byzantion, where seas and continents meet each other. You build your New Rome on the peninsula with seven hills; it takes you seven years until its grandeur matches its beauty, to make it worthy of an imperial capital. You opt for eternity like your predecessor; you call your city after your own name: Constantinople.

Imagine the city becoming the capital of the first state to adopt Christianity as the official religion. Imagine being an Emperor, of what came later to be known as Byzantium after the original name of its capital, trying to impress not only Rome but also God through your city. You crown the city with monuments chosen from all around the world, but you add your jewels in the form of churches such as no one has encountered before. You build your empire large and strong like your greatest work, Hagia Sophia; you gain the secret admiration but obvious envy of the world: they come to see it, they come to raid it, they come to live in it—you end up with neighboring colonies of the Italian city states, living with North Africans, Macedonians, Mesopotamians, Persians, Arabs under and against your rule, threatening yet coexisting, mingling but not mixing, like the waters surrounding your city. Imagine when one of the threats becomes too big to be ignored, by the Muslims who are too different to be tolerated, so that the now crumbled but turned-Christian Europe unites in arms to wage a series of wars against those threatening your religion and your empire. Imagine the disappointment when years later these Latin armies stop to rest on their way back from the forth of their crusades, staying for over five decades, plundering your beautiful city of all its riches that you have worked so hard to build. Imagine the double disappointment when the biggest danger of all arrives outside your great walls, and when you call out for help from your coreligionist Europeans, none comes to save the city that they so admired and so plundered two and a half centuries ago. Imagine not being able to endure one of the toughest raids that history has ever seen; imagine Constantinople falling.

Imagine the city through the eyes of the conqueror. Your name is Mehmet, after your prophet Mohammed, who said once that it would be the greatest victory for Islam to take over Constantinople. Imagine you are only 21 years old, already ruling over a state that stretches from Crimea to Kosovo, having already won over some of the greatest empires, including the Byzantine that reigned over one and a half millennia in the region. When it is time to name your own empire, imagine the confidence in entertaining the idea of calling yourself the Emperor of Rome, but then deciding on the name of your forefathers, to carve the word Ottoman in history for more than four centuries to come.

1071

The defeat of the Byzantine army by the Seljuk Turkish state at Manzigert; beginning of Turkish advancement in Asia Minor

1204–1261

Sack of Constantinople by the Latin armies of the Fourth Crusade; major looting of the city

1453

Fall of Constantinople and the end of the Byzantine Empire; Conquest of Istanbul, new capital of the Ottoman Empire

1454

Sultan Mehmed II recognizes the Patriarch of Constantinople as leader of the Rum *millet*

1599

The Ecumenical Patriarchate moves to Fanar on the Golden Horn

---

Imagine the city, through the eyes of the city-dweller. You are a Christian Orthodox Roman citizen; there are many around you, but you are one of the ruling majority. You speak Greek; you call yourself Romios, after Romeos, meaning Roman. You live in the city that is the capital of your empire, the center of your religion, with your Ecumenical Patriarchate, reigning over the entire Eastern Church. Just as you think that your empire rules all over the civilized world, your city suddenly gets sacked by the people of another order, another belief. You fear for your people's safety, you fear for your city's integrity, you fear for your religion's continuity. You hear that the Sultan, who entered the city mounted on his white horse, summoned the Patriarch, along with the other religious leaders, to his tent. You stop your advance mourning when you hear that they were set free after pledging to be loyal to the Sultan and to make sure that their people would do the same. You are relieved to hear that the Patriarch is now in charge of not only the religious but also the administrative, legal, and social affairs of the Orthodox community. Your Patriarch is an Ethnarch; your community is millet-i Rum.

Imagine the city, again as a Rum, few centuries later, through the eyes of its elite. You are a Fanariot, named after the neighborhood where the Patriarchate is now located. You are not only close to the Orthodox religious order, you are also high up in the ranks of the Ottoman imperial order. Sultans and viziers trust you to translate their secret state documents, they let you run regions far from the center, they confide in you their financial troubles and allow you to solve them, they make you represent the Empire abroad, they bestow upon you titles given to nobody else; you can be the Dragoman of the Porte, Voyvoda of Moldavia, Governor of Samos, Ambassador to Great Britain, making you the closest to nobility in an empire where there is no aristocratic tradition. Imagine the embarrassment when some among you use their power to start up a rebellion, even though they were told not to do so by the Patriarch on threat of excommunication. Imagine the trembling when the Ottomans punish the Patriarch when the event takes place nonetheless, by hanging him outside the door of his own patriarchal church, alongside fellow families of Fanariots, who were the respected elites of Ottoman society for centuries. Realize the connection of all this with what was going on in the Peloponnese, where mainland Greeks engaged in a rebellion that eventually led to the independence of the Greek state, first among the many national movements to follow. Watch the European Powers embrace the new nation as Ancient Greece reborn, not acknowledging the historical legacy that took place in the City. Wonder why.

> **1821**
> Revolt in Moldavia-Wallachia led by Filiki Eteria, suppressed by the Ottomans;
> Rebellion in Morea evolves into national struggle and leads to Greek independence
>
> **1838**
> Commercial Treaty signed with Great Britain
>
> **1839**
> The Edict of Reorganization (Tanzimat) constitutes equal rights between Ottoman subjects;
> period of Ottoman modernization
>
> **1840**
> Establishment of local administrative councils for the representation of non-Muslims
>
> **1856**
> The Edict of Reform (Islahat) confirms and extends the Tanzimat;
> increased level of involvement of non-Muslim communities in governmental posts
>
> **1876**
> The first Ottoman Constitution and the first constitutional monarchy (Meşrutiyet)
>
> **1878**
> The Congress of Berlin grants further rights to non-Muslim Ottomans
>
> **1908**
> The second Ottoman constitutional monarchy (Meşrutiyet); Young Turk Revolution

Imagine the city, at the turn of the last century. You are an Ottoman Rum merchant, specializing in shipping trade with the British. Business is good ever since capital started flowing in the city following the signing of the British Trade Union in 1838. There are wars in action all over the region, bringing not only tradesmen and diplomats but also exiles and refugees to the city. You live in Pera, the new quarter located across the old peninsula of Constantinople, a little further from Galata, which was built by the Genoese. This is the cosmopolitan center of fashion, modernity, and high culture in the city. All European nations have their consulates, branches of their companies, their own post offices, churches, synagogues, schools, foundations, community centers, along with luxury hotels, operas, ballrooms, patisseries, cafés, florists, and boutiques that cater to a Westernized taste. Walk down the Grand Rue du Pera, the main street cut through with a tramway, hearing all the languages of Babel from the well-dressed, well-mannered, civilized multicultural crowd of visitors and Istanbulites, residents and foreigners, all existing side by side, like the seas of the city, mingling but not mixing. Imagine the institutionalization of this social order by a group of Young Turks from Salonika taking over the Ottoman rule with a silent revolution, writing a constitution to guarantee the equal rights of all the religious communities of the millet, thereby planting the seeds of their own individual struggle for liberation for an independent Turkish nation.

Imagine the city through the eyes of a Rum under the new Turkish Republic. It is the late 1930s. You still control most of the economy in Istanbul. Business is going well, you are only competing with the Jews and the Armenians, the two other non-Muslim communities officially recognized as minorities under the Treaty of Lausanne. It is rather calm after the signing of a friendship treaty between the two leaders of Greece and Turkey, Venizelos and Atatürk. Imagine working hard to secure your wealth and investing it in a house in Mega Revma (now Arnavutköy), in a shop in Pera (now Beyoğlu), and in your summer house on the island of Halki (now Heybeli), only a half-hour boat ride outside the city. You have a good quality of life, not only economically but also socially and culturally: your daughter goes to Zappeion, your son to Zografeion, two eminent schools built by the generous funds of the wealthy Rum bankers whose names they bear. You hope they will become medical doctors like their uncles, taking care of their grandmother, who is spending her last years in the Baloukli hospital and nursing home with her Rum friends. You imagine reading their names in the Greek newspapers published in the city, making you as proud as their mother, who is a famous poet and writer. Think of the possibility of the Rum element flourishing in the new Republic, resembling the ideal of the Organization of Constantinople a few decades ago, of creating a Hellenic–Ottoman Empire, which now can be realized within a democratic state. Think what your future in the City might offer; think of an Istanbulite cosmopolitan utopia.

1999
Major earthquake in Turkey followed by another in Greece; period of rapprochement; Greece lifts its veto over Turkey's EU candidacy

2005
Turkey starts talks for EU accession

2008
Partial return of properties seized from minorities in Turkey

Imagine the city of Istanbul through the eyes of its current residents. You are a Muslim Turk growing up in the aftermath of the military coup of 1980, during the period of depoliticization, economic opening, inflation, and mass migration. Imagine the city growing with the speed of light at the same time as its fabric is being destroyed in the darkness of silence. As forests are wiped out for villas and skyscrapers, neighborhoods are being demolished for the passing of new highways; witness the development of a nostalgia for an Istanbul lost. Realize that not only have local Istanbulites become a minority, but also that the local minorities have ceased to reside in Istanbul. Imagine the city as a cosmopolitan center, a meeting place of language groups, ethnicities, religions, cultural orientations. As you turn your face to your past, imagine this becoming a way for the future: imagine recreating an Istanbul with the Rum, the Armenian, the Jew, the Latin, the Ottoman, the Byzantine, the cosmopolitan becoming ours once more. Think of an Istanbulite cosmopolitan nostalgia.

> IMAGINE ASKING YOURSELF:
>
> WHEN THEY WERE LIVING TOGETHER HAPPILY FOR SO LONG, HOW DID THE GREEKS AND TURKS BECOME ENEMIES ALL OF A SUDDEN;
>
> REALLY, WHY DID THE *GREEKS LEAVE* ISTANBUL?

Flashback to the turn of the last century: you are a Rum living in Istanbul all over again in your memory. Imagine reading the local Greek newspaper one day, say in 1912, reporting on the war in the Balkans, where the Ottoman lands in Europe fall prey to the nationalistic demands of Bulgaria, Serbia, and Greece. Imagine the dissolution of the imperial order that defined you for generations as an Ottoman Rum, and the success of the small kingdom of Greece, a nation that takes your religion and your language at the heart of its organization. Imagine the two entities fighting against each other, as they did several times before, during, and after World War I. In the early 1920s, when the Greek army starts advancing into the Western lands of Asia Minor, to claim its share from the Treaty of Sèvres, imagine them being pushed back by an army of national struggle for liberating Turkey, an offspring of the Young Turks. Imagine the catastrophe when hundreds of thousands rush toward the Aegean Sea, fleeing the advancing Turkish troops, the fire, and the destruction chasing them. It is September 1922. Imagine staying behind with those celebrating this tragedy as victory, a victory that calls the truce, liberates Asia Minor, establishes Turkey as an independent state and, one year later, as a Republic, with Mustafa Kemal as its founder.

1912
First Balkan War waged by Greece, Bulgaria, Serbia, and Montenegro against the Ottomans

1914
First World War breaks out; annexation of Cyprus by Great Britain

1915
Battles of WWI alongside bloody clashes and civil strife rage in Ottoman lands; additional acts of deportation and massacre result in the death of millions of Anatolians, amounting to the near annihiliation of Armenians

1918
Mudros Armistice ends World War I;
Allied occupation of Istanbul

1919
Paris Peace Conference designates the regions of the Ottoman Empire to be occupied;
Greek troops land in Smyrna and advance through Western Asia Minor;
beginning of the Turkish National Struggle in Asia Minor

1920
First Turkish National Assembly founded in Ankara;
Treaty of Sevres signed between the Allies and the Ottomans, not ratified by Ankara

1922
Greek army is defeated by the Turkish Liberation forces who capture all of Asia Minor;
the Great Catastrophe and the burning of Smyrna;
abolition of the Ottoman government and the Sultanate;
departure of leading Ottoman Christians from Istanbul

As a prelude to the birth of the new nation, imagine hearing that a Treaty was signed in Lausanne that dictated your old nation to leave the country. Disheartening and disappointing as it may sound, imagine that they would take more than a million people away from the lands they plowed, the wine they grew, the water they drank, the fruit they ate, the neighbors they loved, the air they inhaled for as long as they knew themselves and their ancestors to have been there, to be tucked in a ship toward a land they not know. Imagine sitting inside a tent in Greece months later with the thin clothes you were wearing when you were torn away from home, thinking whether the jam you made that day was still warm or whether the neighbors forgot to feed the cat you left behind. Imagine you are a Rum still in Istanbul, unable to feel relieved that these things are not happening to you, that you are held exempt from the forced exchange of population between Greece and Turkey.

Imagine the changes that take place in a lifetime to be beyond your imagination. Witness an Empire fade away, watch a new nation come into being, experience the implementation of new constitutions, institutions, laws, manners, customs. Watch the highly visible transformation in the calendar, alphabet, headgear, clothing, and in every other aspect of daily life. You will not run into your priest on the street wearing black anymore; nor will you come across an imam in his garb. It is for time to show if this version of a secularist republic will allow more freedom for the minority communities than they enjoyed under the multireligious theocracy that the Ottomans have been. Wait in agony or in excitement; prepare for the gray days ahead.

PROLOGUE xvii

> **1923**
> Treaty of Lausanne fixes the boundaries between Greece and Turkey;
> forced exchange of populations between Greece and Turkey;
> Allied forces leave Istanbul;
> declaration of the Turkish Republic
>
> **1924**
> Greece becomes a republic, followed by a series of military coups;
> Caliphate abolished by the Turkish parliament
>
> **1926**
> Civil Code accepted in Turkey, along with secularism as a fundamental principle
>
> **1928**
> New Turkish constitution eliminates state religion
>
> **1930**
> The Ankara Convention, aka Greek–Turkish friendship treaty
>
> **1934**
> The signing of Balkan Pact;
> period of détente between Greece and Turkey
>
> **1939**
> Metaxas dictatorship in Greece; beginning of WWII
>
> **1940**
> Italian forces invade Northern Greece;
> Greece enters the WWII with the Allies
>
> **1942**
> Occupation of Greece by German, Italian, Bulgarian forces;
> foundation of National Liberation Front
>
> **1944**
> The end of the occupation of Greece
>
> **1946**
> Outbreak of Civil War in Greece to last for 3 years

Imagine the city as no longer the capital of the nation. After a millennium and a half, for the first time, Istanbul is to become the second city. Imagine the effort of building a new city from scratch in order to overshadow the old center, in order to symbolize the fresh birth of a nation in Ankara, in the middle of Anatolia, distant from the ashes of the Empire. Imagine the head of state, father of the nation, boycotting the city of Istanbul while preaching nationalism over cosmopolitanism, and not going there for over a decade, until he reaches his deathbed in 1938. Hear the rumors that Atatürk did not want to be replaced by İnönü. Witness the latter's hardline politics becoming further hardened during World War II, from which, you have to give it to him, he managed to spare the country. Tremble when one day they decide to draft all boys over 20 years of age, with immediate effect upon being caught, to send them to the depths of Anatolia. Wait for news from your son for two years. Decide that as soon as he gets back, you will leave for another place where your children will be safe. Question your decision every day, suffer sleeplessness from fear of ambiguity every night. Imagine living in the city nevertheless, making do as life goes on. Imagine you are a loyal, regular, tax-paying Turkish citizen, who wakes up one day only to find out that you are going to have to pay an incredibly high amount to the government, in cash and in one installment, as something called Wealth Tax. Imagine finding out that this is an arbitrarily imposed tax, where the amount is determined in accordance with the religion of the taxpayer, ranking highest to lowest from Greek Orthodox to Jewish, Armenian, Other Christian, Dönme, and Muslim. Sell all your property at much below its market value to avoid being forced to go to a labor camp far into the mountains of Eastern Anatolia, fearing what would happen to you there, with this taking place during World War II. Realize that this nation is not really built on the basis of secular markers like citizenship, but that religion is still a discriminating factor despite all claims, promises, constitutions, and international treaties signed to establish otherwise.

Imagine yourself about one decade later, again in Istanbul, when the news of the civil clashes between the Turkish and Greek Cypriots on the island in the Mediterranean turn into an anti-Greek campaign in the press. Imagine your child being hit by a stranger on the street for talking to his mother in Greek rather than Turkish. Imagine the anger for being scrutinized by people who came from elsewhere not knowing even the basics about you: that those living in Istanbul were the local Rum community, native to the city since its foundation, whereas those in Greece were called Yunan and were not really related to you, except in language and religion, as it is the case with the Cypriot Rum, with whom the Rum of Istanbul had no connection. Imagine the impossibility of trying to explain this to the crowd that is even more angry about this situation than you are, further agitated by the rumor that the Greeks bombed the late Mustafa Kemal's house in Salonika. Imagine the mob holding sticks and hammers in their hands, determined to tear down anything and everything that belonged to Greeks, Cypriots, Christians, whatever. Get up after that traumatic and sleepless night, on 7 September, year 1955, to be shocked by the unimaginable sight of Istanbul with thousands of buildings destroyed, looted, burned down; imagine walking past the shattered shop windows, vandalized hospitals, plundered churches, broken down houses, ruined schools, and the graves of your grandparents opened up, turned inside out. The rumor turns out to be false, the bomb having been planted by a Turk, damages get partially covered by the government, the environment eventually calms down; but the harm is done: fear of tomorrow settles among the Rum of Istanbul; flight to another land starts being imagined.

1929
Great fire destroys the Rum-dominated neighborhood of Tatavla in Istanbul;
Tatavla renamed Kurtuluş (Liberation)

1938
Law passed in Turkey restricts the professions that may be practiced by non-Muslim minorities

1938
Death of Mustafa Kemal Atatürk; İnönü becomes president of Turkey

1941
Drafting of all non-Muslim men between 18 and 45 in Turkey

1942
Wealth Tax in Turkey imposed in order to tax individual wartime profiteering;
deportation of thousands who could not pay taxes to a labor camp in Askale in Eastern Anatolia

1955
Outbreak of armed struggle in Cyprus;
Septemvriana (6–7 September events) in Istanbul cause massive destruction and looting

1958
Hellenic Union of Constantinopolitans shut down;
Expulsion of leading Rum Polites with Greek nationality

1960
Military coup in Turkey;
Yassıada trials find Prime Minister Menderes and two ministers guilty as charged, leading to their execution by hanging

1964
Major civil strife and bloodshed in Cyprus;
Turkey unilaterally annuls the 1930 Ankara Convention over the Cypriot issue;
Expulsions of Rum Polites with Greek citizenship by thousands as their residence and work permits of get canceled

1974
Demostrations against Istanbul Rum following the invasion of Northern Cyprus by Turkish army

Imagine leaving behind the horror of that September night, soothing down your fear, rebuilding your business, and restoring your house in the decade that follows. Imagine reading your name published in the newspaper, in a list that includes people who have to leave the country within two weeks. It is because you hold a Greek passport, and because your residence permit that is automatically renewed is no longer valid, owing to the Turkish government's unilateral decision to cancel the friendship agreement that was signed 34 years ago. The year is 1964, with the bloody civil war waging wild in Cyprus again. Imagine suddenly becoming an illegally residing foreigner in a city where you and your children were born, where your parents and grandparents are buried. Imagine having to leave behind your relatives, your friends, your business, your life, your city, taking with you a small suitcase containing only your personal items and nothing valuable—except for your memory of the city.

Imagine the city of Athens through the eyes of the new arrival: the biggest city of Greece, the capital of both its ancient and modern versions, booming as a result of internal migration, starting to become secure and stable after long years of occupation and civil war, only to last, however, a few more years until the junta of 1967. You rent a tiny apartment overlooking the cemented streets of central Athens, trying to get used to the idea of not being able to see the Bosphorus view from your large living room ever again. Imagine selling sandwiches on the street, reaching a low after being the most renowned restaurateur in Istanbul only a short time ago. Your children are having difficulty in school for not knowing enough about the heroic deeds of the Greeks during Tourkokratia or the mythological characters of a pagan past or the correct pronunciation of the words in the Athenian demotic as opposed to the forms used in Istanbul Greek or Rumca or Politika. Imagine trying to explain to the Athenians that you are not simply other Hellenes, but Romioi from the City, that you are from the Konstantinoupolites or, for short, Polites, bearing the identity of the city. Ignore the ignorance of Elladites, Greeks from Greece, and try to excuse them for asking if you were also baptized and if you had churches back there. Try to make them realize that you come from the city, the only one known to Greeks as the City, which is the center of Christian Orthodoxy, capital of the Byzantine Empire, throne of the Patriarch, location of Hagia Sophia, crown jewel of Greek civilization. Realize yourself that the only way the Elladites relate to your city is in their imagination of a Greek Constantinople, which in time will be theirs once more. Imagine that they do not know anything about its multicultural heritage and the cosmopolitan culture that the Polites helped maintain. Look around yourself, see only Greeks. Start imagining living without the other.

Imagine a certain part of the city full of Rum Polites, call it Paleo Faliro, or if you so prefer, Istanbulistan. Recreate there your practice of everyday life as in the city you left behind. Imagine shopping for food from the charcuterie, buying treats flown in daily, sitting in coffeeshops and patisseries named after famous Rum establishments of Istanbul, eating fresh fish from the Bosphorus grilled by the best chef from the City, chatting with friends continuously bringing up intricate details of your life as it was back then and how it turned out to be now. Build up your business, make sure that your children study well to secure their place in society, let them socialize with other children of Polites in the sports clubs, foundations, educational institutions that are self-funded by the community. Imagine them getting married to other Polites and raising their children in accordance with the ways of Istanbul. Criticize the Athenians, Elladites, Mikrasiates, and others for not knowing those ways. Every day, imagine a return to your birthplace, but do not dare to make this trip on any given day for several decades. Imagine suffering from permanent homesickness, not being able to cure it for years.

> **1952**
> Greece and Turkey become members of NATO
> **1967**
> Military coup in Greece
> **1974**
> Invasion of Cyprus/Peace Maneuver by the Turkish army and navy;
> split of Cyprus into North and South, corresponding to Turkish and Greek zones;
> end of the Greek junta followed by a civil government led by Konstantionos Karamanlis
> **1981**
> Greece becomes a member state of the European Community
> **1983**
> Declaration of the Northern Cypriot Republic of Cyprus
> **1987**
> Crisis between Greece and Turkey over the Aegean shelf
> **1988**
> Davos convention starts a period of cordial relations between Greece and Turkey
> **1996**
> Crisis over the Aegean islet of Kardak/Imia
> **1997–98**
> Crisis over Cyprus's purchase of S-300 missiles from Russia
> **1998**
> Crisis over the capture of the Kurdish PKK leader Abdullah Öcalan
> **1999**
> Earthquakes in Turkey and Greece initiate a period of rapprochement

Imagine being an Istanbulite in Athens, this time at the turn of the twenty-first century. You are a Turkish woman in Greece, trying to open your ears to both sides of the story in bilateral relations. Imagine you are an anthropology student from Harvard, trying to reconcile between your personal position and trends in the discipline, putting to the fore what the people you study are telling you. The people you study come from the city that is your home. Hear them talk about their home, your shared place of longing. Listen to their parallel histories, broken pasts, changing perspectives. Meet the man who decides to tell his story to make a change; talk to the woman who is too bitter to talk. Feel the weight of what you learn, blend these things with what you know, compose stories, and write them down. Share the story of your fieldwork as made up from stories you were told. Always remember that there will be another story, many stories that compete, contrast, or overlap with the story you end up telling. Imagine the city, through the stories told about it. Enjoy the stories.

Acknowledgments

There are many people involved in the creation of stories. My acknowledgments have to start with the Rum Polites, the protagonists in the stories, whose sincerity and kindness made this work possible. Although they will need to remain incognito in this publication, I wholeheartedly thank each and every one of them. It would be my ultimate fulfillment if with this work I can return at least a fraction of the sense of gratitude that they have given me along the way.

This book is based on research that I conducted for my doctoral dissertation, which I defended to a distinguished committee composed of my dear advisors Michael Herzfeld, Nur Yalman, and Engseng Ho. I remain grateful for the valuable guidance of my professors at that time and their continued support since then. I am especially thankful for the generous commentary provided by Michael Herzfeld, which certainly extends way beyond the wonderful blurb in the back cover. Among my mentors, I feel exceptionally indebted to Cemal Kafadar, whose involvement in this work cannot be sufficiently acknowledged.

Financial support was made available by a combination of funding agencies at various stages of research and writing: the Center for Middle Eastern Studies and the Center for European Studies at Harvard University, the Mellon Foundation, the Krupp Foundation, American Research Institute in Turkey, Alexander Onassis Public Benefit Foundation, Cora du Bois Fellowship, and Migration Research Center at Koç University. I would like to thank them, as well as Istanbul Bilgi University, for the institutional affiliation during the rewriting phase. In addition, I am grateful to the series editors, reviewers, referees, copyeditors, and all staff, who worked on the manuscript during the publication process.

The stories represented here were shared in various forms over the years and received constructive and considerate comments from many on different occasions. That feedback formed the basis for the challenging process of revising the manuscript years after its initial writing. During this period, I enjoyed to have around me colleagues, friends, and especially my family, who have offered their support during the difficult endeavor of rewriting for reflecting on the many changes in the social, political, and the scholarly scene that had an impact on the community, the city, and their study. My thankfulness forces me to spare them from the privileged burden of having their names publicized here, and I clearly carry the entire responsibility for any omittance, mistake, inaccuracy, or oversight that may offend anyone in any way, despite the best of my efforts and intentions.

This book could not have been completed without the endless cups of *duble orta* at Bebek Kahve, of *quattro* at Starbucks Cambridge Broadway, and of *μέτριο χωρής γάλα* at Eleftheroudakis Café Athens.

Contents

1 Introduction: Basics and Beginnings 1

2 Cosmopolitan Knowledge: Impressions from Everyday Life in Athens 41

3 Exclusive Diversity and the Ambiguity of Being Out of Place 67

4 Resolutionary Recollections: Event, Memory, and Sharing the Suffering 133

5 Capital of Memory: Cosmopolitanist Nostalgia in Istanbul 171

Epilogue 207

Bibliography 223

Index 253

CHAPTER 1

Introduction: Basics and Beginnings

It all starts with a story. A story of an encounter, surprising, baffling. A story that shakes expectations, creates curiosity, invites an opening, establishes a promise. A story that changes life, starts a new orientation, determines a direction. Some have to wait for that story to come along. I have been lucky with my story; it happened before I even started waiting for it. Then it opened a road for me to walk along for many years to follow. A road with a tale. A trail of stories. The tale is composed of stories of cosmopolitanism told in the diaspora of the City, about the cultural identity of a community—the Rum Polites, primarily those residing in Athens—with respect to their everyday life, their social relations with others, their constructions of history, their traumatic memories of violence and displacement, and their attachment to the urban cosmopolitan legacy of the City. It is a tale I would like to tell in the following few hundred pages. It all starts with a story on the roadside.

THE ROADSIDE STORY

It was the day of my arrival in Athens. I had left my suitcases in the room of a small hotel that was recommended to me at the airport. I did not know my way around in Athens, but I knew my destination: Paleo Faliro, the neighborhood dominated by the community that I wanted to study.

It was the summer of 1998, my first year in graduate school. I had decided to spend some time in Greece for language training and for testing the feasibility of conducting the kind of fieldwork I had in mind. My intention was to research the Greek Orthodox Rum minority from Istanbul who moved to Athens after being forced to leave Turkey. Having received various warnings about the kind of problems I should be prepared to face, I thought I would want to see the situation for myself. Would it really be difficult for a Turkish woman to investigate matters of political significance in Greece? Times were not great: that summer was marked by heightened tension between Greece and Turkey over Cyprus's purchase of S-300 missiles. With the Imia/Kardak crisis of 1996 still fresh in people's minds, the idea of a Turk doing research in Greece was bound to raise eyebrows. As it often happens in anthropology, the motivations of the fieldworker could be regarded with suspicion, both by the state agencies and by the people themselves. Having little concern about the former, I set out to measure the reactions of the latter, the Rum Polites in Athens.

So I started walking around Paleo Faliro. This being noon, and not the right time to call my contacts in their homes because of the *siesta* break, I had not much else to do besides stroll. On my way to an air-conditioned coffeeshop to escape the dizzying summer heat, I passed by two men on the side of the street. Otherwise unremarkable middle-aged men sitting on their motorcycles, these two drew my attention because they were talking loudly in Turkish. This was surprising to me, but I did not react, except for an unavoidable smile after overhearing a funny pun in slang. This did not escape them. One of them turned and said to me, with a slightly aggressive tone, in Greek: "What are you laughing at?" (*Ti yelas;*). I was not sure how to respond; my competence in Greek was not sufficient to enable me to work my way around any potential tension—which, if previous warnings were to prove correct, could easily arise out of this situation. I could not come up with anything better than to mumble in Turkish: "Sorry, I just heard what you said, so...."

This changed their attitude immediately. I had now their full attention and curiosity, so I continued: "I just came from Istanbul this morning, and when I heard Turkish being spoken...." My faltering explanation was interrupted by the men: "Oooh, so you came from Istanbul today? Why don't you say so? Welcome, welcome!" The exchange took off with everybody talking simultaneously; they were as excited as I was surprised. One of them lowered his voice and asked, as if in confidence: "So you are not one of those Anatolians (*Anadolulu*), right? You *are* from Istanbul, right?

Where exactly?" My family was living in Ayazpaşa at that time, which made them smile in approval: Ayazpaşa is an old neighborhood in Pera that lies next to Taksim and Cihangir, where many Rum families used to live. The other one mocked him saying that it was obvious from my Istanbul Turkish that I was indeed from the City. Their Turkish was no less fluent or no more accented than mine, even though they insisted that they had gone rusty. Some more questions followed inquiring into how far back my origins went in Istanbul, and it seemed to have pleased them that I, like my parents and grandparents, was born and raised in Istanbul, but also had family connections to Salonika and Crete. Then they said that although they came from Istanbul, they both had origins in Cappadocia, which explained their flawless Turkish.

"There are many of us here," said one of the men, "everybody in Faliro is Turkish—well, Turkish speaking; they should really put up a flag there someday soon" (*bayrak asacağız yakında buraya neredeyse zaten*). When I told them of my intention to write about the Istanbul Rum community in Athens, they became even more enthusiastic: "This is wonderful," they said, stealing half-sentences from each other, "come and we'll show you around, we did the same last year with a journalist who came from Turkey, we'll introduce you to people." One of them produced a notebook and took a pen from the other to scribble down his phone numbers, insisting that I had to call him in case I needed something. As he handed the piece of paper to me, he also gave me a warning: "I give you my mother's number as well, she also speaks Turkish. But if you call me at home, and I am not there, don't worry. My wife does not understand, she is infidel (*gavur*), you know?"

The conversation stopped there, the same way it started, with laughter. As I was leaving the scene, I realized that this was the story of the beginning. The story ended with a promise: I decided to research the Istanbul Rum community in Athens.

Stories of Basics

These two men were part of the community that I chose to study. I call them the Rum Polites; they are often referred to as Constantinopolitan Greeks in English, as *Konstantinoupolites* or *Polites* in Greek, and as *İstanbullu Rum* in Turkish. Among these multireferential possibilities and several others, Rum Polites, the term I prefer to use to designate the community, combines two of the most widely used emic terms of self-designation. By formulating this term my intention is threefold: to avoid confusion with other groups with similar names, to hint at their bilingual culture, and to acknowledge their self-emphasized identity as Istanbulites (Polites).[1] The first term *Rum* is the Turkish word for *Romios*, a derivative of the word *Romeos* meaning Roman, after Eastern Roman or Byzantine. Today it designates an ethno-religious category of the Greek Orthodox in Turkey, as well as the wider Middle East. The word Rum also has a territorial connotation (*Rumeli, Diyar-ı Rum*) of the former Byzantine and subsequently Ottoman lands in Asia Minor and the Balkans (see Ergül 2012; Kafadar 2007). I have privileged *Rum* over its Greek or English alternatives in order to avoid a confusion of the term with the widely familiar use of *Romios* in the Greek context as in the binary construct Romeic–Hellenic. Another confusion would arise with the use of Rum only, in which case the Rum Polites could be conflated with other Rum communities from former Byzantine/Ottoman lands outside of Greece, such as Asia Minor, Egypt, or Cyprus. The second term *Polites*, on the other hand, has a further significance in indicating an attachment to an urban legacy as the word *Poli* means city as well as Istanbul, *the* City.[2] These points that came up in the brief encounter at the side of the road constituted the main lines of research throughout my four-year fieldwork in Athens (2000–04) and built the thrust of the arguments that I am making in this book. This is why I started with the story that started my fieldwork. This is an ethnography of stories, whereby stories lead to theoretical arguments. Before telling more stories, let me first introduce the community of Rum Polites.

Any introduction to the Rum Polites has to start by addressing their diversity. Relating back to the Eastern Romans, even to the founders of the city of Byzantion, Rum Polites are one of, if not the oldest of, the resident communities in Istanbul. While they were always numerous and well-established within the urban society, constituting a quarter of the city population at the turn of the twentieth century, their numbers fell sharply in recent decades.[3] The Rum Polites today are dispersed not only between Istanbul and Athens but are also spread all over the world. Among them, some have Turkish citizenship, some Greek, some both. Some are in-between, trying to cancel one and obtain the other. There are many different groups from within or linked to the Rum Polites, such as *Fanariots*,[4] *Karamanlides*,[5] *Mikrasiates*,[6] *Imvriotes*,[7] or *Süryani Assyrians*.[8] Their mother tongue is mostly the demotic Greek, although with a large vocabulary unknown to non-Istanbulites, so some consider it to be a different dialect or even a language called *Politika* or *Romeika*, as I will discuss in detail in later chapters along with samples in oral and written form. Many are bilingual in Greek and Turkish, most are fluent in both languages, while there are some living in Greece who have never learned Greek, or a few who grew up also speaking French at home.[9] They trace their origins in Istanbul for several generations, although many have mixed with people coming from elsewhere, like Cappadocia, Crete, Bulgaria, Russia, Egypt, or the Aegean islands. They have also intermarried with others, so there are a number of Rum–Armenians, Rum–Muslims, Rum–Jews, Rum–Levantines, and so on. The vast majority are members of the Greek Orthodox Church and adhere to a tradition of Orthodoxy maintained by the Ecumenical Patriarchate,[10] located since its inception in Istanbul. There are a few exceptions who are followers of national Orthodox churches, such as the Bulgarian, Albanian, or Russian churches, as well as a small number of Catholics and other Christians.[11] Religion, though, has been the basic criterion for bureaucratic purposes in both nation-states: Rum Polites are recognized as a non-Muslim minority in the Turkish Republic, a legal status they do not have in Greece through being *omoyenia*—of the same religion and descent as the majority of Greece's population.

The history of the Rum Polites community is intrinsically linked to that of the city. From its foundation as Byzantium in sixth-century BC,[12] the settlement along the shores of Bosphorus has always housed a Greek-speaking population. It was with its reinstatement as the capital of the Eastern Roman Empire by Emperor Constantine in 324–330 AD that the city took the name Constantinople, the City of Constantine, or New Rome. Shortly thereafter, in 392, Christianity was recognized as the state religion for the first time in the world, and the city became the patriarchal seat of the Orthodox Church. Constantinople flourished as a cosmopolitan center thanks to its immediate contacts with the neighboring colonies of Venetians and Genoans, for its settled communities of mixed backgrounds, and for being the political seat as well as the economic, cultural, religious, and geographical center of an Empire that stretched over three continents for more than a millennium. Of the many sieges the city endured, including the one cited as the worst plunder in 1204, only the one in 1453 was conclusive: Constantinople changed from being the capital of the deceased Byzantine Empire to that of the thriving Ottoman Empire.

While many of the residents had already fled the city, died, or been dispersed in the course of the Sack/Conquest, the Ottomans eventually decided to keep the remaining population by giving the communities a certain level of autonomy in their religious, judiciary, educational, and other internal affairs. The Christian Orthodox, who identified themselves as descendants of Romans (Romeos) and were recognized as such by the Ottomans (Rum), were under the leadership of their Ethnarch, the Ecumenical Patriarch. They later came to constitute the *Rum millet*[13] with a specific status granted to them by the Grande Porte. Prospering economically as merchants, Rum Polites then transferred this power to the political realm and started to become influential within the Ottoman administration. After the transfer of the Patriarchate to the Fanar region on the Golden Horn, the Fanariot families came to constitute the noble elite of the Rum millet, reigning for about two centuries. With their exclusive right to become the official translators to the Court and their privilege to become governors of certain regions of the Empire, they were the closest thing to royalty in an empire with no aristocratic tradition. Titles were not the only claim to fame among the Rum Polites; they had proven themselves to be very successful in many different sectors ranging from international trade to medicine. Rum Polites have also been active in the cultural realm; it was largely thanks to their contribution that Istanbul became a notable intellectual, artistic, and literary center of the region. Of great significance was also the rise of a quasi-bourgeois class, who consisted largely of Rum Polites. Mainly centered in Pera, these elite classes left their imprint on the urban social environment by mixing local cultural diversity with Western influences, thereby creating a unique version of cosmopolitan modernity that became visible in the changing lifestyles and fashion of consumption at the end of the nineteenth century.[14] The heyday of economic and political power of the Rum Polites started deteriorating, however, with the demise of the imperial orders and the rise of Balkan nationalism. With the Greek revolt/revolution and the formation of the independent state, the attitude of the Ottoman administration toward the Fanariots gradually worsened. Although there was much suspicion, fewer privileges, and more discrimination, however, the Sultans still appointed Fanariots to positions such as ambassadorships to Greece or Great Britain,[15] and most of the trade and finance sector of the Empire was controlled by Rum Polites. This is shown as one of the main reasons why the Rum residents of Istanbul were held exempt from the agreement on the Forced

Exchange of Populations signed with the Treaty of Lausanne in 1923, although this was hardly an undisputed matter.

The last of the peace treaties in the aftermath of World War I, the Treaty of Lausanne signed on 24 July 1923 is recognized as the birthright of the Turkish Republic for granting its international recognition, as well as for shaping the contours of the kind of state it would become. If the publication of the Protocol on the Forced Exchange of Populations more than six months before the Treaty was not sufficient indication of the aspirations for national unity and homogeneity of Turkey, then the events that followed made it quite clear. After several Acts restricting the scope to which the Treaty was to be applied in the immediate aftermath of its signing,[16] Rum Polites were forced to give up the provisions that recognized their minority rights under Article 42 as early as 1925,[17] which opened the road for the subsequent troubles they endured: their right to practice any profession was taken away in 1932,[18] the guarantee of equality before law was overridden with a discriminative and arbitrarily applied Wealth Tax in 1942,[19] their right to hold property and reside in the country was canceled in 1964,[20] and their security and lives were threatened on many occasions, notably in September 1955[21] and August 1974.[22] These and many other pressures of a political, social, and economic nature, which can be placed under the rubric of "Turkification,"[23] forced the Rum Polites to leave Istanbul for other locations, especially Athens. Although there have been glimpses of better conditions, coinciding with periods of Greek–Turkish rapprochement, the entire twentieth century has been a continuous story of the dramatic collapse of the Rum Polites in Istanbul, a story that however still remains unfamiliar to many in Greece and Turkey.

Introductory Stories

This book investigates the cultural identity of the aforementioned community of the Rum Polites, primarily those residing in Athens, with respect to the ways in which they define this identity in terms of their everyday life, their social relations to others, their constructions of history, their traumatic memories of violence and displacement, and their attachment to the urban cosmopolitan legacy of Istanbul. There are many realms where these themes can be observed, and the story above highlights some of them by bringing out the intricate layers of Rum Polites cultural identity.

Let me start where the two men did, who first inquired into the specifics of where I came from. The search into the Rum Polites identity starts, likewise, with a question on place of origin. This is an identity that is territorial to begin with; it is related to a certain geography that is specified even within Istanbul. This connection to location may be so strong that it overrides ethnic or religious differences between Istanbulites, who share a cultural unity within diversity, such that Istanbulite becomes an independent identity in its own right. Thus the enthusiasm of these two men over our common origins is a recurrent theme in the way the Rum Polites relate to the other resident communities of Istanbul—whether Turkish, Jewish, Armenian, *Levantine*,[24] *White Russian*,[25] or any other. I call this adherence to a specific kind of multicultural existence "exclusive diversity," whereby inclusion is restricted to those who, regardless of their specific ethnic, religious, or socioeconomic backgrounds, can claim their birthright in Istanbul—a cause for exclusivity in and of itself. By the same token, this cultural identity that is exclusive to Istanbulites excludes non-Istanbulites such as those whom the men called "Anatolians." Although the reference here was to Mikrasiates, it had a connotation to a wider discourse based on a duality between Istanbul and Anatolia, corresponding to urban versus rural, West versus East,[26] clearly implying a superiority of the former over the latter. With the double meaning of the word *Polites*, the category of villager is often used as a means of otherization and might be extended to all non-Istanbulites (i.e., non-polites, non-urbanites, thus villagers, or provincials), including the Athenians, Elladites, as well as Mikrasiates, thereby cutting across commonalities of religion, ethnicity, language, or nationality. This differentiation was ironically expressed by the man in the story calling his wife an infidel (*gavur*), a word of insult that is used to refer to non-Muslims in Turkey as well as in the larger Muslim world and to designate them as foreigners and outsiders. With a discursive shift where he replaced religion with origin, the man I met that day was dramatically reversing conventional categories of insiders and outsiders: I had to be *the* outsider in the circle as a legal stranger, a Turk, a Muslim, a woman, and as a tourist on her first day in Athens, yet the men incorporated me as one of them for being from Istanbul, whereas the wife—a Greek, a Christian Orthodox, a family member, a resident of Athens—was pushed to the status of outsider by way of her inability to identify with Istanbul. Although this was a rhetorical device used in the service of kindness and politeness, it was indicative of the difference between the Rum Polites and Elladites in the ways in which they relate to the Turks in general. By verbally performing an ability to resist seeing me categorically as a Turk, these two men proved wrong those warnings about how a Turk could be received in

Greece. This was only one such occasion where I witnessed the Rum Polites position themselves in reaction to any modular understanding of Greeks and Turks and against the simplistic oppositions between the two; by rendering the assumed divisions between them flexible, they carve themselves a place not only between but beyond the Greek–Turkish dualism that they further pluralize by virtue of their own exclusive diversity.

Identification with Istanbul becomes visible in many realms of life; here, speaking the language of the city is emphasized as an important dimension. Language first indicates origin: it is an index to culture—speaking non-accented Istanbul Turkish means possessing Istanbul culture. Secondly, it differentiates: ability to speak Turkish helps separate Rum Polites from Elladites—here referred to as gavur. But most importantly, knowing Turkish means knowing the ways of the other: beyond a simple claim to linguistic competence, this is a knowledge of life in the city, of the metropolis, of urban diversity—a notion that I call "cosmopolitan knowledge."

Finally, the flag: their joke about putting a flag in Paleo Faliro as the neighborhood of Turkish-speaking Rum Polites meant that they were reproducing Istanbul symbolically in that neighborhood of Athens: Paleo Faliro is almost a diaspora defined in terms of a city; it is a place of belonging to the City with a strong sense of locality that transgresses notions of ethnicity, religion, or citizenship. By extension, this can be evaluated as giving a higher status to Istanbul than just another city: *the* City is a city with a flag, with a dominant identity, with a diaspora. Even though he does not seem to refer to an actual national flag, there is a flag of Constantinople, rather of the Ecumenical Patriarchate in Istanbul that features the double-headed black eagle representing Byzantium.[27] Though not a symbol of Paleo Faliro, this yellow and black flag is a frequent sight around the neighborhood, hanging high and bold over every institution, association, and community building that either belongs to Rum Polites or relates to Istanbul. So it is that two of the major sports clubs of Greece use this flag as their team banner: AEK, which stands for *Athlitiki Enosi Konstantinoupoliton* (Athletic Union of Istanbulites), of Athens and PAOK (*Panthessalonikeios Athlitikos Omilos Konstantinoupoliton*, United Salonican Athletic Union of Istanbulites) of Thessaloniki were both founded in Istanbul as Pera and Hermes, respectively, and were transferred to Greece in the 1920s. These are just two among the many organizations that had been established by the Rum Polites in contribution to the athletic, artistic, professional, or intellectual life in Istanbul. Parallel to the story of the Rum Polites in the last few centuries, many of these institutions faded away, a few of them continue to exist in their birthplace in a dwindling state, and some were imported to other cities where they live on in the diaspora of the City.

More can be said about this story, and there will be more stories to tell. Before that, though, I give an outline of the book and of the other stories to come.

Outlining Stories

Throughout my fieldwork I collected many other stories, like the one on the roadside, and they shall constitute, throughout this book, the main framework for talking about Rum Polites as well as the pathways to analysis, leading—in subtle or straightforward fashion—to an argument regarding the cultural identity of the Rum Polites. The stories are scattered, the themes make up an assorted and unfinished whole, and the chapters are steps in an endless endeavor of bringing together sprinkled pieces of information about a dispersed community, rather than the other way around. Others write books to prove a theoretical point and use their research as a proof for their final conclusions. In this book I tell the story of my study, perhaps the first of its kind, in order to lead not to an end but a beginning: to introduce the community ethnographically, to call for further research, and to revisit the existing anthropological theory critically in ways that are inspired by a fieldwork on the Rum Polites. The chapters in the book are not stretches of the same linear road driving to a fixed target, but rather a set of diverse paths with crosscutting points of departure and arrival that came about when exploring a vast field where only a few have ever walked before.

The book starts with a prologue. The prologue is about major events in relevant history, which are narrated from the perspective of differently named and anonymous actors in history. For unlike the seemingly smooth flow of events in a chronology, historical actors have parallel, overlapping, or clashing stories that make up their broken, discontinuous pasts. By juxtaposing dates, facts, data, narrative, events, and commentary, I stress that political history is too pertinent to be considered as background and too fragmented to be conveyed with a single plot.

In the next chapter, I walk around Paleo Faliro, the center of my fieldwork in Athens, and tell stories of Rum Polites' everyday life along the way. By noting some of the general ethnographical aspects of daily culture of the Rum Polites, I introduce the concept of cosmopolitan knowledge, an extension of the notion of metropolitan knowledge (Rotenberg 2002), but with a nuanced specification given that the practice of everyday life (de Certeau 1988) of the Rum Polites takes as its reference not the present city itself, but another city of their nonbeing yet belonging, one that is far away in space as well as in time. It is this connection to an Istanbul past that brings the Rum Polites together in Athens, while it further delineates them from the Greeks of Greece. By juxtaposing stories, personal narratives, impressions, everyday observations, tales, and narratives, I intend to stress that cultural life is too complex to be taken as a totality and too variable to be treated as coherent.

Chapter 3 is about the ways in which perceptions of others play into the conceptualizations of Rum Polites identity. Rum Polites in Athens not only differentiate themselves from Athenians, Anatolians, or other Greeks in Greece, but they also display a certain level of fragmentation among themselves. I call this tendency a commitment to exclusive diversity. The notion of exclusivity is based, somewhat ironically, on a regard for multicultural diversity that is specific and exclusive to Istanbul. Within this exclusive diversity, their relations with the Turks become significantly ambiguous—a complicated matrix that I attempt to untangle through further stories of my experiences with the Rum Polites as well as their relations with other Turks and Greeks. Characteristic of such relations is the resistance of the Rum Polites to complying with the binarism of Greekness versus Turkishness, dominant in both popular and official discourses; they instead forge a pluralization of the duality that is taken for granted on both ends. Here I entertain an ethnographic adjustment of the term *disemia* (Herzfeld 1997) to enable its application to the specific case of the Rum Polites. I then bring together some of these conceptual threads and deliberate on the categorization of the Rum Polites. Rather than an intention to force the community into the existing conventional labels, such as minority, migrant, and refugee, I test these categories against the ethnographic information I gathered about the Rum Polites. It follows that the categories widely used in social sciences remain inadequate in characterizing the Rum Polites accurately, because these take the nation-state as their point of reference. Rum Polites not only have a reluctant relation to the current nation-states of Greece and Turkey but also tend to identify themselves with the cosmopolitan legacy of the City that flourished before and beyond the premise of nationalisms. While their present is tainted by negative experiences with extreme nationalism, they rely on a cosmopolitan, supranational idea of the city in the reconstructions of their past in Istanbul. That they display an attachment to the city rather than a country, while rendering their categorization unviable, invites a significant reassessment of the assumptions commonly made in both social theory and official discourses. With that, Rum Polites present a good case to resist what is known as "methodological nationalism" and enable an opening into a possibility of "methodological cosmopolitanism" (Beck and Sznaider 2006). I demonstrate this with respect to the concept of diaspora: while according to both academic and official categorizations the Rum would be considered a diaspora *in* Istanbul for being Greeks outside Greece, the Rum Polites consider themselves to be in the diaspora *of* Istanbul when they live outside of their home city, in Greece, or elsewhere in the world. Rum Polites elsewhere than Istanbul, then, live in a "diaspora of the City." I then offer to investigate the notion of an Istanbul diaspora by describing its wider dimensions as constructed by former residents of the city from different ethnic and religious backgrounds. By juxtaposing narratives of interpersonal relations featuring exclusivity and diversity, I stress that cultural identity is too multifaceted to fit into any prescribed categorization and too malleable not to defy any primordialist assumption.

Chapter 4 is an exploration into the traumatic recent past of the Rum Polites. As a displaced community, the Rum Polites have endured various instances of personal and collective suffering, which remain little known to Greeks and Turks alike. Through their stories of violence, I relate to the ways in which they build on their past as a means to come to terms with the present, while at the same time analyzing how these ways of dealing with their suffering reflect into how they position themselves vis-à-vis others, especially the Turks. Apart from reconciling the boundaries with Turkish others, an attention to traumatic past also reveals the internal divisions within the community of Rum Polites. I show this through a discussion of a diagnostic event (Moore 1987) of commemoration where I participated as an observant. I then reflect on how my disposition to their suffering might have affected their conceptualization of my place relative to the boundaries they draw around the community, which in turn provided me with additional insights into the degree of flexibility of the Rum Polites identity. By juxtaposing remembrances of private memories and public displays of commemoration, I stress that experiences of violence and loss are too significant to be overheard, too loud to be silenced.

Chapter 5 is about contemporary discourses and acts of nostalgia directed toward the idea(l) of a cosmopolitan Istanbul. While I elaborate on the specific ways in which the Rum Polites conceptualize Istanbul as their homeland and point of reference, I also reflect on how the other Istanbulite communities, past and present, living in and out of Istanbul, relate to the city discursively as a source for identity. I focus on different types of cosmopolitanism in Istanbul, which I extract from the writings of Rum Polites, to help frame this multireferential concept contextually as a way of differentiating experiential modes of cosmopolitanism.

In line with major anthropological analysis (Prato 2009; Harris 2011), this chapter, or rather this book, is not about cosmopolitanism or multiculturalism as a political project of social management to be imposed upon people from different backgrounds sharing the same space. It is about understanding how people give meaning to their everyday diverse experiences and generate contested emic definitions of what constitutes cosmopolitan living. The case of Rum Polites and Istanbul offers endless opportunities to approach these concepts that have infinitely been analyzed, interpreted, and redefined and gives us clues as to how such debates in social theory can be grounded through ethnographic analyses of actual cultural realities. By juxtaposing narratives of cosmopolitanist nostalgia gathered from current and past Istanbulites, both in the city and abroad, I intend to show that the city is such a sophisticatedly composite entity that its culture, history, and identity cannot be described without multiple representations of daily life in the city.

In the epilogue, I attempt an update of the social, political, cultural, historical, and urban contexts within which the study is situated. I first reflect on the current state and the recent changes of, as well as possible prospects for, the community of Rum Polites and their city of Istanbul. By juxtaposing various meanings attached to cosmopolitan city in different contexts and by different actors throughout the book, I indicate that local and emic definitions are too relevant to social reality to be ignored by social theory. I conclude with the argument that a more comprehensive understanding of the widely debated concepts like diaspora and cosmopolitanism can be achieved through paying much overdue attention to the present manifestations of the historical city and to the ways in which alternative identities are formulated, not only based on recent post-national creations but also on the basis of older cultural forms that preceded and resisted the nation-state. Stories of the City attest to this point.

THE SCOPE OF THE STORIES

In this book I present an ethnographic case study of the Rum Polites community in Athens. By following their personal memories, everyday experiences, discourses of identification, and social interaction, I show how the Rum Polites may be regarded as living in the diaspora of the city of Istanbul as an exclusive cultural minority despite their primordial continuity with the majority of Athenians.

At an analytical level, I further advance the argument that the city has an identity, which cannot be reduced to the identity of those living in the city. The link between city and identity can also be explored outside the city, in the ways in which people linked to that city relate to it as a source of identity. In specific cases, like that of Istanbul, the identity of the city can override other, more commonly acknowledged bases of identification, such as nation or ethnicity, to become the primary determining factor in the self-inflicted cultural delineation of a community, such as the Rum Polites. If identity is about cultural difference in the making, then the city is a contested ground for altering or reifying multiple identities, including its own.

There are inevitable limits to the scope of this study. This work, admittedly, does not aspire to be a comprehensive encyclopedic reference study of the entire history and present of Rum Polites. With its deep historical, religious, social, cultural, and many other dimensions, this subject is too vast to be explored in one piece of research, let alone by one researcher. The task would appear even more enormous when it is considered that not many studies have been conducted on the community, apart from a few notable works in economic or political history and a collection of monographs regarding single neighborhoods, institutions, and events.[28] Yet there is a fairly large body of writing by Rum Polites, Greek, and Turkish writers who take the cultural life of the Rum Polites as their subject. It has been one of my objectives to bring together these scattered resources toward generating further research on the Rum Polites.

A major issue that I had to deal with has been the historical frame of this study. I was often asked, by Rum Polites as well as others, how far back in the past I was going to cover in my work and if I was going to research into the long history of the Rum Polites community. My answer regarding periodization seemed to please them: I decided to go wherever and whenever I was led by the Rum Polites. That is to say that I followed the Rum Polites I met in present time, into whichever recent or distant eras and events they chose to privilege as important, rather than imposing any particular timeline to my research. For my work is not about what happened to the Rum Polites in the past, but about how they think today about what has happened in the past and how their history informs their present as a community.

In that regard, my stance may be evaluated as non-historicist but hopefully as being historically perceptive in the sense that I have not outweighed the claims of Rum Polites about their historical trajectory in favor of accuracy as established by scholars of history. The reasons behind this decision are informed by an ethnographic sensitivity, as the next story is intended to demonstrate.

The Story of Historians

While I was still at the fieldwork stage, I was invited to present at a university conference in Istanbul. When I shared some views about the long past of the Rum Polites in Istanbul, including the claim of some to be descendants of the Eastern Roman founders of the city, the auditorium filled with Byzantine and Ottoman historians shook with laughter. They later said that I should dismiss such claims, that it was impossible for them to be established as fact by any historical evidence, because they simply could not be true.

A few years later, when I was giving a seminar to a more diverse audience of Istanbulites, I replied to a question about historical origins of the Rum Polites by stating that, according to historians, most of the community today was probably formed through internal migration during Ottoman times and it was not really possible to date them much earlier than the sixteenth century. Upon hearing this, a young lady commented, somewhat angrily, "I don't know who those historians are that you are citing. But they are wrong! I know this for sure because my family came from Byzantium. This is the reality. Because we are from here, we did not come from elsewhere!"

I see no dilemma here in terms of feeling the need to determine who is right and which fact speaks to the historical truth. For I believe that both statements are self-convinced as they each contain a value of truth at different levels. These levels can be recognized through an ethnographically informed perspective to history, and this argument has already been variously demonstrated through anthropological studies in the historical lands of the Mediterranean/Middle Eastern region. Andrew Shryock states, by paraphrasing Dumont, that history is the means by which a community reveals itself for what it is. His ethnographic account of the Balga in Jordan reveals how the will to connect to a point of origin in history is not simply a search for an ancestral lineage, but in a more general sense "the political community in which the ancestors lived" (1997, 65). Rum Polites may or may not be proven to be direct descendants of families that lived during the Eastern Roman Empire in Constantinople. But it is important to understand that such an insistence unveils other values of truth related to an identification with a cultural heritage of a political community, both temporally and spatially. This is not to say that historical truth does not exist or has no value, but that there are other values of truth that have often been overlooked and thus need to be released through an ethnographic intervention. One approach to doing this is presenting indigenous notions of history, as David Sutton did in the Greek island of Kalymnos, as another way of categorizing the past and bringing it to bear on the present (Sutton 1998). After all, "good ethnography should be informed by history, because society is in constant flux and culture is being constantly constituted," Henk Driessen confirms in his work on the Spanish Moroccan borderlands, further stating that "just as the present informs the past, the past should inform the present" (1992, 8). Therefore, the anthropologist cannot disregard the importance of the past, though his/her approach is unlike that of an historian. In agreement with Giordano, "the anthropologist's history is nearly always 'actualised history'—a past that is more or less intentionally 'mobilised' in the present," usually carried out with specific aims in the realms of everyday life, as a sense of belonging or identity, as a counterdiscourse against unacceptable conditions (2012, 24, emphases in the original).

With this complementary balance between anthropological and historical approaches to the interlinked notions of past and present in mind, the stories I tell about Rum Polites contain actualized histories observed across various realms. The first two chapters (Chaps. 2 and 3) provide a focus on the ethnographic present of the Rum Polites in Athens. While noting the contemporary, I stay constantly aware that, for the Rum Polites, the past is an intrinsic part of the present as much as it is part of the everyday social practice and discourse. References to their history entail remembrances of their city, conflating time and space in an Istanbul past as the basic dimension of the Rum Polites identity. Memories, stories, time-honored everyday habits all come to signal their version of history— one that rivals the dominant official and popular historical constructions. The next two chapters (Chaps. 4 and 5) thus deal with the past of the Rum

Polites in Istanbul, favoring the periods, places, and events they favor, whether in the way they tell the story of their history or in the way it was told by others.

Although I paid attention to different historical eras, the period that I ended up writing about most was that of the present, the present that I was able to witness personally—that is, my fieldwork years between 2000 and 2004 in Athens, with another two years both ways as pre- and post-research time. After this intensive research period, I moved to Istanbul where I maintained contact not only with many of my informants in Athens but with far more in the extended Rum Polites community of Istanbul. This book is a revised and expanded version written after some ten years following the completion of the initial dissertation study. In the epilogue, I will be reflecting on the changing dynamics of the community over the course of almost two decades of my engagement and investigate the possibilities for their future—again, the visions that Rum Polites have about their own future.

There will be some who would wish that I would have more to say on religion. The Rum Polites are by and large a Christian Orthodox community, and their connection to the Ecumenical Patriarchate as well as their status as a religious minority in Turkey renders the issue highly relevant. I can only speculate on the reasons why the subject of religiosity did not come up often enough in my conversations with the Rum Polites, and I do not rule out that my limited knowledge of and interest in the topic was one of them. When it did, religion was mentioned and thus treated as a form of sociability: Sunday churchgoing was a major social event in Istanbul; religious feasts are important occasions for bringing together friends and family and to cook together. Rituals such as visits to holy water springs (*ayazma*) or shrines during their Saint's days were significant markers of the cosmopolitan life of Istanbul, which was known and shared by residents of other beliefs as well (Albera and Couroucli 2012; Barkan and Barkey 2014). Such stories are not absent from the book, yet their analysis was performed not in terms of evaluating their religious content per se, but by acknowledging rituals and religious practices as grounds for recognizing the cultural differences that mark the Rum Polites identity.

Just as my limited personal concern for the question of religion (and shall I add, gender[29]) might have shaped the kind of information I gathered, my attention to other aspects of life undoubtedly tilted the balance in the scales of my stories. Food is but one of these. My interest in the consumption of food and drinks, especially coffee and sweets, happily coincided with that of the Rum Polites and created a major topic of discussion in our numerous patisserie-café meetings. Rather than devoting an entire section to the ethnographic data on Rum Polites cuisine, known as *Politiki Kouzina*, I chose to scatter some of the food-related stories throughout the book—I hope this will result in a more appetizing process of reading. Notwithstanding my declared bias, however, this focus was as significant as it was enjoyable: the Rum Polites were renowned as pastry and chocolate makers, restaurateurs, and wine- and coffeehouse owners in Istanbul. Not only did they dominate the sector with their expert chefs trained in Europe, they also furnished the city with spaces like the patisserie-café that stood as landmarks of a cosmopolitan version of modernity a century ago (Örs 2002). These places of consumption, as well as their Rum Polites owners, chefs, and customers, have almost disappeared in Istanbul but are revitalized today under the rubric of a nostalgic turn to cosmopolitanism. For Rum Polites and current Istanbulites alike, the patisserie-cafés stand as symbols of a lost and dearly remembered past Istanbul. Throughout my research, conversations in or about these places of consumption and sociability became moments of reflection on history, identity, and modernity.[30] They further provided a good opportunity for displaying differences between the Rum Polites and Elladites in terms of their habits of cooking and consumption, which often was translated into contrasts in their respective attitudes toward life. The centrality of food in the lives of Rum Polites helped me to tackle fundamental issues of identity. It also allowed me access to an additional cross-segment of the Rum Polites population, enabling me to cover a more diverse sample of the community than I would if I had focused on, say, the jewelry trade or shipping, two of the other sectors where the Rum Polites have been eminent.

STORIES OF METHODS

The issue of comprehensiveness has been a constant concern throughout this fieldwork, and one that has been left unresolved. While this may well be inevitable, it certainly is not dismissible: no geographical or theoretical bounding will eliminate the possibility of finding ever more complexity "within," as Strathern (1991) maintains, and as Falzon reminds us: "But to be explicit about the necessity of leaving certain things 'out of bounds,' would alleviate this predicament, by turning what feels like an illicit incompleteness into an actual methodological decision, one which the ethnographer reflects upon and takes responsibility for" (2009, 34). I am aware that whatever scope or whichever set of informants or information one may choose, this work, as perhaps all ethnographic accounts, is far from being perfectly representative of the cultural variety revealed through fieldwork.

My fieldwork encompassed a displaced and dispersed people living in two multimillion cities in two different countries. Although I ended up focusing mostly on Athens, where the largest part of the community is residing, I had to be constantly in touch with their home community in Istanbul, in a criss-crossing fashion reflecting the moves of the Rum Polites themselves. Rum Polites who now live in other places, such as Thessaloniki, England, Germany, the USA, or Australia, had to be left out of the scope of this book, though a follow-up study of the Rum Polites diaspora would be an important endeavor.[31]

Focusing on Athens was far from being a solution to the problem. First of all, there is no way of accurately determining the size of the Rum Polites population. Being of the same religion, language, and ethnicity, Rum Polites are not considered a minority in Greece, nor are they officially seen as a separate group for demographic purposes. My attempts at finding official or reliable statistical data based on birthplace have thus proven unsuccessful. Instead, I arrived at a conservative estimate of 50,000 as the number of Istanbul-born Rum Polites living in Athens, although others would often guess six-digit numbers. This includes men and women of all ages, professions, income level, political orientation, and social standing, who live all over Athens, albeit with a concentration in the southern suburb of Paleo Faliro and surrounding neighborhoods. With different time frames and reasons for coming to Athens from Istanbul, it was difficult to maintain a wide-enough gaze to be able to observe the Rum Polites in their multiplicity and diversity, let alone to reach conclusions based on any universally accepted criteria that apply to the entirety of the community of Rum Polites.

This problem is not unfamiliar to anthropologists, especially those working in urban settings. Many researchers recognize that urban ethnographies are necessarily—like any ethnography—partial, incomplete accounts (Bestor 2002). It is a lack of completeness that covers all aspects of research, and not only representation; it can be argued that in cities particularly, incompleteness is a methodological inevitability: "People construct a composite of cities and places, communities and groups in cities that is their own. Even at the level of communities, there is only partial agreement between direct neighbors about the boundaries of the composite of the community each holds" (Fischer and Kokkalaki 2013, 114). Invoking the influential work of Fredrik Barth (1969) on the importance of boundaries in the ontological construction of group identities, ethnic or otherwise, the city always reminds us to be aware that neighborhoods do not contain bounded communities, communities are never mutually exclusive, and borders are often patchy and permeable. Thinking and writing about cultural difference, especially in an urban context, requires an approach inspired by Marjorie Shostak: "an approach that is not afraid to leave the cultural story unfinished" (Davis and Konner 2011, 2).

Fieldwork in the city faces many other similar methodological challenges,[32] inviting basic questions regarding the very practicality of it: how to locate people, how to get to them in traffic, how to ask for their time in a hectic and busy environment, how to establish long-term rapport out of fleeting contacts, how to get to know the social contexts within which the community is located, how to observe their relationships with others, when others are so many and so varied. Issues shift from technical to epistemological, however, as anthropologists increasingly pay attention to the difference between carrying out what Prato and Pardo (2013, 81) describe as "'simply' (more or less classical) anthropological research *in* urban areas" and realizing urban anthropology as anthropology *of* the city, where the city itself is also subject to ethnographic study. What distinguishes urban anthropology is not only the size of its field or the range of social phenomena studied; it is rather the anthropologist's explicit reflection on the implications of the urban context in which these phenomena occur, and an understanding of how social life is experienced within urban contexts (Jaffe and de Koning 2016).

The current work would be categorized as urban anthropology not only because it was conducted in two cities with a focus on an urban community. More, it deals with the city as the main point of reference in the identification of a dispersed community, one where the city takes on the role of being the dimension of definition if not determination of the social boundaries and the cultural content of what constitutes the community. The city in this study is more than a physical space; it is a place "of meaning and identity" (Prato and Pardo 2013, 97). This meaning and identity of the city is not secondary: it is a primary source of urban culture and identity *in* and *of* itself.

The city, then, is taken up here as an object of ethnographic research—which introduces additional challenges, not only methodologically but also epistemologically, relating to adopting the urban as an alternative point of reference or premise for revisiting social theory. Accepting the city (in general, and older non-Western urban centers in particular) as an object of study opens up a venue through which to critique methodological nationalism and to call into question the Western bias embedded in disciplinary conventions of presuming an organic link between city and urbanization, industrialization, and nationalization, thereby inviting their dissociation and reconceptualization.

This study privileges ethnographic fieldwork as the primary research method, the "diagnostic methodology" of all anthropology (Herzfeld 2013, 118). The object of ethnography is "the demonstrated achievement of *intimate relations with informants*," which "requires protracted and often repeated stays 'in the field' to experience in person what Pardo calls 'strong continuous interaction'" (1996, 11), revealed through depictions of "minute details as expressing encompassing social and political processes" (Herzfeld 2013, 119, emphases in the original). I understand ethnographic fieldwork as a flexible and broad set of methods that entail the widest range of possible routes to arrive at interpretations of emic meanings that in turn inform etic concepts in social sciences. With that, I share the conviction of many urban ethnographers that there is a demonstrable analytical and theoretical relevance of in-depth empirically based research to developing a deeper comprehension of the complex processes between local, national, and regional contexts, and everyday forms of urban cultural life.

Over four years of continuous residence in Athens, with intermittent field trips to Istanbul, and several years of frequent visits for various durations before and after, my fieldwork on the Rum Polites entailed a great deal of observance (engaged or noninvolved, focused or select, of people, objects, performances, events, surroundings, and appearances), conversing (informal, open-ended, semi-structured, descriptive, "encounter,"[33] focus group interviews, life stories, chitchat, gossip), participation (in events, meals, daily routines, cooking, presentations, performances, seminars, research groups, ceremonies, rituals), analyses (words, language, narratives, discourses, tales, myths, cookbooks, novels, biographies, memoirs, images, tastes, sounds, smells, statistics, surveys, membership records, poems, films, documentaries, newspapers, scholarly work, social networks)—and more. My interactions with informants ranging in age from 9 to 90 were conducted in durations varying from 10 minutes to over 10 years. It is an eclecticism that releases urban anthropological fieldwork that is characterized by flexibility and serendipity—concepts that release "the art of making unsought finding" (Van Andel 1994, 631) or the "accidental wisdom" (Calhoun 2004) of qualitative methods in grounded theory, whose value has been noted variously (Jaffe and de Koning 2016; Rivoal and Salazar 2013; Pieke 2000).

Rooted in the ideal of participant observation, then, the combination of field techniques and the choice of ethnographic fieldwork as an eclectic methodological choice rests on a deliberate decision, to follow Falzon, of "privileging an engaged, contextually rich, and nuanced type of qualitative social research, in which fine grained daily interactions constitute the lifeblood of the data produced" (2009, 1). With this being my ultimate target of methodological achievement, it was the following story of a beginning that gave my research a jump start.

The Story of the Beginning

"Are you not from Istanbul?" asked my classmate in our second term of Modern Greek classes at Harvard. "The reason I am asking is because my professor is from Istanbul as well." I must have looked rather unwilling when he said he thought that I would want to meet just anybody from my hometown, so he continued in a somewhat dismissive manner: "But he is Greek. Would you still like to meet him?" As he was somewhat confused, almost apologetic about the fact that his Istanbulite professor was not Turkish, he seemed surprised when my reaction turned from indifferent to enthusiastic. Little did he know that his reluctant proposition came to me as a blessing: it was around this time that I was trying to formulate my research topic in the form of a prospectus that I was due to defend in a couple of months. Although I had read everything I could find on the Rum Polites, which did not amount to an awful lot, I could use all the insight I could get. I must have made it quite clear that I was very interested in meeting the professor as soon as possible, for the very next day we established contact, first by email and then by phone, in order to schedule a meeting at his office by the end of the week.

"*Hoşgeldin!*" exclaimed the friendly, gray-haired scientist as he welcomed me in flawless Turkish. I was positively surprised; our emails and phone conversations had all been conducted in English, so I was not sure of the level of his connection to Istanbul. He explained himself; he in fact told me his entire life story along with rich information about the Rum Polites in Istanbul and in Athens in the two hours that followed. It turned out that I was very lucky: not only was I able to conduct my first interview at such a preliminary stage of my fieldwork, I had also by coincidence met an important figure from among the Rum Polites, who was to become a key informant throughout my research in the following years.

This meeting was the first step of the ladder that was to lead me to one of the significant segments of my research. Through what is sometimes called the snowballing method, I came to meet a good number of people constituting the intellectual elite of the Rum Polites. This professor first introduced me to an eminent person in Istanbul, who then led me to a well-known journalist in Athens. He made sure that I became familiar with a number of personalities and institutions there, and these threads, along with some more independent contacts of my own, were woven into a large network of people who came to constitute my main informants. Some of them, like the professor I met that day, were internationally acclaimed academics who were teaching and researching in the USA, Turkey, Greece, France, or elsewhere as scholars in various fields. Some others were independent business people, owning small- to mid-sized establishments that operated in a range of fields from tourism to architecture. Most of them had finished at least their secondary education in Istanbul and kept their relations with the city alive even after years of being settled in Athens. Varying in age between 40 and 60, they comprised the generation of Rum Polites who were born and bred in Istanbul during the grand days of the community in the city, while they also bore witness to the vanishing of the Rum Polites from Istanbul following the tragic events they personally experienced. Although some of them knew each other already from Istanbul, their connection was mostly established or strengthened in Athens through their efforts to build networks of Rum Polites around professional, scientific, or other social causes. Most kept vivid ties to the city, were constantly in touch with friends and family residing in Istanbul, and often traveled there for vacation or on business. Given the heightened level of interaction between Greece and Turkey during the time when my fieldwork was conducted, they found more occasions to function in their capacity to fill the increased demand for journalists, translators, traders, teachers, and the like. A few of them even moved back to Istanbul. I had the chance to encounter this core network of informants in different settings and under different circumstances during my zigzags between the two cities. Our common course of connecting the cities brought us closer in mobility.

Meeting informants through informants' introductions was one of the main methods of sampling I used throughout my fieldwork, but it was complemented with another equally important one: coincidence. Though not exactly a textbook research method, I came to cherish it as an important source of ethnographic knowledge. The first benefit of coincidence, I found, is the fact that it is random, thus unmotivated or non-preselected. In this capacity, it might serve as a correction for bias in sampling: snowballing inevitably leads to the recognition of a certain set of informants and exposes the researcher to the kinds of issues that they select to be important (Bernard 2006). While a sociological method might be to use "control sampling" (ibid., 185) by coding the information from informants as to their age, gender, profession, economic standing, and the like, a more ethnographically constructed aim would be to interact with a wider variety of people within the communities under study. For apart from offering a corrective dimension, it is also useful as an additional source that helps fill in the blanks of the systematically gathered information about social networks. Coincidence opens a legitimate door to the unexpected, to serendipity, exposing "the importance of the contingent and accidental in fieldwork" (Crapanzano 2010, 60). The next story is intended to demonstrate these benefits of coincidence as an integral part of fieldwork.

THE MINI-MARKET STORY

The story takes place in Pangrati, a neighborhood in central Athens. It was yet another hot summer day, and I just wanted to buy something cold to drink, so I stopped at the first tiny little vendor I came to. This was a very small shop, basically a *periptero* (kiosk) carved into an otherwise unused building, which seemed like a temporary arrangement. Past the shaky shelves displaying small items like batteries, cigarette packs, and *frappé*[34] cups, there was a refrigerated cupboard from which I took a cherry juice. I approached the table with the cash register and the pile of newspapers and magazines, where the salesman was having a conversation with a customer. This was an elderly lady, a widow wearing all black, who was voicing her opinion about the main topic in the headlines those days: identity (*taftotita*). The issue arose when the PASOK government passed a bill on removing the religion section from the national identification cards, which culminated in a crisis between the Greek state and the Greek national church headed by Archbishop Christodoulos, who did not shy away from making some of his always daring remarks on the essential nature of Greek identity. This identity was, as the elderly lady wearing a big cross around her neck concurred, fundamentally Christian Orthodox and therefore had to be clearly stated on the identification card of every citizen. The conflictual nature of this statement arose from the fact that not every citizen of Greece was necessarily of the same religion; in addition to the larger number of Muslims in the North, there are smaller groups of Catholics, Protestants, Jews, and others who either have another faith, or none, or prefer the section to be absent in the name of privacy and religious freedom. Although the debate was initiated neither by these unofficial minorities nor by the neo-Orthodox fundamentalists, it became a matter of public discussion that highlighted important aspects about religious as well as political tendencies in Greek society, where all fronts became participants. The conversation I was witnessing would be, therefore, less than unusual, had the salesman not started shouting in agitation: "These priests (*papades*) here are outrageous! They can only speak like this here in this country. They say anything they feel like. Only in Greece! I've lived all over the place: France, England, Turkey—not even in Africa is it like this!" The lady walked out, but he continued along the same lines for another five minutes in my presence, in a self-talking mode. When he mentioned Turkey again, I asked him where in Turkey he used to live. "Fanari, Konstantinoupolis," he replied, with a proud undertone to his voice, underlining his regional alliance to the patriarchal neighborhood Fanar in the old Istanbul. When I told him that I was also from Istanbul, he immediately shifted to Turkish and said, "We could not get used to this place" (*Biz buraya alışamadık*), and started telling me his intriguing life story, which was only interrupted when other customers walked in. I left with the juice that he insisted on my accepting without charge.

This was just one instance that was generated by mere coincidence. It is an ethnographically significant situation in the sense that it reveals important information about a contemporary public debate in Greek society and shows how a Rum positions himself in relation to these issues that happen to be very central to this study. But this anecdote would not be relevant on its own, if it did not add to the greater body of ethnographic material that was collected through other methods. For anybody could have such an encounter, it is not uncommon for a tourist who spends a couple of hours in a city to make sweeping judgments about the nature of that society—indeed this is how cultural stereotypes are easily maintained. Anthropologists instead tend to resist generalizations through the multiplicity of the ethnographic situations they encounter throughout the much longer duration of fieldwork. It is this attunement to diversity that makes anthropology more interesting for me. If much of the fun and fulfillment of fieldwork is about surprise, then coincidence is but one means of getting there.

Writing Stories

This book reflects a preoccupation with the much debated issue of ethnographic writing. I tell stories; I include texts produced by my informants, by social scientists and philosophers, by authors and poets, in an attempt to achieve a polyphonic representation of a wider sense of culture. This is appropriate, I find, given that the cultural framework I study is very much based on a sense of pluralism, multiplicity, and hybridity. While this is not too dissimilar to what Marcus (1986) labeled as the "putting things together" of vignettes, travelogues, media images, texts, and literature of a wide variety, I am aware that this is not at all an easy way of producing good ethnography. The notion of culture as an "assemblage" of partial translations and of relational truths may well lead to superficiality (Borneman and Hammoudi 2009). I am concerned, then, like many anthropologists of my generation, with the predicament of "writing culture" (Clifford 1986), the style of writing and the role it plays in the power of representation. Yet I am also worried about trends where any excess textualism tends to replace ethnographic knowledge obtained from encounters and experience-based fieldwork.

I tell stories to overcome this tension: storytelling allows the gist of ethnographic information to be transmitted, along with a descriptive angle that allows the reader to imagine the fieldwork situation and also to witness the actual encounter with the anthropologist "being there" in person.[35] Storytelling does not limit reflexivity, nor carry the pretense of absolute objectivity or factual truth; it brings raw experience-based data out into the open and lets it ripen for interpretation and discussion. Stories may further be treated as expressions of culturally specific forms that are embedded in social relations and structures, sources of counternarratives to underline misleading generalizations, reveal hidden or marginalized histories, disclose revisionist understandings of a phenomenon or an event, correct commonly misused analytical categories, or refute historical claims based on other types of evidence (Maynes et al. 2008). The stories of Rum Polites may be read to highlight any or all of these dimensions. In an ethnography of diverse stories of encounter and displacement, there are many options, lots of choices to make. My inclination was to privilege the decisions made by my informants over those of the governments, historians, and other anthropologists, including my own. When I cited works, I paid attention to privileging those of Rum Polites authors. Rather than just attempting to give voice to the Rum Polites, my concern was to hear them well, hear them right. I listened to them in good will. I tried to write what I heard in a way that would also sound right to them.

I reflexively need to admit, however, that this decision has not always proven to be easy to implement. I became all too aware that my own disposition might have had an effect on how I listen. I cannot say that I am not biased toward peaceful, respectful, and rightful coexistence, to nondiscrimination, to the replacement of prejudices with refined cultural understanding as the main dimension underlying communication between peoples. Some of what I heard was music to my ears. Unwittingly, I might have tuned in to those voices to some extent, while at the same time I might have tuned out some of the ultranationalistic, fanatical comments that are absorbed into the nationalistic background noise that is still loud in both countries. Although I did not intentionally avoid such discourse, it might also have prevented itself from being heard by a Turkish researcher working in Greece. My position as a Turk could have functioned as a brake pedal controlling the speed of our interactions; instead, it worked as a catalyst in driving the conversation into deliberations about Greeks and Turks. Similarly, my being from Istanbul added an important dimension that could be overlooked by other researchers. It allowed me to operate on the fine and wobbly line between insiders and outsiders to the Rum Polites—it was a good place to be, with a clear view on matters of identity. I might be accused of overemphasizing the cosmopolitan, open, urbanite, supranational, multicultural aspects of Rum Polites cultural identity. Others might argue that the Rum Polites are characteristically a closed, conservative, traditionalist community that is bitter about its past. The fact is that both exist, as I try to convey in the chapters to follow. But the question is what to underline—or as Kenneth Burke (Hyman 1964) might have it, to decide on the principles of selecting and ordering from within the variety of cultural reality. Not everybody in the group will share the same characteristics or adhere to the same cultural reality—hence the stress on diversity of the Rum Polites community and on their resistance to homogeneity ascribed by nationalism.

What then is the main dimension that renders the Rum Polites culturally different, what makes them significant, what are the grounds for their distinction, what distinguishes them from other cultural groups? Stories of partition, rejection, and discrimination are significant when silenced; Rum Polites stand as living witnesses to a history untold. But they tell their history differently than others might expect them to their stories do not contribute to the narrative canon of enmity, ethnic hatred, and hostility between Greeks and Turks. Rum Polites tell stories that complicate these two entities and obscure their opposition. Their critical approach to the historical and the contemporary, when coupled with their familiarity with both sides of the equation, enables them to overcome the dichotomy between Turkey and Greece by way of turning their in-between status into having an intermediary and mediating function that could ease the problems associated with the division. At a time when attempts at reaching the same end remain limited to announcements of cultural similarity and friendship, lending an ear to the stories told by Rum Polites would be a good place to start looking more closely at exactly what divides the categories of Greeks, Turks, and any other social group by extension. Through their stories the Rum Polites extend an invitation to look beyond conventions, nationalistic or otherwise, in order to recognize those cultural forms that are overlooked, unrecognized, forgotten. In making their stories the focus of the book, I accept this invitation and further extend it to the attention of researchers to come. Only this will prevent them from disappearing.

Notes

1. In using the term Rum Polites, I have encountered some grammatical problems. It is a combination of one Turkish (Rum) and one Greek (Polites) word, where the former is singular and the latter is plural. I decided it would be difficult for readers to follow if I were to decline the term each time I used it, so I tried to be consistent with the form Rum Polites as much as possible, shifting to other combinations only when necessary. Rather than implying conflation, my only aim with this decision was to avoid confusion.
2. To designate current-day Istanbul, the word Konstantinoupoli (Constantinople) is preferred in Greek. The word Poli is also used, in capitalized version, not only as an abbreviation but also as a reminder of the city's position as the largest and most important urban center in the Greek world and beyond—a status it retains in the religious/symbolic realm as the seat of the Ecumenical Patriarchate of Christian Orthodoxy. The misleading debate over Istanbul versus Constantinople, pursued as claims to

national ownership in certain circles within both Greece and Turkey, is going to be omitted from this book, which aims to provide a more nuanced understanding of the issues regarding city and identity. I have preferred Istanbul, as the dominant official usage in English, translated Poli as City, and used Constantinople when referring to the Byzantine period. Where it did not matter, I may have used the names interchangeably, void of any political intent or conviction.

3. Different census records in Istanbul have counted the Rum Polites differently over the years, using varying bases of identification. The numbers are estimated to be around 200,000 during the last few decades of the nineteenth century, while they reportedly exceeded 300,000 at the beginning of the twentieth (cf. Alexandris 1983, 49–51). In the aftermath of wars and migrations, in 1924 there were still more than 270,000 in a city of just over a million inhabitants (Alexandris 1983, 142), while the 1927 official survey of the Turkish Republic indicates over 100,000 Orthodox Rum in Istanbul, making up about 15% of the population (Dündar 2000). Today, there are some 2000 Rum in an Istanbul of over fifteen million. The largest center today is Athens with several tens of thousands of Rum Polites, although smaller groups of Rum Polites are found in various parts of the world.

4. *Fanariots* are an Ottoman Christian elite who ascended to power in multiple political arenas between the 1660s and 1821 (Philliou 2008, 151). They are named after their residence in the region of Fanar, the location of the Ecumenical Patriarchate.

5. *Karamanlides* or *Karamanli* are a community of Turcophone Christian Orthodox who come from the Central Anatolia/Cappadocia region. They write in Turkish with Greek letters using a language called *Karamanlica* or *Karamanlidika*. Based on their religion, however, they were considered Greeks and a great majority of them were sent to Greece during the forced exchange of populations. Some of them have moved to Istanbul, where they learned the Greek language and mixed with the Rum. See Balta (2010).

6. *Mikrasiates* or "Anatolians," as used above, refers to the people from Asia Minor, that is, the Christian Orthodox Rum refugees from the Greek–Turkish war (called the Catastrophe or Liberation War, respectively) or people who were held as part of the Forced Exchange of Populations in accordance with the Convention signed as part of the Treaty of Lausanne in 1923. Part of the Rum Polites in Istanbul, like those of the islands of Imvros and Tenedos, and the Muslim populations of Western Thrace were held exempt from the forced exchange, yet still had to migrate to Athens later on, increasingly in the second half of the twentieth century.

7. *Imvriotes*, Greek Orthodox residents of the island of *Imvros* (Gökçeada) as well as neighboring *Tenedos* (Bozcaada), located at the entrance of the Dardanelles Strait, were held exempt from the 1923 Forced Exchange of Populations. Like the Rum Polites, Imvriotes also endured many dramatic changes throughout the twentieth century, which resulted in a drastic fall of their population in the islands. Even though differences and discrepancies remained intact between them, they stayed in close contact with the Rum Polites after their migration to either Istanbul or to Athens. For more, see Babül (2006), Tansuğ (2012), and Tsimouris (2001).
8. *Süryani Assyrians*, and the related groups of Syriacs, Arameans, and Chaldeans, are also partially members of the Greek Orthodox Church. They originate from ancient populations in Southeastern Asia Minor and speak different Sami languages. Although they do not have the same origins as the Rum Polites, they were often classified as such by the Turkish state because of their common religion. Some of them were included in the Exchange of Populations, while those who remained in Turkey (especially the population in Antioch/Hatay, which was not within Turkish borders at the time of the Exchange) have partially joined the Rum Polites in Istanbul, sending their children to Rum schools and taking over some community duties such as maintaining and guarding the churches. There are a few hundred Assyrians in Athens who live close to the community of Rum Polites, and many continue speaking Turkish without having learned any Greek. For a few studies on the subject, see Zubaida (2000), Husry (1974), and Al-Rasheed (1998).
9. French was often spoken in families of mixed origin, where couples would revert to French as the common language of communication. More broadly, French has been the lingua franca until the first half of the twentieth century, and fluency in this language indicated good education and elite status in Istanbul society.
10. *Ecumenical* has come to be a somewhat polemical term, but I use it without any allusion to that political discussion taking place in Turkey. For the purposes of this work, it is taken as the correct and preferred emic form as this is how the Rum Polites refer to their own denomination. For more on the Patriarchate, see Benlisoy and Macar (1996) and Inalcik (1991), among others.
11. As a movement born in Byzantine Constantinople, the Rum Catholic Church is an interesting case. Although they are Catholics, they practice not the Latin but the Rum/Byzantine tradition of the Eastern Church. Their website insists that they should not be confused with the Roman Catholics (www.rumkatkilise.org). For a detailed study of some of these communities, see Macar (2002).

12. Exactly who founded the city, and when, remains disputed among historians. Rum Polites scholars Yerasimos (2000) and Alexandris (1983) also differ in their dates of foundation, citing 680 and 658, respectively.
13. For selected accounts on *Rum milleti* or *millet-i Rum* during the Ottoman period, see Gondicas and Issawi (1999), Stathi (1999), Anagnostopoulou (1997), Barkey (2008), Benlisoy and Benlisoy (2001), Exertzoglou (1996), Roudometof (1998), Özil (2016), Anastassiadou (2009), Kamouzis (2013), and Kechriotis (2005).
14. For selected historical accounts of the period, see Svolopoulos (1994), Eldem (1999), Zürcher (1998), Exertzoglu (1996, 1999, 2003), and Yerasimos (1996). See also Örs (2002).
15. Constantine Mousouros served as the Ottoman Ambassador to the Greek Kingdom (1840–1848); later followed by John Photiadis in the 1860s, they both served their country through difficult times in Greek–Ottoman relations. The Ottoman ambassadorship to Greek Britain was also held by Rum Polites throughout much of the nineteenth century: Constantine Mousouros (1856–1891), Constantine Anthopoulos (1891–1902), Stephen Mousouros (1902–1907). For other distinguished Fanariots and Rum Polites in the service of the Ottoman Grand Porte, see Sözen (2000), Alexandris (1983), Phillou (2010), and Janos (2005).
16. Restrictions of the applications provisioned by the Treaty of Lausanne in 1923 include (1) retracting the borders of the city to those of the municipality of Istanbul, which forced otherwise exempt thousands to leave; (2) the one-sided establishment of the category of *etablis* to refer to those who could prove continuous residence since before 1918; (3) the denial of the right to return to the Rum Polites who had temporarily left during the war or the Allied Occupation, and the confiscation of their property; (4) various constraints and intimidation imposed on the Ecumenical Patriarchate, and the de facto instituting of the Turkish Orthodox Patriarchate in Galata; and (5) the dismissal, punishment, or expulsion of many hundreds of Rum Polites from Istanbul and the islands of Imvros and Tenedos, among others. For more, see Alexandris (1983) and Oran (2004).
17. Restrictions in 1925: Commissions composed of minorities were asked to give a written statement declaring that they were denouncing their minority rights in the name of equality in the Turkish Republic, which was done first by the Jews, then by the Armenians, and finally and with much difficulty, by the Rum Orthodox (Alexandris 1983, 138).
18. Restrictions on the Professions of Minorities: Law no. 2007, dated 11 June 1932, titled "Law on the arts and services in Turkey rendered exclusive to Turkish citizens," prohibited a wide range of professions to non-Turks, including those of barber, waiter, singer, construction worker, stockbroker, plumber, driver, and so on. For the full text of the law, see Aktar (2000,

120). This act caused thousands of Greek national Rum Polites to remain jobless and migrate to Athens (Alexandris 1983, 185).
19. Wealth Tax: Law no. 4305, dated 11 November 1942, titled "Wealth Tax Law," was enforced when a commission calculated the tax amount to be paid by distributing the taxpayers into four categories (Muslim, non-Muslim, Foreigner, Dönme). Lists were made public in a month, due dates were just 15 days later, and no delays or appeals were allowed. Those who could not pay their taxes in full were subjected to *haciz*, and if the amount from sales did not cover the debt, they were sent to a labor camp in Eastern Turkey, where they had to work under very harsh conditions until they paid their taxes. This measure was only applied to non-Muslims, of whom 21 died while in the camp. After international pressure, the law was canceled on 15 March 1944. See Ökte (1951), Akar (1992), and Aktar (1996, 2000).
20. 1964 Expulsions: The İnönü government one-sidedly annulled the so-called friendship treaty signed between Atatürk and Venizelos in 1930, on 16 March 1964, followed by the cancelation of a series of similar treaties (Demir and Akar 1994, 55–57). Then the property titles of the Greek Rum were annulled and their bank accounts were frozen. Finally, their residence permits were canceled, and they were forced to leave the country within 15 days. Including their families and dependants, over 40,000 Rum Polites are estimated to have left. See Demir and Akar (1994).
21. Events of 6–7 September 1955: The overnight pogrom known as *Septemvriana* in Greek. Attacks by mobs on Rum-owned private and public buildings in Istanbul, Izmir, Imvros, and Tenedos. See Chap. 4 for more.
22. 1974 Cyprus Events: Turkish Military Forces landed in Northern Cyprus to engage in what is called Peace Maneuver or Invasion or Occupation, as a result of which the island split into two zones between Greek and Turkish Cypriots. This led to demonstrations against the Rum Polites in Istanbul.
23. With roots in the late Ottoman Empire (see Yıldız 2001; Ersanlı 2003; Landau 1981), Turkification is the process of establishing the political and economic supremacy of the ethnically Turkish and Muslim Sunni population in Turkey. For analytical approaches to the effects of Turkification with respect to minority policies, see, for example, Aktar (2000, 2009), Bali (1999), Akar (1992), and Güven (2005).
24. *Levantine* are multireligious, multicultural families who trace their origins back to medieval times in the Levant, the port cities of the Eastern Mediterranean. See Bareilles (2003), Yorulmaz (1994–1995), and Scognamillo (2009), among others.
25. *White Russians* are migrants from the Russian Empire who escaped before or after the Bolshevik Revolution of 1917. See Deleon (1995).

26. In the context of Istanbul, West and East correspond quite literally to Europe and Asia, the continents on the two shores of the Bosphorus Strait.
27. The symbolism of the double-headed eagle has ancient Near-Eastern origins (Collins 2010) and is still used today in the region and worldwide in various forms. The version used here is a black figure on a bright yellow background and is recognizable as a reference to Orthodox Church (Kokkonis-Lambropoulos and Korres-Zografos 1997; Zapheriou 1947).
28. There is a limited but rising literature on contemporary Rum Polites, including Anastassiadou-Dumont and Dumont (2003), Akgönül (2007), Yücel (2016), and Yücel and Yıldız (2014).
29. Both gender and religion are intrinsic parts of cultural identity and are therefore expected to be underlined in an ethnography. Even though I may not think of them as two of my salient characteristics, my being a woman and a non-practicing or secular Muslim is likely to have been taken for granted by my informants. because they were hardly ever reflected upon during the fieldwork, it is hard for me to consider reflexively what effect they may have made on the ethnographic encounter, although one can be certain that they did.
30. It would be impossible to do justice to the great literature in anthropology of food and drink (for a review, see Mintz and Du Bois 2002). Some of the recent works include Marovelli (2014), Srinivas (2013), Yasmeen (2013), and Beriss and Sutton (2007), among others.
31. An international conference with the objective of bringing together Rum Polites worldwide took place in Istanbul in July 2006. Proceedings of the widely attended conference were published in Turkish and in Greek. See Benlisoy (2012).
32. For methodological challenges anthropologists face when doing fieldwork in the city, see, for example, Foster and Kemper (1974), Pardo and Prato (2012), Prato and Pardo (2013), Rogers and Vertovec (1995), and Sanjek (1990).
33. I conducted what I call "encounter interviews" with small groups of people from both parts of the Rum Polites, living in Istanbul and in Athens, who came together to talk about their shared experiences. I found that this not only eased the difficulty of reciting bittersweet memories of displacement but also made it more desirable to display their recollections to an audience that shared and understood them without being judgmental. I also believe that this way of having an open conversation limited the bias involved in the ethnographic encounter in comparison with the potential bias in an interview between one informant and the researcher.
34. *Frappé* is a particular kind of iced coffee that is widely consumed in Greece all year round.

35. This is the title of a renowned essay by Clifford Geertz (1988), which has been taken up recently in several works on the subject. See Hannerz (2003), Borneman and Hammoudi (2009), Watson (1999).

BIBLIOGRAPHY

Akar, R. (1992). *Varlık Vergisi Kanunu: Tek Parti Rejiminde Azınlık Karşıtı Politika Örneği*. İstanbul: Belge Yayinlari.
Aktar, A. (2009). Turkification Policies in the Early Republican Era. In C. Dufft (Ed.), *Turkish Literature and Cultural Memory: "Multiculturalism" as a Literary Theme After 1980* (pp. 29–62). Wiesbaden: Harrassowitz Verlag.
Akgönül, S. (2007). *Türkiye Rumları: Ulus-Devlet Çağından Küreselleşme Çağına Bir Azınlığın Yok Oluş Süreci*. İstanbul: İletişim.
Aktar, A. (1996). Economic Nationalism in Turkey: The Formative Years, 1912–1925. *Boğaziçi Journal, Review of Social and Administrative Studies*, *10*(1–2), 263–290.
Aktar, A. (2000). *Varlık Vergisi ve "Türkleştirme" Politikaları*. İstanbul: İletişim Yayınları.
Albera, D., & Couroucli, M. (2012). *Sharing Sacred Spaces in the Mediterranean: Christians, Muslims, and Jews at Shrines and Sanctuaries*. Bloomington, IN: Indiana University Press.
Alexandris, A. (1983). *The Greek Minority of Istanbul and Greek-Turkish Relations, 1918–1974*. Athens: Center for Asia Minor Studies.
Anagnostopoulou, S. (1997). *Mikra Asia, 19os ai.–1919: Oi ellinoorthodoxes koinotites. Apo to millet ton Romion sto Elliniko ethnos*. Athens: Ellinika Grammata.
Anastasiadou-Dumont, M., & Dumont, P. (2003). *Une mémoire pour la Ville: La communauté grecque d'Istanbul en 2003*. Istanbul: OUI.
Anastassiadou, M. (2009). Greek Orthodox Immigrants and Modes of Integration within the Urban Society of Istanbul (1850–1923). *Mediterranean Historical Review*, *24*(2), 151–167.
Babül, E. (2006). Claiming a Place Through Memories of Belonging: Politics of Recognition on the Island of Imbros. *New Perspectives on Turkey*, *34*, 47–65.
Bali, R. (1999). *Cumhuriyet Yıllarında Türkiye Yahudileri: Bir Türkleştirme Serüveni, 1923–1945*. Cağaloğlu, İstanbul: İletişim.
Balta, E. (2010). *Beyond the Language Frontier: Studies on the Karamanlis and the Karamanlidika Printing*. Istanbul: Isis Press.
Bareilles, B. (2003). *İstanbul'un Frenk ve Levanten Mahalleleri: Pera, Galata, Banliyöler*. İstanbul: Güncel Yayıncılık.
Barkan, E., & Barkey, K. (2014). *Choreographies of Shared Sacred Sites*. New York: Columbia University Press.

Barkey, K. (2008). *Empire of Difference: The Ottomans in Comparative Perspective*. Cambridge: Cambridge University Press.
Barth, F. (1969). *Ethnic Groups and Boundaries*. Boston: Little Brown and Company.
Beck, U., & Sznaider, N. (2006). Unpacking Cosmopolitanism for the Social Sciences: A Research Agenda. *The British Journal of Sociology, 57*(1), 1–23.
Benlisoy, F. (Ed.). (2012). *İstanbul Rumları: Bugün ve Yarın*. İstanbul: Zoğrafyon Lisesi Mezunları Derneği.
Benlisoy, F., & Benlisoy, S. (2001). Millet-i Rum'dan Helen Ulusuna 1856–1922. In *Cumhuriyet'e Devreden Düşünce Mirası: Tanzimat ve Meşrutiyet'in Birikimi: I* (pp. 367–376). İstanbul: İletişim.
Beriss, D., & Sutton, D. E. (2007). *The Restaurants Book: Ethnographies of Where We Eat*. Oxford: Berg.
Bernard, R. H. (2006). *Research Methods in Anthropology: Qualitative and Quantitative Approaches*. Lanham and New York: Altamira Press.
Bestor, T. (2002). Networks, Neighborhoods, and Markets: Fieldwork in Tokyo. In G. Gmelch & W. P. Zenner (Eds.), *Urban Life: Readings in the Anthropology of the City*. Prospect Heights, IL: Waveland Press.
Borneman, J., & Hammoudi, A. (2009). *Being There: The Fieldwork Encounter and the Making of Truth*. Berkeley: University of California Press.
Calhoun, C. (2004). Accidental Wisdom. *Book Forum*. Retrieved from http://www.bookforum.com/archive/sum_04/calhoun.html
Clifford, J. (1986). Introduction: Partial Truths. In J. Clifford & G. Marcus (Eds.), *Writing Culture: The Poetics and Politics of Ethnography* (pp. 1–26). Berkeley: University of California Press.
Collins, B. J. (2010). Animal Mastery in Hittite Art and Texts. In D. B. Counts & B. Arnold (Eds.), *The Master of Animals in Old World Iconography* (pp. 59–74). Budapest: Archaeolingua Foundation.
Crapanzano, V. (2010). At the Heart of the Discipline: Critical Reflections on Fieldwork. In J. Davies & D. Spencer (Eds.), *Emotions in the Field: The Psychology and the Anthropology of the Fieldwork Experience* (pp. 55–78). Stanford: Stanford University Press.
Davis, S. H., & Konner, M. (2011). *Being There: Learning to Live Cross-Culturally*. Cambridge, MA: Harvard University Press.
De Certeau, M. (1988). *The Practice of Everyday Life*. Berkeley: University of California Press.
Deleon, J. (1995). *The White Russians in Istanbul*. İstanbul: Remzi.
Demir, H., & Akar, R. (1994). *İstanbul'un Son Sürgünleri*. İstanbul: İletişim.
Driessen, H. (1992). *On the Spanish-Moroccan Frontier: A Study in Ritual, Power, and Ethnicity*. New York and Oxford: Berg.
Dündar, F. (2000). *Türkiye Nüfus Sayımlarında Azınlıklar*. İstanbul: Çiviyazıları.
Eldem, E. (1999). *French Trade in Istanbul in the Eighteenth Century*. Leiden: Brill.

Ergül, F. A. (2012). The Ottoman Identity: Turkish, Muslim or Rum? *Middle Eastern Studies, 48*(4), 629–645.
Ersanlı, B. (2003). *İktidar ve Tarih: Türkiye'de Resmi Tarih Tezinin Oluşumu, 1929–1937.* İstanbul: İletişim.
Exertzoglou, H. (1996). *Ethniki Taftotita stin Konstantinoupoli ton 19o aiona.* Athens: Nefeli.
Exertzoglou, H. (1999). The Development of a Greek Ottoman Bourgeoisie: Investment Patterns in the Ottoman Empire, 1850–1914. In D. Gondicas & C. Issawi (Eds.), *Ottoman Greeks in the Age of Nationalism* (pp. 89–114). Princeton: The Darwin Press.
Exertzoglou, H. (2003). The Cultural Uses of Consumption: Negotiating Class, Gender, and Nation in the Ottoman Urban Centers during the 19th Century. *International Journal of Middle East Studies, 35*(1), 77–101.
Falzon, M.-A. (2009). *Multi-Sited Ethnography: Theory, Praxis and Locality in Contemporary Research.* Farnham: Ashgate.
Fischer, M., & Kokolaki, M. (2013). Comments and Reflections. *Urbanites, 3*(2), 114–117.
Foster, G. M., & Kemper, R. V. (1974). *Anthropologists in Cities.* Boston: Little, Brown.
Geertz, C. (1988). *Works and Lives: The Anthropologist as Author.* Stanford, CA: Stanford University Press.
Giordano, C. (2012). Anthropology Meets History: Investigating European Societies. *Anthropological Journal of European Cultures, 21*(2), 20–34.
Gondicas, D., & Issawi, C. (1999). *Ottoman Greeks in the Age of Nationalism: Politics, Economy, and Society in the Nineteenth Century.* Princeton, NJ: Darwin Press.
Güven, D. (2005). *Cumhuriyet Dönemi Azınlık Politikaları Bağlamında 6–7 Eylül Olayları.* İstanbul: Tarih Vakfı Yayınları.
Hannerz, U. (2003). Being There... and There... and There!: Reflections on Multi-Site Ethnography. *Ethnography, 4*(2), 201–216.
Harris, R. (2011). Multiculturalism: Theoretical Challenges from Anthropology. *Urbanities, 1*(1), 70–75.
Herzfeld, M. (1997). *Cultural Intimacy: Social Poetics in the Nation-State.* New York: Routledge.
Herzfeld, M. (2013). Comments. *Urbanities, 3*(2), 118–120.
Husry, K. S. (1974). The Assyrian Affair of 1933. *International Journal of Middle East Studies, 5*(2), 161–176.
Hyman, S. E. (Ed.). (1964). *Perspectives by Incongruity by Kenneth Burke.* Bloomington: Indiana University Press.
İnalcık, H. (1991). The Status of the Greek Orthodox Patriarch under the Ottomans. *Turcica: Revue d'Etudes Turques, 21–23,* 407–436.
Jaffe, R., & de Koning, A. (2016). *Introducing Urban Anthropology.* New York: Routledge.

Janos, D. (2005). Panaiotis Nicousios and Alexander Mavrocordatos: The Rise of the Phanariots and the Office of Grand Dragoman in the Ottoman Administration in the Second Half of the Seventeenth Century. *Archivum Ottomanicum, 23,* 177–196.

Kafadar, C. (2007). A Rome of One's Own: Reflections on Cultural Geography and Identity in the Lands of Rum. *Muqarnas Online, 24*(1), 7–25.

Kamouzis, D. (2013). Elites and the Formation of National Identity: The Case of the Greek Orthodox *Millet* (Mid-Nineteenth Century to 1922). In B. Fortna, S. Katsikas, D. Kamouzis, & P. Konortas (Eds.), *State-Nationalisms in the Ottoman Empire, Greece and Turkey: Orthodox and Muslims, 1830–1945.* London: Routledge.

Kechriotis, V. (2005). *The Greeks of Izmir at the End of the Empire: A Non-Muslim Ottoman Community between Autonomy and Patriotism.* Unpublished Ph.D. dissertation, University of Leiden, Germany.

Kokkonis-Lambropoulos, E., & Korres-Zografos, K. (1997). Greek Flags, Arms and Insignia. In E. Kokkonis & G. Tsiveriotis (Eds.), *In Memory of Panos Kokkonis* (pp. 47–51). Athens, Greece: Elias Coconis.

Landau, J. M. (1981). *Pan-Turkism in Turkey: A Study of Irredentism.* Hamden, CT: Archon Books.

Macar, E. (2002). *İstanbul'un Yok Olmuş İki Cemaati: Doğu Ritli Katolik Rumlar ve Bulgarlar.* Istanbul: İletişim.

Marcus, G. (1986). Contemporary Problems of Ethnography in the Modern World System. In J. Clifford & G. Marcus (Eds.), *Writing Culture: The Poetics and Politics of Ethnography* (pp. 165–193). Berkeley: University of California Press.

Marovelli, B. (2014). 'Meat Smells Like Corpses': Sensory Perceptions in a Sicilian Urban Marketplace. *Urbanites, 7*(2), 21–38.

Maynes, M. J., Pierce, J. L., & Laslett, B. (2008). *Telling Stories: The Use of Personal Narratives in the Social Sciences and History.* Ithaca: Cornell University Press.

Mintz, S. W., & Du Bois, C. M. (2002). The Anthropology of Food and Eating. *Annual Review of Anthropology, 31*(1), 99–119.

Moore, S. F. (1987). Explaining the Present: Theoretical Dilemmas in Processual Ethnography. *American Ethnologist, 14*(4), 727–736.

Ökte, F. (1951). *Varlık Vergisi Faciası.* İstanbul: Nebioğlu Yayınevi.

Oran, B. (2004). *Türkiye'de Azınlıklar: Kavramlar, Teori, Lozan, İç Mevzuat, İçtihat, Uygulama.* Cağaloğlu, İstanbul: İletişim.

Örs, İ. R. (2002). Coffeehouses, Cosmopolitanism and Pluralizing Modernities in Istanbul. *Journal of Mediterranean Studies, 12*(1), 119–145.

Özil, A. (2016). *Anadolu Rumları: Osmanlı İmparatorluğu'nun Son Döneminde Millet Sistemini Yeniden Düşünmek.* İstanbul: Kitap Yayınevi.

Pardo, I. (1996). *Managing Existence in Naples: Morality, Action and Structure.* Cambridge: Cambridge University Press.

Philliou, C. (2008). Communities on the Verge: Unraveling the Phanariot Ascendancy in Ottoman Governance. *Comparative Studies in Society and History, 51*(01), 151.
Philliou, C. (2010). *Biography of an Empire: Governing Ottomans in an Age of Revolution*. Berkeley, CA: University of California Press.
Pieke, F. (2000). Serendipity: Reflections on Fieldwork in China. In P. Dresch, W. James, & D. Parkin (Eds.), *Anthropologists in a Wider World: Essays on Field Research* (pp. 129–150). New York: Berghahn Books.
Prato, G. B. (2009). Introduction – Beyond Multiculturalism: Anthropology at the Intersections between the Local, the National and the Global. In G. B. Prato (Ed.), *Beyond Multiculturalism: Views from Anthropology* (pp. 1–19). London: Routledge.
Prato, G. B., & Pardo, I. (2013). Urban Anthropology. *Urbanities, 3*(2), 80–110.
Rivoal, I., & Salazar, N. (2013). Contemporary Ethnographic Practice and the Value of Serendipity. *Social Anthropology, 21*, 178–185.
Rogers, A., & Vertovec, S. (1995). *The Urban Context: Ethnicity, Social Networks and Situational Analysis*. London: Berg.
Rotenberg, R. (2002). The Metropolis and Everyday Life. In G. Gmelch & W. P. Zenner (Eds.), *Urban Life: Readings in the Anthropology of the City* (pp. 60–81). Chicago: Waveland Press.
Roudometof, V. (1998). From Rum Millet to Greek Nation: Enlightenment, Secularization, and National Identity in Ottoman Balkan Society, 1453–1821. *Journal of Modern Greek Studies, 16*(1), 11–48.
Sanjek, R. (1990). Urban Anthropology in the 1980s: A World View. *Annual Review of Anthropology, 19*, 151–186.
Scognamillo, G. (2009/1990). *Bir Levantenin Beyoğlu Anıları*. İstanbul: Metis Yayınları.
Shryock, A. (1997). *Nationalism and the Genealogical Imagination: Oral History and Textual Authority in Tribal Jordan*. Berkeley: University of California Press.
Sözen, Z. (2000). *Fenerli Beyler: 110 Yılın Öyküsü 1711–1821*. Istanbul: Aybay.
Srinivas, T. (2013). Towards Cultural Translation: Rethinking the Dynamics of Religious Pluralism and Globalisation Through the Sathya Sai Movement. In R. Hefner, J. Hutchinson, S. Mels, & C. Timmermann (Eds.), *Religions in Movement: The Local and the Global in Contemporary Faith Traditions* (pp. 230–245). New York: Routledge.
Stathi, P. (1999). *19.Yüzyıl İstanbul'unda Gayrimüslimler*. Istanbul: Tarih Vakfı Yayınları.
Strathern, M. (1991). *Partial Connections*. Savage, MD: Rowman & Littlefield.
Sutton, D. (1998). *Memories Cast in Stone*. Oxford: Berg.
Svolopoulos, K. (1994). *Konstantinoupoli, 1856–1908: H Akmi tou Ellinismou*. Athens: Ekdoseis Athinon.

Tansuğ, F. (Ed.). (2012). *İmroz Rumları: Gökçeada Üzerine*. Istanbul: Heyamola.
Tsimouris, G. (2001). Reconstructing "Home" among the "Enemy": The Greeks of Gokseada (Imvros) after Lausanne. *Balkanologie*, 5(1–2), 257–289.
Van Andel, P. (1994). Anatomy of the Unsought Finding. Serendipity: Origin, History, Domains, Traditions, Appearances, Patterns and Programmability. *The British Journal for the Philosophy of Science*, 45(2), 631–648.
Watson, C. W. (Ed.). (1999). *Being There: Fieldwork in Anthropology*. London: Pluto Press.
Yasmeen, G. (2013). Not "From Scratch": Thai Food Systems and "Public Eating". In C. Counihan & P. van Esterik (Eds.), *Food and Culture: A Reader*. London: Routledge.
Yerasimos, S. (1996). *İstanbul, 1914–1923: Kaybolup Giden Bir Dünyanın Başkenti Ya Da Yaşlı İmparatorlukların Can Çekişmesi*. İstanbul: İletişim.
Yerasimos, S. (2000). *İstanbul: İmparatorluklar Başkenti*. İstanbul: Türkiye Ekonomik Ve Toplumsal Tarih Vakfı Yurt Yayınları.
Yıldız, A. (2001). *Türk Ulusal Kimliğinin Etno-Seküler Sınırları 1919–1938*. İstanbul: İletişim.
Yıldız, S., & Yücel, H. (2014). İstanbul'da ve İmroz'da Rum Olmak, Atina'da Rum Kalmak. *Alternatif Politika*, 6(2), 148–194.
Yorulmaz, A. (1994). *Ayvalık'ı Gezerken*. Ayvalık: Geylan Kitabevi.
Yücel, H. (Ed.). (2016). *Rum olmak, Rum kalmak*. İstanbul: İstos Yayın.
Zapheriou, N. (1947). *H Elliniki simaia apo tin arhaiotita os simera*. Athens: Elefteri Skepsis.
Zubaida, S. (2000). Contested Nations: Iraq and the Assyrians. *Nations and Nationalism*, 6(3), 363–382.
Zürcher, E. J. (1998). *Turkey: A Modern History*. London: I.B. Tauris.

CHAPTER 2

Cosmopolitan Knowledge: Impressions from Everyday Life in Athens

As Constantine Cavafy famously mused once upon a time about Alexandria, the Rum Polites of Istanbul left to go to another land across the sea, hoping to find another city, perhaps better than theirs. Yet the city followed them. And perhaps, as Italo Calvino's Marco Polo imagined once, they understood their city better after feeling lost in unfamiliar quarters of distant cities. Some lives changed radically upon displacement from Istanbul; some found new lives in Athens. Still, the invisible city followed them.

This chapter highlights aspects of Rum Polites' lives in Athens through a selection of ethnographic stories that pertain to their life in Istanbul. Through presenting material in the form of anecdotes, personal experiences, interviews, and other oral or written sources, I paint an impressionistic picture of the Rum Polites' neighborhoods, their everyday rhythms, their language, ideas about food, clothing habits, rituals, and special celebrations. Thus, I stroll from the street into a bookstore, from the church yard onto a fishing boat, from homes to restaurants, covering a range of activities scattered over the temporal and spatial spectrum of life in the city.

In trying to make cultural sense of the daily life experiences of the Rum Polites in Athens, I set out from the theoretical framework provided by Michel de Certeau (1988). Much like him, my intention here is to trace the interlacings of a concrete sense of everyday life where the basic gestures of ways of operating are deployed and repeated from day to day across the different daily functions like meals, dressing, receiving guests, and so on, which are narrated under the rubric of everyday practices of the Rum Polites community in Athens. Carrying this point further, I aim to show how, insofar as these privately generated life narratives become publicly positioned and outwardly oriented, they help formulate the cultural differences between the Rum Polites and the Athenians and become the basis of a perceived separation of identity.

In thinking about the Rum Polites identity in relation to everyday urban experience, I find the conceptual tools provided by Robert Rotenberg (1992) to be particularly appropriate. His notion of metropolitan knowledge as a dispersed, shared knowledge of the urban world that forms the silent backdrop of everyday life is relevant for the Rum Polites: it is knowledge of the City that defines what it means to be from Istanbul, or the ways in which they identify themselves and others as Rum Polites. Yet there is an adjustment to be made in the term, as in the case of Rum Polites in Athens metropolitan knowledge relates not to Athens but rather to knowing the ways of Istanbul, the original city they left behind. I therefore coin the related term "cosmopolitan knowledge" that refers to both urban knowledge, that is, knowledge of the city, and a specific knowledge of Istanbul or the City. As with the situation of loss in Michel de Certeau's Paris, knowledge here is based on memory, except that in this case loss is not a result of demolition but of displacement. Still, what is intimately known and shared remains absent from the regular flow of life in the city where they currently live: "the wordless histories of walking, dress, housing, or cooking shape neighborhoods on behalf of absences; they trace out memories that no longer have place" (de Certeau 1988, 142). These practices are best understood as tactics, because the place of a tactic belongs to the other, and because a tactic insinuates itself into the other's place. Cosmopolitan knowledge thus conditions the manner of relating to another place, via the city of memory, so that remembering detailed information about the city becomes a way of staying in connection with it. Such knowledge, then, forms a kind of cultural capital among the Rum Polites in Athens and operates as a basis for "distinction," *à la* Bourdieu (1984), in helping to distinguish the Rum Polites among the immediate presence of other Greek Athenians.

The Bookstore Story

It was early afternoon and I was strolling around Faliro,[1] the neighborhood where I lived along with a majority of Rum Polites in Athens. I was walking up and down one of the main streets, Agios Alexandros, as I often did during my fieldwork as it was also where most Rum Polites shops and social centers were to be found. Once a chic upscale seaside suburb, Paleo Faliro had transformed itself rapidly into a circumcenter residential neighborhood with a high population density. The large villas with lush green gardens and palm trees gave way to high-rise buildings called *polikatikies*. When the Rum Polites started arriving in Athens *en masse* in the mid-1960s, they moved to this seaside neighborhood because it reportedly reminded them of other seaside neighborhoods of Istanbul. The earlier arrivals who were settled in more central and less expensive areas, such as Patissia, Ambelokipi, or Kaisariani, also moved to new apartment buildings in Faliro[2] (*"mazeftikan ekei"*—gathered there) to constitute what an informant calls "Istanbulistan," making for a "particularly lively community" by the mid-1970s.[3] Many Rum Polites who live in Faliro say that they indeed prefer this part of the city so that they can be closer to other Rum Polites and have easy access to all the Istanbul goodies: anything from *baklava*[4] to daily *yufka*[5] and seasonal fish from the Bosphorus can be found in the many delicatessen shops, restaurants, and patisseries in Faliro, which bear names like Rio, Riviera, or Palet after the former Rum establishments in Istanbul, or use place names like Imvros or *Prinkiponissia*[6] that signal the shop's identity to the customers. This is certainly good for business, as confirmed by various shop owners, to the extent that some use these names without being actually connected to Istanbul at all. In any case, Faliro is a part of town where one would come to find Turkish newspapers in the kiosks called *periptera*, to book a bus tour to Istanbul from Rum Polites travel agents, to hear Turkish spoken occasionally on the streets, or just to watch Rum Polites in the afternoon gathering around the coffeeshops in the *plateia*, go for a promenade along the seafront Poseidonos street, or walk up and down Agios Alexandros, as I was doing that day.

It was around half past two in the afternoon of a pleasantly warm spring Thursday. There was no time for interviews or small talk, as the shopkeepers were preparing to close down for the lunch/siesta break. So I was strolling around, killing time before I went home for lunch, and it was at this moment that a book caught my eye in a bookshop window: *O Ellinismos tis*

Konstantinoupolis (Hellenism of Istanbul) screamed the glossy hardcover, featuring an old sketch of Istanbul imposed on a yellowish background. I was excited because I knew the author, Soula Bozi, well. I asked the shop assistant if I could kindly have a moment to look at the book. She told me that she had already closed the cash till, but I was welcome to browse until she packed up to leave. Observing my interest in this particular volume, she said it would actually be better for me to come back in the afternoon in any case, because there would be a presentation by the author herself. Pleased about the lucky coincidence, I thanked her for the information and left the store, only to return a couple of hours later.

At six in the afternoon, the immediate surroundings of the bookshop were much more crowded and lively than they had been at lunch time. Tuesday, Thursday, and Friday are the only days when Athenians can shop in the afternoon, and many were taking advantage of the longer opening hours to do their shopping before the weekend. After edging past the crowded café of the *plateia* where the waitresses were carefully but rapidly ferrying trays laden with tall iced coffee *frappé* glasses to the tables, I passed the fishmonger who was sprinkling water over his fresh *fagri* and fish-farm *tsipoura* and then the greengrocer, where a woman was telling her husband that, since the tomatoes were almost yellow and outrageously expensive, it would make more sense to go to the *laiki agora* (the open-air farmers' market) next morning. I made a note to myself to reschedule my day in order to go to the *laiki agora*; it was only on Fridays that one had the chance to pick up reasonably priced fresh produce in my neighborhood. It was not to be missed, also for an additional reason: the next day, I remembered, was the beginning of the forty-day fasting period before Easter during which the Orthodox were not to eat any animal products. So today was "broiling Thursday" (*tsiknopempti*) when Greeks would invade grill restaurants and *kebap* places en masse to make sure they consumed enough meat to make it through the next month and a half. That was why, I realized, there was so much activity on the streets, and of course, the fishmonger was busier than usual as fish is the only such product that can be legitimately consumed to alleviate the vegetarian diet—a hard-to-swallow concept in Greece.[7]

Leaving the hectic streets behind, I entered the little bookstore. The book I was interested in was already piled up next to the cashier, who told me that the presentation was to take place upstairs. A narrow climb took me to a half-floor surrounded by shelves full of books, looking like a cozy reading room, and probably recently converted from a former storage area as evidenced by the fresh smell of wood varnish. There were about thirty chairs facing the table at which the author was sitting in waiting. She smiled upon seeing me come in and said, "Welcome to you all! It is nice to see friendly faces here." I sat down with the others, around seven at that point, and watched the room slowly filling up. Some were familiar faces: an employee of the Turkish airline in Athens, a translator of bestsellers from Turkish to Greek, a retired man who is never absent from any occasion having to do with Istanbul or Turkey—all were Rum Polites, but none had any contact with each other. A little while later two women and a child walked in and sat down behind me. From the way they were talking, it was obvious that they were not from Istanbul themselves, but had somehow developed an interest in the history of the City. They asked me whether the lady across from us was the author of the book, and whether she was from Istanbul herself. Yes, I said, she is an independent researcher who has published various books in Greek and Turkish, among them a book on Istanbul cuisine, called *Politiki Kouzina*. They said that this was very interesting, that they liked Anatolian (Eastern) food, and that they had roots in Asia Minor but had never been to Istanbul. Before I had the chance to respond, the author announced that we were about to start.

This was not going to be a presentation, she said, rather a little informal talk, and therefore she was happy to see many friends there, whether these were people she had already met or not. She thought that we were all there because of our love for this most beautiful of cities, and it was exactly for this reason that she had started researching and writing about Istanbul. She had left her hometown relatively late, in 1980, following the military coup that hunted down the leftists of the day, after having finished university and built a career in several branches of art and literature. Her Turkish was excellent, she stated, turning toward me as I nodded, and she kept her ties to Istanbul vivid through visiting often enough to maintain her personal relations with her Turkish friends there.

As she spoke more people were coming in, apologetically moving past the author's desk in front of the listeners, making their way to the few chairs remaining. By the end the room was so full that one of the people who came in last, a middle-aged man who apparently knew the author, sat down next to her at the speaker's table. He then began to partake in the conversation, which had already shifted to the level of chatting together about the subject matter of the book. With his wit and knowledge, he contributed so much to the process that at some point one of the listeners asked the speaker's identity. "I am just a doctor, not a historian," he said, "it's just that I am from the City, so I know about history"—and he laughed.⁸

Knowing about the history of Istanbul is a central dimension of being Istanbulite, as I was told repeatedly by different Rum Polites. A demonstration of this knowledge is important to many, and they display it at every opportunity. In this context of a book presentation where it was appropriate to exchange knowledge, the listeners were busily engaged in talking about the most intricate details concerning the past in Istanbul, as if they had entered a competition on who knows what better. But this did not seem to disturb the author; it looked as if this was the very discussion she wanted to ignite. "We are the last generation who know about Istanbul" (*Imaste i teleftea yenia pou kserei yia tin Poli*), she said at some point, adding that it is important to record the things we know in order to complement the documented history of the city: "We are compiling a mosaic, so that we don't forget ... so that we are not forgotten" (*Simplironoume ena mosaiko na min ksehasoume ... ksehastoume*).

Then the author started listing the resources she had used for writing the book, which comprised an impressive number of archives in both Greece and Turkey, including some that are rarely opened to researchers. The doctor who was sitting beside the author interrupted her nicely and said, although not in these exact words, the following: "This is all very well done, a very neat piece of work in a historical sense. Bravo! There have to be more studies like that, and we are much delayed in demonstrating the grandiosity of our City. There is something else that is more important, however. These are the stories we have, the living history we represent: our experiences, our knowledge of daily life, our cuisine, our famous chocolate—did you know for example that Catherine Deneuve said she ate the best *mille feuille* in one of our Rum patisseries in Istanbul? You know things that are not documented as history. Somebody has to come and talk to us, collect our stories, that would be a much more or equally important task to accomplish, don't you think?"

Everybody in the audience nodded and sighed in what looked like strong appreciation of this comment. The author, too, said that she totally agreed and that she was indeed engaged in a project of collecting oral accounts from Rum Polites women in Athens, and she knew of few others doing similar work. I was in fact the very person she was referring to, sitting there with my mouth open in amazement. The doctor had basically summarized my main motivation and ambition for the task I had undertaken in my fieldwork, expressing not only its legitimacy but also its significance and importance from the point of view of a person who was "just an Istanbulite, not a historian," or an ethnographer for that matter. Once the presentation ended and everybody got up for some coffee, I walked over to him and introduced myself. "I am here intending to do exactly what you said should be done," I said, "Would you care to meet?"

The Boat Story

We exchanged phone numbers, and then some phone calls, until we were finally able to get together. It was already after Easter by that time, and the weather was significantly warmer. He told me to come to the church in Glifada, a major suburb in southern Athens, and from there we would go somewhere by the sea. About fifteen minutes after the time set for our appointment, I saw him arriving on a moped. He apologized for the delay, but he had had to check out the accident site around the corner. Not to do the "*elliniko*," he joked, hinting teasingly that it is regarded as a "very Greek thing to do" to stop and watch when an accident happens. He reminded me that he was a medical doctor, so he could only leave the scene when his colleagues arrived. Anyhow, he said, "jump on the bike if you don't mind. We are going to the marina."

The Glifada marina lies right across the main square from where we had met. There are a number coffeeshops at the docks, but he drove straight to one of the quays and stopped in front of a fairly large professional fishing boat. "Here we can talk in peace," he said, "everywhere else it would be crowded." He pointed out that it was the day of the patron saints of the Glifada church, Konstantinos and Helene; hence there was a huge *paniyiri*, a street fiesta and market, in front of the church. An important name day celebrated by millions throughout Greece, the day is an occasion that attracts many believers, shoppers, and beggars, who would fill up the entire area around the church increasingly toward the evening. But we were away from all these inside the boat, which he said he shared with a friend of his. After offering me a soft drink, he started to tell me his story.

"I am sixty-six years old and I am from Istanbul," he started off proudly. Born and bred in the city, on one of the islands in the Sea of Marmara, he said that this meant he had spent "the most important years of his life there," because "a person builds up his character in his first years and he belongs to the place where he is born and spends these first years of his life." This then is the person's character and it does not change except for major life traumas such as the death of one's parents. As for his own character, he stated the following: "I can say that I have the character of the City, that I am a Rum Politis." A bit later he came back to the subject, saying that he had roots in Istanbul, and that his parents were also Rum Polites: "*Anadan babadan* Rum I am," he noted, using the Turkish phrase that means "from both mother and father."

"*Anadan babadan*," a relatively recognizable expression in Greece, was the first of the Turkish phrases he increasingly used throughout the interview—an interview which soon proved to be the most linguistically interesting one I had yet conducted. He was not simply borrowing from Turkish, or switching between languages, but also combining Greek and Turkish words and rules of grammar in such a way that only speakers of both languages would be able to understand. I told him at the end of our conversation—and he agreed wholeheartedly—that he was demonstrating a fine way of speaking *Politika*,[9] the Greek that is spoken by Rum Polites in Istanbul, which they continue to speak among themselves in Athens today. We started out speaking Greek, but gradually he shifted more and more to Politika as soon as he saw that I was comfortable in understanding it. This seemed to please him and perhaps even surprised him; no wonder, for the whole conversation would have been extremely dizzying for anybody who was not an able Politika speaker, a situation which also applies to some Rum Polites. He was shifting to the other language halfway through the sentence, making up words that do not exist in either language, using the grammatical rules of both of them, and alluding to little details in the Rum Polites life of Istanbul that are indicated by a certain jargon or terminology.

Two examples can demonstrate this: "***Aslında** paidikos heirirgos eimai, alla edo san **genel cerrah** doulevo*" ("In fact, I am a pediatrician-surgeon but I work here as a general surgeon"); "*Doulepsame **omuz omuza**. Autos eihe ena **hayvanat bahçesi** me dio **aslania**. Sto **Burgazi***" ("We worked side by side, shoulder-to-shoulder. He had a zoo with two lions. On Burgaz island"). The words and part-words in bold are Turkish. Here it is obvious that he is not adopting a set pattern of shifting between Turkish and Greek; neither is it only about a preferred language in terminology, as he uses both Greek and Turkish medical titles within one sentence, nor is it about the difficulty of finding the right word in either language. This could be the case for the expression *omuz omuza*, which is rather hard to translate, but does not apply to words like "zoo" or "in fact." The cases of ***aslania*** (*liondaria*) and ***Burgazi*** (*Antigoni*) are particularly interesting as they were formed through adding Greek suffixes to Turkish roots, although they have their Greek equivalents in common use, as indicated here in parentheses. These are just a few examples of the pattern he and others used in their colloquial speech, which is also paralleled in the literature created by the Rum Polites.[10]

All in all, it was most amusing for me to listen to him talk like this, which he acknowledged also by saying that it had been a very good idea to come down to the boat for this interview. "We would not be able to scream like that," he said—we could not talk so comfortably. This was coming from somebody who told me during the course of the interview that it was one of the elements of the "minority character," and he used the phrase in English, to whisper softly in public. He was talking about a fear that came from being different than others, first for not being Muslim, then for not being Turkish, which left its mark on the character of the Rum in Istanbul. As he made clear a little later, he was also alluding to the campaign in Turkey during the first decades of the Republic and up until the 1960s, called "Citizen, speak Turkish!" (*Vatandaş Türkçe konuş!*).[11] During this time many Rum Polites were harassed in public and were forced to speak Turkish instead of their mother tongue, and many children had to keep their mouths shut in fear since they spoke only Greek. Rather than an incentive to learn Turkish, though, this campaign became another source of anxiety for Rum Polites and led them to start thinking about leaving Istanbul. With an ironic twist, this unpleasant experience in Istanbul is still reflected in the way they speak in Greece: criticizing the Athenians for being loud and fussy, the Rum Polites have incorporated the habit originally induced by political pressure such that it has become part of their *habitus*, a marker of polite identity, a sign of good manners, a demarcation of the Rum Polites from other Greek speakers in Greece. It is at these many levels that "talking in tongues" becomes but one of the ways in which practices of everyday life get translated into a sense of distinction by the Rum Polites. The following stories will allude to some others.

The Easter Bread Story

"Don't bring presents anymore," said the wife upon opening the door. "As if we were strangers; you are not a guest!" I was holding an Easter bread in my hand, carefully wrapped by the owner of the patisserie. "But it is *politiko tsoureki*," I said by way of excusing myself—a valid excuse that she confirmed with her approving smile.

It was just after Easter, and I was paying a visit to the Manolidis family. I was responding to an invitation: one of the many gatherings at the Athens home of this middle-aged Rum Polites couple. Mr. Manolidis was a noted scholar and had acted both as an advisor and an informant during my fieldwork on the Rum Polites in Athens. He and his wife had been very welcoming to me throughout my stay in Athens over the years, and we had met on many occasions. This time, it was a dinner in honor of a Turkish couple who were visiting from Istanbul, and they had thought it would be nice if I joined them that evening. Also present were another couple of Rum Polites origin, with whom I had cordial relations. Since we were acquainted from before, I greeted them first, and afterward Mrs. Manolidis introduced me to the visiting Turkish couple: "This is Ilay. She is our daughter here." Then turning toward her husband, she added somewhat teasingly: "She brought us *paskalya çöreği*!"

To me there is nothing more appropriate than bringing something to eat to a house where I am visiting, especially if it is something sweet and if I am invited over for a meal. Perhaps it is a result of my upbringing in Turkey, an incorporation of the well-known saying "*tatlı yiyelim, tatlı konuşalım*" (let's eat sweet, talk sweet),[12] which my hostess would appreciate as correct manners. There is nothing more appropriate to her, however, than looking upset that I brought something with me; not only is it a sign of her unconditional hospitality, of not expecting anything else from visitors than their good company, but it is also a suggestion of my status as a young woman, a student who is away from her home and family, a fact she emphasized even more when she called me their daughter.

At a deeper level, however, we both knew we had an understanding. I had not only brought an Easter bread around the time of Easter,[13] I had also brought the right Easter bread, made according to an original Istanbul recipe by a Rum patisserie chef from Istanbul. Throughout Greece the so-called *politiko tsoureki* is acclaimed for its particular smell and taste stemming from the special spice called *mahlepi*, and it is recognized as a specialty of Rum Polites patisseries. My decision to buy it from a certain patisserie in our neighborhood, therefore, was significant in showing my commitment to the legacy of Istanbulite cuisine, and to our common roots, which we would acknowledge through sharing this good food. It was also a reminder of the many conversations we had had about other food elements associated with the Istanbul cuisine, underscoring our common taste as well as our common cultural orientation.

When I arrived, the others were already sipping their tea from tulip-shaped glasses while examining a book that the Turkish couple had brought with them. It was a recently published glossy hardcover including detailed maps from nineteenth-century Istanbul. The four Rum Polites were engaged in a competition of demonstrating knowledge about the neighborhoods represented on the maps, finding the houses where they, their parents, their relatives and friends lived, discussing the best ways of getting there, and assessing the changes the city underwent in the decades following the making of these maps. Every now and then they would turn to me and say something along the lines of "you are too young to know how much Istanbul has changed since then." They would show the same attitude when one of them could not remember the location of a particular shop or building, and they would recall further details and stories in order to remind the others, coming up with an enormous amount of diverse information by way of showing off their intimate connection to their home city where they no longer lived. The Turkish couple and I, although having much more immediate and current ties to Istanbul than they who moved away nearly thirty years ago, were watching this scene with mixed feelings of admiration and embarrassment while the conversation somehow led them to sing jingles from once-popular advertisements on Turkish television. The evening became a theatrical occasion for them to connect to the memories of their times in Istanbul, both spatially, in terms of missing their city from afar, but also temporally, in the sense of reminiscences of a time eternally lost. It was on this occasion—which resembled a reunion of Istanbulites of different pasts, backgrounds, and ages—that a particularly grounded nostalgia was being generated.

This evening was different in significance from other times when I talked about Istanbul with Rum Polites. Unlike the Manolidis family and their guests, many Istanbulites have not retained living ties with their city and have never gone back to Istanbul since they left for Athens a couple of decades ago. My meetings with them often turned into an interview of somebody reporting on the current situation of their home city. That somebody was I; it was me that they had to figure out, to apprehend, to "place" somewhere before they entrusted me with their personal stories, which was what I was after. Our conversation, therefore, often started with questions about where I lived, where I went to school, which part of the city I was associated with, and finally, what I could tell them about the neighborhood they used to live in. Then they would ask me specific questions about particular roads, buildings, locations, shops—especially food shops; they would draw a virtual map of their past surroundings, which they then wanted to compare to the picture that I was there to paint for them: of the new, contemporary, actual Istanbul they had yet to encounter. This exchange was almost always sentimental in a bittersweet fashion. My description would mostly reassure them of the accuracy of their recollection, of the beauty and the uniqueness of their home city, and yet at the same time increase their longing and the deeply felt pain of partition from their loved one. Sometimes, though, a total disenchantment and disappointment would take place as a result. Perhaps the most striking example of this happened with Elena, a woman psychic who had not been back to Istanbul in more than twenty years. We met at her apartment in Paleo Faliro. After an hour-long conversation about Istanbul, she asked me where I preferred to go to swim. I had to say that, sadly, there was hardly any possibility for swimming in Istanbul anymore, that I was lucky to have had the experience of spending my summers swimming in Marmara or the Bosphorus during my childhood years, but that Istanbulites today had to travel long hours to reach a beach with clean waters along any of the three seashores surrounding the city of Istanbul. Although I paid special attention to making this an understatement, this piece of information shocked her. She kept asking about particular beaches, not believing that they would also be polluted: "How about the Suadiye, Bostancı area? That's where we went most as kids. But I also heard that there are many houses there now. Not even the Princes Islands? Come on, this is open sea. These were the clearest waters; my uncle was fishing for lobster there without needing goggles. The Bosphorus cannot be polluted though, with all the strong current! Especially not Büyükdere, up north toward the Black Sea. We used to go there with my brother; it was his favorite place. Don't you go to Büyükdere at least?" She insisted, so I had no option but to tell her the truth: the seashore she was talking about was cut off by a massive transit road, which was built in front of the row of landmark seaside houses and fish restaurants, leaving no trace of the once well-known beach with golden fine sand. Her negative surprise turned into grief and disappointment as she announced that she would never want to go back to Istanbul again. "Her Istanbul was lost forever," she said. It was at that point that her husband came into the room and joined us. The conversation conveniently shifted to the subject of food, and an engaged discussion of what they were eating in Istanbul, where it would be best, how there is no way of getting anything similar in Athens, why it was that people paid more attention to food in Istanbul than in Greece, and so on. Once again, food had its tranquilizing effect on a potentially grim situation, serving as a mediator between the pain of partition and the pleasure of internalizing a city through consuming it.

Particular food items can be especially significant in terms of their relation to memory and identity. Easter bread is but one such case in point. Not only does it mark a certain time frame that ritualistically structures nostalgia around a certain religious ceremony, it also gains local meaning for invoking the geographically laden flavors from Istanbul. Just as much as it marks a certain Istanbul identity, it denotes an important affiliation with and an appreciation of and a knowledge of Greek Orthodox culture. Although it is a regular item to be found in many Istanbul patisseries as part of the standard menu, a part of the local city tradition, the reduction in the number of Rum Orthodox chefs over the years has diminished the crucial factor of religious symbolism in the preparation of *tsoureki* in Istanbul. "*Tsoureki* has left its hometown with the Rum Polites," claimed the retired Dionysos one day in Istanbul. Being a strong opponent of the community leaving Istanbul for Athens, he chuckled with the difficulty of accepting the harsh fact that the real *politiko tsoureki* can now be best found in Rum Polites patisseries of Athens around the time of Easter, verified by the strong *mahlepi* smell that came from the Easter bread I brought with me from Athens to Istanbul. "Let me prepare some tea for this," he said as he made his way into the kitchen, and I could not help but notice the change in his voice—a shiver as if he were chewing on something that was very hard to swallow.

The Dinner Story

"I always bring my rice from Turkey!" announced our young hostess when one of the guests commented on the quality of her pilaf. "We bring our meat from there," the guest responded as he turned to his wife, whispering that next time they also had to bring rice with them from Istanbul as the pilaf cooked in Athens never tasted the same. We were sitting at a round dining table furnished with silver cutlery, crystal wine glasses, fine china plates, and a carefully starched and ironed white linen tablecloth, indulging ourselves in a rich selection of specialty dishes. Our entire focus was the food; we were not only commenting about how delicious the dishes were but also discussing at length how they were prepared, which ingredients were used, where one would best buy them, other times we had had the same dish, how differently they would make this elsewhere, and so on. The hostess was the discussion leader; her respectable status as the acclaimed chef of the night was being strengthened by her authoritative knowledge about the particularities of the food she prepared for us. She indeed paid extraordinary attention and managed to impress twenty-five of her closest friends, who were all from Istanbul and were also quite careful with their food. "It is not possible to get *nar ekşisi* anywhere here," she complained, referring to a sour sauce made from pomegranate, a specialty from Southern Turkey, "so I asked my sister-in-law to bring me some." Her Circassian chicken was delicious, as was her Albanian liver, both difficult-to-prepare landmark dishes of the multicultural Istanbul cuisine. She knew how to give in, however, when she thought she would not be able to reach perfection. Pointing to a pastry dish, *börek*, she admitted that she had commissioned her mother to make it. "My mother has origins from Thrace," she explained, "there is no way of competing with her in this particular situation."

The dinner continued with more food talk of this sort, and just as the conversation was about to loosen up to other sorts of stories, the desserts came to the table. Once again, the guests started investigating at length into the nature of what was in front of them. One of the plates received special attention: it was the quince dessert that is available throughout the winter in Istanbul, especially in fish restaurants, but is almost unknown in Greece. But there was another reason why the dessert was especially celebrated: it was served with *kaymak*. Kaymak is a kind of thick cream which is served as an accompaniment of several winter desserts, but which it is impossible to get outside Turkey. Our hostess had to order it from a Rum Polites patisserie weeks in advance in order to be able to serve her dessert appropriately that night. "I know that kaymak does not travel," said one of the guests, while swallowing the last bite of the *kaymaklı ayva* that he claimed he missed badly, "but I have no idea why our Rum Polites patisseries cannot make it here." Nobody knew the answer to this question, so I had to step in. Just a few weeks back, I had interviewed a Rum pastry-maker in Athens, who told me that the biggest difficulty in reaching the same quality as the patiseries in Istanbul lay in the fact that the most basic ingredients are not available in Greece. Kaymak was a special case, because it needed to be processed in massive machines to reach the consistency required, but even if he were to settle for something less than perfect by trying to make it in his own little workshop at the patisserie, he would not find the special kind of milk that had to be used for kaymak. Water buffalo (*manda*) milk was not easy to find in Greece, because that type of animal was not raised except in the highlands in northern Thrace, so the patisseries could only acquire a small amount upon special order, which would only suffice for a few rolls at a time.[14]

Many Rum Polites, like those who were gathered on this occasion, are accustomed to making comparisons between Istanbul and Athens in favor of the former, which they then would incorporate with their general unease about living in Greece at a broader level. This would almost certainly be the case in questions concerning food. Much like Loxandra's infamous shout, "What kind of a place is this? You can't find anything to eat!" (*Topos einai aftos? Tipota de vriskeis na fas!*), depicted in Ioardanidou's 1963 novel, a certain condemnation ("What do you expect?") of Athenian life standards would usually mark the dominating discourse on such occasions when Istanbulites were present. A memoir-cookbook puts such conversation in writing (Chalkousi 2002, 42):

> The Rum Polites laid their tables also in Athens (*ksanastrothikan kai stin Athina ta politika trapezia*), with all the family around for dinner. The pot, however, did not cook the same food. It had a different taste, or more correctly, it did not have any. "Useless here the meat, the vegetables without any substance" (*akiro vre edo pera to kreas, ta zerzevatia horis ousia*) and the fruit did not smell at all. If you asked Aunt Katingo, nothing was worth eating anymore.

THE PARTY STORY

My neighbor from downstairs knocked on the door one afternoon and asked if my husband and I were free that Friday night. "We invited several close friends; we'll have something to eat, so you should come." I gladly accepted; this was a friendly young couple with two small children, and although we kept running into each other every day and said on a number of occasions that we had to get together, we had never managed to do so. They were both born and bred in Istanbul, but had gone to Paris for their university studies. I had met other members of the family independently on various occasions, and it was most entertaining for all of us to discover "how small a world" we lived in.

That Friday was in fact a special evening. Although they did not alert us to it, I came to realize that it was the name day (*yiorti*) of our host. The Orthodox celebrate the days of the saints after whom they take their names. In Greece, a name day is still more important than somebody's birthday, certainly a more communal and ritualistic celebration that, say, all Michaels would observe on November 8 regardless of their religiosity, age, or social standing.[15] It is customary to give a small present to the persons who celebrate (*yiortazoun*), who then have to treat their friends to something to eat, usually by distributing sweets. On this occasion, my neighbor chose to invite his friends over for dinner and had kindly asked my husband and me to come along as well.

We knocked on their door early-ish by Greek standards, around nine o'clock, and we were indeed second to arrive after the hostess's brother and his wife. While we were passing along the present and the package of Turkish delight that I had brought with me from Istanbul, I was shifting into a mode of panic and embarrassment. Contrary to what I had expected, the setting was very formal: the house was decorated, candles were lit, the table was furnished in the fanciest way, but the scariest thing of all was that everybody was dressed up in an alarmingly smart fashion. Our hostess was wearing a black cocktail dress beautified with an elegant pin, her brother's wife had a long silk chiffon dress in a dark color, and the men were chic in casual suits and colorful ties. We had changed for the occasion but our apparel could by no means be described as festive. I was wearing a woolen dress, and it might have been from the unexpected excitement that I started to feel very warm. I told them that their apartment was significantly warmer than our freezing top floor at this time, which was true, and asked for their permission to go up quickly and put on something different. Our hostess smiled in recognition of my main motive, and whispered to me in Turkish, "Will you put on something more *abiye* (fancy)?," making me feel less disturbed by the misunderstanding that had led to this for me uncomfortable situation. And I was struck by the astonishing resemblance of this situation to the story that I had just read in a book written by Rum Polites author Faidon Alevropoulos (1982).

Entitled *Nora*, the story takes place in the 1960s in Athens. The main character Dimitris is the only son of a Rum Polites family that has recently migrated from Istanbul to Athens. The story opens with the remark that this is going to be the first Athenian party for twenty-year-old Dimitris. There is a great deal of excitement at home, and much expectancy about what a distinguished gathering it will be. The mother is carefully ironing her son's shirt, instructing him to shave properly, and not be late. Dimitris is taken to the party by a friend of his, whose girlfriend is bringing Nora, a prospective match for Dimitris. He is excited himself, thinking of the parties they used to have in Istanbul. His mother makes sure that he is well dressed, tells him to greet everybody properly, not to jump on the food as if he is facing starvation, and to make sure that he asks the hostess to dance with him before he dances with anybody else. She hands over the present she has bought for the hostess on his behalf, a diary with leather binding, and crosses herself three times as she waves her son goodbye. Dimitris pities her, even while thinking that Athenian parties are bound to be much "cooler" than the formally conservative Istanbul soirees, but as it turns out, he is in for a surprise. First, he sees that his friend is wearing beige cotton trousers and a green sweater in great contrast to the tweed suit and bow tie of Dimitris. When they arrive at the party house, a random person opens the door and lets them in without any introductions. The room is packed, so Dimitris has a hard time even finding the hostess in order to thank her for the invitation and give her the present, which is hardly appreciated. When he asks about the girl he was supposed to meet there, his friend tells him that Nora is a name they use for making sure single guys show up at parties. In short order, his friends disappear in the back room along with some other couples, leaving Dimitris alone to become very bored. And hungry because, unlike Istanbul parties where mothers ensure an abundance of good food, all that is available is a pathetic amount of popcorn and nuts. So he leaves the party to get some *souvlaki* at the joint around the corner, and it is there that he receives a great surprise: the girl hosting the party is sitting there alone, writing in the diary he gave her as a present. He first thinks of attracting her attention, but seeing her careless gaze going past him, he decides to pay for his souvlaki and leave. Thus ends the night of his first ever Athenian party.

I recalled this amusing story because of its reference to the differences in dressing and eating at social gatherings organized by Athenians and Istanbulites. Stimulated by my small embarrassing episode, I was to become increasingly alert to such differences throughout my fieldwork. The attunement to dress was even more important in the context of church visits. One Easter I spent in Istanbul, I met with a Rum friend of mine who was visiting from Athens. We were at the Patriarchate for the afternoon service on Good Friday. There were many who had arrived from Greece for the Easter holidays, "tourists" as she called them, indicating that these were Elladites and not Rum Polites. She claimed that the difference was visible in the way they were dressed: "Look at them," she said, "they would not dress like that even in their small villages. This is the Patriarchate, this is Istanbul. No Istanbulite would come here like that. We always used to dress up for church. 'Suit, good coat, like that' (*Tayyör falan yani. İyi palto ... Öyle*)."

The difference in ways of dressing up for festive and religious occasions is taken here as indicative of a whole other set of cultural distinctions that are made. Being at the Patriarchate for Easter is posited as something of an honor, and the failure of the Elladites to show their respect by the way they are dressed is attributed to their usually being in their own villages or islands for the Easter vacation. What is evoked here with regard to manners and ways of knowing how to act in a particular setting is an urban–rural distinction in the sense of a center–periphery tension, especially as this happens to be both in the city and at the center—inside old Istanbul, in the City, *eis tin Poli*, in Fanar, at the Patriarchate, the center of Orthodox Christianity. This is where cosmopolitan knowledge acts as a way of differentiating between self and others on the basis of knowing the unpretentious ways of displaying self. At a different level, this distinction stresses a relationship of belonging: my friend *knows* what to wear for the Patriarchate, because she *belongs* there. She remembers how her mother used to dress her as a child, how family friends used to come to church sporting their smartest dresses which they bought for the occasion. Because of this knowledge based on her past there, the place belongs to her, to her memories; it is her own church, her city, so the Elladites not knowing the ways of the City are glossed as "tourists," who do not possess that very notion of cosmopolitan knowledge.

Family Stories

The strategic use of everyday signs like food and dress indicates the ability to act appropriately in social situations. This is linked to presumptions about others' social position and capacity of having absorbed or being comfortable in that culture, thus belonging to that culture. The reverse also applies, however, when people wish to underline subversively that they do not know or that they do not belong. Replying to the question of where in Istanbul one can eat the Easter lamb on a spit, a Rum said to me that they did not know "such Greek ways" of doing things. Here he was reversing what otherwise could be considered a Greek Easter tradition, thus a lack of an important religious ritual, into a statement of how these are rather new inventions that are only fit for the Greek countryside. In this sense, not knowing can be taken to mean not having learned new things, thus not having deviated from the old, the original. An extension of this point can often be found in statements regarding the conservative character of the Rum Polites. As an old stereotype that has surfaced variously throughout history, this image can be utilized as part of a self-inflicted discourse of "we the Rum Polites are old-fashioned, we did not grow up in such free ways; this is not what we saw in our parents," especially in referring to intersex relations. Some Rum Polites women might comment self-critically on this conservatism. To repeat the words of a married informant in her fifties: "Forget about traveling without their husbands. These women won't even go to a coffeeshop on their own. In this day and age, here in Athens. Impossible!" At the same time, most of the Rum Polites women would state that they disapprove of the ways in which Athenian women go out, talk, dress, court as they please, evaluating these not as signs of gender equality or liberty, but rather as an indication of not having been brought up properly, of lacking the right manners, of not having learned modesty in the correct or proper family environment.

Proper upbringing by the family, being from a *good* family, and an analogous set of family values form a crucial dimension of demarcation for Rum Polites, and they become most important when their children start having relationships with the other sex. A Rum Polites woman working in Athens for a couple of years gave an explanation for not courting with anybody during that time by saying, "After all, we brought with us Turkish [good] manners/upbringing" (*ne de olsa Türk terbiyesi almışız*). Her mother's friend, who told me this story in Istanbul, seemed to reserve a certain sense of approval and pride for her being rather choosy with men. She also asked me if it was true that the girls, thus the parents, in Greece were much more "free-spirited," indicating with a gesture of swinging her right hand in circles that this was an understatement regarding their questionable standards of morality. Marriage patterns are indeed an issue for Rum Polites as the diminishing community in Istanbul does not offer a large number of eligible bachelors. Religion, though, is not necessarily the only factor here. Although they live in Athens, Rum Polites can be looked down upon by the larger community if they get married to non-Istanbulite Orthodox Greeks; they are considered to have married out. While this value judgment is gradually losing its influence in the selection of a spouse, many recently married Rum Polites told me that they were often asked whether they "took one of our own" (*pires dhikia mas*).[16]

Preference of spouse according to origin is believed to be a deteriorating practice among the Rum Polites in Athens, but it is still possible to encounter otherwise. I remember an instance when I went out with a few young Rum Polites friends in their early thirties, who had recently migrated to Athens after finishing their education in Istanbul. When we were returning home, one of the young men started a conversation with the two Athenian women in our group, which shifted to the subject of cooking. The women were uninterested, but he insisted, aided by the few extra drinks he had enjoyed that evening, in dwelling on the topic along the lines of "Are you telling me that you don't know how to make *paçanga böreği*?"[17] When we talked next day, my friend was ashamed but not apologetic about it: "Perhaps I insisted too much. After all, they are Athenian girls, what do they know of *paçanga*? *Eşek hoşaftan ne anlar*![18] But make no mistake, they would not know anything. You get married to these women, you stay hungry. Not their fault perhaps. They just don't know."

This is yet another example of how knowledge of food can be considered a marker of Rum Polites boundaries. Another important example is that of table manners. Consider this entry in a memoir-cookbook:

> "C'mon, not even how to eat do they know these [people] here" (*oute na fane den kseroun oi edo*), however much we mocked them [by slurping] they would not get it (*ti tous lipithikame den katalavane*). Do not even mention the restaurants, where they ate like animals (*haivania*). A! On this point all the Rum Polites would agree. ... Where is it heard that they throw fork and bread at your face like villagers (*san tous kourides*),[19] that they do not bring knives and plates for everybody separately? Where is the politeness of our *garçon*? (Chalkousi 2002, 89)

Politeness is a matter of respect, of modesty, and of being a proper person for the Rum Polites, such that conflation becomes easy between these all-too-interlinked qualities. When he was visiting me one afternoon, Vangelis, a sixty-year-old man living in Faliro, took off his shoes at the doorstep. I told him that this was not necessary, but he would not listen. "The streets are too dirty here in Athens, nobody cleans up after their dogs," he said and added: "There is no way I can enter an Istanbulite's home without taking my shoes off. Forget the others; they would not even notice." With a brief but telling conversation, Vangelis managed to illustrate a distinction important to the Rum Polites. The distinction was not about the degree of cleanliness; surely it could not be generalized that the Athenians had dirtier houses or cared less about tidiness than Istanbul residents. The distinction was about the importance laid on practicing certain habits about cleanliness, such as taking off shoes at the doorstep, that were part of the generally accepted codes of conduct in Istanbul.[20] The continuation of these habitual practices in Athens was significant in marking the differences in the ways of everyday life between the two, thereby contributing to the repeated idea of the Rum Polites not understanding the Athenians, and perhaps to a greater extent, vice versa.

Stories of Everyday Life

The definitions of us and them are as flexible and as rigid as the boundaries within the community. What is important here for me is to note the extent to which this demarcation occurs through the workings of memory and practice in everyday life. In this chapter I walked, to use the terminology of Michel de Certeau, through the swarming structure of the street, alluding to activities punctuated by spaces and relationships. Walking was a multisensory experience of place (Feld and Basso 2009) and worked as a sensory method that enabled me to witness urban sounds, images, smells, and movements—a range of embodied sensations that Goonewardena (2005) called the "urban sensorium." I focused on how culinary virtuosities seek to establish the plural language of stratified histories, of multiple relationships between enjoyment and manipulation, of fundamental languages spelled out in everyday details.

De Certeau's work echoes others, such as Lefebvre (1991a, 1991b), in their recognition of the ways in which ordinary people appropriate urban space in their everyday life. In that sense, urban practice becomes a subset of spatial practice (Lefebvre 2003) and informs an exploration into how through such urban practices a specific location in space can be coded as a particular place, one that provides an anchor and a meaning to the sense of identity (Orum and Chen 2003). The Rum Polites in Athens add another twist to this discussion: by their urban practices, they are using urban space and attaching meanings of spatiality, in action and in discourse, with reference to another city, such that their practices of daily life immediately take on a translocal dimension. As Appadurai (1996) would have it, it becomes only possible to know *here* because of its relation to there. Although this denotes—by definition—a way of contesting the intended structures of signification in Athens, replacing them with those of Istanbul leads to a transgression of the local and the everyday. To apply the Lefebvrian terminology (Lefebvre 2003, 38), the Rum Polites for whom Istanbul is the *topos* turn neighborhoods like Faliro through their urban practices into a homologous or analogous place that becomes *isotopy*, a part of the *same place*. Such practices further code Athens as a *heterotopy*, marked by differences that situate it with respect to the initial place. The differential in question is to be traced in everyday life practices here that are implicating life elsewhere, in their original topos, in the City.

The attachment to places is rooted in social experience (Herzfeld 1991), and I demonstrate this in the context of Athens, which most Rum Polites repeatedly convey as the city of their non-attachment. Their everyday experiences refer to another city to which they belong, one that is far in space and lost in time, one that lives in their memory through a continuously refreshed and delicately contested cosmopolitan knowledge. Robert Rotenberg writes that "the metropolis generates a particular knowledge of one's identity and the identity of others, all of which is bound up in the issue of who considers himself or herself to be a metropolitan" (2002, 96). Rotenberg's analysis of Vienna might have applied to this case better if the greater part of the Rum Polites were still living in Istanbul. The fact that they are not, however, gives all the more importance to the way in which cosmopolitan knowledge about Istanbul becomes a kind of cultural capital, a way of practicing distinction, through which the Rum Polites can identify each other as belonging to the City and reassure themselves in their identity of being Istanbulites, while at the same time underlining their differences from Athenians on an everyday basis. Here considering themselves as Polites is not enough: possessing cosmopolitan knowledge—that is, a recognition of the city ways and their practice in everyday life—becomes necessary. What is displayed through these practices of distinction is an attachment to Istanbul, the invisible city in memory, rendering itself visible in the pin on the black cocktail dress, in the smell emanating from the *mahlepi*, in the clinging heavy pronunciation of the L, and in the joy of finding *kaymak* in Athens, where it does not belong. Like those birds that lay their eggs only in other species' nests, to follow de Certeau's phrasing again, memory produces in a place that does not belong to it. Being away from Istanbul intensifies the remembered knowledge of it, allowing the maintenance of an exclusive cultural identity that renders the Rum Polites distinct.

In sum, these are the threads of thought that I would like to draw from such stories in order to weave the rest of this volume: the practice of everyday life of the Rum Polites in Athens is guided by a set of habits, manners, and dispositions that are based on a shared sense of knowledge. This knowledge is derived from remembered lived experiences in Istanbul; it is an Istanbul-specific form of urban knowledge that I call cosmopolitan knowledge, which is exclusive to those who have maintained or would like to maintain their connection to Istanbul, and thus leads to a delineation of the Rum Polites from other Athenians who are not Istanbulites. This delineation is often perceived as distinction, thus the Rum Polites can be seen as a culturally distinct community within the wider Greek society. The community, however, is far from being internally unified and easily describable, as I demonstrate in the next chapter.

Notes

1. There are two neighborhoods bearing the name of Faliro: Paleo (old) Faliro and Neo (New) Faliro. When no specification is made, the use of Faliro refers to Paleo Faliro.
2. Population increase in Paleo Faliro intensified during the 1951–1961 period, at 71.84% in relation to the previous decade (41.9%), with the rate becoming stable at around 50% until 1981, when it dropped to 15.20%. This jump in the 1950s is to be attributed to internal migration within the city. The percentage is not very high in relation to other neighborhoods that received migration from rural areas, such as Argiroupoli at 846%, A.Dimitrio at 362%, and N.Liosio at 483%, while the Athens average is around 35% for the period between 1951 and 1971 (Kotzamanis 1997).
3. The official website of the municipality of Paleo Faliro, www.palaiofaliro.gr.
4. *Baklava* is a pastry dessert that is popular in Turkish and Middle Eastern cuisine as well as in Greece, especially after the influx from Asia Minor. Rum Polites prefer to consume baklava from Istanbul, describing the Asia Minor or Greek variants as "less refined" or "too oily and sweet." For a long time, baklava from renowned Istanbul stores was brought in by the initiative of individuals, until the ongoing popularity of the product led the companies to open branches in Athens, which were franchised and run by Rum Polites as well.
5. *Yufka* is a very thin pastry used for the making of pies and sweets, which needs to be used when fresh. Although similar kinds of pastry, such as phyllo pastry, are basics in Greek cooking, fresh yufka cannot be obtained in Athens and is flown in by daily morning flights from Istanbul.
6. The Greek name for Istanbul's Princes islands, a group of islands in the Marmara Sea.
7. Anthropologists have provided much ethnographic evidence indicating the importance of meat consumption in Greek cuisine (see, e.g., Herzfeld 1985; Sutton 2001). Recent work also suggests that attitudes toward food are changing—for example, with the increasing popularity of the idea of healthy Mediterranean cuisine (see Trichopoulou et al. 2003; Yiakoumaki 2006; Kizos et al. 2011).

8. For a brilliant discussion on non-historian historians, see Papailias (2005, 47–53).
9. For dictionaries and other literature on Politika in Greek, see Zachariadis (2014).
10. Rum Polites literature refers to the body of written work produced and published in Greece and in Greek by writers who were born and raised in Istanbul. It is loosely linked to the literature of the Rum in Istanbul. See Vaios (1998, 2000).
11. For more, see Çağaptay (2006) and Aslan (2007), among others.
12. See also Cowan for similar "sweet tooth" situations in Northern Greece (1990, 66).
13. Greek Easter bread differs from similar types consumed in other Orthodox countries. The conventional day for eating *tsoureki* (often decorated with red-dyed eggs that symbolize Jesus Christ's blood and resurrection) would be on Easter Sunday according to the Christian Orthodox calendar. A similar version is popular and is available for a longer time in Rum Polites patisseries in Athens, famously known as *politiko tsoureki*, and all year round in many patisseries of Istanbul, where the religious connection has been lost despite the ongoing use of the name (*Paskalya çöreği*).
14. Some two years after the anecdote took place, a renowned baklava chain from Istanbul opened branches in Athens. It carries kaymak that is flown daily from Istanbul. Some Rum Polites still claim that it just does not taste the same as it does in the City.
15. See forthcoming publications by Renee Hirschon, who is conducting a research project on this very topic in 2017.
16. Maintenance of regional preferences in marriage patterns is also common among Mikrasiates and other populations in Greece (Hirschon 1989, 160).
17. A rather complicated pastry dish traditional to Istanbul cuisine.
18. Phrase in Turkish that is used when it needs to be underlined that a person is not able to appreciate something nice due to ignorance. A near translation would be: How would a donkey understand anything about [the taste of] *hoşaf* [a sweet fruit juice]?
19. *Kourides* literally means Kurds. Here it is used as part of a larger discourse against villagers, uneducated or unmannered masses who migrated to Istanbul from rural parts of Turkey, mainly from the Eastern regions where Kurds are omnipresent. The notion of Kurd is adopted here as a negative stereotype of a person who would not have manners because he is a newcomer to the city, thus does not have cosmopolitan knowledge. The waiters they refer to here would not actually be Kurds; the term is stretched to mean villager in a wide sense that would also include *Elladites* or Athenians.

20. Taking off one's shoes at the doorstep can be a form of politeness but is also a matter of informality (one would not take off one's shoes when invited to a formal dinner party and wear borrowed slippers under a nice dress or suit) and of comfort (one might take off one's shoes at one's own or a close relative's house for convenience), yet it is not necessary unless the host lays much importance on this custom. Later, when I visited this informant's house, I did not forget to take off my own shoes, on which he commented, "This is an Ottoman house, as you know" (*Burası Osmanlı evi biliyorsun*), invoking a self-stereotype about his behavior, which he also accepted to have rather conservative connotations. Ironically, in Istanbul today, leaving one's shoes outside the entrance door of a house (as in a mosque) might also be interpreted as a kind of conservatism that is associated with a Muslim or rural household.

BIBLIOGRAPHY

Alevropoulos, F. (1982). *Nora*. Athens.
Appadurai, A. (1996). *Modernity at Large: Cultural Dimensions of Globalization*. Minneapolis: University of Minnesota Press.
Aslan, S. (2007). 'Citizen, Speak Turkish!': A Nation in the Making. *Nationalism and Ethnic Politics, 13*(2), 245–272.
Bourdieu, P. (1984). *Distinction: A Social Critique of the Judgement of Taste*. Cambridge, MA: Harvard University Press.
Çağaptay, S. (2006). *Islam, Secularism and Nationalism in Modern Turkey: Who Is a Turk?* London: Routledge.
Chalkousi, X. (2002). *Mirodies kai yevseis tis Polis … kai stin korfi kanela*. Athens: Tsoukatou.
Cowan, J. K. (1990). *Dance and the Body Politic in Northern Greece*. Princeton, NJ: Princeton University Press.
De Certeau, M. (1988). *The Practice of Everyday Life*. Berkeley: University of California Press.
Goonewardena, K. (2005). The Urban Sensorium: Space, Ideology and the Aestheticization of Politics. *Antipode, 37*(1), 46–71.
Herzfeld, M. (1985). *The Poetics of Manhood: Contest and Identity in a Cretan Mountain Village*. Princeton, NJ: Princeton University Press.
Herzfeld, M. (1991). *A Place in History: Social and Monumental Time in a Cretan Town*. Princeton, NJ: Princeton University Press.
Hirschon, R. (1989). *Heirs of the Greek Catastrophe: The Social Life of Asia Minor Refugees in Piraeus*. Oxford: Clarendon Press.
Kizos, T., et al. (2011). Survival Strategies of Farm Households and Multifunctional Farms in Greece. *The Geographical Journal, 177*(4), 335–346. https://doi.org/10.1111/j.1475-4959.2011.00403.x.

Kotzamanis, V. (1997). Athènes, 1848–1995. *Revue de Recherches Sociales, 92–93*, 3–30.
Lefebvre, H. (2003). *The Urban Revolution*. Minneapolis: University of Minnesota Press.
Orum, A. M., & Chen, X. (2003). *The World of Cities: Places in Comparative and Historical Perspective*. Malden, MA: Blackwell Publishers.
Papailias, P. (2005). *Genres of Recollection: Archival Poetics and Modern Greece*. New York: Palgrave Macmillan.
Rotenberg, R. (1992). *Time and Order in Metropolitan Vienna: A Seizure of Schedules*. Washington: Smithsonian Institution Press.
Rotenberg, R. (2002). The Metropolis and Everyday Life. In G. Gmelch & W. P. Zenner (Eds.), *Urban Life: Readings in the Anthropology of the City* (pp. 60–81). Chicago: Waveland Press.
Sutton, D. E. (2001). *Remembrance of Repasts: An Anthropology of Food and Memory*. Oxford: Berg.
Trichopoulou, A., Costacou, T., Bamia, C., & Trichopoulos, D. (2003). Adherence to a Mediterranean Diet and Survival in a Greek Population. *New England Journal of Medicine, 348*(26), 2599–2608.
Vaios, C. (1998). *Anthologia Konstantinoupoliton poiiton tou eikostou aiona*. Athens: Tsokatou.
Vaios, C. (2000). *H Konstantinoupoli diigetai… (Anthologia tou eikostou aiona)*. Athens: Tsoukatou.
Yiakoumaki, V. (2006). Local, Ethnic, and Rural Food: On the Emergence of Cultural Diversity and Its Integration in the European Union. *Journal of Modern Greek Studies, 24*(2), 415–445. https://doi.org/10.1353/mgs.2006.0030.
Zachariadis, N. (2014). *Lexiko tou Konstantinupolitikou Idiomatos*. Athens: Gavrilidis.

CHAPTER 3

Exclusive Diversity and the Ambiguity of Being Out of Place

THE STORY OF THE LANDLORD

Sitting comfortably on the kilim-covered cushions scattered around the low copper plate that was to serve as a table, we were nibbling on the *nan* bread while waiting for our dishes at an Indian restaurant in the Psirri district of central Athens. I was there with my friend Stratos from Cyprus, his girlfriend Niki, a Greek from South Africa, and my husband, who can best be described as a German Athenian. We had decided to go to one of the new places that have opened during the last few years in this area where the ever-growing immigrant communities are concentrated. Having lived in different parts of the world, all of us had an occasional craving for something other than what one would get in the regular tavernas and restaurants in Greece. "I miss spicy hot food especially," said Niki, remarking upon how bland food generally is in Greece, as she dipped her nan in the crimson red sauce served in a small wooden bowl. Stratos commented on what a good thing it was that there were immigrants from different parts of the world so that Athens could finally boast some degree of the linguistic, demographic, and of course culinary variety that he was so accustomed to from the many years he spent in London. The conversation shifted to the topic of immigration, and we continued talking about how the trend has accelerated in recent years to make Greece the highest migration receiving country in the EU, how this has entirely changed the outlook of the city, how the bureaucratic structure and the Greek society have

© The Author(s) 2018
İ.R. Örs, *Diaspora of the City*, Palgrave Studies in Urban Anthropology, https://doi.org/10.1057/978-1-137-55486-4_3

been unable to cope with this drastic change in population, and how the incomers are being negatively perceived and discriminated against, the Albanians especially.[1]

Stratos was curious to find out from me about how the Rum Polites have dealt with social integration into Athenian society, as he had heard about the many difficulties they had had to face when they first arrived in Greece. I could confirm that based on what I knew about the Rum Polites, but these difficulties were essentially different from those experienced by the current economic immigrants or political refugees, and I explained why the Rum Polites had to be considered separately from these groups. But then I had to ask him back: "Who did you hear that from? Do you know any Rum Polites who told you stories of that sort?"

"Forget it," he said, making a swift gesture with his hand as if he was chasing away an invisible fly: "This is my landlord. He is an old man, generally very kind, but he is super anti-Turkish. Even by Cypriot standards!" We all laughed at this ironic last comment that he made in acknowledgment of my presence, but actually he was being serious. "I would be reluctant to introduce you to him. For your sake. He might make you upset," he said.

I told Stratos that I would not mind meeting his landlord, as long as he agreed to meeting with me. I was insisting, for I had a hunch. To begin with, it would be more interesting for me to take up the challenge of getting to know somebody like this, for all the informants I had met thus far had been very open-minded individuals who were superbly nice to me, without any concerns about my Turkish background. It was obvious that this would not always be the case. And I did have a hunch, and I mentioned it to Stratos as well: "Could it be that he is exaggerating his anti-Turkish stance because you are from Cyprus? I think he would want to meet me. Do ask him when you can."

This turned out to be a correct instinct. By noon the following day, I had received a phone call from Stratos. "I cannot believe this," he said, "but he wants to meet you immediately. How did you know?"

Now Stratos was very interested in the encounter himself, and I was looking forward to a promising interview. So I duly went in the afternoon, and together we went upstairs to his landlord's apartment. The door was opened by a man of about 80, once tall but shrunken by age, frail but energetic looking, who with a big smile across his wrinkled face let out an impressive "*Hoşgeldin!*" (Welcome!) and gave me a hug. I glanced over at Stratos, who looked amazed by this grand entrance, yet had to be content with a short

"*Yia sou*" (Hi) himself. We were shown to the living room, where we were told to make ourselves comfortable on the large couches. These were of a rather firm type, with mahogany carving on the legs and frames, which matched the dining ensemble and the essential glass-doored *vitrin*, where valuable objects like icons, china, and silver were displayed. This type of furniture was fashionable some 30 years ago, now more *passé* than *retro*, but was quite common in the houses of Rum Polites of this older generation. Here they looked rather well-kept, and I could not help but notice that the cloth covers protecting the furniture had just been removed for the visitors.

While I was paying attention to the interior, I was also going through the usual greetings with our host, which included polite refusals of the many different kinds of food and drink that he was insistently offering us. In the end the negotiations were finalized when he brought us some tea, which he swore that he had already boiling on the stove,[2] to accompany the baklava that somebody had brought him recently from Istanbul. After confirming with me that its source was one of the oldest and still the best of baklava shops in Istanbul, he turned to Stratos for explication: "You probably never had this kind before. This is the real thing!" He was not having any as he had diabetes, but he made sure that Stratos was able to appreciate it: "Isn't it the best baklava you've ever had?" There is no modesty with the Rum Polites, I thought to myself, when it comes to what their City has to offer. I was in no position to escape stuffing myself—not only did I need to demonstrate that I was homesick by eating baklava, but I also was "far too thin" for his standards, as he repeatedly told me as if to underline the temporary grandpa role that he suddenly found suited him. He continued along family lines: Are your parents back there? Do you have brothers and sisters? Younger or older? When are you completing your studies? I was trying to keep pace by making my answers long enough to be polite to him but short enough for the sake of Stratos, who was starting to get bored as the conversation was being carried out in Turkish on the old man's initiative. Suddenly he remembered Stratos's existence. "Oh I forgot about you," he said. "You don't mind that we are speaking Turkish, do you? We have so much to talk about from the good old City. If you want, you can go to your place and do your own thing, and I can continue chatting here with Ilay." Though not entirely unpuzzled by being bluntly excluded from the encounter, Stratos said that he had some work to do anyway, so he would check back with us in a little while. When he left, the old man turned to me and said that it was better that way, and Stratos would not mind. "He's a good kid, but there are things that I can tell you, but you know, he won't understand." (*Einai kalo paidi, alla einai kapia pramata pou boro na se leo-alla kseris, den tha katalavi ekinos.*) I nodded. I understood what he meant, but he put it into words for me anyway: He is from Cyprus. But he is too young to remember how it was before they parted, the two communities. We knew how to live well together, Greeks and Turks, but they ruined it for us. It's all politics. And all politics evolves around this Cyprus. That little island ruined it for us as well. You will find that we Polites do not get along with the Cypriots. They are full of hatred for the Turks. That is what they were told, that Turks were evil, that they were barbarian. These kids are too young to know otherwise. This is a good kid. But be careful with the Cypriots in general.

He continued a little more along the same lines, while I listened to him with a smiling and nodding façade that I hoped was masking my amazement. He was in fact voicing a very familiar discourse about Greek–Turkish relations and Cyprus. Once upon a time, it went, Greeks and Turks were living happily and peacefully side by side. Then came the evil (and this evil could be disguised in many forms: wars, the Great Powers, nationalism, Young Turks, Islamic fanaticism, populism, uneducated rural people migrating to the city, the Cyprus events, etc.) and inserted tensions between them. This hurt especially the population of Istanbul: throughout the second half of the twentieth century, almost all of the painful events experienced by the Rum Polites coincided with periods of heightened conflict in Cyprus. The Rum Polites had no connections to the Cypriot Greeks, but for the Turkish state everything from their name (the former are Rum of Istanbul, the latter are Rum from Cyprus in official Turkish terminology) to their religion, and by extension, their interests, their political affiliations, and their stance toward Turkey and the Turks were not differentiable. Having suffered from being categorized in the same breath with the Cypriots, therefore, the Rum Polites strongly underlined how they differed from them in terms of language (*Chipriaka*), cultural sophistication ("peasants"), and, indeed, in terms of their relations with the Turks ("fanatics").

As is to be expected, tense relations within the "trouble triangle" (Aktar et al. 2010) between Greeks, Turks, and Cypriots do not allow this rhetoric to be part of the dominant official discourse. But the words that my Rum informant uttered in front of a Greek Cypriot and a Turk were all pronounced in a tone that signaled a resemblance to other conversations I had had with other Rum Polites. It was not how he was repeating this familiar rhetoric that puzzled me, then. It was what Stratos had told me earlier about his being anti-Turkish. Was he simply putting on a theatrical show of being nice to a Turk? Was this just an act of courtesy, a gesture of the infamous Mediterranean hospitality? Would he behave in the same way if I was a more threatening, stereotypical kind of Turk, that is, a strong and dark man with a deep voice and a moustache? Was he just talking to Stratos in this manner, and acting like himself when the Cypriot was away? It was hard to know. He had not seen me, or even asked anything about me before he met me. He had no reason to meet with me, be nice to me, speak Turkish to me, or tell me those very personal and emotional details from his life story as he did for the next three hours. He said a few times that these were not things that he mentioned to anybody and kept going on and on about some very complex, some very painful, or very touching situations he had encountered throughout his life. "We don't bring up such memories with my wife, my sister, or my friends. My son doesn't know these things at all. Otherwise how can you go about your life today, if you continue in the past? *Perasmena ksehasmena.* Bygones are bygones."

I was deeply moved. What was going on felt like a self-inflicted session, which he ignited without my leading to it with questions. It was not a formal interview, for I was thinking that this was going to be a brief initial meeting where we would schedule to meet at some other more convenient time later. It was as if this was the occasion for him to release what he had been keeping inside him for so many years. But why had he been holding back all that time? Was it because he thought he was not going to be understood, or because he wanted to move on, or because he had to act as a victim of the Turks to comply with what he held to be the anti-Turkish sentiments in Greece? Why was he talking to me so differently now? If he did not feel comfortable with me, he would not have entrusted me with such emotional stories. For his flabbergasting narrative could well have been dismissed as fictitious had I not believed implicitly in his candor and truthfulness.

This is why I was disappointed when I heard a couple of days later that he had asked Stratos whether he was sure I was not a spy.

STORIES ON OTHERS

The story above highlights one of the many situations I encountered during my fieldwork when I witnessed Rum Polites displaying varying versions of themselves in differing situations. While this is surely a common phenomenon that applies to many a human condition, my interest here is to analyze these instances of altering Rum Polites selves. This is in order to reach an understanding of the specificity of this ethnographic setting in terms of how changing modes of self-presentation reveal the ways in which cultural codes operate within the intimate privacy of the Rum Polites community in Athens. This way I analyze the internal dynamics of the Rum Polites in Athens, as well as their relations with others, in order to highlight the heterogeneities, diversities, discontinuities, and factionalities that complicate attempts at their characterization and categorization. I further deconstruct the self–other dichotomy by showing the flexibility of both the dividing border between self and other and the assumed internal homogeneity of self and other, which renders them ambiguous.

The notion of ambiguous self or the heterogeneity of Rum Polites identity refers both to an internal diversity of sociological differences and to a willingness to otherize and distantiate the self from others within the community. To describe this situation, I use the term "exclusive diversity" as the ways in which Rum Polites hold their adherence to cosmopolitanism to be a dimension of exclusivity, while at the same time they act selectively in terms of whom they are going to include within this cultural diversity. In this complex matrix that involves many selves and many others, varying historical representations and changing identifications, and an exclusive diversity based on cosmopolitan knowledge that is distinct to those who originate in Istanbul, no single definition of the community is satisfactory for the Rum Polites who tend to resist all conventional categorizations. The search for identity returns to its starting base, to the City.

After my eventful encounter described above, I was soon to find out that Stratos's landlord was not the only one who displayed changing and conflicting positions regarding his relations with others. From that meeting onward, I paid additional attention to the ways in which people acted differently in different situations or in the presence of others. This focus resonated with my knowledge of how this part of the world has been an important venue for the development of anthropological perspectives of self-display (see Herzfeld 1989). In this particular ethnographic case, my presence ignited a special situation in terms of a self–other encounter: as a Turk, I was embodying the ultimate other for a Greek, but as an Istanbulite, I was closer to the intimate self of Rum Polites. Interacting with me, not only as a Turkish Istanbulite but also as a researcher interested in learning about the Rum Polites identity, ignited moments of self-reflection for my informants, during which they critically reasoned about themselves, both individually and collectively.

"So you are basically doing oral history?" asked Panayota after listening to me telling her about my research in Athens. "But this is so difficult, so shaky. Consider my father for example. He was a very well integrated person when he lived in Istanbul. He loved Istanbul, he had only Turkish friends, he would never have left for Greece if he had a choice. He came here, and cursed this place and these people all the time. Twenty years later, he is now telling me that I should watch out when I interact with the Turks because they can be dangerous and so on. What's up with you, I ask him. He got brainwashed here, with TV and newspapers and all that. But in the kind of research you do, where would you put my father? It's a problem."

Panayota is a historian, who came to Athens upon finishing university in Istanbul. Leaning left in her political orientation, she is a member of a circle of Rum Polites intellectuals active in promoting a critical rapprochement between Greeks and Turks. As somebody who would characterize herself as Rum for being cosmopolitan, supranational, and beyond the Greek–Turkish dichotomy, she was voicing disappointment and disturbance about her father's changing position: "It's not that he experienced something traumatic or anything. He came years after we left, so that he could be close to his family, his grandchildren and so on. And he was whining for years about it too!"

My informant was expressing her concern about her father turning "too Greek" in terms of his relation with the Turks. In this, she was referring to the ethnic stereotypes that are widely held in Greece. It is a well-known fact that has been variously acknowledged by anthropologists of modern Greece that "Turk" and "Turkey" are loaded terms that "represent Otherness, more than any other term denoting ethnic category" (Theodossopoulos 2003, 179). As the principal others, the Turks are not only considered to be the later arrivals in the region but also as strangers to Greek history and civilization, as they are further demonized as a backward, corrupt people representing the barbaric East (Koliopoulos and Veremis 2002, 260). The connotations entailed in this ethnic category are noted to be almost always negative: a not exactly human, malevolent, and dangerous figure (C. Stewart 1991; Millas 2001). These stereotypical representations remain the most widely held attitudes about how Greeks think of Turks, or by extension, how the Cypriots think of Turks, as voiced by my informant in the story of the landlord. Countering this view, there is the discourse of cultural proximity and friendship that was ruined by nationalism—a romanticized idea advocated by circles of scholars, intellectuals, associations, and various groups of Rum Polites. Recent studies in Greece or Cyprus demonstrate this phenomenon to be much less straightforward than is popularly suggested.[3]

Rum Polites offer a particularly interesting case in terms of their relations to Turks. Although they vary in their attitudes toward Turkey and Turks, given the major differences in their socioeconomic standing, personal experiences, and political views, their overall dual, hybrid, or in-between status as a community of Greece and Turkey renders any distinction between these two entities less than clear. Their ambivalence fluctuates, as in the case of Panayota's father, through changing phases during a person's life as well. There is much room for flexible shifts within the wide range between the poles of "*Tourkofilos*"[4] and "Hellenified," the latter implying assimilation into the generic anti-Turkish stereotypes held in Greece as a result of living there for a long time. The use of such terms by Rum Polites to refer to each other, including their immediate family members, is significant as it is ironic—an indication of the intricate ways in which the Rum Polites capture and critically comment on the awkwardness of the Greek and Turkish enterprise of estrangement at work.

Rum Polites scholars comment analytically on the nationalist constructions of the Turkish image, for example, in the realm of fiction: "The negative image of 'the other' is not as old as it is supposed to be, and as persistently claimed by the nationalists of the two countries. Nor was the image of 'the other' always negative. The Greeks started to imagine a negative Turk in about 1810 and the Turks conjured up a negative Greek almost a hundred years later. Before this period, 'the other' was not negative, or more precisely, 'the other' did not exist; it had not been imagined or created" (Millas 2000, 179).

Escaping the certainty of such works of nationalist imagination, then, the relations of the Rum Polites with the Turks are marked by a level of ambivalence such that it blurs any attempt at categorical condemnation or stereotyping of an ultimate and undisputedly negative nature. An examination of memoirs by Nikos Apostolidis (1996) illustrates this by demonstrating both an incorporation of generic stereotypical representations of Turks and a certain resistance to them through citing anecdotes of personal experience. The starting lines of the section of his book titled *The Turks as a People* display this duality vividly:

In general lines the Turks as individuals are disciplined, courteous, respectful and appreciative of seniors—especially the educated ... When you offer them some coffee or some help, they will try to return it to you. As a mass, however, they are the worst in the world. With their low level of civilization, they believe blindly in everything they read in the newspapers, anything they hear on the radio and the TV, and all that they are told by the hodjas in the mosque or the officers in the army ... The Turks suffer, get saddened when they see a dog that was killed by somebody or hit by a car. And the reverse: with great apathy and with great pleasure they can massacre one and a half million Armenians and a million Pontiac Greeks, because so they were ordered by their superiors. (Apostolidis 1996, 283–84)

These are the words of a man born in 1911 in Istanbul, who has been living in Athens since 1972. His memoirs entail very detailed information about various aspects of life and people in Istanbul, with intermittent outbursts of convenient generalizations about the Turks. These include overarching statements that link historical claims to the supposed natural Turkish character. Even though the anecdotes that precede these assertions do not lead to the harsh conclusions that follow, and instead serve to prove that there was close contact and affinity between the Rum Polites and the Turks, the author's juxtaposition of history/memory and of personal/generic gives these claims a certain level of perceived validity. In this case, the author chooses to revert to stereotypes, which has the effect of bypassing the ambiguity implied in that duality in the perception of the Turks as a people.

In many other cases, though, writers preserve such ambiguity. The following lines from the journal titled *Kinsterna* published by Rum Polites (vols. 1 and 2, June–December 2002) insightfully bring together conceptualizations of the Rum Polites self and its relations with the ambiguous category of Turks.

> The Turks respected my father very much. He was a deeply polite and dignified person. Real Constantinopolitan. He never offended anyone, he would not quarrel with his friends, naturally did not swear, but he would indirectly claim respect, even obedience, mainly with his attitude. His relations with the Turks were first rate. A diplomat—just like an old Fanariot. He wheedled without showing, he paid always something more "to get his job done," rarely told his views in public. When something bothered him, he put on the act of the furious, with a dim complaint written over his lips. The Turk opposite him—much more innocent—would retreat, deeply worried

that he troubled the "*mösyö*."⁵ ... And these, together with the ringing sound from the glasses of tea that kept going back and forth with head spinning speed—you did not need to have finished one for them to bring you a new one; all the secret is that you have next to you a "fresh" tea. All these, of course, when they want to make you feel like a master. However, it confuses me to remember all that. I did not understand then why the Turks threw us out as suspects, they attacked us with so much barbarism during the *Septemvriana*, although they loved us as fellow urbanites. Were they the same Turks who did all that? Life later gave me—as much as it gave me—the answers that I needed; these images, however, remained in the memory of my spirit indelibly. (Maria Harisiadou 2002, 84–90)

In Greece, where there are persistent negative stereotypes about the Turks, the capacity to "generate certainty in support of prejudice" (Herzfeld 1992, 73) is broken down by the Rum Polites through the ambiguous yet multiple ways in which they relate to their Turkish others. The Rum Polites in Athens are diverse, and do not make up a community that is unified in any sense, and certainly not in terms of their relations with the Turks. Yet their orientations toward others, however varied they may be, underline an important commonality that unifies the Rum Polites as a community of cosmopolitans, in the way Hannerz describes them: as those who share a stance toward diversity, "toward the coexistence of cultures in the individual experience," and for whom participation in this foreign other is significant (Hannerz 1990, 239).

Living in the metropolitan environment of Istanbul, the Rum Polites were exposed to other others in their everyday life. Whether the relations between them were harmonious or not, the coexistence of many different social groups was an intrinsic dimension of the local culture, not least the centuries of tradition in the local cuisine, as described by Bozi in her *Politiki Kouzina* (2003). This is highlighted in the following entry from another cookbook of Istanbul Rum cuisine: "The women of Istanbul were chefs by birth. The art and craft was transferred from mother to daughter and was later enriched by the mother-in-law, the neighbor, the friend, the Karamanli, the *Laz*,⁶ the Armenian, the Turk, and a little bit, by the Jew" (*tin Karamanlou, ti Lazou, tin Armenissa, tin Tourkalitsa kai elahista tin Evreissa*) (Chalkousi 2002, 12).

The most immediate others, such as friends and neighbors, were often members of other non-Muslim minorities, like Armenians and Jews, with whom the Rum Polites participated and competed in many aspects of everyday life, as the memoirs excerpt below demonstrates:

> The Armenians are a very ancient people, much before the period of Alexander the Great. They are hard-working, obstinate, patriotic, but also very jealous. Envious. I am especially referring to the Armenians of Istanbul, who were unimaginably jealous of us.... (Apostolidis 1996, 333)

A woman now in her 60s related to me her childhood memories from when she was living with her family in the Istanbul island of Büyükada (Prince's Island/*Prinkipos*) in the summers. There they had Armenian neighbors, and they actually were on very good terms as far as she could remember. This is why the words of her mother made no sense to her: "My mother had told me that the Armenians had a heavy odor because they used olive oil in their cooking. I was thinking about the smell when playing with the neighbor's children. How terrible for a child, isn't it?" Her mother also warned her not eat anything she was given in that household, a warning that she did not understand until many years later when she herself received a plate of *dolma*[7] from her downstairs neighbors on a special occasion. Seeing this, her Rum neighbor upstairs came over to her house and reminded her not to eat it. "You know, you know," she said. Her friend who was present at the time responded that they were going to throw the food away anyway. After reassuring the neighbor and then urging her to leave, the friend told her friend the story of the perpetuating myth that indicated an ancient clash between Greeks and Armenians.[8]

It is interesting to note here how food in general, and oil in this particular case, can act as means of demarcation of community boundaries. Here it seems to function contrary to conventions: ethnographic cases show that Greeks rely on the exclusive use of olive oil as a way of differentiating themselves from their butter-using others.[9] A joke-puzzle related to me by an informant repeats a similar association between eating and Armenians, while extending the stereotypical representations to other communities of Istanbul:

> What does a Jew do when he finds some money? He trades it, invests it in business. What does an Armenian do? He eats (with) it (*ta troi*).[10] That's for sure. What does a Turk do? He changes his woman (*allazi gommena*). What does a Rum do when he earns some money? He spends it on his household.

The heritage of long centuries of living together established, among other things, persistent stereotypical representations among the different communities of Istanbul. Evelpidis demonstrates the negative side of multiethnic coexistence when he makes the list of different peoples of Istanbul: Rum Polites, he claims, were suspected by everyone (1976, 168):

> In the eyes of the Rum, the Levantine were fake European traditionalist hypocrites; people with fake feelings, foreign language, and with borrowed homelands. The Jews—the *Yahudi*—were parasites who did not recognize the plough and the hammer ... They were cowardly, big-mouth, penny-pinchers (*buçukçulides*), money-grabbers. Those from Aleppo were like Turkish Christians, and the rich ones were hanging out with the Levantine. Albanians, the stubborn villagers, were selling fruit, liver, milk. And the Armenians were the most laughed about among all the unfortunate. For their melancholy and ugliness, their rude ways, their filthy food, their chatter and their fatness, for their treason of giving half to others half to the Turks, even when they were massacred every now and then by the Turks. So much was said about them from mouth to mouth, so that the better ones of them would be ashamed to appear with their own race. They presented themselves as French or English, yet their English and their French were ridiculous. Still they would know something from all the languages of the Babel.

Linking to Prato's critical analysis (2009), the way it is described in these excerpts, multicultural co-living in Istanbul may not sound like a much cherished harmony, yet the quotes are valuable as important notes that add on the complexity of the social experience that many scholars dub as conviviality in the city. Conviviality, literally meaning "living together," refers to something more than multicultural coexistence or urban coresidence and offers more than just a descriptive category that "captures the modes of peaceful and happy togetherness" (Nowicka and Vertovec 2014, 350). In the words of Paul Gilroy, conviviality is "a social pattern in which different metropolitan groups dwell in close proximity but where their racial, linguistic and religious particularities do not—as the logic of ethnic absolutism suggests they must—add up to discontinuities of experience or insuperable problems of communication" (2006, 27). It is the experience of encountering multicultural others in everyday life and showing empathy toward others.

Conviviality is a concept that is used to refer to emic notions of cosmopolitanism in many societies in the Mediterranean area, such as *convivéncia* in Spain (Suarez-Navaz 2004; Mann et al. 1992; Erickson 2011; Arizpe 1998), *civiltà* in Italy (Silvermann 1975; Pardo 1996; Herzfeld

2009), "conflicting conviviality" in Macedonia (Mattioli 2012), or the local versions of conviviality in Syria (Rabo 2012; Marcus 1989) and in Egypt (Bayat 2010). In the case of Turkey, conviviality is considered to be rooted in the cosmopolitanism of the Ottoman Empire (Freitag et al. 2011; Freitag 2014; Gilsenan 1992; Zubaida 2010; Barkey 2005; Meijer 2013). Primarily reflecting itself in port cities (Fuhrmann and Kechriotis 2009; Driessen 2005), conviviality is found to be particularly relevant for describing life in Istanbul as the term emphasizes not only the differences between people and groups but also "the ability of people from different backgrounds to interact in daily life in a shared space, to make and produce socially a collective culture, collective identity and a sense of belonging in a place" (Duru 2015, 246).

For the Rum Polites in Athens, who define their distinct identity through belonging to a cosmopolitan Istanbul, the notion of conviviality takes on another crucial dimension. Despite all clashes and competition that have come with it, the multicultural presence of many different ethnic, religious, linguistic communities in Istanbul is something that they acknowledge as an indispensable dimension of everyday urban experience that the Rum Polites fail to find the equivalent of in Athens. The limited level of multireligiosity in Greece is seen as a sign of a monotonous homogeneity, indicated on an everyday basis. For example, the Rum Polites point to the fact that the Athenians are still debating whether or not they should build a mosque in the city, whereas Istanbul in comparison has hundreds of various churches and synagogues. "You can hardly hear anything other than Greek being spoken here. This is so boring," says Anastasia, who follows all the Turkish channels on her satellite dish. She once said to me that she misses the sound of *ezan* (Islamic call for prayer) so much that she rushes home from work in order to listen to it on Ramadan days, when the call to prayer that signals the break of fast is broadcast on Turkish TV. Knowledge about the special days of other religions is considered to be another sign of cosmopolitanism; there are countless stories of how they visited each other on their respective name days or religious holidays, went to churches and *ayazma*[11] together, and practiced rituals of whichever origin. Some Rum Polites in Athens still call their Armenian, Jewish, or Muslim friends in Istanbul on such occasions. One explanation that Rum Polites give as to why the Athenians lack this kind of multiculturalist experience is that they have no urban tradition. According to stereotypical representations that are voiced not infrequently by the Rum Polites, all Elladites are peasants and all Greece is one big village. "Everybody is obsessed with the question of '*Apo pou eisai?*' (Where do you come from?) because everybody came from some village," a lady told me before relating to me a story: A few years ago, she found herself in a difficult situation when her young son asked his parents why they did not go back to their village for the Easter break as all his friends in school did. The question was normal for a small child, but it was a little hard to handle for his parents as they said they could not find the right words to explain: "Well, we are not from *those* kinds of people."

Those kinds of people are the non-Polites—non-Istanbulite and non-urbanite. The rural–urban cultural clash has been noted extensively as a central theme of elite and public discourses in Istanbul (Keyder 2000), Athens (Faubion 1993), and elsewhere in the rest of a world that is undergoing drastic urbanization. For Rum Polites, the urban–rural division is an important aspect that is further employed to explain the differentiation between the two major Rum communities: the Rum Polites and the Anatolian Rum (*Mikrasiates*). Despite the fact that many of them were also settled in urban centers of Asia Minor before the catastrophic population exchange, and that they also consider themselves to be cosmopolitans (Hirschon 1989, 2003), Rum Polites reserve the ultimate urban status for themselves due to the greatness of their own City.

Thus there is a bittersweet competition between the Rum Polites and Asia Minor Rum in terms of who is more cosmopolitan and modern. This encompasses differences in a variety of realms ranging from schooling to intellectual life and openness to new ideas, from religiosity to culinary traditions. I became familiar with this rivalry when an informant took me to a seminar on the Karamanli language hosted by the Association of Smyrnians. During the entire meeting he made comments such as "Let us stick together and sit by ourselves. We are from Istanbul, we should not mix with the Anatolians," a sentiment he repeated jokingly later to the president of the association, who was a good friend of his. After we left, he reflected on his stance: "We always joke like this among ourselves, but in fact there is a certain level of truth to it. Smyrna was the crown of Asia Minor, and Smyrnians have a strong urban tradition. It kills them when we Polites call them villagers. What can we do? After all, we are the ones from the City." What this ironic exchange brought to light was an ongoing and lively debate that deserves to be taken up in a comparative context of different modes of Rum cosmopolitanism as associated with the Polites, Smyrnians, Pontiacs, Cappadocians, and others—a further dimension of the internal diversity and hybridity of the Rum Polites community that I will be exploring next.

Stories on Selves

A common way in which the Rum Polites talk critically about the wider collectivity is through relating to stereotypical conceptualizations within the community. They do this in a reflexive way by including their first-hand experiences with other Rum Polites, while maintaining a desire to distance themselves from any standardized way of being, from being just like the other community members. Somewhere between the wish to deconstruct and the tendency to dismiss, a Rum intellectual told me one day: "Now I am tired of trying to understand these people. One day they act like this, next day they behave exactly the opposite way. In Istanbul they were of a certain disposition, here they are completely different. I have been trying to figure them out for years, but it is not worth it. Good that you took over the task. When you get to understand these Rum Polites, you can tell me all about it!"

This resonates with other such outbursts by Rum Polites regarding their own complexity and unpredictability. I often heard half-joking, half-serious comments such as "somebody should treat us sociologically," that is, diagnose the social problems of the community, or "we are a tribe worthy of anthropological investigation," that is, an endangered species of rather weird and exotic disposition. I would also be asked why I would bother with the Rum Polites, who are "a confused and lost people themselves" and not worth learning anything from, unlike the "previous generations in Istanbul, who were really culturally superior." When asked to clarify what they meant by such statements, the speakers tended to typecast the Rum Polites and support these views through their own experiences with other Rum Polites, as the following stories are to demonstrate.

Much of the disappointment that my informants experienced upon their arrival in Athens came from disillusionment with the rest of the Rum Polites. Partially because they migrated in a scattered fashion, these stories were less about any solidarity that was formed within the community than they were about individual struggles for survival. "Everybody minded their own business. You could not expect any help from the other," a housewife remembered when talking about her arrival in Athens in the late 1960s, using the Turkish phrase *"kimse kimsenin gözünün yaşına bakmazdı"* (nobody would see the tears in the eyes of others), meaning that nobody would empathize with the others' suffering. I was told by different entrepreneurs that they would prefer to employ Rum Polites, not necessarily out of a sense of responsibility, but because they were more professional, disciplined, knowledgeable, and had a better work ethic than the local Greeks. Those who went out of their way to help the community were not appreciated or offered any help in return when it was they who needed support. Telling me several stories about how Rum Polites betrayed each other upon their arrival in Greece, a pharmacist in his 60s, Petros, started passionately compiling the following adjectives:

> What should I tell you about these? Not trusting each other, not standing up for the other (*birbirlerine güvenmez, birbirini tutmaz*). Cheaters, traitors (*üçkağıttsides*). They did not go through human liberation (*den perasane apo elefteria anthropon*). They are a self-interested bunch. Passive, unpleasant (*Suya sabuna karışmayan, ghourousouzides*).

Various others who left Istanbul at different periods and under different circumstances related to me their stories about how surprised they were with the ways of the other Rum Polites, and often in negative terms. One frequent reference was to the conservativeness or closeness of the Rum Polites. Sofia, a woman in her 40s, who arrived in the 1980s, put it to me in plain Turkish:

> In Istanbul we had our own circles. Our own friends, work milieu, etc. There were always some Rum who lived in their own world, closed into themselves, in their little family circle, church neighborhood, going to Rum schools, you know those who would leave Tatavla only in the summer for the islands, or to go to an *ayazma* in the *yortu* days, that sort of thing. These mostly came here altogether, constructed the same circles here in Athens, gathered in and around Faliro, opened their shops, and continued living in their worlds. Those like us, progressivists, had either been to foreign schools, or were engaged through work or other activities in close interaction with a wider segment of the city. We had a more mixed *parea* (circle of friends), so we had to lose our networks when we came to this town where there were no ways of reestablishing such connections. We are trying to keep up with our *parea* in Istanbul, but it is difficult. I hate that I have to interact with the rest of these people here, just because they are Rum. They are so old-fashioned, conservative (*tutucu, geri kafalı*).

The term "progressivist" used by Sofia applies to a generation of Rum Polites intellectuals who are leftists in their political orientation. As one informant voiced in contempt recently, the story of the leftist movement among the Rum Polites is yet to be written. Comprised of men and women who were in their university years during the 1970s and have participated in the political movements and protests in Turkey, Greece, as well as the rest of the world, some members of this group called themselves progressivist students (*i proödheftiki fitites*) and took part in the foundation of the Student Union of Polites (*Fititiki Enosi Konstantinoupoliton*). This group is not an active political force today, though its loosely connected members are still engaged in cultural and intellectual activities that are based on a politically informed agenda. These range from individual attempts at translating Turkish literature into Greek or compiling anthologies on Istanbul, to more collective efforts of organizing conferences and bringing out journals. The acclaimed journal *Synchrona Themata* that has appeared since 1978 is a product of the work of these Rum Polites.

H Kath 'imas Anatoli is a linked movement that was also forged by a group of Rum Polites intellectuals. Although from different professions, these people shared a common interest in social and historical research, an interest they institutionalized in 1992 as the Research Association of Our Own East (*Etereia Meletis tis Kath 'imas Anatolis* or Etmelan). It organizes various occasions for people from Istanbul, Imvros, and Tenedos to research and study the history of many centuries and the production of contemporary art and literature in the City as well as by the diaspora. Etmelan brings out two journals, called *Kath 'imas Anatoli* and *Kinsterna* (previously *Dexameni*), organizes biannual conferences and yearly seminar series, publishes their proceedings, and consults on and contributes to the production of books, international conferences and exhibits, feature films, and documentaries.

In the realm of community affairs, the level of institutional organization shows a great deal of internal diversification and ambiguity of self among the Rum Polites in Athens. During my fieldwork, I witnessed that this relatively small community was distributed among a few dozen separate organizations, ranging from school alumni societies to neighborhood communities of districts in Istanbul. These would sometimes—but not always—overlap or even cooperate, which meant that altogether they made up for a divided focus on community affairs. A survey conducted among members of these institutions showed that most wished for a union of organizations that would bring all Rum Polites under one roof. In 2006, the Ecumenical Federation of Polites (Oi.Om.Ko.) was established to bring together the activities of 25 Rum Polites organizations around the world. Apart from its main object of strengthening the dispersed Rum Polites community, Oi.Om.Ko. also provides for the disadvantaged among them, giving financial, legal, medical, and other forms of assistance through various projects and programs of academic or philanthropic nature.

Rum Polites in Athens are less than fully engaged in terms of political undertakings, however. The ideological commitment and political institutionalization of Rum Polites in Greece remains somewhat limited.[12] When I asked about the reasons for this, the question was dismissed by my informants, commenting on how family concerns and personal struggles were highly prioritized by the Rum Polites. Others noted that it was better this way, for a political internal division would prove catastrophic for an already dispersed community like the Rum Polites. Noting that the *Pontii* had suffered because of this in the past, one eminent member said to me, "*bir o eksikti zaten!*" (as if we needed that too). Despite generational and other differences, especially those that relate to the reason of displacement from Istanbul, politics was, in general lines, a risky endeavor that the Rum Polites in Athens opted to stay away from.

Some may therefore find not much room for surprise in this distancing from politics, but there is some room for self-criticism—for it is, perhaps, one of the most frequently made comments that the Rum Polites have no common orientation and they fail to unite around a single aim in the interests of their community. This view is verbalized in a letter by Vassilis Hatzopoulos published in the *Anatoli* newspaper (July–August 2004, p. 11):

> The majority of our compatriots, for better or worse turned a page in their lives, regarding Istanbul as a yellow photograph in a family album rather than something alive that needs help and solidarity. Let us take advantage of the mistakes of Turkey and ... act as consultants to each government in Greek–Turkish matters ... We should have made our presence in Greece felt and not only be recognized by them as being excellent in eating and drinking etc., etc..... We have failed greatly as individuals and as institutions to create a political lobby in our new homeland and impose our terms. It is entirely unfair that there are no politicians of Rum Polites origin (not Asia Minor) who could have made their voices heard....

Note that in this statement, as in many others, call for political action is in order to fulfill a sense of responsibility for being Rum Polites. In other words, the point of reference as well as the aim remains Istanbul, as opposed to a wish to get organized politically to gain a political stance within Greek society, for service to Greece, or in pursuit of their own common interests of improving their conditions in Greece.

The political disinclination of Rum Polites supersedes their self-declared weakness or unwillingness to act as an organized political force—certainly not at a party level, but even not as an electorate. It is not much of a disputed self-image of the Rum Polites that they are by and large uninterested in national politics, as this story shows:

> It must have been in the fifties, when this Rum guy went to the *periptero* (kiosk) and asked for a newspaper. The *peripteras* asked what kind he wanted, because you know there were very partisan newspapers then, communist and royalist and so on, and you would be in trouble if you got the wrong one. The guy was confused at first, and then angry: a Greek newspaper I want, do you understand, just a Greek newspaper!

Similar stories would cite the Rum Polites commenting on the civil war in Greece. The following, told to me by a middle-aged writer, illustrates both these points quite well:

> I will tell you yet another thing, and you will be shocked to hear it. There is this woman I know from elementary school in Istanbul. Somehow we were talking about the military coup in Turkey, and I don't know how but I came to mention the *junta* in Greece. She asked me what the term was. She did not even know the Greek word, she was using the Turkish words *askeri idare* or something. "How can this be," I asked, "you were already in Greece during those years!" Can you believe it, she asked which years these were. She paused and then said, "Oh, we were preoccupied then with building our house here in Athens!" She gave me this as an explanation, and as a legitimate one at that. And mind you, this is a typical Rum Polites answer: we were preoccupied with our home. Very very typical!

Another important dimension of diversity that was highly changed and rendered ambiguous through displacement is the socioeconomic standing among Rum Polites. In most cases, migrants or refugees suffer from the often forced and sudden act of displacement mostly in socioeconomic terms. Apart from their loss of actual capital, property, workplace, income, and investments, migrants who find themselves in strange lands realize they are missing those traits that may be even more important for the reestablishment of their standing in the new society: social network, status, value of professional skills, and local knowledge. The Rum Polites faced many such difficulties upon their arrival in Greece, but were most disappointed with not receiving help or even a good reception from the Elladites. Long stories of how they were being cheated by their Greek partners often contain references to an entirely different work ethic from what they were accustomed to in Istanbul, where a handshake would close a deal that the other party would undoubtedly honor. Not knowing local ways of conducting business, some would refrain from working with the Athenians, claiming that they were not trustworthy or knew nothing (i.e., did not possess cosmopolitan knowledge), therefore sticking with other Rum Polites as much as possible. Thanks to their raised levels of education, skill, and (cosmopolitan) knowledge, most of them struggled yet managed to make a decent living for themselves and their families, making sure that their children would study well enough for a much better start. An elderly lady in a retirement home, who grew up in Arnavutköy in a three-story villa overlooking the Bosphorus, for example, worked as a tailor in a two-room apartment until both her daughters graduated from college. The founding director of Oi.Om.Ko., Nikos Uzunoglou, claims that while the vast majority of Rum Polites have been able to get back on their feet and be better off in their lifetime, there are still hundreds who are in need of their fellow Rum Polites' help to survive—a matter proving increasingly difficult given the current financial crisis of Greece.

Perhaps as relevant as their class position is the perceived status of Rum Polites in Greece. The imagery of the wealthy and cultured Rum elite, for example, the Fanariots, utilized by the Rum Polites but also by the Elladites, may not necessarily be based on their actual socioeconomic conditions. Rather, it may relate to a supposed notion based on a combination of an imagination of their historical elite position as the heirs of the Fanariots or Byzantines and the presentation of their cultural sophistication as bearers of an urban cosmopolitan heritage. Let me illustrate this argument with the words of an informant, who was telling me the story of his first marriage:

> She was from a big Athenian family who were very wealthy. At that point, I had no money in my pocket and I did not care. We were all socialists then, so the idea of marrying rich was not necessarily appealing either. But the girl was not spoilt at all. Anyway, we decided to get married. Her family was very excited because I was from Istanbul. This meant a lot to them despite the fact that I was poor. We got married, but had a divorce in about a year. Cultural differences, I would say. Money does not make anybody sophisticated. This is a fact.

Another significant dimension of class or status is residence, which continues to differentiate among Rum Polites in Athens in terms of their specific local origins in Istanbul. Place of birth and origin differentiate at the most micro level of neighborhoods, allowing Rum Polites to be sorted according to their perceived status and social standing. Certain areas of Istanbul populated with Rum residents are thought to represent different types of cosmopolitan living associated with different eras, as I examine in detail elsewhere (Örs 2018) and summarize in Chap. 5. This cosmopolitan association is juxtaposed upon another taxonomy of what is considered a more prestigious place to live in the city, such that districts of Beyoğlu (Cihangir, Pera) rank highest, followed by Şişli (Nişantaşı, Tatavla), for example. Seaside neighborhoods along the Bosphorus (Yeniköy, Arnavutköy, Boyacıköy, Ortaköy) maintain their exclusive position, while those on the Asian side (Çengelköy, Kuzguncuk, Kandilli, Moda) rank somewhat lower in the Europe-biased imagination that belittles them as *karşı taraf*.[13] The persistence of such stereotyping, still used by current Istanbulites, among many Rum Polites in Athens may seem more than ironic but still remains strong enough to confuse preconceived ideas of social standing: as confirmed to me repeatedly, living in an apartment in Pera may well be viewed as being of more distinguished status than living on the Anatolian side, even if in a luxurious *yalı* villa by the water. "Whatever you do, it is simply Anatolian," Sophia said, agreeing with Anna's words: "*Her tarafından Anadolu olduğu belli oluyor*" (It is obvious that it is Anatolian all over!).

A good way of showing the economic dimension of ambiguity related to place is through a focus on Paleo Faliro. The idea of home and the notion of living in a bounded circle merge spatially and conceptually in Faliro, the main neighborhood populated predominantly by Rum Polites. Although it is a decent residential neighborhood with quite high real estate prices and the added value of the seafront, upgraded through mega projects in the wake of the 2004 Olympics with the addition of sport facilities and a luxurious marina, Paleo Faliro is not as elite, exclusive, or expensive as the top areas in the city, such as Kolonaki, Kifissia, or Vouliagmeni—unlike what its status used to be a few decades ago. The loss of its prestigious recent past as a posh summer resort can partially by explained by the migration Athens has received since the 1960s, which led to an increase in the number of high-rise apartment buildings that replaced the large villas.

Yet Faliro is certainly not a gated area or even an isolated suburban neighborhood. It is in fact quite close to the city center—only a ten-minute drive—and people who live there travel everyday to go to work or school, where they interact closely with the rest of the Athenians. This close yet enclosed position of Faliro allows the Rum Polites a certain level of residential ambiguity. It is ironic that when Rum Polites stay in Faliro to continue what they refer to as their "way of life as it was in Istanbul" in order to keep their Constantinopolitanism that is based on cosmopolitanism, which here means openness to others, they are perceived as pursuing enclosed, conservative lives in exclusive settings.

It is sometimes the Rum Polites themselves who adhere to this self-perception. A pastrymaker who lives in the center of Athens told me that he did not even want to go there to be among the Rum Polites, explaining that "they see the world like this" as he put his hands left and right of his face to imitate a horse with blinkers. Another informant, a university professor, warned me that I should not be surprised if I heard Turkish spoken on the streets of Faliro. He was quick to note, however, that these people would never do this in Turkey. "Whatever renders them separate from the rest of the society, they would go for that. They prefer to live in their own world," he remarked. The categorizations of people living further north were even more striking, as they relied on the additional dimension of a class-based Athenian discourse regarding the north–south division. Offering me tea in the beautiful garden of their house in Psihiko, a lady whose daughter I know asked me, with motherly concern, how I could stay down there among the Faliriotes: "They can be very strange. They can make you feel like a stranger, too." Another middle-aged, well-off informant who came to Faliro to meet me for lunch said, after commenting on the physical surroundings of the neighborhood, half-jokingly, "You should move from here. The good Rum Polites live in the northern suburbs (*O kalos Politis meni sta voria proastia!*)."

This ambiguity of class and status is paralleled in more primordial dimensions like ethnicity or language. The memory and knowledge of Istanbul bring not only Rum Polites together. There are many others from the City whose life brought them to Athens. They also live in and around Paleo Faliro. Among them are Assyrians, another Christian Orthodox community from Southeastern Turkey, Armenians, Kurds, as well as Turks. None of these are Grecophones, and some of them are not even interested to learn Greek. An informant related to me the story of an Armenian man married to a Rum woman, both from Istanbul. He never learned Greek, because had no wish to interact with the Greeks whatsoever. They have been living in Athens for over 20 years, I was told. When I asked about the language they spoke at home, the answer was "Turkish, of course. This is why they live in Faliro. So he can go out, do his shopping, find people to talk to."

It is true that one can easily get by with Turkish in Faliro, if necessary. The situation is by no means comparable to that of Chinatown in Manhattan, the Turkish quarter Kreuzberg in Berlin, or the Greek neighborhood in Toronto. But it is a fact that Turkish-speaking persons would have little problem making themselves understood around Faliro. They can walk into *Benito*, for example, a charcuterie named after its Istanbulite owner of Italian Levantine origin, greet them in Turkish, buy fresh *yufka* flown in every other day from Istanbul, and chat about current affairs in Turkey. They can walk into a coiffeur and it is likely that there would be somebody who knows the meaning of *röfle* (Turkish: highlights). I remember an instance when I was out for *kebap*[14] in Faliro with some young Rum Polites who had recently moved to Athens. I asked my friend to request some red pepper as I could not remember the word in Greek. He turned to the waiter and said, "*Pul biber var mı?*" (Turkish: Do you have—a specific kind of—red pepper?). As I burst out laughing, I told my friend that I could have done the same if I'd known they were Rum. "No no, they're Kurds!" (*Yok canım, Kürt bunlar*) he answered, teaching me my first lesson in the multiculturality of the Turkish-speaking community in Athens. Examples can be multiplied. All these little intricacies of daily life make Faliro a center of attraction for the Istanbulites. Many Turks living in Athens, be they diplomats or businessmen, prefer to live around Faliro, or they make sure they spend much time in the neighborhood. "Where else in Athens can you get this service?" explained one young woman. "I walked into a patisserie once, and while shopping I must have told the man that I liked *ramazan pidesi*.[15] Next day he called me at home and said, 'Miss, your *pide* are ready' (*Hanımefendi, pideleriniz hazır*). I had not even ordered them. I could not even imagine having them months away from *ramazan!*"

Although the Rum Polites are not a highly integrated community void of internal clashes, there is something that holds them together sufficiently to stop them from being entirely dispersed. The dilemma voiced by those who choose to reside close to one another is that if they could reconcile their differences and integrate into the larger social structure, their children would start to assimilate, and discontinue what they call the Rum

Polites lifestyle (*Konstantinoupolitiki zoi*)—an honored heritage they struggle to preserve despite the difficulties presented by "all these mixed schools and mixed marriages" (with non-Istanbulites) that one elderly informant identified as being the main perils for his grandchildren. If their children "turn into Elladites," they say, the identity and memory of Istanbul that renders the Rum Polites exclusive and distinct could just disappear.

The National Story

Even after long presentations of ethnographic and historical evidence to show the diversity of Rum Polites, it is not unusual for me to be asked questions begging for more direct answers, such as: "I did not understand one thing. Are these people Turks or Greeks?"

Here I wish to investigate the common tendency to ask simple questions and the difficulty that anthropologists encounter in answering them as a result of their involvement in the multiplicity of cultural realities concerning the communities they study. I will both address that difficulty, by presenting the diversity of ethnographic situations on which an answer can be based, and engage with the nature of the questions themselves in order to highlight their underlying assumptions. Rather than proving that seemingly simple questions are very hard to answer accurately, my intention is to reveal the intricate processes of formulating ethnographically grounded insights on issues of wider concern. For the lessons learned from analyzing the Rum Polites would lead inevitably to questions about other social groups elsewhere, and perhaps inspire ideas on how to go about answering them. This also speaks to attempts from within anthropology to refute methodological nationalism, designated as the assumption that the nation-state as equated to society is the natural social and political form of the modern world (Beck 2000, 2002, 2003, 2004; Wimmer and Glick-Schiller 2002; cf. Fine and Chernilo 2004; Chernilo 2006).

In the following, I discuss the extent to which widely used categories in social sciences are suitable for a successful conceptualization in the case of Rum Polites. Through presenting relevant ethnographic material, I question the assumptions underlying these categories and the limitations these may bring to the understanding of social reality in general and the Rum Polites in particular.

Rum Polites are categorized officially by the nation-states within which they live. In Turkey they are referred to as *İstanbullu Rum*, a non-Muslim minority, which is a legally described and internationally constituted community under the Treaty of Lausanne.[16] In Greece, they are variously noted as *Ellines tis Polis*, or *Konstantinoupolitiki omoyenia*,[17] or as redeemed returning migrants from the diaspora community of Constantinopolitan Greeks. The criterion used in the Treaty of Lausanne to differentiate between populations was religion, and this, arguably, has remained as the single most salient marker in both Greece and Turkey to underline the conceptual boundaries of the nation. Regardless of their legal citizenship status, Rum Polites were always included among the latter in the shifting distinction between *kseni* (outsiders, foreigners) and *dhiki mas* (our own) in Greece (see Herzfeld 1980, 1987), while the Turkish state more often than not applied a policy of their exclusion, exerting its right to define bounded populations, treating the Rum Polites as foreigners on the grounds sometimes of formal citizenship (as in the 1964 expulsion), but always of religion (notably as in the Population Exchange and the Wealth Tax).

In order to determine who the Rum Polites are, the first question that would be asked is whether they are Greeks or Turks. For in this day and age, nationality is largely assumed to be the primary and the predominant source of identity; moreover, national identities are thought of as being mutually exclusive, bounded collectivities within a self and other dichotomy. Rogers Brubaker (2010), among others who argue for the salience of methodological nationalism, states that the nation-state is conceptualized in both social-scientific analysis and political practice as an internally homogeneous, externally bounded political, legal, social, cultural, and economic space. Accordingly, and as designated bureaucratically by citizenship papers, national identity cards, and passports, one can either be Greek or Turkish.

In the case of Rum Polites, the situation has often been far from clear. When living in Istanbul they mostly held Turkish passports as the Rum Polites who had Greek citizenship had to leave the country in the 1960s.[18] When they moved to Athens, in the absence of a single regulation that applied to the entire Rum Polites community, they were evaluated and treated in accordance with their own individual situation. Generally, most Rum Polites maintained their Turkish citizenship, unless there were any particular problems that came with it. The compulsory military service was the most widely experienced problem. Young men who had Turkish passports through their fathers were facing major problems until the two countries reached an agreement that serving in either country would suffice for those who had dual citizenship. But those who left in their teens and twenties still have unresolved issues that prevent them from entering Turkey today. Although many Turks would probably trade their passports for EU citizenship, Rum Polites are still hanging on to theirs in many cases.[19] Often, I was told, the bureaucratic and political barriers were so great that they were discouraged from taking any action. This sometimes led to the failure to renew Turkish passports and a prolonged inability to obtain Greek citizenship, such that people had to spend years "countryless," as a few of my informants put it—that is, without the legal status of being a citizen of any state. For a long time, the general policy in both Greece and Turkey was to keep the corresponding minority statistics stable between the two countries, and applications for either obtaining or relinquishing citizenship were considered accordingly.[20] The "corresponding" minority of Muslims in Western Thrace in Greece, who were also held exempt from the population exchange, presents a comparable case regarding the overlapping aspects of ethnicity, nationality, and religion in identity negotiation (Yağcıoğlu 2004; Grigoriadis 2008; Dragonas 2004; Anagnostou 2001).

Having citizenship and holding on to it is not enough, however, for the Rum Polites to be recognized as Turks by the Turkish authorities. There has never been any initiative by the Turkish government to protect the rights of its citizens in Greece with regard to Turkish nationals of Rum origin, but this discourse has been repeatedly employed for the Muslim-Turks in Greece who do not have Turkish nationality. The discriminatory treatment of the Rum Polites in Turkey and the reluctance on the part of the Turkish state to consider them fully as Turks has become obvious in many instances, as noted before, and the following brief encounter is another illustration of the same point.

This story takes place between the Turkish Ambassador to Greece and a Rum professor who holds only Turkish citizenship, and who related the story to me. During a long conversation that was "very polite and pleasant," where the Ambassador was reflecting on his favorable views on Greek–Turkish relations, he frequently used the terms "us" and "you" when referring to Turks and Greeks, respectively. Each time he was called a Greek (*Yunan*), the professor corrected him by reminding him that he too was a Turkish national, but the Ambassador kept "repeating the same mistake." Finally, the Ambassador gave up trying to correct himself: "Please allow me," he said, "I feel more comfortable [talking to you] this way" (*Rica ederim bırakın ben böyle daha rahat ediyorum*). This is an ironic case where discursive conventions may be so internalized as to override official definitions, even though the person using them might be a high-ranking diplomat. Once again, religion becomes more important for the state than secular markers of national identity such as citizenship.[21]

What is largely unknown, on the other hand, is that having Turkish citizenship is something more than a novelty for many Rum Polites. Their level of involvement with the state of Turkey, or with Turkishness in general, goes beyond a matter of obligation to comply with some bureaucratic nuisance. For many, it remains an important part of their identity. I know a few Rum Polites who travel to Istanbul in order to cast their vote during the Turkish elections. I know many more who fulfill their citizenship duties, such as paying taxes or pension installments, although there is no way for them to get caught after decades of being nonresidents, and even though they know that Turkey is not a welfare state where the benefits they get would be worth the trouble they go through. Many Rum Polites are not deterred by the burdens that come with Turkish citizenship. When a shop owner and his wife told me that their 15-year-old son had, like themselves, only Turkish citizenship, I asked them what he would do when it was time for the boy's military service in a few years. The father said "Good. He should also go and get to know his country a little." Knowing that many Greeks and Turks would do anything in their power to escape the army, I was more than surprised by the non-ironic and non-hesitant way he said this: he had not even moved his hands or changed his facial expression—he was quite serious.

I saw the same solemn attitude evinced by the shop owner when referring to Turkey as his (and by extension, his son's) country reflected in the words of another parent. This time, we were in the house of my informant, who was showing me her family album. She proudly pointed out the picture of her son wearing cap and gown on the occasion of his graduation from a university in England. I noticed the Turkish flag in front of which the entire family was striking a pose. "Both my husband and I are Turkish citizens," she explained without my asking, "and so are all our children. Everybody was posing next to their flag, so this is that picture." She was so clear in making this point that I got the impression there was nothing ambivalent to her about it. I asked her whether they posed in front of the Greek flag as well, since their son also holds a Greek passport. "Of course not," she said, and went on turning the pages of the album. Her look made me feel embarrassed about the question in my own gaze, so I turned my eyes to the next picture featuring three of her grandchildren.

It is not only their continuing formal relations with the Turkish state—or more generally, Turkishness—that makes it difficult for Rum Polites to be categorized as simply Turks or Greeks. It is also their encounters with Greek nationalism and the ways in which it operates in Greece, which is contributing to their ambiguous position in relation to the Greek nation. A set of examples drawn from the experiences of Rum Polites children in Greek schools is highly illustrative. The memoirs of Chalkousi highlight those early shocks in schoolyards, which were "full of small fanatic anti-Turks (*Tourkofagous*)," for example, when they found out that March 25 was not only the rebirth of Christ (*Evangelismos*) but also the great national celebration of the rebirth of the nation (*palliyenisia*), of which they "had no idea" (*den ihame habari*) (Chalkousi 2002, 101). A humorous example of Rum Polites encounters with nationalism can be found in a scene from the movie *Politiki Kouzina*, when the father of the protagonist Fani, then a nine-year-old child, is called in to the police station because of some unruly behavior on the part of his son. "We have information about you, Mr. Iakovidis; we know that deep inside you are a patriot. In addition, however, you have to keep your eyes open. You have to protect the child from a thousand and two dangers," says the officer, meeting the wide-eyed gaze of the boy's father, and gives him the recipe for becoming a good patriot in a Greece under military rule: "I will write here some places for you to take the kid. You will start from the Royal Gardens, then you will go and see the Anaktora, and afterwards you will visit the Military Museum. So that he learns about the battles of Greeks. The child has to become a patriot." After a brief moment of silence, he adds: "Twice a week, after the meal."

Many of my informants who gave me their feedback on the movie commented that these scenes were highly demonstrative of their own experiences. They did not see their situation as something to be remedied, they said, it was nationalism that was the real sickness. As one of them put it, "They thought it was an insult that we were not exactly like them. For me it's far from it. My biggest fear is that my own child will turn into one of those fanatics under the influence of his friends, the Greek kids here (*i edo Ellinopouli*)."

Despite these complexities, it is less likely for most Rum Polites to call themselves Turks (or to admit to being called this[22]) than Greeks. Rum Polites have been, more often than not, categorized as Greeks (here: *Hellenes, Ellines, Yunan*), both in Turkey and in Greece, and many in Athens would be content with this: Rum Polites would not accept that they are less than Greek, much as they would insist that they are a distinct kind of Greek, standing for the diversification of the category Greek.

A good number of Rum Polites would carry this point further and carve out for themselves a third option beyond being simply Greek or Turkish. One man said to me that he felt both Greek and Turkish, while he maintained his critical distance from both: "I have two ears.[23] When I go to Turkey I use my Greek ear; and when I am in Greece, I listen with my Turkish ear. My brain brings the two together; I am both Grekoturkish and Turkogreek." This echoes the dual frame of reference found among displaced peoples elsewhere (Guarnizo 1997; Rouse 1992), revealing an orientational bifocality in the sociocultural domain (Vertovec 2007; Portes 2007). But it does not stop there. In other cases, combination may well become confusion: "In Greece, I am a foreigner but not minority. Turkey is my homeland but I am treated as a foreigner. What bothers me is the nationalist paradigm." Someone else referred to the same situation, but insisted that he did not fall into either of these two categories: "I have a personal, private relationship to the Orthodox religion and to Istanbul. I find that these are my sources for identity. I don't accept being characterized by any other criteria—nationalistic or ethnic. Orthodoxy, as you know, is Ecumenical; it is beyond national divisions. Ethnic nationalism, anyway, is the biggest evil for me (*Zaten etnik milliyetçilik bence her kötülüğün başı*). I am an Orthodox Rum from Istanbul, that's it."

Rum Polites, then, cannot be fully *sorted* with respect to either the Greek or the Turkish state; they retain a categorical confusion, often inflicted by themselves, sometimes imposed by others, and always strengthened by the social and historical conditions within which they live. Many Rum Polites declare themselves to be more comfortable with displaying not a nationally but a culturally defined identity, resembling a certain "cultural citizenship" defined within "a dual process of self-making and being made" (Ong 1996, 78). While this may not be true for all Rum Polites, as noted above, the fact that there is a significant group among them who turn their position in-between nation-states into a statement of their status beyond nations makes it difficult to give an answer to the dualistic question of whether the Rum Polites are Greeks or Turks. Being a community that suffered under the premise of nationalism in its recent past, and presenting a plurality in their cultural disposition toward complicating the notions of "Greek" and "Turk" as singularistic and mutually exclusive categories, perhaps the Rum Polites would be better served by a different response than opting for simply choosing one of the two.

The Minority Story

The Rum Polites are often referred to as a religious minority in Turkey. But how accurate is this designation to describe their social status in Turkish society? The category of minority gained popularity in the aftermath of the World War I with the application of the so-called Wilson principles and was used to designate social groups that could be differentiated by a criterion such as religion, ethnicity, language, or sect, from the demographically and politically dominant group within a nation. The newly independent states signed international treaties to ensure the rights of the people living within their borders, whom they were to therewith designate as minorities. In the case of Turkey, the Treaty of Lausanne served the reification of an ongoing state of classification from the Ottoman period, when the *reaya* was delineated into distinct religious groups called *millet*.[24] The minority category is often applied to the Rum Polites living in Turkey as they are officially recognized as *Rum azınlık* in state terminology. The transition from this religious criterion to an ethnic one came about during the era of national struggles in the Balkans, and single nation-states quickly adopted the same criterion as the underlying basis of their national communities (Todorova 1997). Thus Turkey became a nation of the Turks, meaning Muslims of a Sunnite order, and Greece became the country of Greeks, that is, Christian Orthodox.[25] With a practice of naming that conflated ethnicity, religion, nation, and citizenship, the state apparatus defined the majority as natural citizens and the rest of the citizens as minorities.[26]

Naming a social group a minority is to constitute it as a politically marginal and economically disadvantaged community. Politics of naming reveal the workings of a "governmentality that conducts the minority as compliant, marginal, or excluded" (Demetriou 2013, 70). The Rum Polites had a well-established status and a recognition of their deep-rooted history in Istanbul during the Ottoman era. Their relatively advantageous stance within the newly formed Turkish society, however, started deteriorating as soon as they were recognized as a minority within the nation-state of Turkey. Whether the acts that followed could be interpreted as attempts at reducing them to the less privileged position implied by the category of minority can be a point of discussion, but that they certainly led to that result is a matter beyond dispute. This resonates with the point that being granted rights on the basis of having a culture and a cultural identity may lead to complex and contradictory consequences (Cowan 2006, 18). In any case, ironically or not, the international efforts to secure minority rights within the new (democratic, secular) Republic of Turkey eventually led to a worsening of the political, economic, cultural, and social conditions of the Rum Polites as they lost the rights and privileges they had had under the imperial (dictatorial, hierarchical) order of the Ottoman Empire.

The legal framework had taken its course in its diffusion into society, but ambiguity regarding the social status of the Rum Polites was preserved in the realm of everyday life for much longer. An interesting set of anecdotes from the schoolyard, the very place of political acculturation, highlights the complexity of social practices of exclusion and marginality. Though as children they had experienced harsh situations of harassment in Turkey, several informants told me, where they were "a minority of course," their good friends would always take on the task of protecting them from those "confused kids." Similarly, an informant noted that one day he was given the task of placing flowers in front of the statue of Atatürk at a national day of mourning commemoration: "My friends told me that I was more a child of this country (*bu vatanın evladı*) than they. They would be honored if I did this on behalf of them, they said, and I could not refuse." This story is indicative of what I was told many times: the religious division that rendered the Rum Polites official minorities might have meant they were subjected to discrimination from the state. But as far as the wider society surrounding them was concerned, it was often acknowledged as their special social position and their cultural distinction.

With an ironic twist of their fate with nationalism, the Rum Polites were included in the Greek state through the same criteria on the basis of which they were excluded from the Turkish nation as minorities. Again, if those criteria did not consist of fixed markers such as ethnicity, language, and religion, but attachment or belonging, then there would be much reason to consider the Rum Polites as a cultural minority in Greek society, a status they were given neither by the state nor by the people of Greece. There are other categories that were entertained as being suited for the case of Rum Polites in Athens, and it is those that I would like to revisit in the next section.

The Migrating Story

More than two decades ago, Harrell-Bond and Voutira (1992) argued that relatively little attention has been paid to forced displacement, uprootings, exiles, migrations, and related phenomena by the academic establishment, although such phenomena and the events that give rise to them are a standard feature of human experience. Their concern was echoed by many others who noted a new era of intensified and diversified migration processes in the wake of the end of the millennium (Glick-Schiller et al. 1992; van Hear 1998; Massey 1999). In spite of the recent rise in anthropological interest toward the study of refugees, immigrants, and other forms of "transnational living" (Guarnizo 2003), it would be difficult to argue for their becoming part of the mainstream concerns within the discipline. Studies of displacement, it could be argued, are still a matter out of place. This observation could be further duplicated: anthropology, both as an academic enterprise and as the work of anthropologists, positions the cultural experiences of uprooting at the margins. Thus some of the important contributions in this field, including those with an intention to assist the efforts of policy-makers and humanitarian organizations, have dealt with the people in question as being in transition, in a liminal state, and as strangers in misery facing the social problem of acceptance by the host society. One common denominator in all these studies is the treatment of the migrant groups as being marginal to the rest of the society. Whether such marginality is caused by being fewer in number, having an unproportional access to political power, economical disadvantage, or a result of dominant norms and value systems, those who are labeled under rubrics such as migrants or refugees are almost always considered to be part of a social problem or a political issue that needs to be addressed, examined, and resolved.

Migration in Greece has long been categorized under two main threads: (1) the out-migration of guest workers as expatriate labor force to Western countries and (2) the emigration of repatriating Greeks from the "diaspora." Since the 1990s, a new wave of immigration has brought a major demographic tide to Greece, as migrants from former Soviet Bloc countries started moving into the country. In addition, there is an escalating issue of irregular and often illegal immigration from Southeast Asia and the Middle East, either seeking asylum or refuge in Greece or intending to pass in transit as a gateway to Europe. The current decade is marked by the tragedy of refugees fleeing the civil war in Syria, who suffered greatly while trying to escape to Europe via the Turkish–Greek Aegean sea border, adding another chapter to the long history of human smuggling in the region (İçduygu 2004; Triandafyllidou 2009). The number of international migrants in Greece today is estimated to exceed one million people—nearly 10% of the population—a figure that would be multiplied if the undocumented, illegal, and transient migrants or refugees were taken into account. Recent scholarship addressing the old and new waves of migration in Mediterranean Europe includes Andersson (2014), Ben-Yehoyada (2015), Friese (2010), and Pascale (2010).

The definitions of migrant, refugee, or exile used throughout the literature are often based on their officially recognized versions, as reinstated by international laws such as the 1951 Geneva Convention and as applied through various UN organizations. It is important to recognize, however, that such definitions were formulated and came into practice within the framework of a system of nation-states, as part of the process that has arisen as a by-product of the transformation of empires into nation-states (Zolberg 1983). These cases need to be contextualized in the national order of things, instead of taking this order as a given to such an extent that it becomes invisible (Malkki 1995).

In considering the applicability of the categories of displacement on different groups, the situation of Rum Polites may be contrasted to other cases in Greece where the newcomers share the same religion and descent as the majority. The migration waves from Eastern European countries like Albania and Romania were partially based on the premise that the only European country in the Christian Orthodox realm would offer a relatively easier refuge and better options for integration. Most of these immigrants initially entered Greece illegally, but were counting on the easing of the terms for obtaining a residence permit and citizenship by proving that they were of Greek descent. The notion that this was an act of repatriation was not disputed, however, as both political authorities and Greek society were reluctant to accept these people as anything more than cheap labor.[27]

Another comparable situation where the migrating community was of the same background as the population in the receiving country took place in the context of the forced exchange of populations between Greece and Turkey in the 1920s. Although there were major difficulties that the Asia Minor refugees in Greece and their *mübadil* (lit. exchangee) counterparts in Turkey had to face, the fact that this condition was constituted by the involvement of both states and reified on an international scale provided the legal framework within which these problems could be addressed. On the other hand, designating these groups as refugees contributed to their conception as suffering populations under misery and severe hardship and as victims of the catastrophic tragedy of war, further underlying their initial marginalization by the wider Greek society (Hirschon 1989).

These cases of migration, however, differ from that of Rum Polites. Whatever their circumstances of displacement, Rum Polites have not really been economically or socially isolated as refugees in Greece. Most of them had to leave behind their business, property, or wealth, but this did not always change their ultimate class position: many were able to start again to earn a living and respectable status for themselves and their families. Generally self-employed and involved in trade, as they were back in Istanbul, a good proportion of Rum Polites prospered in their businesses and made sure that their children studied well to become doctors, architects, professors, engineers, and similarly respectable professions. A sample story comes from a family that ran a renowned restaurant business in Pera. When they were expelled in 1964, they had to leave Istanbul within a week, losing their enterprise along with everything they owned and had saved over a lifetime. It was a question of survival in Athens as they had small children at the time. They started selling souvlaki on the street— "Imagine, how terrible, the lowest thing to do for a Rum Politis" (*Düşün, sokakta souvlaki satmak, ne korkunç, bir İstanbullu Rum için en aşağı iştir bu*), as one of my informants related the story to me. But they did very well, moving on to opening a small store in the city center where they catered for the business lunch needs of the Athenians. In a matter of three years, they opened a big restaurant in Kolonaki that became very successful and renowned for "oriental cuisine," to repeat the description used by their son, who is one of the most acclaimed surgeons in Greece.

In the case of Rum Polites, the ambiguities and complexities underlying the course of their displacement contributed to their ambivalent position between the two states. There is no single event to be blamed for the presence of the Rum Polites in Athens. Some of them were expelled, some lost their property and profession, some feared for their security and well-being in the long term, and some chose to live in Greece as they saw a better future there than in Turkey. For whatever reason, they shared and still share the painful experience of uprooting from their homeland, but without the downside of being harshly discriminated against in Greek society. Such cases of maltreatment as they reported were mostly about being teased with words like "*Tourkospori*" or questions as to whether or not they were baptized in Turkey. Though embarrassing for children, such instances were not considered by their parents as posing any kind of danger. They were in fact attributed to the general level of ignorance of the Elladites—their lack of cosmopolitan knowledge. "After all, we were not short of anything they had," said one informant after reflecting on his childhood experiences, and added: "We had something additional for being from the City, but this did not make us less than Greek, and they should know this very well."

Although rare and understudied, there are comparable instances of displacement of peoples who migrated to their supposed "ethnic homelands" (Heleniak 1997) or their "homeland states" (Brubaker 1996). Apart from the aforementioned forced displacement of Asia Minor Greeks, one could mention postwar resettlements (for Germans as *Volksdeutsche, Aussiedler, Vertriebene,* or *Flüchtlinge,* see Benz 1992; Münz and Ohliger 1998; Römhild 1999), of Jews (Ben-Rafael et al. 2006; Remennick 2012), of former colonials (for the case of French from Algeria, see Baussant 2002; Jordi 1995), of disaster fugitives (for Czechs from Ukraine after Tschernobyl, see Valášková et al. 1997), and of various mobilizations in the Balkans or Baltics (for Croats, see Zmegac 2007; for post-Soviet Greeks, see Voutira 2006). Despite the differences among these cases, they seem to share the "double absence" in "the suffering of the immigrant," in the acclaimed words of the famous sociologist Abdelmalek Sayad (2004)—the condition that Bruce Clark (2006) named "twice a stranger," referring to the displacements in Greece and Turkey. This is the common sentiment of being "strangers either way," where the "perception of differences—their own and among the homeland populations"— leads toward a reshaping of their migrant identity through an emphasis on their diversity, and often to the nurture of a feeling of superiority toward the homeland coethnic populations (Zmegac 2007, 33).

As indicated in the earlier anecdote of a Rum man getting married to an Athenian woman from a wealthy family without being asked for his economic condition, there is a conceptualization of the Rum Polites as enjoying the legacy of forming the upper crust in an urban society. Arguably, this perception avoids their being too closely associated with the conditions they encountered during and immediately after the displacement. Another important feature of differentiation from other displaced groups in Greece is their place of origin. The symbolic value of Istanbul as the City is set apart from all other centers of out-migration; this includes not only the countries in Eastern Europe, Africa, Australia, or the Americas but also geographically and historically close places such as Asia Minor. The difference between Asia Minor and Istanbul origins corresponds to the distinction between rural and urban, which in the case of Istanbul gets translated into a clash with *Anatoli* (*Anadolu*, Asia Minor, Orient). Although many of the Asia Minor refugees lived in urban centers and claimed a cosmopolitan identity, the Rum Polites reserve the ultimate urban status for themselves given the greatness of their own City. So the point is not so much one of uprooted Greeks in Greece or of "strangers at home" in comparison to other refugee or migrant groups in Greece (Hirschon 1989, 2003; Tsimouris 2001; Kirtsoglou and Theodossopoulos 2001). More than that their home is elsewhere than in Greece, or that they have a "lost homeland," it is the uniqueness of the home itself that is the most salient element of the Rum Polites identity.

The Diaspora Story

Despite its long history reaching back to ancient times, the condition of diaspora has relatively recently become part of modern social theory, overwhelmingly centering on new diasporic developments that are linked to the larger phenomenon of globalization. Although some important work has emerged in this area[28] to the extent of becoming a fascination and a catch-all concept, it has been importantly noted that contemporary practices of diaspora cannot be reduced to epiphenomena of global capitalism; both old and new diasporas have to be taken into account (Clifford 1997; McCabe et al. 2005; Safran 2007). Similarly, diasporas should not necessarily be regarded as developed out of a nation, or out of its dissolution, although they are indeed caught up with and defined against the norms of nation-states.

Although the definition of what can be described as a diasporic community, experience, and space has been subject to much debate (Smith 1992; Safran 1991; Baumann 2000), the vast majority of theories seem to converge on that last point: diasporas are constituted by members of nations that are dispersed out of their state. Whether that state is existent, imagined, virtual, a relic of the past, or a utopia of the future, it is always a place to which diasporic peoples are supposed to belong. The ties of belonging among the people and between the people and their land are often of a primordial nature; they are usually based on a politically constituted continuity of ethnicity and religion. This assumption arises from a projection of the conditions of the present to other diaspora situations formed within different times and spaces. It has proven to be more appealing to researchers to address this issue with respect to contemporary non-Western diasporic conditions (Ayhan Kaya 2001; Naficy 1991), which were nonetheless studied as being formed within the web of their relations with modernity, technology, and the West. However, diasporas have been variously noted as being complex, hybrid, heterogeneous, ethnic-parochial, and cosmopolitan (Werbner 2010). The older forms of diaspora or current diasporic experiences in historical settings have formed a challenge to those who wished to develop a perspective without imposing on these communities the teleology of the (post-)nationalistic, (late-)modernistic present (Alavi 2015; Calhoun 2002; Falzon 2004; Ghosh 1992; Ho 2006; Rubel and Rossmann 2009; Zubaida 2002).

In the following, I present an argument in parallel to those advanced by recent attempts at presenting ethnographic and historical information about a community in order to discuss its specific conditions in comparison to similar cases and determine what kind of a diaspora, if any, it constitutes. With that, I address the challenge of distancing diaspora studies from the limitations of their present reference points by approaching alternate diasporic conditions formed in different times and spaces. I examine the case of the Rum Polites in Greece from a critically employed perspective of the Greek diaspora, before I draw some conclusions about how to describe the Rum Polites in relation to the categories mentioned.

As composed of Greek-speaking Orthodox Christians, the Greek diaspora is narrowly defined as "Greeks outside Greece." The recently formed cases of diasporic Greek communities, such as Greeks in Australia, the USA, Canada, Latin America, South Africa, England, or Northern and Western Europe, although highly diverse, would fall into this broad category of the Greek diaspora.[29] Problems arise, however, when taking into account those Greek communities who have lived outside the nation-state since a point in time that preceded the foundation of the modern Greek state. The tendency to include them within an unquestioned framework of Greek diaspora has been subject to some criticism, and a correction has been attempted. In his contribution to a volume on the subject, Richard Clogg (1999) wrote that these groups were not a diaspora in the sense of having been formed as a result of migration, voluntary or imposed. Therefore, people of the *Kath 'imas Anatoli* (our own East), and "the now pitifully exiguous Greek community in present-day Turkey (in Istanbul, and even more vestigially, in Imvros and Tenedos)," who are the Rum Polites, were not to be considered part of the Greek diaspora, together with the Greek minority in Southern Albania, as well as the Greek Cypriots. These were rather "the last remnants outside the borders of the Greek state" (Clogg 1999, 8). This formulation entails the use of words like "last" or "remnants" and suggests the persistence of an assumption that the normal course of history is toward their integration into the nation-state, and that it is simply a matter of time before this happens. Although I agree with his tendency to remove the Greek state as it is presently constituted from the picture, I find that Clogg does not achieve a radically different perspective on the notion of Greek diaspora by just extending its borders into the vast territories of Kath 'imas Anatoli. As much as he demonstrates a willingness to overcome it, an undercurrent of nation-ridden thinking seems to be influential in Clogg's study of the Greek diaspora. This becomes obvious later in the same article with his closing words: "The history of the Greek people, irrespective of the way in which national boundaries have been drawn, should be seen as part of a seamless entity" (ibid., 17). Far from remedying the issue of reification of historical forms with the concerns of the present, the widening of the state's boundaries lends itself to further nationalistic readings that are not too far off those of the Greek official nationalist ideals. From the point of view of the Greek nation-state, the Rum Polites are part of the "unredeemed" Hellenes of Constantinople. They are an "expatriate," out of homeland, diaspora community because it is assumed that the homeland of Greeks is (in) Greece. Thus, as soon as they move to Greece, they are considered to have "repatriated," to have returned to their homeland.

Rum Polites do not accept these categorizations, simply because they consider their homeland to be Istanbul—neither Greece, nor Turkey, nor Kath 'imas Anatoli. This is the first point to be made. Those who live in Istanbul are at home, not in diaspora and not waiting to be redeemed. Consider this letter published by the newspaper *Anatoli* in Athens and written by an eminent member of the present Rum community in Istanbul, Dimitris Frangopoulos, the former headmaster of the Zografeion High School in Istanbul, and beloved teacher of several generations of Rum Polites. Writing on behalf of "the community which remains in its hearth (*estia*), here in Istanbul, I wish for the strengthening of solidarity between Rum Polites of the Diaspora, and especially of Greece," Frangopoulos makes clear that the reference point remains in "the Queen of cities," which is the "Birthplace" (*Yenetira*) and the "always holy Homeland" (*Patrida*) of all the "compatriot" (*simpatriotes*) Rum Polites. Note that the emphasis is not on a diaspora that *includes* Greece, but on all Rum

Polites outside Istanbul, *especially* in Greece. There is no question in this terminology that Greece is a foreign land, abroad, just like the other places of diaspora with reference to the center, which always remains Istanbul, the City. One of the instances when I encountered this rhetoric was in an interview with a Rum musician in Istanbul, who specialized in playing and singing *rembetiko*.[30] The discussion shifted to the renowned movie *Rembetiko* by Kostas Ferris and the soundtrack song entitled "Hellas, My Mother" (*Mana mou Ellada*). After a brief pause, with which he interrupted the course of our conversation, he said, as if he was revealing a thought he had held back for some time: "This has never been my sentiment" (*Ben hiç öyle bir şey hissetmedim*).

The second related point is that for the Rum Polites migration to Greece is neither an act of repatriation nor an act of return. Rum Polites never lived in Greece: as a community they date much further back than the nation-state of Greece and do not necessarily buy into the myth of origin that they spread out of Ancient Greece. Yet the terminology of return is very much embedded in the official and popular discourses in both Greece and Turkey. I recall an embarrassing instance when my father made a phone call to introduce me to one of his good Rum Polites friends in Istanbul. "I would like you to meet my daughter. She is doing her doctoral research on Greeks who returned to Athens." A friendly voice from the other end of the line corrected him: First of all, it is not Greeks but Rum (*Bir kere Yunanlı değil Rum'dur onlar*). Then, there is no return, but leaving, or rather, being forced to leave (*Dönmek yok ayrılmak var. Hatta ayrılmak yok, ayrılmak zorunda kalmak var*).

Departing from Istanbul to Athens is a displacement, not an act of repatriation, then, and not a matter of willingness to be included in the greater Greek nation. As Neoklis Sarris points out, what many researchers fail to recognize is that Athens is not a point of reference for the Rum Polites in Istanbul. It is often assumed, he states, that Istanbul should have been part of the Athens-based Greek nation—a fantasy held by Athenians rather than the Rum Polites, who also refer to Istanbul as *the* City: "Rum Polites did not move to Athens because of their Greek nationalism, or because they thought they belonged to the Greek nation, but as a consequence of chauvinistic Ottoman despotism, which later took the ugly shape of Turkish nationalism" (1996, 34–35). He argues, in other words, that Rum Polites only left their homeland because they were pushed out of it, not because they regarded it to be less of a homeland than the nation-state of Greece.

Although the idea of Istanbul as a nostalgically missed homeland prevails among the Rum Polites, repatriation is not necessarily a dominant discourse among the Rum Polites in Athens today. In other words, Rum Polites do not sustain an "ideology of return" (Brah 1996, 180) despite their continuing sense of cultural belonging to their place of origin at varying levels. "Too many waters have passed under the bridge," claimed one informant, "I have been here for fourteen years, others for over thirty-five years, our children are born here, we have our businesses, our lives are established here. I miss my home, but I don't know. What can one do there? What school, what job? Difficult." As sad as it might be to admit that return is no longer a viable option, Rum Polites decreasingly recognize their presence in Athens as a problem to be solved—or rather, they continue to live in Athens despite the problems that can never be solved.[31]

Assessment of the possibilities of return has always been a process affected by the specific political and economic factors under changing historical conditions. Although the right to remain in or return to Istanbul was granted to the Rum Polites by article 16 of the Treaty of Lausanne,[32] exerting these rights has not been easily achievable in practice. Still, from around the turn of the century until the 1960s, many Rum Polites continued living and working between the two cities. Some publicly declared their desire to return to Istanbul, but this was not allowed by the Turkish government.[33] There were some who were able to move back; return migration was notable in periods of cordial Greek–Turkish relations especially between 1930–1940 (Alexandris 1983, 174–81) and 1948–1955 (Stamatopoulos 1996). Those who still had family members and properties in Istanbul, of whom there were many, would spend a couple of months there every year, especially in summer. But in the mid-1970s Greece entered a period of stability, which was accelerated after the country's entrance into the EU in 1978. By contrast, Turkey has not performed well on many fronts, especially in the realms that affected the Rum Polites, such as minority rights, security, and economic freedom. Istanbul has changed a lot during the course of a few decades, becoming an unrecognizable place where the old residents have been replaced by masses of migrants from the countryside, who built shanty towns that caused the city to grow exponentially. In spite of all these developments, the number of Rum Polites who visit Istanbul has increased considerably since the beginnings of rapprochement in 1999, a development which, aided by the mild climate in bilateral relations, sparked hopes in many Rum Polites in Greece for the reestablishment of their ties with their City. The process of

Turkey's application for membership in the EU brought with it a range of new opportunities for the Rum Polites, including a chance to resolve some of the outstanding issues.[34] The reluctance to give up Turkish citizenship might be seen in this context as part of the unwillingness of the Rum Polites to destroy their links with the past and, therefore, their hopes for building a future.

This focus on the Rum Polites clearly indicates that, through their self-definition and specific historical and cultural position, they not only resist but also refute the notion of diaspora as presently defined. Judged by any of the standards established by official or academic discourses, the Rum Polites in Athens cannot legitimately be considered to constitute a diaspora group. Residing in Athens, they are not outside current or greater Greece, they are not different from the majority population in terms of their language, religion, or ethnicity, and their presence in the country is not perceived to be temporary either by the host society or by the political authority. By taking Istanbul as the reference point of homeland and as their place of belonging, however, the Rum Polites establish both that they are not in a diaspora community while in Istanbul, because they do not consider their presence in the city as being temporary, and that they do not regard themselves to have returned home while in Athens. This is a way of refuting the assumption that Greeks are naturally at home in Greece, of "inverting the official formula in order to challenge the very logic of statehood" (see Herzfeld 1987, 152).

Rum Polites, then, do not comply with the ascribed, analytical notions of diaspora as established in official, popular, or scholarly discourses. But if they still choose to adopt the term diaspora to describe their condition in Athens, what is it that ethnographic research has to offer to theory in order to make it applicable for a more accurate understanding of cultural reality?

In contemporary studies of diasporas, it is seldom appreciated how much diasporic experience is shaped by absence (Ho 2006). This diagnosis, which applies especially to diasporic experiences in older societies, is an important starting point to address the reasons for the difficulties of applying current theories of diaspora to non-Western and pre-modern cases. As in the case of Hadrami diaspora that Ho studies, the Rum Polites continuously consider the predominance of absences: the absence of habitual practices in everyday life, the loss of a home, the absence of the other, the absence of kaymak, of the sound of ezan, of the smell of coal, of the misty, foggy mornings on the Bosphorus. What describes all these absences is the presence of a sentiment, coded by two emic terms: *gurbet* in Turkish, *xenitia* in Greek, roughly translatable as longing for a home far away.[35] Such cultural codes stand to verify that stories of diaspora dwell on the many complex and layered ways in which home is remembered in strange lands, making the idea of home both an emic and etic category (Stock 2010). For it is this coding of diaspora that is the most difficult to establish; it is a meaning that can be approached only with an ethnographic insight, which helps the researcher see what is not well documented, officially recognized, publicly known, loudly verbalized. Yet it is perhaps the most decisive in determining a people's cultural identity. For such identities are always larger than the categories within which they are placed, both by state officials and by scholars. In the following, I discuss the ways in which and the reasons why the categories mentioned prove to be insufficient, while forcing their limits in a direction that renders them more suited for a description of the Rum Polites.

Theorizing Stories

Social science literature has recently expanded its theoretical horizons to include experiences of transnationalism (Coutin 2006; Eriksen 2007; Bauböck 2006). Even though there is a dynamic and processual view that allows the recognition of changing identities and multiple social relations with notions such as "post-national citizenship" (Soysal 1994) or "transborder citizenship" (Glick-Schiller 2005), the notion of transnational remains embedded in the presumption of the existence of two countries, whether migrants keep their ties with the old, the new, or both of the national states.

Rum Polites in Athens are a displaced people, but they have not been recognized as such. Because studies of displacement occur in what Malkki (1995) calls "the national order of things," or what Löfgren (1989) refers to as "the international cultural grammar of nationhood," the displacement experience of the likes of Rum Polites has not been adequately acknowledged. Appreciation of this particular aspect was blocked because of their ambiguous relations to two national societies and the resulting complexities in situating them entirely under the scope of either of these nation-states.

As "Greeks," the Rum Polites were thought of as being in their natural land in Greece; their displacement was taken as an act of return, of repatriation. Because Istanbul was not in Greece, the Rum Polites there were considered a diaspora community. Such a categorization, which turned out to be misjudged in the face of ethnographic and historical data, was deemed to be proper by the state mechanisms of Greece and Turkey, which, adopting a Western practice of conflation, engaged in a particular naming practice, in an artifact of naming by drawing "nationalist equations of land, language, and people" (Ho 2002, 216). This classification was misjudged particularly because it followed a trend of extending a practice beyond the time and place it was developed, thereby overshadowing attempts at recognizing the diversity of people under the same name and accounting for their mobility over different lands and, with that, recognizing the local cosmopolitans beyond states and nations.

It is argued that modern anthropological categorization of social types is a variant of official principles of classification that are predicated on presuppositions of unitary identities—that is, of individuals as members of bounded groups, of which the most rationalized are the nation-states (Kearney 1995). The case of Rum Polites can be deliberated in this respect. The Rum Polites cannot be accurately or unproblematically described as minorities, migrants, diaspora, in terms of citizenship, in the manner in which these terms are conceptualized by the state, because "the ultimate power of the state is revealed in the actor's rhetorical dependence on the state as a model of legitimacy" (Herzfeld 1987, 152), which is not the case with the Rum Polites. These are not compatible categories, because their *raison d'etre* is, unlike that of the Rum Polites, enmeshed with the nation-state. Rather than taking the nation-states of Greece or Turkey as their point of reference, Rum Polites not only base their identity on an earlier historical period (pre-national) but also (for this would not be enough, given that all nationalities do the same, not to mention the Greek nation-state itself) on a social system (multiethnic empire) that does not comply with the basic premises on which the nation-state is built. The proof of this latter point is their very self, the collective tragedies they experienced in the recent past because they did not fit inside the nation's tightly constructed conceptual boundaries. Their idealized past is not located in a Hellenic Greece, but in the cosmopolitan City as experienced in the heyday of the Byzantine Empire, or the last decades of the Ottoman era—a rich multireligious, multicultural florescence, resembling Sephardic Jewish dreams of Muslim Spain before the expulsions (Boyarin 1992) or the Mediterranean over the centuries, as described by Goitein (Alcalay 1993), as well as other cases presented in more recent scholarship, including by Greene (2000) and Hoerder et al. (2003), among others.

What is it, then, if not the nation or ethnicity, that is the organizing principle or the point of reference for the Rum Polites to describe their situation as diasporic? What would allow for a successful understanding of the specific situation of the Rum Polites, while inviting a critical reassessment of the notion of diaspora for its application to cultural experiences in alternative times and places, and under different institutional circumstances?

The answers lie in the city. For the Rum Polites specifically, it is Istanbul, the City, which is the home of the Rum Polites, the foundation of their history, the source of their culture. Istanbul is the *raison d'etre* of the Rum Polites. Cosmopolitanism is integral to their culture only insofar as it is perceived in the Constantinopolitan way. Diversity defines the Rum Polites community and makes any attempt at categorizing them difficult. After all eliminations, revisions, and corrections, what remains undisputed is the City. The connection to the city both defines and determines but also multiplies and diversifies. It entails all the contradictions, provisions, and discontinuities that make their categorization difficult and thereby allows the accommodation of a complex, sophisticated cultural identity that otherwise cannot be contained conventionally. The City is central, not marginal to Greekness. Ever since its foundation, Constantinople has been the religious, political, economic, and cultural capital of the Greeks. The pivotal importance of Istanbul in Greek imagination has also lent itself to political inclinations of irredentism. It has been the center of the *Megali Idea*, "the capital of dreams," as reclaimed in a famous speech by the first Prime Minister Kolettis to the Constituent Assembly in Athens in 1844. More than a century later, another Prime Minister, Constantine Mitsotakis, said, "We do not go to Constantinople, we return there," showing that although irredentist ambitions were no longer part of foreign policy,[36] the City remained a compass directing the romantic Greek orientation.

For all roads lead to the city built on seven hills, the New Rome. What remains in the capital of the deceased Eastern Roman Empire is what gave rise to its foundation in the first place: Christian Orthodoxy. The Ecumenical Patriarchate, the throne of all the peoples with the Orthodox faith, who always pray with their faces turned to the East, to Istanbul, their point of orientalization.

There the Rum Polites, firmly rooted in a city that proves their Rumness,[37] their Orthodoxy, their Glory, stand against their categorization as dispersed, marginalized, unredeemed Greeks in diaspora. They situate their Rumness in their own home, among multiethnic others.

Cosmopolitanism is not a challenge to their identity; it only strengthens their sense of belonging. They emerge as Polites, urbanites, etymologically urban, and exclusive in their diversity. As they are pushed out of their City, they retain their city identity, maintained and strengthened in memory, practiced by cosmopolitan knowledge in daily life. And they take their City with them wherever they go, building diasporas of the City. In Australia, Canada, America, or elsewhere, they establish Associations of Constantinopolitans. There they foster and continue the legacy of a distinct Rum Polites culture and identity, one that they share with others from Istanbul. The memoirs of a Turkish woman living in the USA show how after years of being scrutinized in various Greek associations across the country, she was surprised to find one where she was welcome. "Oh no, we are not a Hellenic Society here. We are from Istanbul. If you are also from Istanbul, your presence is most appreciated," they told her, without requiring any proof of citizenship or religion for membership.

The answer to the second part of the question also lies in the city: recognizing the city as a basis for diaspora building, and by extension for identity construction, opens up new horizons in those branches of ethnographic studies that were thus far overshadowed by the predominance of Western value systems and the supremacy of the nation-state. The city enables a spatial shrinkage yet a conceptual enlargement by allowing linkages between diverse peoples and experiences, contradictions and complexities, ambiguities and multiplicities, which thus far were attempted to be sorted by the work of nationalism. Situating a study in a cosmopolitan city removes the bias of ethnic and religious continuity in the categories formed through a reference to the state, thereby showing that people appealing to the same space do not have to be of the same background and that their claims may be of conflicting nature. This might help meet the challenge voiced by Clifford: "The diaspora discourse and history currently in the air would be about recovering non-Western, or not-only-Western, models for cosmopolitan life, non-aligned transnationalities struggling within and against nation-states, global technologies, and markets" (1997, 328).

In the specific case of Istanbul, the diaspora community of Istanbul is as multicultural as the city itself. The urban identity is so strong that its imprint is visible on all communities that have ever lived there. Rum Polites are apparently joined with the previously mentioned cases of the Istanbul Armenians called *Bolsohay*, and the Jews from Istanbul living in

Israel, in sharing a common diaspora, in the sense of *gurbet* or *xenitia*, sojourning away from their city as their homeland. This applies to the Istanbulites regardless of their ethnic or religious identity; in that regard, it is a supra-ethnic, supra-religious, supranational identity of the city.

Understanding all these ambiguities and locating them in different aspects of identity among the Rum Polites necessitates walking the fine and wobbly line between insiders and outsiders, which are continuously being redefined and relocated. This difficult task is one that the Rum Polites themselves face on an everyday basis; it involves balancing between the value placed on exclusivity and that placed on diversity. For being Istanbulite in Athens brings with it a double burden: that of displaying openness toward outsiders (here, Elladites or local Greeks) in the name of being cosmopolitan and that of protecting the unique cosmopolitan heritage from the influence of others (here, non-Polites) in the name of keeping their exclusivity. On the one hand, they find it necessary to stick to each other to keep their culture, in order to prevent or delay being entirely assimilated into a homogenized Greek society, but on the other hand, this makes them look like a closed, conservative, confined community.

I have addressed some of the ambiguities in the way different Rum Polites relate to ontological questions concerning their others and their perceptions of themselves. Following Hirschon's notion that "the particular criteria employed in boundary maintenance are part of cultural practice and are used, more or less consciously, to define categories of exclusion and inclusion" (2006, 162; also see Herzfeld 1985), I show that the idea of exclusion is nurtured by a special notion of exclusivity that places cosmopolitan knowledge and the practice of everyday urban life at its center. The term exclusive diversity underlines this selectivity within the multiplicity of others and variety of selves, while rendering the boundaries between them blurred and their relations ambiguous.

Among the multitude of others, the most decisive remains the category of the Turk. As part of cosmopolitan knowledge, the knowledge about the ultimate other, the Turk, is what distinguishes the Rum Polites most starkly from the Elladites. Unlike the Greeks from Greece, the Rum Polites were born in Turkey, grew up in an environment surrounded by many Turks, and have a range of experiences, both good and bad, with them. Though this does not mean a priori that they know the Turks any better than any given Greek, it certainly helps substantiate the claims that are made along these lines. The ability to differentiate within the category of the Turk leads to a differentiation of the Rum Polites from the Greeks, for the sense of a different self, thus constructed, underscores the difference in the perception of others with demonstrations of knowledge about Others. In that sense, the knowledge of the Turk as the significant other establishes what Susan Stewart (1993) characterizes as "longing as belonging"—an other that has a place in the formation of the interior, functioning as *appendage*, an addition to the body which forms an attachment, transforming the very boundary of the self.

At a personal level, my interactions with the Rum Polites focused on those areas within their self that lay closer to the boundaries with others. Those areas are precisely within the realm of what Herzfeld calls cultural intimacy (1997), but in a slightly yet significantly different way, as I intend to demonstrate in the ethnographic examples I have given. In the story of the landlord, the old man acted in a way that my friend Stratos described as "surprisingly and extremely friendly," a manner that went beyond any mere public display of hospitality, as in a short while he made Stratos leave the scene. What we later talked about could best be described as sweet nostalgia for a bitter past, including the suffering that was caused as a result of acts of Turkish friends, which would seemingly not have to be hidden from a Cypriot whom he stereotypically categorized as anti-Turkish. But the way he told me these stories—disappointed but forgiving, angry but understanding, straightforward yet poignant—apparently had to be veiled. So it was not his affinity with the Turks that he wanted to prevent being known by others; it was rather the ambiguity he presented to me in terms of his relations with the Turks, which he amended through the way he talked to Stratos both before and afterward—when he referred to me as a spy—because "he would not understand" the complexity of these relations. As a Cypriot, Stratos would not have (the "correct") knowledge of the Turkish other; he would not possess cosmopolitan knowledge.

The point is not to decide which of the performances were displaying the *true* self of the actors, for the only truth here is that human beings and societies are more complex than what one person might grasp them to be. Encountering different aspects of people, therefore, may come as a surprise to those who know them otherwise. Those expectations were formed through their previous experiences, conversations, and representations of these people, yet were not necessarily based on observations in real-life situations. Through the value I placed on the latter because of being an ethnographer, the outcome of these meetings came much less as a surprise to me than it did to the immediate acquaintances (or even family members) of my informants. Once a certain level of social intimacy was achieved in these personal ethnographic encounters, our discussions easily shifted to issues of politically sensitive concerns on a wider national and international scale. This has not always been the case throughout my fieldwork; but more often than not, my presence provided my informants with an opportunity to explore an aspect of their cultural identity for which they had few outlets. It was no longer a problem to be solved on an individual basis, but an issue that had to be analyzed at a collective level. For this was the kind of cultural intimacy that they could share only to a limited extent with surrounding Greeks, because their cultural intimacy was, I would like to argue, coded differently than that of the latter. In the following, I will present arguments to the effect of inviting a nuancing of the notion of disemia and an ethnographic adjustment of the concept of cultural intimacy to the case of Rum Polites. This attempt also speaks to the later revisions made, especially regarding the historical, geographical, and institutional scope of these two interlinked concepts (Herzfeld 1997).

Disemia is based on a symbolic duality between the official and the private, but ambiguity is not absent from the ways in which Greeks relate to the Turks, Turkey, and the Turkish aspects in their culture. Yet this ambiguity is one that the Greek nation-state constantly struggles with. Treating the Turks as "natural enemies" and the Turkish elements in Greek culture as "its worst failing" (Herzfeld 1987, 29) are the two ingredients in the recipe borrowed from the West for preparation of the idealized modern Greek identity. When cooking it in the privacy of their homes, however, contemporary Greeks do not prevent themselves from adding a few Turkish spices they have been accustomed to using for the last few hundred years. To continue the culinary terminology, the dilemma that marks the political culture of Greeks can be characterized as between eating a dish that is often too bland for themselves and offering food to others that is too piquant for them to digest. The two suggestive ethnographic moments, that of the South African Greek Niki commenting on the mildness of Greek cuisine in an Indian restaurant and of my Rum friend asking the Kurdish waiter for red hot peppers in a kebap place, are not too far off from illustrating this symbolism in everyday practice.

One source of explanation for the ambiguity of political identity among the Rum Polites stems from a resistance (or failure, depending on the intention of the actors) to comply with a too neatly structured formula between Turks and Greeks that is imposed by the official nationalist ideology. In the post-independence period, the indecision of Greeks in Greece in how to relate to Turks was (attempted to be) taken care of by a Greek state that internalized the call of Europe and found a solution to the dilemma by containing these intricacies of social experience within the private realm, where the ambiguity remains situated. The Rum Polites, however, were not only outside the jurisdiction of the Greek state, they were under the domination of the Turkish state. Far from involving them in the process of casting out the Turkish influence in their culture, this situation further contributes to an increased level of ambiguity in their relations with the Turks at present, as it did in the past. Thus the ambiguity in the case of Rum Polites has a different source: rather than characterizing the content of cultural intimacy, or the "cultural stuff" of the interior, it is an ambiguity that is inherent in the very *institutionalization* of the Rum Polites identity, or the complication thereof. Their ambivalent position vis-à-vis two nation-states that are constituted as—not only oppositionally but also ideally—mutually exclusive, as the respective acts of de-Turkification and de-Hellenization suggest, further contributes to the complexity of being formally, and often officially, in-between these two nations.

The duality that characterizes the Greeks in their dealings with the Turks is thus multiplied in the case of Rum Polites through the relative absence of the Greek state structure as the regulating factor, and the inclusion of the Turkish authority as its symbolic opposite, which allows the preservation of ambiguity. Overcoming this ambiguity becomes possible by converting it into diversity, which is in turn enabled by the reliance of the Rum Polites on a cosmopolitan social system instead of a standardizing national state structure. The supposed uniformity of the latter serves the otherization of Elladites by the Rum Polites, who value plurality, through a discourse that resembles what Herzfeld calls village rhetoric: "*Others*' homogeneity marks their fundamental inferiority, *our* internal differentiation a familiar and complex excellence" (Herzfeld 1987, 166; emphasis in the original). This differs, or rather makes the Rum Polites differ, from the nationalist ideology of classification that renders ambiguous as subordinate. In the case of Greece, otherness in the self is regarded to be "a categorical confusion, *matter out of place*" (ibid., 15), but this framework provided by Mary Douglas (1966) plays out differently in the context of Rum Polites. For the Greeks who display a public image of the Hellenic ideal type, the inclusion of Turkish elements is a matter of pollution (ibid., 41). For the Rum Polites it is an internalized matter of identity that is not penalized by the not-so-internalized Greek state ideology.

Being unable to isolate their associations with Turkey, Rum Polites as a whole become a matter out of place, which renders their categorization difficult as I will show later. While this adds to their "ambiguity of being out of place," it does not mean that the Rum Polites are socially marginalized in the societies where they live. For there is a difference in the kind of "matter," depending on what kind of "place" this is a condition of being out of. In this case the place (Istanbul, the City) is one of symbolic purity (for being the center of Orthodoxy, Romiosini, Greekness), and not of pollution (for being Turkey, the East, the Orient). It is the source of *politismos*, of civilization, and not of barbarism or backwardness. Such a reordering in the "global hierarchy of value," to borrow another term from Herzfeld (2004), is clearly illustrated in the two ethnographic examples that I have previously presented. Both the woman who was praising a young girl for not being able to find a suitable husband because she was raised with "Turkish" manners (*terbiye*) and the man who wanted to take off his shoes in accordance with an "Ottoman," if not Muslim, custom were turning their faces toward the East for setting the standards of what was to be considered pure and clean. Athens, in that view, symbolizes a West of cultural degeneration.

Following Burke, "what we want is not terms that avoid ambiguity, but terms that clearly reveal the strategic spots at which ambiguities necessarily arise" (Burke 1969, xviii). In inverting the normative order between what East and West are thought to represent, an anchoring of cultural identity in Istanbul further catalyzes the reduction of the often geographically perceived distance between the self and the other. Therefore, the "otherness in the self" is not a flaw of identity confined to the secret, private realm, and being "out of place" is not something that is evaded. Rather than a condition of marginality or impurity, a (City-based) blending with the not-so-otherized Orient is instead elevated to the level of a characteristic of cultural sophistication defining the very notion of a cosmopolitan self. The Rum Polites thus fill in the vacuum between the two stereotypes of Hellenism and Romiosini while casting an identity for themselves that both incorporates and complicates the two by crossing over the duality with the multiplicity of their identity. This adherence to the plural is supported by the nostalgic reconstruction of a cosmopolitan cultural heritage, a multicultural social system as exemplified in the Byzantine and Ottoman Empires, which is opposed to a singularistic nationalistic idealization of the past.

Notes

1. Migration in Greece has been known to consist of two main threads: (1) the out-migration of guest workers as expatriate labor force to Western countries and (2) the emigration of repatriating Greeks from the "diaspora." Since the 1990s, a new wave of immigration has brought a major demographic tide to Greece, as migrants from former Soviet Bloc countries started moving into the country. Today, over half of the migrant population is of Albanian origin, followed by a number of Eastern Europeans, most of whom are now legalized or naturalized members of Greek society. In addition, there is an escalating issue of irregular and often illegal immigration from Asia and the Middle East, either seeking asylum or refuge in Greece or intending to pass in transit as a gateway to Europe. While the decades of the 1990s and 2000s were dominated by migrants from former Soviet Bloc countries in the Balkans, such as Albania and Romania, the following decade is marked by the tragedy of refugees escaping the civil war in Syria, who suffered greatly while trying to escape to Europe across the Turkish–Greek Aegean sea border. The number of international migrants in Greece today is estimated to exceed one million people—nearly 10% of the population—a figure that would be multiplied if the undocumented, illegal, and transient migrants or refugees were taken into account. Recent scholarship addressing the old and new waves of migration in Mediterranean Europe includes Andersson (2014), Ben-Yehoyada (2015), Friese (2010), and Pascale (2010).
2. Turkish tea is made with two special pots that are placed on top of each other. The upper small pot contains tea leaves while the water is boiled in the bigger pot below. Making Turkish tea is a procedure of cooking. Because tea is the most widely consumed drink in Turkey, making the country rank second in the world in terms of tea consumption, the Rum Polites continue this habit of making and drinking tea in the Turkish way, often using characteristic tulip-shaped glasses, distinguishing themselves further in Greece, where tea consumption is quite low.
3. For Greece, see, for example, Theodossopoulos (2004, 2006), Kirtsoglou and Sistani (2003), Özkırımlı-Sofos (2008), and for Cyprus, see Sant-Cassia (2005), Bryant (2010), Navaro-Yashin (2012), Bryant and Papadakis (2012), and Kızılyürek (2011).
4. *Tourkofilos* (Gr.) literally means Turkish-friendly or friend of the Turks, but when used sarcastically, it may imply negative meanings such as collaborator or traitor.
5. The way the French word *monsieur* is pronounced and written in Turkish.

6. The population from the Black Sea region of Northern Asia Minor. In Greek they are called by their ancient name, *Pontioi*, but the author preferred the terminology used in Turkey.
7. Literally meaning "filled in," *dolma* refers to a set of dishes that are prepared by stuffing a mixture of minced meat or rice into vine or cabbage leaves, peppers, tomatoes, eggplant, or zucchini. They can be cooked in olive oil or butter and served hot or cold. The Turkish word *dolma* is also used in Greece, usually in the plural form *dolmadhes*, along with its Greek equivalent *yemista*.
8. My informant was very embarrassed and reluctant to repeat the myth because she found it to be disgusting and nonsensical. In the end, her husband told me about it, after making me promise that I would not be repeating it to others. In fact, the story is something that many would know about, but their reluctance suggests something about the disposition of my informants. Suffice it to say at this point that the myth is a long-held prejudice indicating rivalry between Armenians and Greeks, with food at its epicenter.
9. For a thorough investigation of dairy products in Greece, see Elia Petridou (2001) and Petridou et al. (2012).
10. It is well known that eating, in both Greek and Turkish, has another commonly used connotation besides its literary meaning. It could be translated as conspicuous spending, spreading, or pocketing as well, but the additional words and gestures that my informant used indicated that in this case he was referring to the consumption of food. See Herzfeld (1985).
11. *Ayazma*: From the Greek word *ayiasma*, a ritual act of purification through sprinkling holy water. The Turkish spelling is preferred here to indicate a more common use of the word in Istanbul: some springs are considered to be sacred in the Orthodox religion. These often have a small church, an associated saint, and a saint's day (*yiorti*). There are more than 500 *ayazma* in Istanbul, a number that rises to a thousand in some accounts. See Atzemoglou (1990).
12. The current generation of Rum Polites has not been noted as influential in Greek politics, whether as electorate, as bureaucrats, or in party politics. The only MP thus far is Kostas Gavroglou, a parliamentary representative of SYRIZA elected in 2015. Since November 2016 he holds the position of Minister of Education, Research, and Religion.
13. Opposite/other side in Turkish, a fixed expression for the Asian shore of the Bosphorus, regardless of the geographical position of the speaker. In Greek, the wording is *apenanti plevra*, designating the Anatolian side as being located across, taking as reference point the original part of Istanbul within the city walls.

14. Kebap is a certain way of preparing meat dishes, which are offered in special restaurants. These restaurants are popular throughout the Middle East, while some regions in Southeastern Turkey are also renowned for their kebap specialties.
15. A special kind of bread that is produced during the month of Ramadan for breaking the fast. It is difficult to find it at any other time, even in Turkey; it is certainly surprising for it to appear in an overwhelmingly Christian country where this kind of fasting is not observed.
16. The Rum Polites were held exempt from the forced exchange of populations in 1923, as established by Article 2 of the Convention between Greece and Turkey that was signed six months before the Treaty: "The following persons shall not be included in the exchange provided for in Article 1: (a) the Greek inhabitants of Constantinople, (b) the Moslem inhabitants of Western Thrace. All Greeks who were already established before October 1918, within the areas under the prefecture of the City of Constantinople, as defined by the law of 1912, shall be considered as Greek inhabitants of Constantinople" (trans. Alexandris 1983, 95).
17. *Omoyenia*: lit. homogenous, of the same kind, roughly translatable as kith and kin.
18. The number of Greek nationals among the Rum Polites was estimated to be around 10,000 before the 1964 expulsions, while this number was reduced to a few hundreds by the end of the decade, comprised of women married to Turkish nationals and the very elderly who were not able to travel.
19. The number of Turkish nationals in Greece is estimated to be around 18,000, with the Rum Polites constituting the vast majority. There are around 25,000 persons born in Istanbul who obtained Greek citizenship later. These numbers are not official or verified through a formal source, but rely on an aggregation of results of individual calculations, partial research data, and various attempts to guesstimate by the Rum Polites.
20. See Tsitselikis (2007) for changing practices of obtaining and losing citizenship in the case of Greece. See Kirişçi (2000) for the Turkish context.
21. This is noteworthy especially in the case of the Turkish state, which is constitutionally a secular system that is supposed to be founded on the principle of separation of religion and state and to have equal distance to all citizens regardless of their religious belief. For the complexities of religion and secularism in Turkey, see Navaro-Yashin (2002), Azak (2010), Özyürek (2006), Gözaydın (2008), Çağaptay (2006), and Silverstein (2011), among others.
22. A full-blown "*Tourkos*" coming from the mouth of a Greek is intended almost invariably as an insult, just as related words such as "became Turkish" (*eyine tourkos* = went crazy) carry a negative meaning. Similarly,

Tourkofilos, a word that literally means Turkish-friendly or friend of the Turks, might be employed to designate the other as a traitor. Those who might be good friends with the Turks may nevertheless be offended by being thus termed. In fact, there have been court cases between some Rum Polites in Athens for the use of these particular words in public.

23. Such puns are widely used as rhetorical devices throughout this part of the world. A similar saying, I have two shoulders, is used by Cretan shepards to indicate that the person abides by two laws, that of the state and his own, by the quick addition of the letter *n* (Herzfeld 1985).

24. Although the main text of the Treaty of Lausanne does not include any direct references to specific communities, presenting instead a generic notion of the rights of all non-Muslim minorities, the practices in its immediate aftermath justified its limitation to the three main religious communities, meaning the Jews, the Christian Orthodox, and the Armenians, and the establishment of a state discourse, if only lip service, regarding their rights being guaranteed under the same treaty. The privileging of religion as the main criterion in this way meant that other groups that could be characterized as minorities for being from a different sect (such as the Alevi) or ethnicity (such as the Kurds) were excluded from the scope of a similar kind of legalization. The history of minority policies pursued in the Turkish Republic is too wide a topic to be examined at length here, but suffice it to say that "minorities" remains one of the highly debated issues in a contemporary Turkey that is at the doorstep of the European Union.

25. There were other criteria deployed during and after the era of national independence in both Turkey and Greece, including but not restricted to language, descent, and national consciousness. The prevalence of religion, however, is still applicable today. When applying for Greek citizenship, for example, applicants who can verify that a blood relative (preferably from the male side) was baptized Orthodox would have a better case (for recent practices, see Triandafyllidou and Veikou 2002).

26. For selected studies of minorities in Greece and Turkey, see Gounaris et al. (1997), Mackridge and Yannakis (1997), Fortna et al. (2013), Akgönül (2013), Memişoğlu (2013), and Demetriou (2013), among others.

27. For some studies on migration in Greece, see, among others, Psimmenos (2000), Lazaridis (2000), Hatziprokopiou (2006), King et al. (1998), and Tziovas (2009).

28. See, for example, Appadurai (1996), Bhabha (1994), Brah (1996), Braziel (2008), Butler (2001), Christou and Mavroudi (2015), Cohen and Van Hear (2008), Hall (1990), Hannerz (1996), Knott and McLaughlin (2010), Kokot et al. (2013), Sheffer (2003), Smith (1994), and Werbner (2002).

29. For studies of diaspora Greeks, see Anagnostou (2001), Anagnostopoulou (1997), Augustinos (1992), Christou (2006), Gondicas and Issawi (1999), Hassiotis et al. (2006), Kouroupou and Balta (2001), Leontis (1995), Moskos (1989), and Tziovas (2009).
30. A music genre associated with anti-authoritarian subcultures called *rebet*, which flourished in the aftermath of the Asia Minor catastrophe and the forced displacement in the 1920s. Owing to a mixture of Turkish and Greek musical heritage in its structure, forms, and vocabulary, rembetiko has become an expression of suffering related to war and partition, Aegean alliances, resistance state domination, and later of internationalism and communism, especially during the dictatorial period in Greece. See Holst-Warhaft (1989).
31. This situation altered after the financial crisis that has hit the Greek economy since 2008. Having a relatively steady economic situation, Turkey became attractive again for offering a variety of options, which allowed some Rum Polites to return and settle down in Istanbul. For more on this trend, see the Epilogue.
32. "No obstacle shall be placed in the way of the inhabitants of the districts exempted from the exchange under Article 2 exercising freely their right to remain in or return to those districts and to enjoy to the full their liberties and rights of property in Turkey and Greece."
33. A large group of wealthy and influential Rum Polites who fled Istanbul during the Greek–Turkish War organized themselves into a relatively powerful pressure group in Athens and urged both governments as well as the League of Nations to recognize their right to go back to Istanbul in 1925. The Turkish side responded by canceling all their rights and properties as well as their citizenship, on the grounds of their absence during a time of national struggle (Alexandris 1983, 119).
34. The changes in the law regarding the right of associations and foundations to hold property is one among the most publicly debated issues. Ownership rights that were recognized by the Treaty of Lausanne have not been executed over the years; and the Turkish parliament had to reconfirm those along with the new laws to be implemented as part of the EU candidacy in 2003. Some improvement is noted after a new law became effective in 2008, allowing the return, repurposing, or restoration of the property that initially belonged to non-Muslim foundations.
35. For *xenitia* in the Greek context, see Seremetakis (1991), for Cyprus see Sant-Cassia (2005). See also Alexiou (1974) for literature, Holst-Warhaft (1989) for music.
36. The *Megali Idea* was an active state policy until the catastrophic defeat of the Greek Army in Asia Minor in 1922 (Skopotea 1988; see also Herzfeld 1992). Today there are still adherents of this view among extreme right

circles. Although these remain marginal, they have some visibility in Greece's mass media. From time to time one hears public statements by eminent individuals that indicate that the idea of taking back Constantinople still has supporters.

37. Here in using the word Rumness I seek to incorporate another meaning implied by the term Romiosini, the condition of being Romios, referring to being intensely Greek, with its emphasis on the post-classical heritage, including Byzantine, Ottoman, and Eastern Orthodox. See also Herzfeld (1997, 182).

Bibliography

Akgönül, S. (2013). *The Minority Concept in the Turkish Context: Practices and Perceptions in Turkey, Greece, and France (Muslim Minorities)*. Leiden: Brill.

Aktar, A., Kızılyürek, N., & Özkırımlı, U. (2010). *Nationalism in the Troubled Triangle: Cyprus, Greece and Turkey*. Basingstoke: Palgrave Macmillan.

Alavi, S. (2015). *Muslim Cosmopolitanism in the Age of Empire*. Cambridge: Harvard University Press.

Alcalay, A. (1993). *After Jews and Arabs: Remaking Levantine Culture*. Minneapolis: University of Minnesota Press.

Alexandris, A. (1983). *The Greek Minority of Istanbul and Greek-Turkish Relations, 1918-1974*. Athens: Center for Asia Minor Studies.

Alexiou, M. (1974). *The Ritual Lament in Greek Tradition*. Cambridge: Cambridge University Press.

Anagnostopoulou, S. (1997). *Mikra Asia, 19os ai.-1919: I ellinoorthodoxes koinotites. Apo to millet ton Romion sto Elliniko ethnos*. Athens: Ellinika Grammata.

Anagnostou, D. (2001). Breaking the Cycle of Nationalism: The EU, Regional Policy and the Minority of Western Thrace, Greece. *South European Society and Politics,* 6(1), 99-124. https://doi.org/10.1080/714004933.

Andersson, R. (2014). *Illegality, Inc.: Clandestine Migration and the Business of Bordering Europe*. Berkeley: University of California Press.

Apostolidis, N. G. (1996). *Anamniseis apo tin Konstantinoupoli*. Athens: Trochalia.

Appadurai, A. (1996). *Modernity at Large: Cultural Dimensions of Globalization*. Minneapolis: University of Minnesota Press.

Arizpe, L. (1998). Conviviability: The Role of Civil Society in Development. In A. Bernard, H. Helmich, & P. B. Lehning (Eds.), *Cultural Diversity and Citizenship*. Paris: OECD Publishing.

Atzemoglou, N. (1990). *Ta Ayiasmata tis Polis*. Athens: Risos.

Augustinos, G. (1992). *The Greeks of Asia Minor: Confession, Community, and Ethnicity in the Nineteenth Century*. Kent: Kent University Press.

Azak, U. (2010). *Islam and Secularism in Turkey: Kemalism, Religion and the Nation State.* London: I.B. Tauris.
Barkey, K. (2005). Islam and Toleration: Studying the Ottoman Imperial Model. *International Journal of Politics, Culture, and Society, 19*(1–2), 5–19.
Bauböck, R. (2006). Towards a Political Theory of Migrant Transnationalism. *International Migration Review, 37*(3), 700–723.
Baumann, M. (2000). Diaspora: Genealogies of Semantics and Transcultural Comparison. *Numen, 47*(3), 313–337.
Beck, U. (2000). *What Is Globalization?* Cambridge, UK: Polity.
Beck, U. (2002). The Cosmopolitan Society and Its Enemies. *Lebenszeiten,* 389–406. https://doi.org/10.1007/978-3-663-10626-5_23.
Beck, U. (2003). Toward a New Critical Theory with a Cosmopolitan Intent. *Constellations, 10*(4), 453–468.
Beck, U. (2004). Cosmopolitical Realism: On the Distinction between Cosmopolitanism in Philosophy and the Social Sciences. *Global Networks, 4*(2), 131–156.
Ben-Rafael, E., et al. (2006). *Building a Diaspora: Russian Jews in Israel, Germany and the USA.* Leiden: Brill.
Ben-Yehoyada, N. (2015). 'Follow Me, and I Will Make You Fishers of Men': The Moral and Political Scales of Migration in the Central Mediterranean. *Journal of the Royal Anthropological Institute, 22,* 183–202.
Benz, W. (1992). Fremde in der Heimat: Flucht-Vertreibung-Integration. In K. Hage (Ed.), *Deutsche im Ausland-Fremde in Deutschland: Migration in Geschichte und Gegenwart* (pp. 374–386). Munich: C.H. Beck.
Boyarin, J. (1992). *The Storm from Paradise: The Politics of Jewish Memory.* Minneapolis: University of Minnesota Press.
Bozi, S. (2003). *Politiki Kouzina: Paradosi aionon.* Athens: Ellinika Grammata.
Brah, A. (1996). *Cartographies of Diaspora: Contesting Identities.* London: Routledge.
Braziel, J. E. (2008). *Diaspora: An Introduction.* Malden, MA: Blackwell.
Brubaker, R. (1996). *Nationalism Reframed: Nationhood and the National Question in the New Europe.* Cambridge: Cambridge University Press.
Bryant, R. (2010). *The Past in Pieces: Belonging in the New Cyprus.* Philadelphia: University of Pennsylvania Press.
Bryant, R., & Papadakis, Y. (2012). *Cyprus and the Politics of Memory: History, Community and Conflict.* London: I.B. Tauris.
Burke, K. (1969). *A Grammar of Motives.* Berkeley: University of California Press.
Butler, K. D. (2001). Defining Diaspora, Refining a Discourse. *Diaspora: A Journal of Transnational Studies, 10*(2), 189–219.
Çağaptay, S. (2006). *Islam, Secularism and Nationalism in Modern Turkey: Who Is a Turk?* London: Routledge.

Calhoun, C. (2002). The Class Consciousness of Frequent Travellers: Towards a Critique of Actually Existing Cosmopolitanism. In S. Vertovec & R. Cohen (Eds.), *Conceiving Cosmopolitanism: Theory, Context, Practice* (pp. 86–109). Oxford: Oxford University Press.

Cassia, P. S. (2005). *Bodies of Evidence: Burial, Memory and the Recovery of Missing Persons in Cyprus.* New York: Berghahn Books.

Chalkousi, X. (2002). *Mirodies kai yevseis tis Polis ... kai stin korfi kanela.* Athens: Tsoukatou.

Chernilo, D. (2006). Social Theory's Methodological Nationalism: Myth and Reality. *European Journal of Social Theory, 9*(1), 5–22.

Christou, A. (2006). Deciphering Diaspora, Translating Transnationalism: Family Dynamics, Identity Constructions and the Legacy of 'Home' in Second-Generation Greek-American Return Migration. *Ethnic and Racial Studies, 29*(6), 1040–1056.

Christou, A., & Mavroudi, E. (Eds.). (2015). *Dismantling Diasporas: Rethinking the Geographies of Diasporic Identity, Connection and Development.* London: Routledge.

Clark, B. (2006). *Twice a Stranger: The Mass Expulsions That Forged Modern Greece and Turkey.* Cambridge, MA: Harvard University Press.

Clifford, J. (1997). *Routes: Travel and Translation in the Late Twentieth Century.* Cambridge: Harvard University Press.

Clogg, R. (Ed.). (1999). *The Greek Diaspora in the Twentieth Century.* London: Macmillan Press.

Coutin, S. B. (2006). Cultural Logics of Belonging and Movement: Transnationalism, Naturalization, and US Immigration Politics. In A. Sharma & A. Gupta (Eds.), *The Anthropology of the State: A Reader.* Malden: Blackwell.

Demetriou, O. (2013). *Capricious Borders: Minority, Population, and Counter-Conduct between Greece and Turkey.* Oxford: Berghahn.

Di Pascale, A. (2010). Migration Control at Sea: The Italian Case. In R. Mitsilegas (Ed.), *Extraterritorial Immigration Control: Legal Challenges* (pp. 274–304). Leiden: Martinus Nijhoff.

Douglas, M. (1966). *Purity and Danger: An Analysis of Concepts of Pollution and Taboo.* London: Routledge and Kegan Paul.

Dragonas, T. (2004). Negotiation of Identities: The Muslim Minority in Western Thrace. *New Perspectives on Turkey, 30*, 1–24.

Driessen, H. (2005). Mediterranean Port Cities: Cosmopolitanism Reconsidered. *History and Anthropology, 16*(1), 129–141. https://doi.org/10.1080/02757 20042000316669.

Duru, D. N. (2015). From Mosaic to Ebru: Conviviality in Multi-Ethnic, Multi-Faith Burgazadası, Istanbul. *South European Society and Politics, 20*(2), 243–263.

Erickson, B. (2011). Utopian Virtues: Muslim Neighbors, Ritual Sociality, and the Politics of Convivencia. *American Ethnologist, 38*(1), 114–131.

Eriksen, E. O. (Ed.). (2007). *Making the European Polity: Reflexive Integration in the EU*. London: Routledge.
Evelpidis, C. (1976). *Politika*. Athens: Papazisis.
Falzon, M.-A. (2004). *Cosmopolitan Connections: The Sindhi Diaspora, 1860–2000*. Leiden: Brill.
Faubion, J. (1993). *Modern Greek Lessons: A Primer in Historical Constructivism*. Princeton: Princeton University Press.
Fine, R., & Chernilo, D. (2004). Between Past and Future: The Equivocations of the New Cosmopolitanism. *Studies in Law Politics and Society, 31*, 25–44.
Fortna, B. C., Katsikas, S., Kamouzis, D., & Konortas, P. (2013). *State-Nationalisms in the Ottoman Empire, Greece and Turkey: Orthodox and Muslims, 1830–1945*. London: Routledge.
Freitag, U. (2014). 'Cosmopolitanism' and 'Conviviality'? Some Conceptual Considerations Concerning the Late Ottoman Empire. *European Journal of Cultural Studies, 17*(4), 375–391.
Freitag, U., Fuhrmann, M., Lafi, N., & Riedler, F. (Eds.). (2011). *The City in the Ottoman Empire: Migration and the Making of Urban Modernity*. London: Routledge.
Friese, H. (2010). The Limits of Hospitality: Political Philosophy, Undocumented Migration and the Local Arena. *European Journal of Social Theory, 13*(3), 323–341.
Ghosh, A. (1992). *In an Antique Land*. London: Granta Books.
Gilroy, P. (2006). *After Empire: Melancholia or Convivial Culture?* Abingdon: Routledge.
Gilsenan, M. (1992). *Recognizing Islam: Religion and Society in the Modern Middle East*. London: I.B. Tauris.
Glick-Schiller, N. (2005). Transnational Migration and the Re-framing of Normative Values. In F. V. Benda-Beckmann, K. V. Benda-Beckmann, & A. M. O. Griffiths (Eds.), *Mobile People, Mobile Law: Expanding Legal Relations in a Contracting World*. Aldershot: Ashgate.
Glick-Schiller, N., Basch, L., & Blanc-Szanton, C. (1992). Transnationalism: A New Analytic Framework for Understanding Migration. *Annals of the New York Academy of Sciences, 645*(1), 1–24.
Gondicas, D., & Issawi, C. (1999). *Ottoman Greeks in the Age of Nationalism: Politics, Economy, and Society in the Nineteenth Century*. Princeton, NJ: Darwin Press.
Gözaydın, İ. (2008). Religion, Politics, and the Politics of Religion in Turkey. In D. Jung & C. Raudvere (Eds.), *Religion, Politics, and Turkey's EU Accession*. New York: Palgrave Macmillan.
Greene, M. (2000). *A Shared World: Christians and Muslims in the Early Modern Mediterranean*. Princeton, NJ: Princeton University Press.
Grigoriadis, I. N. (2008). On the Europeanization of Minority Rights Protection: Comparing the Cases of Greece and Turkey. *Mediterranean Politics, 13*(1), 23–41.

Guarnizo, L. E. (1997). The Emergence of a Transnational Social Formation and the Mirage of Return Migration among Dominican Transmigrants. *Identities: Global Studies in Culture and Power*, 4(2), 281–322.
Guarnizo, L. E. (2003). The Economics of Transnational Living. *International Migration Review*, 37(3), 666–699.
Gounaris, B., Mihailidis, I., & Angelopoulos, G. (Eds.). (1997). *Taftotites stin Makedonia*. Athens: Papazisis.
Hall, S. (1990). Cultural Identity and Diaspora. In J. Rutherford (Ed.), *Identity: Community, Culture, Difference* (pp. 222–237). London: Lawrence & Wishart.
Hannerz, U. (1990). Cosmopolitans and Locals in World Culture. *Theory, Culture & Society*, 7(2), 237–251.
Hannerz, U. (1996). *Transnational Connections: Culture, People, Places*. London: Routledge.
Harisiadou, M. (2002). Tourkia einai edo.... *Kinsterna*, 1–2, 84–90.
Harrell-Bond, B. E., & Voutira, E. (1992). Anthropology and the Study of Refugees. *Anthropology Today*, 8(4), 6–10.
Hassiotis, I., Katsiardi-Hering, O., & Ampatzi, E. (2006). *I Ellines stin Diaspora*. Athens: Vouli ton Ellinon.
Hatziprokopiou, P. (2006). *Globalisation, Migration and Socio-Economic Change in Contemporary Greece: Processes of Social Incorporation of Balkan Immigrants in Thessaloniki*. Amsterdam: Amsterdam University Press.
Heleniak, T. (1997). Internal Migration in Russia during the Economic Transition. *Post-Soviet Geography and Economics*, 38(2), 81–104.
Herzfeld, M. (1985). *The Poetics of Manhood: Contest and Identity in a Cretan Mountain Village*. Princeton, NJ: Princeton University Press.
Herzfeld, M. (1987). *Anthropology Through the Looking-Glass: Critical Ethnography in the Margins of Europe*. Cambridge: Cambridge University Press.
Herzfeld, M. (1992). *The Symbolic Production of Indifference: Exploring the Roots of Western Bureaucracy*. New York: Berg.
Herzfeld, M. (1997). *Portrait of a Greek Imagination: An Ethnographic Biography of Andreas Nenedakis*. Chicago: The University of Chicago Press.
Hirschon, R. (1989). *Heirs of the Greek Catastrophe: The Social Life of Asia Minor Refugees in Piraeus*. Oxford: Clarendon Press.
Hirschon, R. (2003). Unmixing Peoples in the Aegean Region. In R. Hirschon (Ed.), *Crossing the Aegean: An Appraisal of the 1923 Compulsory Population Exchange between Greece and Turkey* (pp. 3–12). Oxford: Berghahn.
Ho, E. (2002). Names beyond Nations: The Making of Local Cosmopolitans. *Études Rurales*, 163/164, 215–231.
Ho, E. (2006). *The Graves of Tarim: Genealogy and Mobility across the Indian Ocean*. Berkeley: University of California Press.
Holst-Warhaft, G. (1989). *Road to Rembetika: Music of a Greek Sub-Culture: Songs of Love, Sorrow, and Hashish*. Limni: Harvey & Co.

Icduygu, A. (2004). Transborder Crime between Turkey and Greece: Human Smuggling and Its Regional Consequences. *Southeast European and Black Sea Studies, 4*(2), 294–314.
Jordi, J.-J. (1995). *1962: L'arrive des Pieds-Noirs.* Paris: Editions Autrement.
Kaya, A. (2001). *Constructing Diasporas: Turkish Diasporic Youth in Berlin.* Bielefeld: Transaction Publishers.
Kearney, M. (1995). The Local and the Global: The Anthropology of Globalization and Transnationalism. *Annual Review of Anthropology, 24*(1), 547–565.
Keyder, Ç. (2000). *İstanbul: Küresel ile yerel arasında.* İstanbul: Metis.
King, R., Iosifides, T., & Myrivili, L. (1998). A Migrant's Story: From Albania to Athens. *Journal of Ethnic and Migration Studies, 24*(1), 159–175.
Kirişçi, K. (2000). Disaggregating Turkish Citizenship and Immigration Practices. *Middle Eastern Studies, 36*(3), 1–22.
Kirtsoglou, E., & Sistani, L. (2003). The Other Then, the Other Now, the Other Within: Stereotypical Images and Narrative Captions of the Turk in Northern and Central Greece. *Journal of Mediterranean Studies, 13*(2), 189–213.
Kirtsoglou, E., & Theodossopoulos, D. (2001). Fading Memories, Flexible Identities: The Rhetoric about the Self and the Other in a Community of 'Christian' Refugees from Anatolia. *Journal of Mediterranean Studies, 11*(2), 395–415.
Kızılyürek, N. (2011). *Paşalar, Papazlar: Kıbrıs Ve Hegemonya.* İstanbul: Kalkedon Yayınları.
Kokot, W., Giordano, C., & Gandelsman-Trier, M. (2013). *Diaspora as a Resource: Comparative Studies in Strategies, Networks and Urban Space.* Vienna: LIT Verlag.
Koliopoulos, J. S., & Veremis, T. M. (2002). *Greece: A Modern Sequel.* New York: New York University Press.
Kouroupou, M., & Balta, E. (2001). *Ellinorthodoxes koinotites tis Kappadokias.* Athens: Center for Asia Minor Studies.
Lazaridis, G. (2000). Filipino and Albanian Women Migrant Workers in Greece: Multiple Layers of Oppression. In F. Anthias & G. Lazaridis (Eds.), *Gender and Migration in Southern Europe: Women on the Move* (pp. 26–34). Oxford: Berg.
Leontis, A. (1995). *Topographies of Hellenism: Mapping a Homeland.* Ithaca: Cornell.
Löfgren, O. (1989). The Nationalization of Culture. *Ethnologia Europaea, 19*(1), 5–24.
Mackridge, P., & Yannakis, E. (Eds.). (1997). *Ourselves and Others: The Development of a Greek Macedonian Cultural Identity since 1912.* Oxford: Berg.
Malkki, L. H. (1995). Refugees and Exile: From "Refugee Studies" to the National Order of Things. *Annual Review of Anthropology, 24*(1), 495–523.
Mann, V. B., Glick, T. F., & Dodds, J. D. (Eds.). (1992). *Convivencia: Jews, Muslims, and Christians in Medieval Spain.* New York: George Braziller.

Marcus, A. (1989). *The Middle East on the Eve of Modernity: Aleppo in the Eighteenth Century*. New York: Columbia University Press.
Massey, D. S. (1999). International Migration at the Dawn of the Twenty-First Century: The Role of the State. *Population and Development Review, 25*(2), 303–322.
McCabe, I. B., Harlaftis, G., Minoglou, I. P., & Cohen, R. (2005). *Diaspora Entrepreneurial Networks: Four Centuries of History*. Oxford: Berg.
Meijer, R. (2013). *Cosmopolitanism, Identity and Authenticity in the Middle East*. Surrey: Curzon.
Memişoğlu, F. (2013). The Legacy of the Nation-State Building Process: Minority Politics in Greece and Turkey. In J. D. Iglesias, N. Stojanović, & S. Weinblum (Eds.), *New Nation-States and National Minorities: A Comparative Perspective* (pp. 169–190). Essex: ECPR Press.
Millas, H. (2000). *Türk Romanı ve Öteki*. İstanbul: Sabancı Üniversitesi Yayınları.
Millas, I. (2001). *Eikones Ellinon Kai Tourkon Scholika Vivlía, Istoriografía, Logotechnía Kai Ethnika Stereotypa*. Athina: Ekdoseis Alexandreia.
Moskos, C. (1989). *Greek Americans: Struggle and Success*. Brunswick: Transaction.
Münz, R., & Ohliger, R. (1998). Long-Distance Citizens: Ethnic Germans and Their Immigrations to Germany. *European Forum*, European University Institute, Centre for Advanced Studies.
Naficy, H. (1991). Exile Discourse and Televisual Fethishization. *Quarterly Review of Film and Video, 13*(1–3), 85–116.
Navaro-Yashin, Y. (2002). *Faces of the State: Secularism and Public Life in Turkey*. Princeton: Princeton University Press.
Navaro-Yashin, Y. (2012). *The Make-Believe Space: Affective Geography in a Postwar Polity*. Durham, NC: Duke University Press.
Nowicka, M., & Vertovec, S. (2014). Comparing Convivialities: Dreams and Realities of Living-with-Difference. *European Journal of Cultural Studies, 17*(4), 341–356.
Ong, A. (1996). Cultural Citizenship as Subject-Making. *Current Anthropology, 37*(5), 737–762.
Örs, İ. R. (2018). Cosmopolitan Nostalgia: Geographies, Histories, and Memories of the Greeks of Istanbul (Rum Polites). In N. F. Onar, S. Pearce, & F. Keyman (Eds.), *Istanbul: Living with Difference in a Global City*. (pp. 81–96). New Brunswick: Rutgers University Press.
Özkırımlı, U., & Sofos, S. A. (2008). *Tormented by History: Nationalism in Greece and Turkey*. New York: Columbia University Press.
Pardo, I. (1996). *Managing Existence in Naples: Morality, Action and Structure*. Cambridge: Cambridge University Press.
Petridou, E. (2001). *Milk Ties: A Commodity Chain Approach to Greek Culture*. Unpublished Ph.D. thesis, University of London.
Petridou, E., West, H. G., Paxson, H., Williams, J., Grasseni, C., & Cleary, S. (2012). Naming Cheese. *Food, Culture & Society, 15*(1), 7–41.

Portes, A. (2007). Migration, Development, and Segmented Assimilation: A Conceptual Review of the Evidence. *The Annals of the American Academy of Political and Social Science, 610*(1), 73–97.

Prato, G. B. (2009). Introduction – Beyond Multiculturalism: Anthropology at the Intersections between the Local, the National and the Global. In G. B. Prato (Ed.), *Beyond Multiculturalism: Views from Anthropology* (pp. 1–19). London: Routledge.

Psimmenos, I. (2000). Making of Periphratic Spaces: The Case of Albanian Undocumented Female Migrants in the Sex Industry of Athens. In F. Anthias & G. Lazaridis (Eds.), *Gender and Migration in Southern Europe: Women on the Move*. Oxford: Berg.

Remennick, L. (2012). *Russian Jews on Three Continents: Identity, Integration, and Conflict*. New Brunswick: Transaction Publishers.

Römhild, R. (1999). Home-Made Cleavages: Ethnonational Discourse, Diasporization, and the Politics of Germanness. *Anthropological Journal on European Cultures, 8*(1), 99–120.

Rossman, A., & Rubel, P. G. (Eds.). (2009). *Translating Cultures: Perspectives on Translation and Anthropology*. Oxford: Berg.

Rouse, R. (1992). Making Sense of Settlement: Class Transformation, Cultural Struggle, and Transnationalism among Mexican Migrants in the United States. *Annals of the New York Academy of Sciences, 645*(1), 25–52.

Safran, W. (1991). Diasporas in Modern Societies: Myths of Homeland and Return. *Diaspora: A Journal of Transnational Studies, 1*(1), 83–99.

Sarris, N. (1996). Introduction. In N. G. Apostolidis (Ed.), *Anamniseis apo tin Konstantinoupoli*. Athens: Trochalia.

Sayad, A. (2004). *The Suffering of the Immigrant*. Cambridge, UK: Polity.

Seremetakis, N. (1991). *The Last Word: Women, Death, and Divination in Inner Mani*. Chicago: University of Chicago Press.

Sheffer, G. (2003). *Diaspora Politics: At Home Abroad*. Cambridge: Cambridge University Press.

Silverman, S. (1975). *Three Bells of Civilization: The Life of an Italian Hill Town*. New York: Columbia University Press.

Silverstein, B. (2011). *Islam and Modernity in Turkey*. New York: Palgrave Macmillan.

Skopotea, E. (1988). *To Prototipo Vasilio kai i Megali Idea: Opseis tou ethnikou problimatos. 1830–1880*. Athens: Polytypo.

Smith, M. P. (1992). Postmodernism, Urban Ethnography, and the New Social Space of Ethnic Identity. *Theory and Society, 21*(4), 493–531.

Smith, A. D. (1994). Ethnic Nationalism and the Plight of Minorities. *Journal of Refugee Studies, 7*(2–3), 186–198.

Soysal, Y. N. (1994). *Limits of Citizenship: Migrants and Postnational Membership in Europe*. Chicago: University of Chicago Press.

Stamatopoulos, K. (1996). *H Teleftaia Analampi: H Konstantinoupolitiki Romiossioni sta Chronia 1948–1955.* Athina: Ekdoseis Domos.
Stewart, C. (1991). *Demons and the Devil: Moral Imagination in Modern Greek Culture.* Princeton: Princeton University Press.
Stewart, S. (1993). *On Longing: Narratives of the Miniature, the Gigantic, the Souvenir, the Collection.* London: Duke University Press.
Stock, F. (2010). Home and Memory. In K. Knott & S. McLoughlin (Eds.), *Diasporas: Concepts, Intersections, Identities* (pp. 24–28). New York: Zed Books.
Suarez-Navaz, L. (2004). *Rebordering the Nation: Boundaries and Citizenship in Southern Europe.* Oxford: Berghahn.
Theodossopoulos, D. (2003). Degrading Others and Honouring Ourselves: Ethnic Stereotypes as Categories and as Explanations. *Journal of Mediterranean Studies, 13*(2), 177–188.
Theodossopoulos, D. (2004). The Turks and Their Nation in the Worldview of Greeks in Patras. *History and Anthropology, 15*(1), 1–28. https://doi.org/10.1080/0275720042000191073.
Theodossopoulos, D. (2006). Introduction: The 'Turks' in the Imagination of the 'Greeks'. *South European Society & Politics, 11*(1), 1–32.
Todorova, M. (1997). *Imagining the Balkans.* New York: Oxford University Press.
Triandafyllidou, A. (2009). Greek Immigration Policy at the Turn of the 21st Century. Lack of Political Will or Purposeful Mismanagement? *European Journal of Migration and Law, 11*(2), 159–177.
Triandafyllidou, A., & Veikou, M. (2002). The Hierarchy of Greekness Ethnic and National Identity Considerations in Greek Immigration Policy. *Ethnicities, 2*(2), 189–208.
Tsimouris, G. (2001). Reconstructing "Home" among the "Enemy": The Greeks of Gokseada (Imvros) after Lausanne. *Balkanologie, 5*(1–2), 257–289.
Tsitselikis, K. (2007). The Pending Modernisation of Islam in Greece: From Millet to Minority Status. *Südosteuropa Zeitschrift fir Gegenwartsforschung, 55*(4), 354.
Tziovas, D. (2009). *Greek Diaspora and Migration since 1700: Society, Politics and Culture.* Farnham: Ashgate.
Valášková, N., Uherek, Z., & Brouček, S. (1997). *Aliens or One's Own People: Czech Immigrants from the Ukraine in the Czech Republic.* Prague: Institute of Ethnology.
Van Hear, N. (1998). *New Diasporas.* London: UCL Press.
Vertovec, S. (2007). *New Directions in the Anthropology of Migration and Multiculturalism.* Oxford: Routledge.
Voutira, E. A. (2006). Post-Soviet Diaspora Politics: The Case of the Soviet Greeks. *Journal of Modern Greek Studies, 24*(2), 379–414.
Werbner, P. (2002). The Place Which Is Diaspora: Citizenship, Religion and Gender in the Making of Chaordic Transnationalism. *Journal of Ethnic and Migration Studies, 28*(1), 119–133.

Werbner, P. (2010). Complex Diasporas. In K. Knott & S. McLoughlin (Eds.), *Diasporas: Concepts, Intersections, Identities* (pp. 74–78). New York: Zed Books.

Wimmer, A., & Schiller, N. G. (2002). Methodological Nationalism and Beyond: Nation-State Building, Migration and the Social Sciences. *Global Networks*, 2(4), 301–334.

Yağcıoğlu, D. (2004). *From Deterioration to Improvement in Western Thrace, Greece: A Political Systems Analysis of a 'Traiadic' Ethnic Conflict*. Unpublished Ph.D. dissertation, George Mason University, Fairfax County.

Zmegac, J. (2007). *Strangers Either Way: The Lives of Croatian Refugees in Their New Home*. Oxford: Berghahn.

Zolberg, A. R. (1983). The Formation of New States as a Refugee-Generating Process. *The Annals of the American Academy of Political and Social Science*, 467(1), 24–38.

Zubaida, S. (2002). Middle Eastern Experiences of Cosmopolitanism. In S. Vertovec & R. Cohen (Eds.), *Conceiving Cosmopolitanism: Theory, Context, Practice*. Oxford: Oxford University Press.

Zubaida, S. (2010, July 20). Cosmopolitan Citizenship in the Middle East. *Open Democracy*. Retrieved from https://www.opendemocracy.net/sami-zubaida/cosmopolitan-citizenship-in-middle-east

CHAPTER 4

Resolutionary Recollections: Event, Memory, and Sharing the Suffering

In this chapter, I focus on the acts and processes of representation with regard to particular tragic events that the Rum Polites experienced throughout the twentieth century and that are largely responsible for their displacement from Istanbul. Through presenting of recollections from a variety of oral and written sources, I explore how the Rum Polites contribute to the nuancing of the official or canonized versions of nationalist history-making through their own alternative narratives of violence in their distant and recent pasts. I show how the Rum Polites deal with their traumatic memories, without downplaying their importance and significance, in ways other than adopting the condemning, stereotyping, and victimizing discourses that characterize dominant national historical narratives. After giving a review of some of the past experiences of violence, I discuss a particular event at length from different angles and positions, which then construct my departing point for a discussion of the relation between memory of suffering and the boundaries of identity among the Rum Polites.

It could be anticipated, with the expectations informed by a nation-state logic, that the Rum Polites would develop a fanatic anti-Turkish stance and a strong discourse of hatred, for sharing the collective trauma from recent personal or communal experiences with the Turks. Official Greek history contains anti-Turkish elements that were meant to justify the struggle for independence from the Ottoman Empire and to sustain

© The Author(s) 2018
İ.R. Örs, *Diaspora of the City*, Palgrave Studies in Urban Anthropology, https://doi.org/10.1057/978-1-137-55486-4_4

the international rivalry with neighboring Turkey. In this history, the "Greeks" in Turkey are assigned a special role: they are expected to pose as witnesses to and as victims of crimes that stand as a proof to the negative stereotype of the Turk. Their recollections of experiences with Turks are to be living evidence of the traumatic cruelty they had to endure over years and centuries. Similarly, Turkish sources and discourses also represent these people as "enemies within," contributing to the function of otherization in nationalist history-writing processes.[1]

Yet there is always a dependable level of diversity in the case of Rum Polites, echoing the words of Italo Calvino, where the evil is mixed, maybe not with good, but with variety, the volatile, the changeable.[2] There is certainly a great amount of sadness, anger, and disappointment within the majority of the Rum Polites community against the Turkish state and the people who have caused or allowed such immense measures of destruction, which eventually led them to leave Istanbul. Yet one should not underestimate the variety of reactions different people may have toward traumatic experiences and how they may choose to cope with them. Earlier, I tried to give a sense of how fragmented a community the Rum Polites constitute and how drastically they differ from each other in their political views, especially toward the Turks. This multiplicity encompasses a wide spectrum of positions, from which extreme ideologies are not excluded. What I wish to underline here, however, is the overwhelming presence of voices that counter the tendency: contrary to what would be stereotypically expected from "Greeks," especially those who suffered as a result of their experiences with the "Turks," the Rum Polites lend themselves toward refuting the inimical discourse, toward emphasizing with the need to arbitrate between such polarities, toward considering the multiple factors that led to the traumatic events, and in this way developing a more mature and sound understanding of the recent past (Örs 2006). Their stories of the events portray different ways of coming to terms with that past, even some reconciliation with their own history. Their stories make up resolutionary recollections of the events.

As Appadurai (1981) suggests, there may be different rules for the use of history, just as there are culturally diverse ways in which the past is seen to inform action and consciousness in the present. It is because they have their own multiple stories of events that most Rum Polites recognize the multiplicity of perceptions for each event. There are many who do not wish to take the pains of dealing with the past. But those who do are inclined to escape a categorical condemnation of the Turks. In this regard, they posit themselves as being different from the official or popular Greek position, offering those valuable nuances that help position them historically in a place where they like to see themselves: not as helpless victims maintaining an adverse discourse, but as rational, constructive, and reconciling actors mediating suffering in order to prevent more suffering.

> *I dive my hands in ink*
> *as chronographer with countless*
> *handwritings and tell tales*
> *unutterable, speechless, endless.*

The above poem is by Savvas Tsilenis (2002), published in the literary journal *Kinsterna* of the Rum Polites. It beautifully expresses the difficulty of reciting remembrances of traumatic events, for the people who experienced them. As seen previously, there are other Rum Polites who relate to the collective experiences of their community by narrating these experiences with the sensibility of an individual who personally endured them. In this section, I bring up stories of personally lived instances by way of recognizing what has been "unutterable" in the tales told by the Rum Polites.

For the current generation of Rum Polites in Athens, the traumatic events that they can personally remember start around the time of World War II. Although Turkey had not taken part in the war, the political environment at the time allowed local governments to use the war as a pretext for taking extraordinary measures and to justify many of their actions. The first major act was the sudden drafting of non-Muslims, which is remembered as having affected many families among the Rum Polites.[3] Another event was of an economic nature: in 1942, a law was passed in the parliament for the collection of a special tax called Wealth Tax in order to cash in a portion of previously accumulated wealth. This tax encompassed wealth in the form of currency, real estate, or any private property. Percentages and amounts were estimated arbitrarily and charged in proportions that varied in accordance with religious and ethnic background. The taxpayers had 15 days to pay, without the right to appeal or to petition for a delay; those who did not gather the often outrageous amounts in cash not only had their property confiscated but were also sent off to a labor camp in the depths of Eastern Anatolia (Aktar 2000, 2011; Ökte 1951; Akar 2006).

The quote below illustrates the dramatic experiences endured by a child during the period of the Wealth Tax.

I was a small child then. The authorities were going to all offices and homes those days, so there was a fearful expectation in every family. My father was already taken to Aşkale. We used to live in Tarlabaşı, so it did not take them too long to come to us. My family was not very rich, and our house was rented, so they did not have too much to seize. This made them angry, I guess. There was an official, a man from Ankara, who brought with him a porter (*hamal*), a big man with wide shoulders I remember, to carry the furniture. This man was Kurdish, he did not know, he was just waiting for orders. The official decided that they would put all our belongings into a room, and lock the door "as a means of precaution." As if we were going to steal our own things. So they took everything away. Not even our tea cups they left behind. And what made me angry most was what they did with my grandfather, who was partially paralyzed. They wanted to take his bed. My mother was crying, asking for mercy for a man who could not walk. So they took him like this, holding the mattress they carried him out and put him on the floor. Before they closed the door of the room, I saw my wooden toy horse inside. I pointed out to it, with tears in my eyes, and the Kurd saw this. He understood. Big man like a bear, but he had a heart. He took the toy and gave it to me. Before I knew it, the official from Ankara stormed in, yelled at the *hamal*, took my horse out of my hands, and threw it inside the room. He slammed the door shut, and sealed it (*mühürledi*). He was very angry, "This room will not be opened by anybody! Understood?" he ordered. So we lived in that house for some time, knowing that everything we had was behind that door, without having any access to it. I can never forget that.

When the war ended, the Wealth Tax was canceled and the labor camps were closed down. After the victory of the Allies, a period of relative calm followed, but before long the civil clashes in Cyprus were to constitute the background to some of the most violent occurrences in the history of the Turkish Republic, this time directed deliberately at the Rum Polites.

The most shocking and horrific events were probably those called *Septemvriana* that happened on the night of 6 September 1955. In a chain of uproar in the streets of Istanbul, Izmir, Marmara, and the Northern Aegean islands, masses of people attacked and destroyed shops, businesses, houses, churches, schools, hospitals, cemeteries, and any other kind of property belonging to Rum Polites. The pretext was the news that a bomb had been placed in Salonika in the house where Mustafa Kemal was born, but the fact that only specific buildings were attacked made it obvious that these were acts of a planned destruction directed against the Rum Polites. The bomb story turned out to be fabricated, but the result was an immense devastation that occurred within the short few hours until military order was established next morning: some 6500 buildings were destroyed, enormous financial damage was incurred, and "an acute sense of insecurity" was inspired among the Rum Polites that became "the death knell for the once prosperous Greek community of Istanbul" (Christidis 2000, 361).

The dates of 6 and 7 September 1955 became a turning point in the history of the Rum Polites in Istanbul, yet the immediate consequences did not measure up to the immensity of shock and destruction ultimately caused by the events: many started packing to leave the city; many more saw that this was the beginning of the end; but most picked up the rubble, reconstructed their place in the city, and carried on with their lives. The demographics did not fall drastically, in fact rose for a period, as shown by population surveys and enrolment records for Rum schools.[4] Most stayed, and some of those who left for Greece came back. Istanbul was experiencing a period of relative stability, and for the Rum it was era of "the last glimmer" (Stamatopoulos 1996). The wishful thinking that this might have been an extraordinary situation never to be repeated must have been shared by quite a few, but these optimists were to be disappointed. Following a near decade of calm waters in the otherwise rough seas between Turkey and Greece, the Rum Polites suffered the biggest blow in 1964, when the civil clashes in Cyprus entered a bloody curve. Perhaps it was not possible to foresee the extent of what was to happen, but according to one informant, these developments did not come out of the blue. He told me his narrative of that fateful decade in Istanbul with the following words:

> In 1950, there was no pressure. After the Wealth Tax the situation had improved. 1955 was the first signal that meant 'pack your things' (*mazeve ta*). The Cypriot events were the issue. Then the 'bad stuff started' (*arhisan ti kakia*). Things that many people don't know. Example: Even if you were Turkish but Christian, the law was such that your money was blocked by the Central Bank. You could not take as much as you wanted, whenever you wanted. You couldn't take the money and leave the country. Of course, there were holes and windows. A Turkish friend could take your money and give to you, etc. Not altogether, of course. This was a significant measure.
>
> Another thing that most people don't know about: the first expulsions were not in 1964, but in 1957. This is how it happened. In Istanbul there was a Hellenic Union of Istanbul (*Elliniki Enosi Konstantinopoleos*)—only Greek passport holders could be members. My father was there. When things happened in Cyprus—they had burned villages, killed people and so on, the Greeks in Istanbul were thought of as spies, that they are sending

money to EOKA, etc. They closed down the EEK within one day in 1957 and they took the members immediately to the military jail in Harbiye. Without a court case, without anything. In order to cause a scare, surely. Eleven members came out later and they sent them out with just one suitcase. Without family, just 'expelled.' So, these are the first expulsions. Before 1964, of course.

The *en masse* deportation of Greeks in 1964 gave rise to the biggest wave of migration of the Rum Polites from Istanbul. Using once again as pretext the bloody events on the island of Cyprus, the Turkish government unilaterally denounced on 16 March 1964 the peace and friendship agreement that was signed between Atatürk and Venizelos in 1930. With that, Greek citizens who legally resided in Istanbul and who were an intrinsic part of the native population amounting to almost a third of the Rum Polites lost their legal guard against discriminative action by the state. Then the Turkish government passed a law (Law number 1062, article 1, *Kararname* number 6/3801, enacted by parliament on 2 November 1964) rendering all Greek passport holders as illegal residents, therefore working and owning property illegally. This was done on unverified charges of the Rum Polites being collaborators with the Greek Cypriot militia who were allegedly fighting for unification with Greece. Starting with the cancelation of their property deeds and their residence permits, in about a fortnight, over 20,000 Rum Polites were forced to abandon the country, their property, their business, their family, simply all their life in Istanbul. They were only allowed to take with them their nonvaluable personal effects, and so they arrived in Greece with no more than twenty dollars in their pockets. The wealth they left behind amounted, according to some estimates, to more than five hundred million dollars. Having been given notice as short as two weeks in most instances, they had not been able to arrange for securing their businesses, wealth, and property, most of which was taken over by the Turkish state[5] (Alexandris 1983, 280–86; Demir and Akar 1994).

Pressures of various sorts continued to be directed at the community of Rum Polites, limiting their economic and cultural activities and inhibiting the functioning of religious, social, and educational institutions (Alexandris 1983, 286–98). This caused the remaining Rum Polites also to leave Istanbul in large numbers, increasingly after the 1974 invasion of Cyprus, when public discourse once again became overtly anti-Greek. Some horror stories that were related to me by the Rum Polites include comments made to them along the lines of "In 1955 we circumcised your priests, now we are going to cut off their heads" (*1955'te papazlarınızın pipisini kesmiştik, simdi kafasını keseceğiz*) or "Then your property, now your life" (*O zaman malınız, şimdi canınız*).

There are many reasons for the displacement of Rum Polites, which remain, although scandalous, largely unknown to the general public in both Turkey and Greece. They found some exposure with the release of a number of popular movies and TV series in Greece and in Turkey, albeit not enough to establish a grounded and widespread discussion leading to a deep understanding and recognition of the events that the Rum Polites suffered in their recent history. Among those events, the best known—in both countries and abroad—still remain the Septemvriana. In the next section, I reflect on the 1955 events through showing how the Rum Polites represent them today.

September Stories

Even though they did not lead to the biggest wave of migration of the Rum Polites from Istanbul, the horrific events of 6–7 September 1955, the Septemvriana, are the most salient in terms of the extent of visible destruction, which found international coverage. Photos showing crowds of men with sticks in front of destroyed stores, ruined cars, burned churches, and opened graves flooded the media, inscribing enduring pictures in the public imagination. These powerful images are used extensively in various sources,[6] be it for informative or provocative reasons, providing a dimension of visuality in the representations of the events.

The recollections of the Rum Polites have additional reality effects by triggering senses other than sight. An informant told me that the most tormenting memory she had was the way Pera smelt the next morning: the disgusting stink of the meat, fish, cheese, eggs, rotten fruit, and cream that were spread all over the street, mixing with the stench of burned tires, plastic, and wool to create an unbearable, piercing odor that remains in her nostrils to this day. Another vividly remembered sense is that of trying to walk on the sticky, muddy mass of textiles, creams, drinks, oil, and heaps of foodstuffs that covered entire streets. And of course, there was the sound:

> Sixth of September, Tuesday, seven o'clock in the evening. We had just closed our shop in the central street of Pera, selling crystal, glassware,

and various kitchen equipment. ...Walking down the street of Pera toward our house in Sıraselviler, we saw the crowd with sticks and canes in their hands, shouting "*Kahrolsun, keratalar gavur, köpekoğlu!*" [Damn the infidel bastards, sons of dogs!] We immediately gathered that it was something serious against us. ...All along the street of Pera, on the horizon one could see the rising smoke and flames. Everywhere they were burning, breaking, tearing apart. They had still not arrived at our shop when Takis went in. He unlocked the door and first of all raised the Turkish flag—for the Cyprus issue was boiling then. Then he took a large paper and wrote 'Cyprus is Turkish,' and pinned it on the flag. He thought that he could save our possessions this way. They, however, had it all written down, they knew who to hit. The orders they were given were such that nothing was to remain intact from among the belongings of the minorities. ...He went across the street and stood opposite the shop and waited to see what would happen. We loved our business very much! In a little while, a group of about fifteen to twenty men. They waived the flag—their flag, cut the shutters of the shop with special tools; it surprised him, they were brand new, produced on the spot. Immediately after that, another group came from behind, again fifteen to twenty people, who entered from the shop window inside and started to break with rage whatever was in front of them ... and the most tragic of all was that Takis opposite was watching thirty years of hard work being, in front of his eyes, all smashed up. (Memoir entries cited in Konstantinou-Kloukina 2003, 479–82)

The image of smashed glass and the terrifying noise of such destruction, the powerful act of "shattering silence" as an infinite inscription of horror in the memory of people experiencing violent events, is a familiar theme in recollections of trauma (Aretxaga 1997). One does not need to go further than one of the best known cases of interethnic violence in history: in fact, *Kristallnacht* is the title of a volume composed of newspaper articles and first-person accounts from the Rum who experienced the Septemvriana. The immediate analogy to the night of 9/10 November 1938 is explained on the back cover:

The crystal night: the outbreak of the pogrom against the Jews of Germany. That night is characterized by the sound of crystal and glass smashed by Nazi gangs. The same terrifying sound will remain forever imprinted in the memory of Greeks of the City who experienced the night of 6/7 September 1955.

The power of the memories of violence is fed here by the living force of unforgetful senses; as much as the passing years might filter out the details of remembrance, what remains are the haunting instances—like scenes from a nightmare—with intensified drops from the minutiae of personal experiences.

> *the less you see and express*
> *your sight in the gaze of others,*
> *the deeper the stabbing wound of witnessing.*

In spite of the enormous level of destruction and pain suffered by the community, the Rum Polites writings about the Septemvriana suggest that there is an attempt to come to terms with the event and to reestablish it in the most realistic way. Rather than simply condemning the Turks altogether or reverting to stereotypes of barbarism based on ethnic hatred, they assess the role of involvement of other parties, seek to understand their possible motivations, while describing the wider situation in Istanbul along with the reactions of other Istanbulites during the course of events. Like Anagnostopoulos, whose poem is cited above, many Rum Polites try to avoid their memories of violent events violating their present, and their relations with others at present. For these people, understanding the multiple dimensions involved in making the other commit the violence is necessary in order to come to terms with their suffering from a violent past.

Christoforos Christidis is a retired diplomat and researcher of Istanbulite origin who wrote a comprehensive work on the Septemvriana (2000). Starting with a chronology of developments leading to the night of 6 September 1955, a detailed description of what happened where, and notes on the day after, he proceeds to a careful analysis of the reasons for and consequences of the September events. He then summarizes these into the following major points: (1) the 6/7 September events were organized in advance; (2) the nationalist bodies that were involved, such as the "Cyprus is Turkish" Association and the "Association for Rehabilitation of Western Thrace Refugees," had close ties with the Turkish government, and with Prime Minister Menderes in particular; (3) the government unsuccessfully tried to blame the communists for the acts; (4) the news reports about the destruction of Atatürk's house were false—the acts were engineered as a pretext for the pogrom; (5) the Patriarchate and other authorities among the Rum minority failed to take the necessary precautions; and (6) the British were involved in planning the events to some extent; an acute clash between Greeks and Turks would benefit the British policy on Cyprus, and it is highly unlikely that the Turks alone were responsible for these far too well-organized events.

The journalist Paleologos writes that, as much as he would like to believe in the innocence of the Turkish government, and as little direct involvement as there might have been, the fire was lit by the populist policies pursued by the Menderes government toward the religious classes repressed under Kemalism; the events were the responsibility of the government even though the role played by fascist groups like "Cyprus is Turkish," the press, the secret services, and the British cannot be underestimated. At the end of the day, the doer of the evil was Turkish chauvinism—a British-inspired act that Ankara played along with for internal reasons (*Tachidromos*, 7 January 1956).

Many Rum Polites thus approach the events analytically, investigating the reasons by taking into account the diversity of positions involved. Some argue that the Greek state was as much to blame as the Turkish, expressing a deep disappointment with the politics of both Turkey and Greece that were adopted at the expense of the Rum Polites in Istanbul. This is the sentiment expressed by film director Tassos Boulmetis, who points out that the Rum Polites had the misfortune of being smashed between two sides: on the one hand, an ethnic-nationalistic (*panethniki*) Turkish politics, which cut out a healthy part of its society, and on the other, a short-sighted and fragmented Greek politics, which led to the diminishing of a healthy section of Hellenism. "If there is anger and fury, then it is directed more to my kind, dear readers, and not to my 'enemies'" (Boulmetis 2004, 28).

Sharing this opinion is also the renowned author Petros Markaris, who claims that, during the civil clashes in Cyprus, "the Turkish superstructure (and not the Turks of Istanbul) saw the omoyenia[7] as an easy and dismissible element for increasing pressure toward Greece," and that "maybe the Turkish politicians would not have hit the omoyenia so mercilessly if they had not overestimated the Greek interest in them," and if they had known that Greece would not hesitate to victimize the Rum Polites for the possibility of unification with Cyprus (Markaris 2002, 12).

Characteristic in this quotation is the differentiation between different levels of Turkish society, rather than an outright rejection of a generic category of the Turks altogether. A widely held disbelief is that those who committed the violent acts were actually not Istanbulites, but some fanatic, unknowledgeable, easily brainwashed masses that were brought in from outside the city—often described as "Anatolians," "rural people," or "wild villagers from the mountains." In addition to appearing in the published memoirs, versions of this phrase are used by many of my informants as a point of either dismissal or defense, but most certainly as an indication of the existence of a negative stereotypical category of the non-Istanbulite in the Rum Polites collective representation. It must be noted that the Rum Polites could not believe that the Turks in their immediate surroundings would commit these acts, which was underlined by a deeper discourse of peaceful multicultural coexistence in the City. This is exemplified in the words of Konstantinou-Kloukina (2003, 452–53):

> The common living of hundreds of years led to the brotherly coexistence of the simple people of the Turks and the Greek minority, who shared their pains and happiness. We the both peoples were born to the same earth. ... Istanbul was a city where Muslims and Christians lived together for many centuries to the point that they influenced one another in matters of religion, customs and traditions. The simple Turkish people lived and worked together harmoniously with the Greek people. And this would stay that way if there were no political pressures and explosive publications and provocative articles against the Greeks, which fanaticized the population and [cultivated] the aggression into extreme measures.

The Rum Polites literature thus indicates the press, provocation, state policies in both countries, as well as non-Istanbulite Turks as responsible for the events. They further blame their own community for not being able to prevent the culmination of events and point their finger at the powerful Rum Polites persons or institutions for not taking any action. The Patriarch himself is not immune to criticism either. He is alleged to have closed himself in his cell during the night of Septemvriana, praying for a miracle to stop the pogrom, as the Church has been accustomed to doing since Byzantine times. It is also claimed that the Patriarch personally knew about what was to happen much earlier as he received phone calls from the mayor and the chief of the police. He was warned not to leave the Patriarchate, so he did not. He neither tried to warn his people in advance nor reacted strongly enough in the aftermath of the events. Therefore, Athinagoras is said to be known as "the small Patriarch" in the eyes of the Rum Polites, because he only cared for his own safety and abandoned his people (Tsoukatou 1999, 155).

There may be many selves and other others to blame for the acts, but in the aftermath of the events, the relations of the Rum Polites with their Turkish friends and neighbors were nevertheless greatly challenged. On the one hand, the Rum Polites were disappointed that their Turkish friends did nothing to warn them in advance and to protect them from the unexpected: "It is noteworthy that all the Turks kept the secret, not even our good friends told us anything, perhaps so that we wouldn't take any measures. No Rum knew anything. Nobody, nobody" (Tsoukatou 1999, 155). Here it is assumed that the Turks had prior knowledge, an assumption not held to be valid by most of my informants. Whether or not this was the case could only be determined after the fact, and in the event of a prior warning, such as the case of this man in his 80s:

> We were still in our house, on the island of Büyükada (*Prinkiponisso*). Mehmet, my business partner and neighbor there, told me something funny that I did not give any meaning then. He told me to take the earlier boat back [from Istanbul] to spend the evening at home with my family. I asked him why, he said "just like that" (*öyle işte*). I laughed, asked him if they wanted to come over for dinner in that case, but he was very detached. Later that night I understood that he knew from before. Our house was not destroyed much but others were totally wrecked. I was so angry. He even had a Rum wife, how could he...? When next afternoon I saw him on the street, I changed my path. He was also looking the other direction, he was embarrassed. I could not forgive him for a long time.

While the situation prior to the events is under speculation, the behavior of Turkish friends during the course of the night is talked and written about extensively and positively. The theme of good Turks who saved the Rum Polites feature the likes of the Turkish neighbor downstairs who stood in front of the crowd to block their entry to the building, saying, "We are all Turks here. There are no Rum here!" to the angry mob. Here is a striking story by Valasiadis (2002, 80–82):

> Around seven in the evening, voices started to be heard: Turks were breaking, tearing, burning churches, unbury the dead and the like. Fear and panic, you understand. ...With all that happening, we were trying to save what we could [from the sports club of Tatavla]. Cups, relics, flags, the registry book of the members, until the mob arrived at our sports club and the first windows were smashed. We escaped from the back side, jumped out of the building onto the field and ran home. At home I saw that the women

were scared, my sister was crying, my father was pale as a ghost. He said that they entered the shop through the front door, and left through the back, destroying everything in between. As we were crying about our fate, there was knocking at the door. We were dead silent, whispering prayers, until we heard "Master Yianni, open, it is Rashid." He came to [the shop of] my father when he was 12, and became like one of us. We fasted, Rashid fasted. We had Easter; Rashid had Easter bread (*tsoureki*). We had Agia Vassili (New Year); he was cutting the pie with us. Turkish seeds, Romeika language, Greek customs. He came in, armed with a wooden stick. "Don't worry Master Yianni. I am here, I am going to stay here." Knocking on the door again. This time Rashid asks who this is, with the stick in his hand. It's Şevket, who comes in with an ax in his hand, saying, "To the house of my neighbors, over my dead body!" Before we closed the door, knockings again. It is Melek Hanım, the elderly widow from the next neighborhood who came to keep company with her friend, my grandma, who had brought her food and drink when she had lost her husband. There were also these kinds of Turks, humans, in those difficult years. When the worst was over, my mother said, "You see? You give knives, you take knives back … you give good, you take back good!"

Simeon Vafiadis from Kuzguncuk, a neighborhood on the Asian side of the Bosphorus, has the following recollection:

Our neighborhood went through this without any damage, thanks to a neighbor and a friend, Ali Rıza, a civil police commissioner. Ali Rıza was a Turk from Crete, and as we found out later on, waited at the entrance of our district and did not let anybody from the horde pass that point. …Around midnight, a boat full of demonstrators arrived in the harbor of Kuzguncuk, but the mayor and a policeman threatened the captain that they would shoot him if he dared dock the boat. (From memoir notes cited in Tsoukatou 1999, 58)

The same thing happened at the shop of Vafiadis when Hasan, a Kurdish porter of Armenian origin, ran there with a friend as soon as he heard what was happening and stood in front all night to make sure nobody caused any harm. After mentioning some other instances and offering a full description of the situation in different parts of the city, Vafiadis claims that the idea in the beginning was to teach a lesson to the infidel (*gavur*), but as usually happens with this kind of mass demonstration, the organizers (i.e., the state and the police) quickly lost control and the outrage started. When one considers that the duration of the events was only four or five hours, he emphasizes, one wonders how they managed to cause such terrible destruction.

Consider now the following paragraphs taken from an interview with a man in his 60s. After painting a beautiful picture of his life in Istanbul for more than half an hour, he paused for a moment to remember another story of the same kind, during which he told me that this was the way he wanted to recall the past, selecting only the good and not the painful memories, because he did not want to spoil the nice conversation we were having. In response I told him that it was surely his decision to choose what to share with me, but that I would not be disturbed to listen to any bad experiences he might have had in Istanbul, if he wanted to discuss rather than restrain them. He said, "Anyway, they were not many," and continued:

> Well, even as a child you understand the things that happen around you. I did not see my father for three years, between 41 and 44. They took him to the army and he did not come back. It was difficult because I was a small kid (*pitsirikas*) and I did not understand why. But then you have a good time and you don't care when you don't think of it. You assume that things must be this way. You don't question. We were in [the island of] Antigoni and I was asking every now and then about my father. Then he came, I was happy, that was it. Only this I remember as a difficult period.

When I then asked him specifically about his experiences of the Septemvriana, he gave me this following answer in good plain Politika:

> *Ta Septemvriana? Diavazoume hikayedes stis efimerides. O Tourkos mas voithise klp. Oloi mas sosate? Pios to ekane tote? Na ehei 10% pou sosane tous Romious, oi 90% ekanan zimia. Ksereis tin istoria? O kapucus üstümden geçersiniz demiş, den tous afise mesa, kurtarmış, sonra gidip onların arasına karışıp öbür evleri yıkmaya gitmiş. O laos fanatismenos. Den itane mono anthellinika vevea, o logos itane kai ftoheia. Biri yer biri bakar, tosa chronia den andehane. Imouna 18, kai imastan sto Gönen kaplıcaları me tin oikogenia mou. Otan arhise to vurun kahpeye, to akousame kai figame gia tin Poli. Ftasame sto Galata, alla epeidi arhise to sıkıyönetim, den mas afisane na vgume, perimename mesto vapouri mehri to proi. To spiti mas den pirazane.*
>
> (Septemvriana? We read stories in the newspapers. The Turk helped us, etc. All of you saved us? Who did it then? Maybe 10 percent saved the Rum, the 90 percent destroyed. Do you know the story? The janitor told them, "you'd have to pass over my dead body," and then he joined the crowd to

go destroy the other houses. Fanaticized people. It was not only anti-Greek of course, the reason was also poverty. One eats, other stares, all these years they could not take it. I was eighteen, and we were in the health resorts in Gönen. When "hit the bastard" started, we heard and we left to come to Istanbul. We arrived in Galata, but because the martial law was instated, they did not allow us to come out, so we waited inside the ship until the morning. Our house was not disturbed.)

In these sections, where he constantly switches between Greek and Turkish while using combination words (*kapucus, hikayedes*),[8] he stresses some of the important dimensions of the recollections that were already mentioned. First, he does not privilege the Septemvriana as the most traumatic experience of his life. Second, he deals with the events by elaborating on the reasons, such as fanaticism and poverty. This does not mean that he downplays the trauma associated with the events. But perhaps it means that he inserts limits in terms of how far to let this trauma define his life, his sense of self, and his conceptualization of others—in this case, the Turks. Like the language he uses, he adopts a cultural disposition that is hybrid and plural, placing his identity beyond the duality between Greeks and Turks, above any simplistic division between good and bad.

In terms of how they represent their traumatic experiences, the Rum Polites in Athens remain highly diverse and divided. The motivation for this division is mainly political: not because there are strong ideological divides, but on the contrary because there is a chaos, or even a vacuum with regard to the political interests of the Rum Polites. I have previously dealt with this issue in Chap. 3, but here I want to take it up again to discuss it from a different angle. The questions I would like to seek an answer to are the following: To what extent are the traumatic past experiences with the Turks effectual in how the Rum Polites shape their identities and political orientation; and in turn, how do these identities and orientations affect the ways in which the Rum Polites deal with their suffering?

There is no causal relationship between the extent of trauma or violence suffered by the individuals and the level of bitterness they keep about the past and about the Turks. I encountered far too many cases of those who endured much personal suffering, but would still not exchange living in Turkey for anything else. Among the strongest advocates of a politics of mediation are people who lost their wealth in the 1940s, then rebuilt it only to see it destroyed in the 1950s, who were expelled in the 1960s but came back only for their lives to be threatened in the 1970s, and so on.

Here is a sample narrative told to me by a patisserie owner who came to Athens as a teenager before his parents did. He explained why:

> I had to come to Athens because of my schooling. My father loved Istanbul very much; he would not leave it for any reason. He was selling clothes; he had a shop in Pera. During the events [of Septemvriana in 1955] his business was totally destroyed. Everybody left after that, but he did not. Then when the Greeks were forced to leave, he did tricks to stay. He had roots in Andros through his father, so he held a Greek citizenship. His sister's husband was French, so he became Catholic and took on French identity, and had himself removed from the list arguing that he was not Orthodox, thus not Greek. Also during the Cyprus events, he would not leave. In Burgaz where they were that summer [of 1974] the soldiers built barriers to prevent the Rum from getting hurt. It was dangerous. But my father would not leave. My mother was scared though, for herself, for her children, and later her grandchildren, so this was a topic about which they continuously fought those days. In the end, my father could not resist anymore, and they also moved. But my father was very annoyed, he did not like Athens, kept criticizing the people, the town, everything. He fell ill and died shortly thereafter. He just could not live anywhere else.

This is just one of the many stories to show that negative experiences in a place or with a people do not have to change one's positive relations with them. The reverse also holds true, proving the same point: that a person has very negative attitudes about the Turks does not necessarily mean that these are based on painful experiences. Perhaps this is more true than not. Those who promote extreme views are not those who can demonstrate more personal suffering even if they might try to. There are some books by Rum Polites that demonstrate a highly conflict-ridden take on past events and/or were published with the explicit aim of lobbying against Turkey. One of them is titled *He Wanted Me to Live: Turks 1922–1975. Barbarians of All Times*, where the author talks about the Septemvriana only during the last three pages, mentioning some stories that he heard from others. He himself did not even hear anything during that night, thanks to the strong southerly wind he suspects, but mainly because the family of Mahmud Bey, who were their friendly neighbors, convinced the crowd to change their path, swearing that all the neighboring houses belonged to Turks (Volovonis 1988, 122). Similarly, the edited volume titled *Dying a Hundred Times … Septemvriana 1955: The 'Night of Crystals' [Kristallnacht] for the Hellenism of the City* (Tsoukatou 1999) includes several first-person accounts of the fateful night where Turkish neighbors and friends covered for the Rum Polites. Among them are names that are known for their fanatic anti-Turkish stance, as confirmed to me by some of my informants.

The multiplicity in the ways in which the Rum Polites relate to their trauma suggests that in this case there is no linear correspondence between the nature of individual experiences and how people choose to deal with them. It is rather the political stance or the social status of the actors that informs the way they posit themselves in relation to the traumatic events, and thereby to the Turks. The question at stake is not so much how great a loss was suffered by individuals or how much they were affected by all that happened. That they present their recent past one way or another is perhaps of more significance in terms of showing how they seek to construct their identity from out of the tragedy.

Sally Falk Moore forcefully argues for the necessity of integrating historical information in ethnography and suggests ways that can make this endeavor practically possible. She posits that certain kinds of events can be treated as a preferred form of raw data. These should in no sense be staged for the sake of the anthropologist; the analysis should include local commentaries on the event; the event should be "diagnostic"—that is, one that reveals ongoing contests, conflicts, and competitions as well as the efforts to prevent, suppress, or repress these. "This kind of event," she claims, "is a telling historical sign visible in fieldwork" (1987, 730).

I will now turn to an event of the sort that Moore prescribes: it is in no way staged for me; there are local commentaries that reveal both the internal conflicts within the community and the attempts at mediating these tendencies. Furthermore, it brings to light some of the changes in the way the community members perceive a particular historical event, while it also links the past with the present. This is the commemoration held on the 49th anniversary of the Septemvriana in Athens.

The Story of Commemoration

It is eight o'clock in the evening, 6 September 2004. I am on my way to the National War Museum in central Athens. Tonight the amphitheater of the museum is to house a special event organized by several associations of Rum Polites in order to commemorate the tragic events that took place in Istanbul in 1955. The program for the evening titled "Ta Septemvriana: 49 Years" was published in all community newspapers, followed by the announcement that entrance was free. Still, I am surprised by the size of the turnout. There are probably a couple of thousands cramped in the hall, leaving no possibility for latecomers like me to find an empty seat in the amphitheater or even a place to stand in the foyer that is also overflowing with people. Some are hopelessly trying to push their way through, moving their heads around to catch an empty spot from which they can see what is going on inside. Many look like they have given up the effort, opting for standing around in the entrance area which in fact provides them with a better opportunity to catch up with their acquaintances. These free-floating people are made up of a few hundred men and women, middle-aged and above, all dressed up beyond the relatively casual code of the Athenian summer. With ties and jackets, dresses and jewelry, they run to greet what looks like an old friend they have not seen for a long time, then they turn back to the group they came with, probably to give some extra information about the person who has just left their company. Their looks and laughter tell me that the air in the room is heavy with gossip.

I make my way through the stirring crowd toward the end of the hall to join those trying to get a peek inside. Among them I spot a good friend of the family and walk over to greet him. "What's up Ilay?" (*N'aber Ilay?*) he calls out in Turkish, and I answer, "How are you?" (*Ti kanete?*) in Greek. I do this without realizing it in the moment, but what happens is this: Among ourselves we always speak Turkish with this person; not only because he is fluent in Turkish owing to his Karamanli origins but also because I got to know him originally through an Istanbul connection before I moved to Athens, or even spoke any Greek. Since we started out talking Turkish to each other, it stayed this way in the following years, except when there were others with us who did not speak Turkish. Yet in this particular situation of a public event in Greece, my tendency would be to shift to Greek—a tendency probably strengthened by an undercurrent of not wishing to invite the gaze of those others gathered there to commemorate a day of suffering caused by the Turks. My self-imposed carefulness to not cause any sort of disturbance—for him more than myself—is probably an exaggeration in this case, for he is the one who keeps shifting back and forth between Turkish and Greek as much as I try to stick to the latter. We carry on with the conversation anyhow. After some small talk, I comment on how crowded it is, but he does not seem to take pride in the successful turnout. "Our alumni associations did not participate," he shrugs. Some fifteen Rum Polites associations were taking part in the organization, including Sillogos Konstantinoupoliton and Neos Kyklos

Konstantinoupoliton, but obviously this gathering did not represent the entire organized body of the Rum Polites. "We did not think that this was timely," he explains. "Why do something now, on the forty-ninth anniversary of Septemvriana, rather than making an effort to do something really good next year?" Every year there is some small gathering on this day, he tells me, so there is no purpose in enlarging the scale like this: "This is just a show." For next year we have a much better occasion in mind; we will bring together researchers, scholars from Turkey, and from here, there will be a symposium, a discussion, he says, "we'll have a reconciliation (*simfilosi*)—there already is a commonality, but we want to put our stamp on it, and bring it to the fore even further." Meanwhile two people take the stage for the book reading. He informs me that the young woman is a member of parliament and the man a famous actor. When I ask if they originate from Istanbul, he answers negatively: "*yok canım!*" The two take turns reading, but it is very hard to hear. The noise from the foyer is very loud and distracting, and the occasional warnings of "ssshhhhhh!" from the crowd remain ineffective. He turns to me a few minutes later and murmurs that he cannot stand it any longer, then leaves the room. I try to move a little further in to listen, but more importantly to watch the audience. People seem to be attentive, yet somewhat unreadable, in striking contrast to the rather theatrically executed reading on stage. Occasionally I see a few heads nod, lips moving in a whisper, hear the odd tongue click against the teeth to produce the sound "ts-ts-ts" in reaction to the paragraphs cited from the Septemvriana memoirs. "Yes, Agia Triada was smoking," says one woman to the next; another shakes her head in disagreement with what she hears being said about something particular that happened in Tatavla. A tense yet not charged atmosphere prevails throughout the reading of these bitter accounts from the tragic events, but things loosen up when the showing of the short movie starts. Titled *Double Memory* (*Dipli Mnimi*), it is an awarded documentary created by two Rum Polites about twin sisters called Fofo and Loulou, who were born in Istanbul in 1916, during "the time of the Sultan." Their witty way of telling stories about daily life in Istanbul against a backdrop of family pictures and the beautiful scenery of the city triggers a much more relaxed and expressive crowd than before, this time actively engaging with the film through laughter, applause, and deep sighs. As the movie comes to an end, I see the man in front of me wiping tears from his eyes. Then he turns around with a smile on his face and joins the rest of the people leaving the hall. The foyer is more hectic now than ever. I leave the reunion and go back home.

When I met up with this same family friend two days later, he went on with the conversation we had been forced to interrupt, but with an added touch of gossip: "What a show it was, wasn't it? People dressed up, acting seriously ... so pathetic!" Yet there was little value to this gathering, he found, as nothing new had been offered. He reiterated the need for a symposium next year so that "people can get something out of it. But these associations won't do it that way. All they want is to show off." He said he did not take part in any of their meetings, except maybe the ceremonial cutting of the New Year's bread, because he cannot stand their fights over whether they should have an excursion to Cappadocia or Kefalonia. What they are talking about is so trivial, yet they make such a big deal out of everything, he said, and this makes it impossible for them to get together to make important decisions about things that really matter. "If they could ever get together, we would even have a member of parliament representing us," he argued before he ended his words with a Turkish phrase: "These would fit neither village nor town" (*Bunlardan ne köy olur, ne kasaba*). After a pause he added: "Aren't we urbanites/Istanbulites after all?" (*Polites den eimaste?*)

I wondered if this intriguing word play was intended—or if he simply came up with it on the spot wanting to refer to the ineffectiveness of the community by way of invoking a self-stereotype. Whatever the case, the phrasing was more than appropriate: on the one hand, the Rum Polites did not fit any category because they were so diverse and divided, and on the other, they did not fit in Athens because it was too small a settlement—like a village or town relative to the grand Istanbul—to contain the Rum Polites. Although I cannot be sure whether or not he meant to include me when he said "Aren't we Polites?" his final shift of second person plural from the constant use of third left me to think that this might have been the case.

STORIES ON SHARING SUFFERING

According to Wendy James (1997), escaping any kind of reductionism in the anthropology of emotions is to treat language as a vehicle of conscious and self-critical inquiry into the common roots of feeling and experience. Moreover, while the study of emotional experience cannot be simply reduced to a scrutiny of words, language cannot be removed from an engagement with emotional life. This is why I tended to be quite attentive to the ways in which words were used when the Rum Polites shared with me their sensitive journeys to a traumatic past. For a commonly encountered issue in an anthropology of emotions is that of the involvement of the researcher, which becomes extremely important to balance in cases of violence and suffering. This task becomes all the more difficult when the researcher belongs to an ethnic, national, or religious category that the informants consider as the cause of their suffering.[9]

In cases of interethnic violence, suffering is shared at an ethnic/national level. Ethnic others, especially if they are held to be responsible for the violent acts, are regarded to be inherently evil and thus incapable of appreciating the consequences. Thus the line between those who suffer and those who do not corresponds to the divide between self and other, a divide that becomes naturalized, thus further strengthened, through the very tragedy itself.

But it might very well be the case that history may, for purposes of the present day, be used as a means of reconciliation with the other. Memories of tragedy could offer all the more dramatic a display for all the more radical acts of overcoming the past. As unforgettable as it might be, the past may be rendered flexible terrain by the plow of the present in order to cultivate a fertile future. Therefore the sentence by David Lowenthal that "there can be no certainty that the past ever existed, let alone in the form we conceive it, but sanity and security require us to believe that it did" (1985, xxii) can be reversed: a certain past might be remembered differently in order to escape the insanity of the present and to cope with the insecurity of the future. While this by no means verifies historical reality as such, it certainly reveals some of the cultural and political parameters of the present; and these are the focus of this anthropological work.

When analyzing the commemoration event, therefore, I had to rely on more varied sources of data than my own impressions or the feedback of my family friend; to follow Moore, I had to find more commentary on the event that was not affected by the presence of the anthropologist. A review article published in the *Anatoli*, one of the Rum Polites newspapers, provided me with valuable information to that end. Published on the second page of the September 2004 issue and entitled *Commemoration Event for the Septemvriana: Major Collaboration Gives Way to Positive Problematization and Hopes for Overcoming*, the article was written by a reader who used the initials G.K. Mentioning the unexpectedly large turnout, the inadequate size of the venue, and the details of the program for the anniversary, the author stated that this was the first time that the Rum Polites associations had "dared" organize such a public event for the occasion. The main reason was apparently the date: the beginning of September came just at the end of the summer holidays, when most people still had not caught up with their course of daily life in the city. To make up for the inconvenient juncture, the Sillogos Konstantinoupoliton, the largest and the oldest of the Rum Polites associations, had been advancing a project of "informing Greek public opinion" in recent years. Although this year's public meeting did not seem to suffer from bad timing, many issues had been raised by the Rum Polites who were present at the occasion. These mainly concerned the cooperation between Rum Polites institutions, and what such events should entail in the future. Some said that they knew all of this, but that the Elladites had to be informed, whereas others commented that each time they left such occasions "deeply afflicted, in low spirits." In the subsequent section, the article brought up the question of what should be done:

> If the only aim is to bring up the collective memory of suffering, then organizations such as this year's are suitable. But they run the danger of becoming 'tiring' when repeated. Yet this choice is [about] maintaining and consolidating 'the psychology of the defeat' (*i psichologia tis ittas*) that has penetrated into the subconscious of the Constantinopolitan. The result is that people avoid the unpleasant feelings invited by commemoration events. On the other hand, gathering at events that are 'signed' by many institutions creates anticipation for something more advanced. Overthrowing the 'psychology of the defeat' is neither easy, nor can it be achieved for the entirety of the community in question. However it would be preferable for the Polites associations to dare to move toward overthrowing this psychology as much as possible. Such a move would be *'the assessment' of the role of the Turkish state* in the Septemvriana, in cooperation with Turkish researchers who have specific studies on that subject. This move would have many positive dimensions that are not currently present. There are already signs of concern for the Septemvriana and generally for anti-minority politics on the part of Turkish society. It is a development that we should utilize more actively. Next year when the Septemvriana reach their fiftieth anniversary will be a good opportunity for transcending the usual (*ipervasi ton kathieromenon*). (Emphases in the original)

On the other hand, there are outspoken attempts by the Rum Polites at breaking down stereotypical representations of the Turks. Consider the following excerpt taken from the commemorative editorial of the September 1991 issue of the monthly community newspaper *Eptalofos* published in Athens by Rum Polites:

> Such serious events [like Septemvriana] should not be confronted only by condemning and blaming those in power. It is the responsibility of us all to face the matters calmly and objectively and try as much as possible to abolish the inclination to use any sort of violence like the other side does. Let us stress to as many Turks as possible that, in the final analysis, these actions are not suitable for civilized people, and that they damage not only us, but also themselves, even the very mob that committed the crime, although they are not in the position to realize it. This is necessary to do, because in Turkey, alongside those fanatic anti-Greeks, there are some who think correctly and don't approve of what has happened. All of us have to partake in developing relations with those healthy-thinking [people] and in expanding the circle toward those who can help us in this endeavor. Several organizations of Greek–Turkish friendship are engaged in doing this: why shouldn't our newspapers and associations work on it as well?

With regard to the position to be taken in relations with the Turks and with the events themselves, the paragraph above is very clear. What remains hidden between the lines, however, is a subtle critique directed against certain groups within the community who are not of the same opinion. As hinted in the last sentence, many of the Rum Polites newspapers and associations follow varying lines of politics, which sometimes leads to public quarrels or even legal disputes within the community. The same variety applies to the Rum Polites institutions with regard to their handling of collective suffering, and there are many people who do not wish to be involved with these institutions because of their divergences on this highly sensitive point.

These stories indicate that the Rum Polites do not follow the path of nationalists in lending their social memory to the service of the construction of national narratives. Similarly, they resist a simple inimical discourse against the Turks that could invoke uniform stereotypical representations. They are thus dealing with their collective suffering in ways that allow them to consider the multiplicity of dimensions surrounding the tragic events, thereby avoiding an outright condemnation of the Turks as enemy. While this probably does not eliminate the pain, it potentially helps them deal with it so that they can move on with their lives in less conflict-ridden ways.

It is evident that some Rum Polites' way of dealing with suffering is to avoid talking about it. The fact is that I could not have access to those who successfully practice their decision not to tell. It has happened to me a few times that my informants wave their hand in the air, as if wanting to chase an invisible fly, when the conversation brings us to certain sensitive topics, indicating that they would rather skip talking about them. In these cases I respected their silence; I did not find it right to push people over the limits they impose on themselves just because I wanted information for my dissertation. Besides, silence can be indicative of embodied memory—observing violence from the way it is inscribed on people without talking about it (Das 1995), which can be very telling and instructive at times. During an interview, an elderly lady suddenly wanted to change the subject: "I was bitter when I left the City. I would not want to trouble you with these memories now," she said, telling me that she would much prefer for the young generation to know of the good times. A little later the conversation came back to a point where she volunteered to recite the culmination of events leading to her partition from Istanbul. It was one of the most compelling and shocking stories that I had heard, and I have not since encountered any other such case, yet she initially wished to keep it to herself.

My conversations with members of the second generation, that is, the Rum Polites born in Athens to Istanbul-born parents, suggest that this is a commonly encountered situation. Rum Polites often do not share their experiences with their children, even when they are asked to recite their memories. They only bring up the topic when they are with their Rum Polites friends from Istanbul, but to the frustration of the children, they mostly talk in Turkish so that nobody else can understand. Once I found myself in an uncomfortable situation during an interview where the grandchild was also present. When walking me to the door, this granddaughter whispered to me that she had never heard these things before and that she would be surprised if even her mother knew these stories that her grandmother had just told me.

According to what criteria, then, do witnesses choose their preferred audience for sharing their remembrances? Besides the conviction that those who did not suffer in a similar context cannot empathize with the experience, the decision might be based on an ordering of others in terms of their emotional proximity to self. The right to share one's suffering is granted with respect to the other's ability to empathize, which is based on a familiarity with, thus readiness to understand, both the physical and the psychological circumstances in which the events took place. In the case of my candidacy to become the privileged listener to the stories of the often difficult encounters of the Rum Polites with their often difficult past, the situation was rather complex. Even though I was familiar with the setting of collective suffering of the Rum Polites, I had little room to draw any experiential parallels in my own version of the lived past.

Having grown up in Istanbul in the aftermath of the 1980 coup period where the military-led state organization made sure that the young people learned as little as possible about recent history and politics, I spent most of my teenager years as a member of the so-called Generation X who had little knowledge about the deep cultural and political divisions that prevailed in Turkish society. Of the many issues that were deliberately disguised from the youth, that of the minorities was perhaps the most salient. My circle of family and friends always included non-Muslims and other minorities, but there was never a discussion of the problems they experienced because of their different backgrounds, whether at present or in the past. Nor was this a topic of public debate until recently. Thus when I started learning about the tragic events that the Rum Polites encountered, I was shaken by a set of very strong emotions such as anger, disappointment, embarrassment, and heartfelt pain. This disposition only intensified in time, especially during my fieldwork: the more I learned about what had happened, the more I realized how little was known about these matters, and the more I felt the weight of responsibility to let people know. But then the same problem came up: Was it my place to announce the suffering endured by the Rum Polites, and even if it was, to what extent could I correctly understand and represent it? I remember coming back from meetings with Rum Polites and being unable to record the interview right away because I was too touched by the stories I had just heard. Sometimes I even found that the people themselves were much cooler toward their own pain than I could ever be. Once one of my informants empathetically noted that I was affected by what she was telling me, so she gave me a warning, saying, "Are you allowing yourself to get sad about other people's stories? You cannot remain objective if you do that. Think like this: *c'est la vie*! Anything can happen in life."

As it turned out, objectivity and impartiality were out of question in my case; during the course of my research, I became increasingly sensitive to these kinds of issues. The best I could do, I decided, was to accept my position reflexively and to think of ways of making use of this sensitivity to arrive at new kinds of ethnographic understanding. For example, I could investigate the dynamics of my stance regarding the self–other divide maintained by the relative position to suffering. Could I partake in the community delineated by suffering, by suffering for and with the Rum Polites, even if I categorically was the Other? In other words, would my wish to share give me the right to share?

In the next section, I describe an ethnographic moment that was to construct a framework for putting these questions in perspective.

The Story of a Movie

I was moving toward the end of my research. Or more accurately, I had decided to take a break from my research in order to finish writing my dissertation. Toward the end of 2003, I left Athens for a transatlantic trip in order to attend a conference and later stop off at Harvard to meet with my advisers and arrange for my extended stay there during the upcoming Spring term. I was away for just three weeks, yet when I returned to Athens, I saw that much had changed. Something had happened in the meantime that had made the headlines in the newspapers and on TV and had become the topic all my friends and informants were talking about with great excitement: *Politiki Kouzina*. This was the title of a movie that I had been anticipating for some time. Written and directed by Tassos Boulmetis, an Istanbul-born Rum who came to Athens as a small child, the film was an autobiographical account reflecting on the life of Rum Polites who were expelled from Istanbul in 1964. The story was told as a tale involving not only partition, nostalgia, and sadness but also a great degree of humor, romance, and cooking—hence the name of the movie: *Istanbul Cuisine*.[10] This much I knew, because some of my informants had taken part in the making of the movie either as actors or as consultants. But what I did not know was what nobody expected: the movie was to become a blockbuster success, with about a million people going to the cinema to see it in the space of just two weeks. It was equally well-received by the art critics: *Politiki Kouzina* took eight awards, including for the best film and the best director, in Thessaloniki, the country's most important film festival. The soundtrack became one of those hits you could hear being played everywhere, from radio stations to shops and cafés. The international press also acknowledged the new craze in Greece, comparing the movie with the likes of *Zorba the Greek* and *My Big Fat Greek Wedding*.

By the time I was back in Athens, everybody had already seen the movie. "Have you seen the movie yet?" was the first sentence people would utter when I called them or met with them, sometimes even before they greeted me. Upon my negative reply, they would go on to tell me about the movie and advise me to go and see it immediately. There was no doubt that I was going to do so, but I decided to give it some time. That I had not seen the movie was giving people more incentive to give me feedback, to which I could listen at length without needing to voice my own opinion. This way, I managed to collect a range of very interesting reactions to the movie over a week's time. Almost everybody that I talked with showed great excitement and made positive remarks about the film. Those who had not known much about the Rum Polites became informed, and those who were familiar with the topic opined that it was a sensitive and balanced way of approaching a politically charged issue. Either way, many must have come to understand what an important yet neglected subject this was, as they declared that my work was going to be crucial—but that it was such a difficult task. I surely knew that, but hearing it from my own informants, including those who had so far not been convinced that research on the Rum Polites was worthwhile, made me all the more aware of it. I decided to go and see the movie on Wednesday.

That day I had a lunch appointment with a friend who was also a scholar and a key informant. He said that I had to have a full stomach because the cooking scenes in the movie were bound to make me hungry, so we went to a small restaurant that was run by Rum Polites, conveniently located near the theater where I was going to catch the movie. Over *yaprakia*, *keftedakia*, and *çerkez tavuğu*,[11] I told him about my trip to the USA, my conference, the feedback I got from my advisors. While we were having our *yoghourtlou*,[12] he told me his impressions of the movie, and how others around him reacted to it. During *ekmek*[13] we discussed some of my future projects for further research on the Rum Polites. I shared with him the growing sense of responsibility I was feeling while writing up the anecdotes I'd collected, knowing that this was to become the first ethnographic publication of its kind, with expectations having risen since the release of the movie made the Rum Polites into a matter of public debate in Greece. We were having Turkish coffee[14] when the owner of the restaurant came over and joined us, shifting the conversation from Politiki Kouzina to his own Istanbul cuisine in the restaurant and to a brief narrative of the years he spent in Istanbul. He did not know anything about either of us, the work we did, our background or interests. Still, he shared his memories freely and openly, and without making them into statements of any politically or even emotionally charged nature. What he told us entailed recollections of tragedy and suffering, but his laughing face indicated that he was more than at ease with remembering his past in Istanbul. When I later pointed this out to my friend, he asked me a rhetorical question, knowing that my answer would be positive: "But was this not what you've seen in everybody? Only the Greeks would make a fuss about these events, because they see things superficially and out of context. We are different, and you know that."

He was referring to the locals in Greece when he said "Greeks," that is, Yunanlılar or Elladites as opposed to Rum or Polites. Even if he was not using both of these sets of terms, I was certain of what he meant: he was continuously invoking such comparisons, frequently and on various occasions, but always at the expense of the former. His criticisms of "Greeks" in every aspect of life, ranging from their eating habits to their business ethics, could sometimes be so harsh that I would feel the need to talk down his judgments. But in this case, he was not overstating: my experiences with the Rum Polites had indeed shown me that they could approach their own tragedy with an unbiased disposition that would be surprising to many outside the community. My friend was suggesting that "Greeks" were among these outsiders, and I was worried that I could also be included in that category. Although he did not seem to imply this, pointing out that "we" as Polites were different, I was less than relieved with regard to my confusion about my position vis-à-vis the Rum Polites and their suffering.

Little did I know that during the next few hours this perplexity would further evolve into a total turmoil of emotions. For as much as I thought I knew what to expect from the movie, it turned out I was in for a surprise. It was an early afternoon showing, the theater was not full, and I was there by myself. So I took out my notepad, thinking I could scribble down some notes while watching. This did not happen. Instead, I burst into tears that lasted almost the entire duration of the movie. I had no way of guessing this was to come; I do not normally cry even when watching sentimental movies, and this one was not in that a category. Although it told the sad story of a forced displacement, which had tragic consequences for the people involved, the scenario was entirely enmeshed in the often humorous flow of everyday life, creating an enjoyable and even entertaining effect that caused the audience to break out laughing quite often. But then the next scene would be so delicately touching that I would start weeping again. I had entirely lost control.

My emotional state remained the same until hours after the film had finished, and I could not even ask myself why. Later I came to terms with it. It was a time when I was looking back on my fieldwork, trying to make sense of the varied stories I had collected, looking for the right way of handling the highly sensitive material. In the process I gave a lot of thought to where I would fit in all of this, not only in terms of my personal relationship with my informants but my position toward their stories. Analyzing them required a certain level of objectivity on my part; thus, I was trying to enforce some degree of disengagement on myself, since actual detachment did not seem to be an option for me. Yet there was always this question in my mind: How much could my informants resist thinking of me as yet another Turk, one of those who caused them to suffer? To what extent could I empathize with their suffering so that I could feel, and make them feel, that I understood them? If not, how could I responsibly represent their stories to others, how could my representation be valid? The lines uttered by the characters in the movie invoked memories of the words of my informants, reminded me of the weight of sharing the stories that always ended on a light note. I myself could not take them lightly, precisely because I was not from within the community, yet I had to approach them in a rational, unbiased, and balanced fashion, at least to the degree achieved by the movie that I had just seen. Seeing the movie right after the emotive discussion at lunch had further stirred up all my already entangled thoughts, so I had let go of my self-control and cried.

Two days later I met with another friend and informant for dinner, in yet another restaurant owned by Rum Polites. The unavoidable subject came soon enough, right after the arrival of our drinks. While I was mixing the *rakı* with water and ice in our tall glasses, she asked the question that she seemed to have been waiting for: "So? What did you think?" I told her that I liked the movie, but that I was not able to give a critical account of it, since I was very much touched by it. By way of an answer she told me that she also had cried a lot during the movie, so we started a detailed discussion on which parts affected us most. Then she paused for a moment and said: "But I don't understand. Why did *you* cry?"

Her emphasis was disheartening, although I knew that she did not want to intimidate me with it. But I was not to give in to my emotions once again; after all, I had spent the last two days thinking about that very question. So I told her that I did not understand it either, but maybe she could help me figure it out. Why would she not wonder why she herself cried? She was a young child in 1964, and nobody in her family was expelled as they all held Turkish passports. Moving to Athens was for her a voluntary decision that she took with her husband for better job prospects, and it was only after the loss of her father that her mother left Istanbul to join her in Athens. In short, she did not have any first-hand experience of the expulsions in 1964, nor did she personally suffer as a result of them, or any other atrocities for that matter. "But," she said, "many people I know did!" That makes two of us, I mused, but we stopped there, leaving the issue of suffering and identity unresolved, as the fish we'd ordered was approaching our table.

Our brief discussion left me even more baffled than before. When I shared this with another informant, she thought that it was very natural I had cried. "Of course, you are very involved by now!" (*Tabii, sen çok involvedsun artık*), she said, using the English word *involved* for emphasis. "We all cried," she added. This time my crying had worked as a means of inclusion; crying meant caring, and feeling the suffering. Rum Polites were more vulnerable than other people, and this particular friend judged that the level of my involvement allowed me to cross the border.

Stories of Involvement

During her fieldwork among the Bedouin, Lila Abu-Lughod (1986, 20–21) experiences a situation analogous to the one I described above. She finds herself crying aloud at a funeral in the village, unable to control her—perhaps previously stored—emotions that find an occasion to pour out, to the perplexity of her informants. Reflecting later on that situation, Abu-Lughod speculates on a number of reasons for her outburst, each of which is overshadowed by the outcome: the expression of the involvement of the ethnographer in cultural manifestations of sadness and empathy. In an ethnography that investigates the local ways of communicating and sharing sentiments, an emotive moment such as crying in public becomes an insightful opening into the central questions of boundary making and the position of the ethnographer vis-à-vis the community.

All anthropological studies pay attention to the relationship between the ethnographer and the informants, though for different reasons, and perhaps some more than others. The earlier ideals of a distant and objective observer position have been abandoned in favor of acknowledging and understanding the specific subjectivities that are intrinsic to the configuration of the connection between the ethnographer and the community, where the dimensions of selfhood in the former are linked to the questions of identity in the latter. In reflexive anthropology, the ethnographer is a "boundary-crosser" (Reed-Danahay 1997, 3), who, rather than engaging in some apolitical self-infliction, makes use of this ambivalent position of being an insider–outsider as an opening to a "radical consciousness of self in facing the political dimensions of fieldwork and constructing knowledge" (Okely and Callaway 1992, 33).

That cultural boundaries are sufficiently flexible as to render less than dichotomous the division between insiders and outsiders of the community is no longer a novel statement in anthropology today. But it should always be important to establish, ethnographically, which criteria are employed in the drawing of social boundaries and which cultural factors are used to determine what and who is to be considered an insider or an outsider, and why, how, and under which circumstances exceptions and modifications to these rules of conduct take place.

Studying a community that is not easily distinguished from the wider society through obvious or publicly accepted markers such as language, ethnicity, or religion, my attention inevitably turned to rather private and intimate areas when investigating the cultural identity of the Rum Polites. If practices of everyday life and cosmopolitan knowledge are the two pillars upholding the distinction of the Rum Polites, the third element contributing to their institution as a separate cultural entity, I wish to argue, is the way they approach their own suffering as a community.[15]

Given their troublesome past, Rum Polites have often been characterized as victims—of Turkish chauvinism, of Greek irredentism, of ultranationalism, of British interests in Cyprus, and of anything else, including their own vulnerability. They are portrayed as helpless bearers of human tragedy, with anonymous wrinkled faces of silence and misery that are transposed against pictures of violent gangs smashing windows during the Septemvriana. For the displaced part of the community in Greece, there is a popular saying similar to the description of the Asia Minor refugees as suffering from being "twice a stranger" (Clark 2006): there they called us *gavur*, here they call us *tourkospori* (Turkish seed). These representations of the Rum Polites may be the dominant theme in the mass media, coffee-table books, and website forums that seek to lobby for the survival of an endangered species.

But as we have seen above, this kind of "victimization" is not the way in which the Rum Polites choose to represent themselves. My intention in this chapter has been, in parallel, to point out the different ways used by the Rum Polites for approaching their own violent experiences in the past.

I have therefore tried to state the narrative of the past through the words of the Rum Polites, expressed orally or in writing, while paying attention to the particular effects that my presence might have on the specific versions of this narrative that may have been preferred over others. In doing that, I have been careful to take into account that the problem of representing suffering in proper language affects almost all social anthropology, not merely that which seeks to describe extremes of victimhood (Benthall 1997, 1). With my treatment of two events, the commemoration of Septemvriana and the screening of *Politiki Kouzina*, I intended to engage in the intricate dynamics within the community at different levels and different times with a living discourse that reflects upon the connection between events and experience (James 1997, 115).

The above analyses are aimed at showing that the right to suffering or the right to share suffering, in the case of Rum Polites, is not simply given on the premise of national or ethnic continuity. It might, however, be extended on the basis of another kind of origin, namely, that of the city. Originating in Istanbul brings those who live far away from it together in the diaspora of the City. In a community that makes longing for the city into a strong dimension of belonging, the forced distance from home becomes the most salient kind of suffering. This experience of the painful present is one that distances past resentments, as distance from the city becomes a means of coming closer to those who would otherwise be considered others. That the Rum Polites acknowledge the experience of displacement to be an experience of intense suffering, whether the reasons for it are voluntary or enforced, indicates the dual importance of my being an Istanbulite as well: not only has it been important during my fieldwork in shaping the ways in which I communicated with my informants, it has also been significant as providing a mutual basis for the pain of partition that defined our common identity as Istanbulites abroad. Whether that eventually enabled me to cross the line delineating insiders from outsiders, or not, I feel that it helped me to see better the porous boundaries around the community of Rum Polites.

Historical representations, as cultural productions, provide the means through which persons live the boundaries between themselves and those identified as others, so that socially marked others can be embraced to be incorporated into "us" (Holland and Lave 2001, 14). In the next chapter, I show that the presentation of Istanbul as a historical cosmopolitan center provides its past and present inhabitants with a discourse that enables the construction of an "us" as an identity of Istanbulites, one that remains exclusive to those who have a right to the city. This right to the city is not transferable by religion or ethnicity; for the Rum Polites, the Elladites, Mikrasiates, or villagers are others to Istanbul, regardless of whether or not they had comparable cases of traumatic memories of a homeland far away. It is the pain of longing for a lost Istanbul that unites those living far away from the City. In this sense, the diaspora of Istanbul is as open to diversity as the city itself, and those who have a right to the City may have the right to suffer in the way that the Rum Polites do.

Notes

1. For critical readings of Greek nationalist history with its anti-Turkish dimensions, and vice versa, see Theodossopoulos (2003, 36), Herzfeld (1985, 19), Brown and Hamilakis (2003), Millas (2001), Dragonas et al. (2005), Özsüer (2012, 2015), and Fortna et al. (2013).
2. "It's a story that sooner or later I'll also end up telling, but in the midst of all the others,

    not giving more importance to one than to another, not putting any special passion into it beyond the pleasure of narrating and remembering, because even remembering evil can be a pleasure when the evil is mixed, I won't say with good, but with variety, the volatile, the changeable, in other words with what I can also call good, which is the pleasure of seeing things from a distance and narrating them as what is past."

    Italo Calvino, *If on a Winter's Night a Traveler*, Harcourt Brace & Company, 1981.

3. Forced conscription of 1941–1942: In the name of national security, all non-Muslim men between the ages of 20 and 45 were drafted into the Turkish army's nonmilitary services (*amele taburu*) with a decree published on 8 May 1941, which was implemented with immediate effect and without any regard for their personal situation. See Bali (2008) and Göçek (2016, 322).
4. Zografyon Lycee for Boys, located in Pera, publishes its student enrollment statistics on its website http://www.zografyon.k12.tr. There were around 550 students registered in the year 1955–1956, a number that kept increasing steadily until it passed 700 by 1960. The fall recorded after the 1964 expulsions is the most drastic: from over 650 in 1964–1965, only 500 came back to school in 1965–1966. Also see Alexandris (1983, 326–31).
5. On the fiftieth anniversary of the 1964 expulsions, a number of academic events took place in Turkey and Greece, including an exhibit entitled "20

Dolar, 20 Kilo" by the Babil Association (http://www.babilder.org/wp-content/uploads/2015/10/KatalogTR_internet.pdf), and an international conference that took place from 30 October to 1 November 2014 at Istanbul Bilgi University (http://www.bilgi.edu.tr/en/news-and-events/news/4192/1964-expulsions-and-the-istanbul-rum/), which were covered in various sources including a dedicated issue of *Altüst* (http://www.altust.org/2014/05/12incisayicikti), as well as a forthcoming volume (Örs et al. 2018).

6. On the fiftieth anniversary of the Septemvriana, a photo exhibit took place in Istanbul, which was vandalized by members of ultranationalist groups (*Zaman*, 7 September 2005). The photos and the documents exhibited were published by the History Foundation (2005).
7. *Omoyenia* is used here to refer to the Greek Orthodox community in Istanbul.
8. *Kapıcı* (doorman, janitor) acquires an -s in order to resemble a masculine noun in Greek. *Hikaye* (story, anecdote) follows the same pattern to become *hikayes* and then gets pluralized as *hikayedes*, here used to mean implausible tales with little, if any, truth value.
9. For comparative ethnographic cases on social dimensions of suffering, see Kleinman et al. (1997).
10. This would be the meaning closest to the words Politiki Kouzina, but it was not translated as such. The English title of the movie is "A Touch of Spice," which was taken as a basis for the Turkish title as well: "Bir Tutam Baharat." Despite much anticipation voiced in the press, the planned showing of the movie in Turkish theaters never took place except for a few private screenings.
11. Starter (*meze*) dishes from the Istanbul cuisine: meatballs, stuffed vine leaves, chicken with walnut cream.
12. A special kind of kebap from the Bursa region, made with thin slices of meat placed over pita bread and served with tomato sauce and yoghurt.
13. A special kind of dessert that is known as *ekmek kadayıfı* in Turkish. When the dessert came to Greece with the Asia Minor refugees, the name was shortened to just *ekmek* (bread). In fact, this specifies what kind of *kadayıfı* it is, as the texture of this dessert resembles that of bread. There is a trend of dropping the second word from dual combinations when Turkish food names are used in Greece, where the remaining word is usually just the adjective. Other examples are *yogourtlou* (*kebap*) seen above and *peynirli* (*pide*), where a certain kind of pita bread is known as "with cheese" throughout Greece, even though it might not have cheese inside.
14. What is called Turkish coffee throughout Turkey and parts of the Balkans and the Middle East was renamed in Greece as Greek coffee through a nationalistic campaign in the aftermath of the 1974 invasion of Northern

Cyprus by the Turkish army. Many Rum Polites (and a few Greeks still) prefer to call the coffee Turkish, however, whether because this is what they are accustomed to calling it, or in reaction to the reasons for the name change. Some reconciliatory attempts to rename it Byzantine—somewhere in the middle, as it were—can be dismissed as misguided because coffee was not consumed as a drink until after the Eastern Rome disintegrated. It became popular in the Ottoman Empire during the sixteenth century (Hattox 1985).

15. For a discussion of competitive suffering in Greece, see Dubish (1995).

Bibliography

Abu-Lughod, L. (1986). *Veiled Sentiments: Honor and Poetry in a Bedouin Society*. Berkeley: University of California Press.
Akar, R. (2006). *Aşkale Yolcuları: Varlık Vergisi Ve Çalışma Kampları*. İstanbul: Mephisto Yayınları.
Aktar, A. (2000). *Varlık Vergisi Ve "Türkleştirme" Politikaları*. İstanbul: İletişim Yayınları.
Aktar, A., Hacıdimitriadis, Y., & Kandemir, F. (2011). *Yorgo Hacıdimitriadis'in Aşkale-Erzurum Günlüğü, 1943*. İstanbul: İletisim Yayınları.
Alexandris, A. (1983). *The Greek Minority of Istanbul and Greek-Turkish Relations, 1918–1974*. Athens: Center for Asia Minor Studies.
Appadurai, A. (1981). The Past as a Scarce Resource. *Man, 16*(2), 201.
Aretxaga, B. (1997). *Shattering Silence: Women, Nationalism, and Political Subjectivity in Northern Ireland*. Princeton, NJ: Princeton University Press.
Bali, R. (2008). *II. Dünya Savaşında Gayrimüslimlerin Askerlik Serüveni: Yirmi Kur'a Nafıa Askerleri*. İstanbul: Kitabevi.
Benthall, J. (1997). Speaking of Suffering. *Anthropology Today, 13*(3), 1–2.
Boulmetis, T. (2004). *Politiki Kouzina*. Athens: Ellinika Grammata.
Brown, K. S., & Hamilakis, Y. (2003). *The Usable Past: Greek Metahistories*. Lanham, MD: Lexington Books.
Christidis, C. (2000). *Ta Septemvriana*. Athens: Kentro Mikrasiastikon Spoudon.
Clark, B. (2006). *Twice a Stranger: The Mass Expulsions That Forged Modern Greece and Turkey*. Cambridge, MA: Harvard University Press.
Das, V. (1995). *Critical Events: An Anthropological Perspective on Contemporary India*. Delhi: Oxford University Press.
Demir, H., & Akar, R. (1994). *İstanbul'un Son Sürgünleri*. İstanbul: İletişim.
Dragonas, T., Ersanli, B., & Frangoudaki, A. (2005). Greek and Turkish Students' Views on History, the Nation and Democracy. In T. G. Dragonas & F. Birtek (Eds.), *Citizenship and the Nation-State in Greece and Turkey* (pp. 161–189). London: Routledge.

Dubish, J. (1995). *In a Different Place: Pilgrimage, Gender, and Politics of a Greek Island Shrine*. Princeton, NJ: Princeton University Press.
Fortna, B. C., Katsikas, S., Kamouzis, D., & Konortas, P. (2013). *State-Nationalisms in the Ottoman Empire, Greece and Turkey: Orthodox and Muslims, 1830–1945*. London: Routledge.
Göçek, F. M. (2016). *Denial of Violence: Ottoman Past, Turkish Present, and Collective Violence against the Armenians, 1789–2009*. Oxford: Oxford University Press.
Hattox, R. S. (1985). *Coffee and Coffeehouses: The Origins of a Social Beverage in the Medieval Near East*. Seattle: Distributed by University of Washington Press.
Herzfeld, M. (1985). *The Poetics of Manhood: Contest and Identity in a Cretan Mountain Village*. Princeton, NJ: Princeton University Press.
Holland, D. C., & Lave, J. (2001). *History in Person: Enduring Struggles, Contentious Practice, Intimate Identities*. Santa Fe, NM: School of American Research Press.
James, W. (1997). The Names of Fear: Memory, History, and the Ethnography of Feeling among Uduk Refugees. *Journal of Royal Anthropological Institute, 3*, 115–131.
Kleinman, A., Das, V., & Lock, M. M. (1997). *Social Suffering*. Berkeley: University of California Press.
Konstantinou-Kloukina, A. (2003). *Opou lipon… mia fora kai enan kairo stin Poli, 1949–1958*. Athens: Ikaros.
Lowenthal, D. (1985). *The Past Is a Foreign Country*. Cambridge: Cambridge University Press.
Markaris, P. (2002). Introduction. In N. Valasiadis (Ed.), *Kai sta Tatavla Hioni*. Athens: Ekdoseis Gavrilidis.
Millas, I. (2001). *Eikones Ellinon Kai Tourkon Scholika Vivlia, Istoriografia, Logotechnia Kai Ethnika Stereotypa*. Athina: Ekdoseis Alexandreia.
Moore, S. F. (1987). Explaining the Present: Theoretical Dilemmas in Processual Ethnography. *American Ethnologist, 14*(4), 727–736.
Okely, J., & Callaway, H. (1992). *Anthropology and Autobiography*. London: Routledge.
Ökte, F. (1951). *Varlık Vergisi Faciası*. İstanbul: Nebioğlu Yayınevi.
Örs, I. R. (2006). Beyond the Greek and Turkish Dichotomy: The Rum Polites of Istanbul and Athens. *South European Society and Politics, 11*(1), 79–94. https://doi.org/10.1080/13608740500470349.
Örs, İ. R. (2018). Introduction. In İ. R. Örs, S. Akgonul, C. Aktar, & E. Macar (Eds.), *1964 Expulsions: A Turning Point in the Homogenization of Turkish Society*. Istanbul: Istanbul Bilgi University Press.
Özsüer, E. (2012). Türk-Yunan İlişkilerinde "Biz" ve "Öteki" Önyargılarının Dinamikleri. *Avrasya İncelemeleri Dergisi, I*(2), 269–309.

Özsüer, E. (2015). The "Other" Face of History: Re-comprehending History in the Example of Turkey and Greece. *Turkish History Education Journal, 4*(2), 165–201.

Reed-Danahay, D. (1997). *Auto/Ethnography: Rewriting the Self and the Social.* Oxford: Berg.

Stamatopoulos, K. (1996). *H Teleftaia Analampi: H Konstantinoupolitiki Romiossioni sta Chronia 1948–1955.* Athina: Ekdoseis Domos.

Theodossopoulos, D. (2003). Degrading Others and Honouring Ourselves: Ethnic Stereotypes as Categories and as Explanations. *Journal of Mediterranean Studies, 13*(2), 177–188.

Tsilenis, S. (2002). Oramata Panselinou. *Kinsterna, 1–2,* 17.

Tsoukatou, E. (1999). *H "nihta ton kristallon" tou Ellinismou tis Polis.* Athens: Tsoukatou.

Valasiadis, N. (2002). *Kai sta Tatavla Hioni.* Athens: Ekdoseis Gavrilidis.

Volovonis, N. (1988). *Ithele na Ziso. Tourkoi, 1922–1945: Varvaroi olon ton Epochon.* Athens.

CHAPTER 5

Capital of Memory: Cosmopolitanist Nostalgia in Istanbul

The city is as real as it is imagined. Rooted presence for many generations, rendered absent by the roughness of displacement, becomes a memory cast in stone with an invisible ink. The inaccuracy of descriptions falls unnoticed; images are overwritten as nicer photos get taken. The tense impressions on grandparents' faces become smoother as the family pictures fade. The bitter incidents of yesterday become sweet memories of the present. Nostalgia is not what it used to be, as the common saying goes, and neither is the city.

The city of nostalgia is marketed first to those who imagine it because they do not know it. Popular, commercial images circulate in Greece to cater to their romantic appetite for a lost but redeemable, otherized but not yet so distant homeland. The city of their desires, dreams, and fears shows up on the cover of novels, front pages of magazines, cinema posters, elevator tunes, travel agency brochures. Turn the pages of *Donna* (2003), a women's lifestyle magazine, and find the article written by Katerina Koliou, calling readers to "enjoy a spring getaway to the city of contrasts, where the cosmopolitan atmosphere breathes in the exhilarating scents of the East!" Or buy the daily *To Vima* of 23 April 2003, together with the free *National Geographic* issue from May 1915, featuring a cover story dedicated to Istanbul. Note that this differs from what Donna Haraway (1989, 267) calls a colonial–national aesthetic established by *National Geographic*, where romantic accounts of the past have

© The Author(s) 2018
İ.R. Örs, *Diaspora of the City*, Palgrave Studies in Urban Anthropology, https://doi.org/10.1057/978-1-137-55486-4_5

171

usually been toward the pastoral, traditional, countryside, natural world. Do not be surprised that the first of the series, as with subsequent issues, is concentrated in historical nostalgic representations of urban centers. Learn from author Edwin A. Grosvenor that the "magical" word Constantinople is synonymous with a mixture of ethnicities and an encounter of religions, that "it is cosmopolitan, more than any other capital of humanity, at present but also in the past," and that "if you are resident in this city, four languages are just about enough to get by." Be relieved to find out that one of these is Greek. Compare this to another article, among many others, published in the *GEO* magazine of the newspaper *Eleftherotipia* (15 September 2001). Read: "Polis, our soul—a landmark of the visible and invisible: soaked in the humidity of time and its wrinkles that furrow her face. A bridge that connects us to the past, the umbilical cord to uneven knowledge, a marginal balance among reality, nostalgia, and fantasy."

Then leave Greece for Istanbul, to listen to the voices from within. Hear how people talk about a city that they know, yet no longer recognize. Watch how they look at buildings or entire districts now and imagine their old versions, notice how they transform the current to comply with the images of the old. Read the books they write on how it was, and what has since changed. Mind the gap between now and then, feel the void of reasoning explaining the loss. Do not ask how it all disappeared.

Relive the Istanbulite *belle époque*, pick any date, say, from the 1880s to the 1960s. Be part of the urban society in peaceful, respectful, civilized, multicultural coexistence. Live in a world capital, the biggest and most important city of the region, then as always during its uninterrupted one and a half millennia. Become a member of the Ottoman merchant class, the new bourgeoisie, or the Europeanized upper classes. Don't forget to wear your hat, straighten your tie, and shine your shoes when walking along the *Grand Rue de Pera* on your way from your home in Cihangir to the tango night in Pera Palas, with customary stops at the patisserie-cafés scattered along the tram-lined street.

You may have any cultural background you like, but make sure you interact with those who are not your kind. Remember you live in a city that is the center of attraction for people and products, ideas, and lifestyles. Feel privileged in having everything at your disposal: the best of East and West come together in this hub via the trade routes and are added to the wonderful local resources. Cherish the waters, trees, fish, strawberries, and artichokes of Istanbul, the likes of which are to be found nowhere. Or no longer. Miss the taste of fruits you never had, look for the springs that have long become contaminated.

Forget that this is the time of regional and continental wars, bloody revolutions and even bloodier repressions, forced migrations, expulsions, capitulations, dissolutions, massacres, poverty, discriminations, catastrophe, and all sorts of human suffering. Never mind the reasons that brought the influx of people to the city, just celebrate diversity. Buy milk from the Bulgarian milkman, liver from the Albanian vendor, have these carried home by the Kurdish hamal, and go to *Rejans* to taste the yellow vodka prepared by the Russian waitress who actually is a princess in exile.

Now wake up. Realize that what you see today is different from what you imagine. Look for people, find out that the population of the city has grown more than tenfold since then. Listen to their languages ... hear only one: Turkish, albeit with many accents. You have to go to some run-down parts of the city to hear Kurdish, Arabic, or, these days, Russian spoken by a new wave of immigrants involved in suitcase trade. The patisseries have closed down, replaced by lahmacun-cafés, and you hate that smell. You prefer the new venues that are remakes of old establishments. You go to *Pano's* wine shop, even though it is no longer owned by a Rum but a man from Anatolia, or to the recently restored *Markiz*, although it is now more like a nightclub for youth and has lost the Parisian chic atmosphere that used to prevail.

You cannot hear Greek; you would not know where it would be spoken except in your imagination. You are not even sure you would not confuse it with Italian or Spanish for the sound of it. Of course, you recognize it from the songs of Angela Dimitriou and Sakis Rouvas, which you hear being played as background music in supermarkets, shopping centers, "traditional" Rum tavernas where you can dance on the table and break plates "like the Greeks do." You decide to visit Greece for the first time. Their ouzo is just like rakı, after all, they also drink Turkish coffee. We are so much alike, you think, Greeks and Turks. Really, why did the Rum *leave* Istanbul to *return* to Greece?

Read:
> Gustave Flaubert, who visited Istanbul 102 years before my birth, was struck by the variety of life in its teeming streets; in one of his letters he predicted that in a century's time it would be the capital of the world.
> The reverse came true:
> After the Ottoman Empire collapsed, the world almost forgot that Istanbul existed.

> The city into which I was born was poorer, shabbier, and more isolated than it had ever been before in its two-thousand-year history. For me it has always been a city of ruins and of end-of-empire melancholy.

These lines were written by Orhan Pamuk, the most internationally acclaimed author of contemporary Turkey and the 2006 Nobel Laureate in Literature. They are taken from his book *Istanbul: Memories and the City* (2003). Primarily a novelist, with *Istanbul* Pamuk joined the ranks of authors who have some personalized words to say about their city. His autobiography also contributed to the ever-increasing literature on Istanbul in which the city appears as more than just the setting or the context but features as the main protagonist, a text to be written and to be read. Pamuk in fact borrowed words from other writers to describe his city, to decipher its text: Westerners such as Nerval, Gautier, and Flaubert are woven together in Pamuk's narrative with Turkish masters like Tanpınar, Koçu, and Yahya Kemal.

Selim İleri, another bestselling author, also wrote some of his many books as both a memoir and a literature review of Istanbul. Comparing works of prose and poetry across generations, he shared the feelings of nostalgia and melancholy imparted by Pamuk. "It is almost impossible today to get hold of that Istanbul," he wrote in his *Istanbul Hatıralar Kolonyası* (2006): the "Istanbul we lost took its strength from its cosmopolitanism. Cosmopolitanism pointed to the variety of all kinds and details in that Istanbul; to the coexistence of history, of the present, and of tomorrow. East and West belonged to Istanbul. And now?"

Now is the time for "cosmopolitanist nostalgia," a generic term used here to denote the wide array of past-oriented discourses preoccupied with describing Istanbul as a cosmopolitan city. The authors describing old Istanbul converge on the point that this was a world city of amazing multicultural delights and tend to note regretfully its presumed loss. To paraphrase Fine, who states that "we do not live in a cosmopolitan age, but we live in an age of cosmopolitanism" (2008, 19), Istanbul as represented in this nostalgia literature may not be living its cosmopolitan age at present, but through an abundance of the very nostalgic narratives related to its past and visions for its future, the city might well be said to be in an age of cosmopolitanism. Novels, articles, movies, television series, and exhibits seeking to demonstrate the cosmopolitan character of old Istanbul follow each other in swift succession. These paint a nostalgically constructed picture of the city from the gaze of locals and travelers, making the "multicultural" a dominant theme in post-1980 Turkish literature and public intellectual discourses (Dufft 2009; see also Millas 2006, 2011). Most major publishing houses now have special series about Istanbul, where they bring out polished versions of earlier works from dusty archives, such as Sadri Sema's *Eski İstanbul'dan Hatıralar* (Memories from Old Istanbul), originally published in *Vatan* newspaper in 1952 (1994 [1991]) or the translation of the *Unveiled Women of Stamboul* by Demetra Vaka (2003 [1923]), or encourage new writers to focus on the urban social fabric of Istanbul. Some of these are harsh criticisms directed at the massive destruction that the city underwent as a result of national and municipal policies of developmentalism, but many authors choose to describe an idealized image of a much loved but long lost Istanbul they claim to remember well. Specific focus on neighborhoods with a multicultural past gives rise to a number of monographs, including but not restricted to Galata and Pera (Akın 1998), Büyükada (Tanrıverdi 2003), Balat (Deleon 2004), Tatavla and environs (Yentürk 2001), and a series written by Orhan Türker and published by Sel Yayıncılık on Galata/Karaköy (2000), Pera/Beyoğlu (2016), Tatavla/Kurtuluş (2010a), Psomatia/Samatya (2010b), Mega Revma/Arnavutköy (1999), Fanari/Fener (2001), Halkidona/Kadıköy (2008), Therapia/Tarabya (2006), Nihori/Yeniköy (2004a), Prinkipo/Büyükada (2004b), Antigoni/Burgaz (2007), and Halki/Heybeli (2003).

Note that the old names of these neighborhoods are in Greek, because these are areas that were dominated by a Rum population. In fact, the Rum Polites play an important role in this nostalgic literature about the cosmopolitan old Istanbul. They usually feature the well-dressed *madame*, the polite *monsieur*, hatmakers, florists, patisserie owners, rich bankers, jewelers, friends, and neighbors who were good cooks and spoke Turkish fluently albeit with a charming accent—but this remains just about all of what the reader may find out about the Rum Polites of Istanbul. An excerpt from a short story by Leyla Erbil illustrates this point well: Erbil travels back in time in Istanbul and visits her once favorite Patisserie Trianon in Pera, owned by a Rum couple, whose names she does not know. "*Rumca*" (Rum language), she writes, "constituted a light, sweet background poem in Trianon during all the time we spent in that patisserie. Those days the city was anyway a poetic city laced with the mixture of our voices with theirs" (2000, 14). She speculates that it must have been because of the 6–7 September events and the resulting destruction of

Istanbul and Pera that the couple ran away. Erbil confesses to be puzzled as to why she would miss, after all these years, "a crazy couple who kept talking with a language, a culture, which I did not know or understand at all" (ibid., 15).

In powerfully expressing her mixed emotions of longing for a past she barely knew, Erbil in fact summarizes a stance widely held stance throughout the entire literature toward the Rum Polites, namely, the tendency to portray them as the major figures in the cosmopolitan fabric of urban life, a *Leitmotif* of a shapeless kind. The Rum Polites are the nameless protagonists in the stories about old Istanbul; they are the people who disappear from a story that finishes without anybody knowing the end. If cosmopolitan Istanbul is a fairy tale that is no more, than the Rum are the absent protagonists embodying the very story of its disappearance.

Often reduced to the sweet notes of a background symphony, or the colors of an urban mosaic, the Rum of Istanbul remain an overrepresented yet understudied community in Turkish popular literature. Despite growing research on the lost Ottoman cosmopolitanism (Hanley 2008; Coller 2011; Nelson 2007; Freitag 2014), the Rum Polites, along with other minority communities, are remembered only as part of what is forgotten in Turkish social memory.[1]

Defending cosmopolitanist nostalgia against calls by scholars for its dismissal is necessary to be able to recognize it as a potential source of ethnographic information on public and private expressions of historical identification. If nostalgic discourses point to the question of whether or not there is a cosmopolitan moment in Istanbul now, then this must form the starting point of a research agenda that investigates under what conditions, subject to what limits, and by which actors cosmopolitanism appears (Beck and Sznaider 2006). It is my conviction that a concept like cosmopolitanism, which by definition involves plurality and diversity, can be expected to have a multiplicity of changing meanings with respect to different social groups, time frames, or spatial and political contexts. Here my aim is to unlock some of these meanings of cosmopolitanism as they appear in the nostalgic discourses by contextualizing the Istanbul cosmopolitan in its various manifestations.

In the following, I start with a critical analysis of cosmopolitanist nostalgia in contemporary Istanbul, juxtaposing different perspectives in a contested manner as each position seeks to describe its own version of the city's history with a vision toward its projected future. Some of these visions are utilized for commercial or political purposes of developing or branding Istanbul in certain ways, while some others are facilitators for forging a resistance against policies and practices that lead to the destruction of present riches and potential restoration of the city to its idealized image in the past. This constantly changing debate takes place in an increasingly controversial and conflicted public space, where competing notions of cosmopolitanism partake in challenging questions regarding the identity of the city. The Rum Polites play a pivotal role as both protagonists and as participants, which renders their overdue inclusion an essential contribution in these conversations.

Criticizing Nostalgic Stories

In *Traveling Cultures*, James Clifford talks about rewriting Paris in the period of 1920s and 1930s through a set of travel encounters that portray the city as "a place of departures, arrivals, transits" (1997, 90). In fact, many great urban centers could be understood as specific, powerful sites of dwelling or traveling, and their literary and historical representation could be made possible through "working with intersecting *histories*—discrepant detours and returns" (ibid., 104).

Istanbul is one such city that has attracted travelers, nomads, refugees, and immigrants from all walks of life, for various reasons, continuously over a couple of thousand years. Regardless of whether they settled down or eventually left, Istanbul has always been more than just another point of passage for travelers worldwide. These travelers resemble the cosmopolitans who were often utilized as central figures in narratives in eighteenth- and nineteenth-century romantic novels, where cosmopolitanism appears as something grounded in the local, the particular (Wohlgemut 2009).

One of the main criticisms directed against cosmopolitanist nostalgia concerns its non-referential nature: the public nostalgic discourses in Istanbul rarely specify what exactly they romanticize. Their sense of loss upon which nostalgia is based, as Boym (2007) maintains, is not properly remembered, nor does one necessarily know where to look for what is lost. They display what Kendall et al. (2009) call a "sampling style of cosmopolitanism," one that remains on the surface, that is witnessed in passing, almost in accidental fashion. Such an experience of cosmopolitanist outlook "implies engagement and contact, but only as a form of temporary, fleeting connection" (ibid., 115). This style points to a brittle form of engagement, a weak form of cosmopolitanism that may easily be abandoned when people feel threatened in terms of their selfhood, socioeconomic or political position, or security (ibid., 118).

Nostalgic accounts mostly remain both apersonal and ahistorical: they do not offer an indication as to when and where in Istanbul cosmopolitan culture prevailed, what kind of cosmopolitanism Istanbul used to have, who the cosmopolitans were, and how they disappeared. This non-referential nostalgia, although cosmopolitanist, leaves many questions regarding the very nature of cosmopolitanism unanswered. If, for example, there was such a recognized, celebrated, quintessentialized level of cosmopolitanism reigning in Istanbul until recently, how did it give rise to its own dissolution, to the tragic destruction of the very cosmopolitan order it endorsed? How within such a cosmopolitanist landscape could a pogrom like that of 6–7 September 1955 take place? How could large amounts of wealth be seized from minorities by the force of law? How could a campaign that promotes the sole use of the Turkish language in public prevail for years in the multilingual environment of cosmopolitan Istanbul?

In cosmopolitanist nostalgia such questions remain largely uninvestigated, absent, or lost—like the cosmopolitans themselves. Cosmopolitanist nostalgia is apersonal because, in spite of the popularity of the nostalgic discourses—or perhaps because of them—there is little effort made toward understanding the subjectivities involved in the loss of pluralism. Minorities are presented as remnants of the past, but paradoxically remain "both ubiquitous and unacknowledged, both remembered nostalgically and rejected ideologically" (Mills et al. 2011, 135). The city is pictured, as Roland Barthes would have it, as "a place of our meeting with the other" (1981, 96), yet the faces or stories of these others are rarely heard. Relatively few people ask the questions of *who* and *why* regarding the claimed disappearance of the cosmopolitan fabric and, more specifically, of the Rum Polites community. What happened to the Rum Polites and others who made the place so cosmopolitan remains mysterious to the bearers of nostalgia. It is as if one day people saw that the Rum shops and patisseries were closed down. The Rum Polites had left all of a sudden, without telling anyone about it. Nobody understood how; they never found out where they had gone. The old Istanbul was a fairy tale, and the princess had disappeared.

In the case of Rum Polites, the discourse that puts them in the center of a cosmopolitan picture of Istanbul is one that seeks to evoke some feeling of sympathy, as toward an endangered flower species. Reacting to those in Turkey who see them as a color contributing to the multicultural decoration of the city, the Rum Polites say that they resent being objectified, as if they were "a vase or a decorative item" (*sanki bir vazo, bir süsmüşüz gibi*), being reduced to a mechanical or abstract role they are made to play, an empty place they have to fill in the cultural rainbow of Istanbul. This popular idea of "minorities as the disappearing colors" (Kırca 2000) is met with ironical critique by non-Muslim intellectuals in Turkey today: Roni Margulies (2009) thanks the elites for their benevolence; Rıfat Bali (2002) criticizes narratives that talk about a sudden loss as if Istanbul's cosmopolitan fabric just evaporated; Mario Levi (1999) finds that the minorities are "not more than symbols" in this sentimental picture. As Cohen (1985) reminds us, in our everyday discourse, the past, itself symbolic, is recalled to us symbolically. While the image of Rum Polites serves to express symbolically a cosmopolitan past, it also acts as an indicator of the discontinuity of past and present.

Within these nostalgic discourses, the kind of Istanbulite cosmopolitanism that is described is quintessentialist in the sense that no conditions are deemed necessary to claim its existence; it is taken for granted, unconditionally accepted as a given. What we are confronted with is an idealized image of social harmony within an ageless multiculturalist urban system, which is not much criticized with regard to its limits. This is evident in popular discourses that display what could be called a showcase cosmopolitanism, detected from the everyday life on the streets of the city. The sociological gaze typically remains limited to a quick look at pedestrians: their dress, language, and gestures appearing suggestive of different class, ethnic, and religious backgrounds, all of which is indexed to an essentialized Istanbulite cosmopolitanism. Accounts of well-known orientalists or travelers, for example, operate at this level: the letters of Lady Montagu or the memoirs of Pierre Loti and Nerval all bear witness to the anonymous multiculturality of the boulevards of Istanbul. Like these travelers, many of the supporters of popular nostalgia engage in what Fish (1997) calls "boutique multiculturalism," characterized by a superficial and cosmetic appreciation or sympathy toward different traditions and cultures than their own.

Another major critique directed against cosmopolitanist nostalgia is that it is ahistorical, or not a reliable source of information about the past. The historical validity of these discourses cannot be questioned against historians' accounts, because such discourses tend to lump together different periods (Byzantine, Venetian, Ottoman, and early Republican) without much regard to the different modalities of cultural mix. Statements are also rarely verified in light of primary data like statistics or archival evidence that could offer concrete criteria for cosmopolitanism. Without any definition of the concept or determination of its pointers, claims about the cosmopolitanness of Istanbul become only as valid as those that contend otherwise.

On the other hand, it can also be argued that narratives of nostalgia and cosmopolitanist discourses do not need to be (and often do not claim to be) authoritative sources of accurate factual information about the past. While nostalgia has been regarded as "dangerous misuse of history trading on conveniently reassuring images of the past, thereby suppressing both its variety and its negative aspects" (Shaw and Chase 1989, 1), contemporary anthropologists are analyzing nostalgia as affect, discourse, or cultural practice that mediates collective identities (Bissell 2005; Bryant 2008), or as a critique of the present (Parla 2009). For an analysis of nostalgic discourses taken as ethnographic sources, the question of whether the past they depict was truly cosmopolitan or not is somewhat redundant. If we agree with Kathleen Stewart that "nostalgia is a cultural practice, not a given content" (1998, 227), then we can admit that the forms, meanings, and effects of nostalgia shift with the context. Nostalgia, as a way of representing the past for purposes of identification, is not so much about validity as it is about identity.

Identifying Nostalgic Stories

The questions that have to be asked and answered, therefore, must be contextual: To what extent are these nostalgic representations contemporary, that is, shaped and conditioned by the present? What is relevant within the current sociopolitical context that explains the popularity of cosmopolitanist nostalgia in Istanbul at the turn of the twenty-first century? Nostalgic representations of a cosmopolitan past in Istanbul indicate that a certain historical legacy is used to sustain the present in Turkey. Should we then not ask, as Michael Herzfeld did with regard to modern Hellenism (1987, 5), *why* bearers of nostalgia should find it necessary to appeal to the past in this way? One can multiply these questions asked by Ange and Berliner (2015, 8) in relation to the cosmopolitanist nostalgia in Istanbul: Who is participating in these discursive practices and with what kinds of motivation? What and whose purposes does it serve to claim that Istanbul was once a major multicultural urban center? What is the significance of yearning for a certain mode of history today? Why the insistence on the loss of cosmopolitanism in Istanbul now?

According to Rıfat Bali (1999), the largest group of bearers of cosmopolitanist nostalgia are the urban elite since the late 1980s. This group—composed of well-educated, secular, left-leaning democrats—started rediscovering the disappearing faces of their city while forging an increasing affinity with the city's multicultural social and physical heritage that was seen to be suffering due to the multiple perils of state-led Turkification and rent–profit commercialization, as well as rural–urban migration. This elite fosters a city identity or an Istanbulite consciousness that is based on the belief that old, cosmopolitan Istanbul was a much more refined and civilized, bearing elements urbane, cultured, cosmopolitan, European, and modern "civilization." Paradoxically enough, those civilized elements that are recognized today to have been embodied by the then prominent non-Muslims segments of urban society, are the same minorities that were regarded by the elites of the last generation to be threats to the ideals of the Republic that foresaw a similar style of Western civilization for Turkish society.

This discourse of cosmopolitanism as multiethnic coexistence coincided with the image chosen to represent Istanbul in international platforms. One such occasion was when Istanbul became the 2010 European Capital of Culture, a title granted by the European Union. A leading figure in this endeavor, Cengiz Aktar, summarized the relevance of Istanbul's legacy in an article titled "*Cosmopolist*" published in the journal *Istanbul*. After noting that the negative imaging of the Turk as the Muslim, the Oriental, and the barbarian has been internalized in the European subconscious, Aktar suggested that this could be changed through a focus on Istanbul (Aktar 2002, 52):

> Ever since its foundation, Cosmopolist Istanbul has been a city that bore different cultures, religions, and languages, which has always been able to synthesize them. In this synthesis no element has been regarded to be more superior to the other and political or administrative authorities have been able to keep the same distance toward all of them. This is some kind of pre-secular secularism. As the capital of classical and multiethnic empires, Istanbul is a city that absorbed this quality, politically and culturally. The institutional memory of this quality is present in this city.

In this passage, cosmopolitanism is clearly taken to be a sign of a capacity to be European, modern, and "civilized." While bringing Turkey closer to the West in this way, this view also suggests that the EU, because it is built on multicultural premises, must acknowledge the extraordinary cosmopolitan heritage of Istanbul and thus embrace the Turks as Europeans.

Major international events such as the 2010 European Capital of Culture, the Olympic Games, or the Istanbul Biennale thus serve as venues for what has been named as "palimpsestation" of the city or the museumization of a multicultural urban culture (Iğsız 2015; Göktürk et al. 2010; Gürsel 2012). This comes with the premise that branding Istanbul as a cosmopolitan center would prove Turkey's ability to acknowledge and embrace internal diversity and to conform to EU standards by displaying European civility.

A related development where a European-oriented international outlook is observable is in Turkey–Greece relations, which entered an era of rapprochement in 1999. This coincided with a period of increased efforts by the Turkish state to become a member in the EU in the first two terms of the AKP government (2002–2008). Greece lifted its long-standing veto on Turkey's accession, opening up a public debate regarding the compatibility of Turks with European values, whereas Turkey was engaged in proving that its place was in Europe and nowhere else. If forging an agreement with Greece—geographically and culturally the most proximate European country—was one way of approaching the EU, modifying state politics pursued against minorities was another. While virtually none of the enduring issues were solved, the positive climate between Greece and Turkey would make it less likely for the Rum Polites to be subjected to pressure aimed at adjusting the balance in bilateral relations. As controversial, problematic, and flimsy as Turkish minority politics have been in general, not least at present,[2] popular narratives of cosmopolitanist nostalgia featuring non-Muslim communities are certainly not irrelevant to public debates taking place in the wider discursive space in Turkey.

It is at this juncture that a focus on cosmopolitan Istanbul becomes doubly important: anti-minority policies in Turkey, with regard to non-Muslims generally and to Rum Polites specifically, can be seen as an indispensable dimension of the nation-state's efforts to eradicate multiculturalism as a remainder from an imperial past by replacing it with a uniform national culture under the dominance of the Sunni Muslim Turk—a process often addressed as "Turkification." The stark contrast between nationalism and cosmopolitanism that marked the beginning of the Republican period appears to have been abandoned, as some of the nostalgia accounts attest, for a compromising approach where the latter is appropriated in the name of national interests, which are seen to lie within the international, multicultural European community, thereby circumventing the homogenizing, impoverishing, traumatizing effects of nationalism. Such an anti-nationalist version of cosmopolitan nostalgia appeals to the current generation of European-minded, secular, democrat urban elite classes because it provides its adherents with a refuge from pressing issues and challenges of the present, and with a potential shortcut toward building the desired future.

What we encounter here is not only an emphasis on what Svetlana Boym (2001) would call the "restorative" function of nostalgia by indicating a wish to resubmit to a cosmopolitan past but also a "reflective" dimension where the bearers of nostalgia are more critically aware of their present circumstances. As such, the urban elite, feeling that their value systems and lifestyles are threatened, and their present is on shaky ground, turn to their recent history with a "nostalgia for a balanced past" (Herzfeld 1991) in search of assurance that a different future can be possible. Nostalgia, as Boyer maintains (2006), always carries with it a politics of the future.

Here, the newly found sympathy on the part of the urban middle classes toward the city's non-Muslims turns to empathy whereby older residents present themselves to have turned into minorities amidst the upsurge of non-Istanbulite migrants. The increasing rate of departure of non-Muslims from the 1960s onward coincides with the arrival of Kurds, Arabs, Georgians, Syrians, and others from neighboring Middle Eastern or Eastern European provinces and countries in consequent waves of economic or political displacement. Within the ever-shrinking category of local Istanbulites gone astray inside an enormous and anonymous population, the urban elite positions itself symbolically against these developments by dismissing the newcomers using culturally schematized terms like *maganda* or *arabesk* (see Öncü 2005; Stokes 1992). A dismissive narrative mourning the replacement of the Rum patisserie-café with smelly *lahmacun*[3] houses is a common feature of nostalgic discourses. Uniting in a class-based cultural and ideological front against the migrants (Erman and Coşkun-Yıldar 2007), the urban elite takes refuge in "ghetto" neighborhoods where such exclusionist discourses are constantly being reproduced (Neyzi 2009, 8) alongside a yearning and mourning for the non-Muslim minorities, or their ghosts, as the city's lost cosmopolitans. Conveniently forgetting that their own rise in urban society a few generations ago coincided with, if not benefitted from, the departure of non-Muslims from Istanbul, this Western-educated, modernist, Muslim yet secularist elite, known also as "white Turks," confronted with new types of otherness, especially of Islamists and Kurds, find escape in a nostalgia for the "former others," who are now harmlessly few and therefore easily tolerable (Akgönül 2013; Secor 2002, 2004).

There is a very strong Western European bias that amounts to the equating of Istanbul's cosmopolitan golden age to the era of Ottoman modernization. Thus, the present diversity of the massive Istanbul population is not seen to contain elements of the cosmopolitanism that is being nostalgically reminisced. Although the new population of Istanbul is also highly varied, this is hardly considered to be a cosmopolitan situation. The changing social urban context is not taken to lead to much of what Vertovec (2007) describes as the diversification of an already existing diversity; on the contrary, it is regarded to be an impoverishment in demographic and cultural terms. The new population of primarily "Anatolian," that is, of rural or Eastern background, is resisted to be included among the local Istanbulites; regardless of how many years they may have lived in the city, their inability to link themselves to any of the native communities casts a doubt as to their ability to become properly urban.

In other terms, in the eyes of the urban elite upholding these nostalgic representations of the past, the newcomers may not belong to Istanbul for they do not know the ways of the City, they do not possess "cosmopolitan knowledge." This selective disposition is, whether intended or not, inherently charged politically as it relates to dominant cultural schemes of symbolic power (Hage 1998) that determine how a certain group of others are preferred over other others. Similar to the case in London, the cosmopolitan city accommodates and at the same time produces different kinds of strangers, but remains "bound in the dynamics of class and status that construct acceptable and unacceptable forms of difference" (Hatziprokopiou 2009, 27). This means that not all kinds of strangers are constructed as different, nor are all forms of difference deemed to produce others; rather, strangers are produced as outsiders, internal others, or enemies (Balibar 2006). Just as in the case of Rum Polites in Athens, who selectively evaluate who they prefer to include in their community, the cosmopolitanist discourses in Istanbul also adhere to a notion of "exclusive diversity," one that does not include economic immigrants or minorities of poor or rural origin. In other words, this is a case where exclusive diversity excludes through the work of cosmopolitan knowledge, which becomes the cultural capital, a means for distinction of an urban status among Istanbulites, old or new.

Narratives that promote an idealized cosmopolitanism are not monopolized by European-oriented liberal elites; more conservative and religious segments of urban society also partake in this endeavor, albeit with other visions about the past and the future. A nostalgic yearning for the Ottoman Empire, in which a Turkish Muslim dynasty ruled over a multicultural population (at times referred to as "neo-Ottomanism"), is evident in different realms of cultural and policy production. Grand festivities now take place to celebrate the Conquest of Istanbul on 29 May, a day that the Greek world commemorates as the Fall of Constantinople, which is clearly an act of inventing tradition that parades an "ownership" of the city by supporters of both Islamism and nationalism. A revival of Ottoman cultural forms and imagery as fashionable is observable in all aspects of everyday life, ranging from popular TV series to city landmarks and changing names of sports clubs. This glorification of the Ottoman past, a trend that was certainly absent and unutterable in the first decades of the Republic, comes with an elevated discourse of "tolerance" where the Sultans generously allowed their different subjects to coexist.[4]

As a political discourse, however, tolerance not only indicates a criticism of intolerance or a stance against prejudice but also an intrinsic disapproval of the tolerated (Mills 2011) that is only half-heartedly accommodated, and an assumption that difference is perceived negatively (Bryant 2016). Tolerance may simply mean retraction of persecution, but in fact disguises the possibility of it, thereby concealing the potential mistreatment of minorities (Kaya 2013). In the words of Kasbarian, this "nostalgia tends to gloss over the structural and everyday discrimination minorities experienced under the Ottoman regime, and it infantilizes and fossilizes the remaining communities as a historical relic" (2016, 210). In this mode of imperial cosmopolitanism, the minorities are, once again, not more than ornate symbols of an idealized past: the severe conditions of non-Muslims in the Empire, who endured arbitrary rule that often met with discrimination, are omitted from the rosy picture.

The nostalgic image of cosmopolitan Istanbul, then, is utilized to advance various political objectives. State and local governments of all political convictions may adopt cosmopolitanist discourses in order to brush over their shameful record on minority rights, seeking to save face or to delay the implementation of reforms. Put differently, addressing actual minority problems and taking action for preserving cultural diversity is not part of the cosmopolitanist agenda, but showing off with a multiculturalist heritage, or bemoaning the loss of minorities in an age of new majority populations from provincial, conservative backgrounds with no appreciation of urban cosmopolitanism, is. Whether advanced by the state or by the civil society, this kind of charitable attitude does not achieve much in terms of contributing to aspirations for a just, free, egalitarian, and democratic Turkey.

Spatializing Nostalgic Stories

The aforementioned shortfalls of cosmopolitanist nostalgia are visible in the physical urban landscape. Popular discourses have rendered fashionable those sites of multicultural coresidence that have long been deserted by their previous Rum, Armenian, or Jewish occupants and have been left to decay after being repopulated by poorer rural immigrants (Biner 2007). Upon their rediscovery by the urban elite, neighborhoods like Galata, Fanar, Ortaköy, or Cihangir that were previously populated by Rum Polites and other minorities began to be restored and reclaimed as representations of a lost but retrievable cosmopolitan urban past. Yet during this process, little if any discussion took place regarding the disregarded legal and economic rights of the minorities in these districts. Without a critical approach to anti-minority policies, attempts to reinstate the cosmopolitan fabric remain limited to cosmetic modifications: during the window dressing of houses that used to be owned by Rum Polites, questions of how these houses changed hands, when property rights were transferred overnight by the imposition of unconstitutional laws, continue to linger. The reasons for the loss of cosmopolitanism, for the absence of the minorities so beloved in nostalgic narratives, and for the ruined state of empty buildings remain unexplained.

Debates on preserving the physical surroundings or architectural landmarks in the city constitute visible manifestations of cosmopolitanist nostalgia and competing ideological narratives. Religious sites of Istanbul make a convincing case in displaying the spectrum: Hagia Sophia (Ayasofya) is the world-renowned Byzantine church that served as a mosque during the Ottoman era, but has been used since 1934 as a museum advertised as a symbol of the multicultural heritage of Istanbul for global consumption. Writing about a show of dervishes taking place there on the eve of the Millennium that was broadcast worldwide, journalist Nilgün Cerrahoğlu states that Ayasofya was "dominated by an atmosphere of multicultural peace" (*Milliyet*, 27 December 1999). In Greece a version of Hagia Sophia without its current minarets stands as a strong sign for reclaiming Constantinople as "our own," a policy advanced by the extreme rightists and religious fundamentalists, while their Turkish counterparts voice their demand to turn it into a mosque again.[5]

There is also a parallel heated public debate every now and then for building a mosque in Taksim Square, which would be located opposite Hagia Triada, the largest functioning Orthodox church of Istanbul, whose dome currently dominates the area. In 2013, this central square of Istanbul staged one of the most important political protest movements in recent Turkish history, which became renowned worldwide as the Gezi events. The plans to rebuild the Ottoman military barracks as the facade for a luxury hotel and a shopping mall in Gezi Park were based on a certain imagination of Istanbul's imperial past and its commercial future, but this clashed with multiple rival views of pluralism among social actors demonstrating their right to the city (Örs 2014). The Gezi events became the pivotal point in the resistance of Istanbulites against ongoing rent-oriented development policies and antagonistic mega projects of urban gentrification under cover of Istanbul's glorious past (Keyder 2000; Öncü 1999, 2007). Yet the process of resistance is far from being successfully concluded as a particularly vulgar program continues being implemented under the rubric of *kentsel dönüşüm* (urban transformation), where no culturally, historically, or naturally significant site is spared from massive housing, transport, or industrial projects. Public reactions to such destruction, as in the neighborhoods of Tarlabaşı,[6] Sulukule,[7] and Yedikule,[8] led to organizations of civil initiatives such as *Kuzey Ormanları Direnişi*,[9] which center on promoting an appreciation and preservation of the cosmopolitan heritage and identity of Istanbul.

These struggles with a cosmopolitan state of mind are attempting to take a more processual view with "a mode of managing meaning" (Hannerz 1990, 238), thereby engaging in an "immersive style of cosmopolitanism" that can be described as reflecting "a conscious pattern of action which is based on learning and cultivating engagements for the purpose of change, self-knowledge or improvement" (Kendall et al. 2009, 119). This comes to show how in Istanbul, as in many other metropolis settings, "the production and reproduction of the 'cosmopolitan city' involves a symbolic and material territorialisation of difference" (Young et al. 2006, 1689), where neoliberal and entrepreneurial forms of urban governance determine the distinction between acceptable and unacceptable difference and accordingly choose which parts of the city will be marketed as packaged diversity and which others will be condemned to being spaces of exclusion, neglect, and even destruction. The local settings are sites where alterity and strangeness can be noticed as that which cannot be recognized and can make people, in Sennett's words, dislodge from their own subjective categories of difference (2005). In the immersive style of cosmopolitanism, such experience does not lead to fear and anxiety but to action. Current and former Istanbulites from all walks of life are participating in cosmopolitanist practices and discourses in various ways, for different reasons: they either perpetuate an essentialized, timeless, non-referential cosmopolitan image of Istanbul, leaving it vulnerable to deliberate uses and abuses for meeting political and material interests, or actively resist such destructive tendencies in pursuit of preserving the legacy of the city, exerting pressure on governments and corporates through inducing public opinion to be sensitive to, or at least more aware of, the issues of the city and its people. As Ange and Berliner maintain, especially when used for social and political concerns, nostalgic discourses and practices may bond diverse categories of actors and constitute "a source of mnemonic convergence" in favor of stories of clashes and misunderstandings between multiple pasts (2015, 9–10). All limitations aside, cosmopolitanist nostalgia is a set of discourses that serve various groups and individuals in Turkish society differently and, with that, result in bringing the current residents of Istanbul closer to the Rum Polites who used to inhabit their city, whether symbolically or substantially.

In a discursive space where overlapping definitions of cosmopolitanism converge in such contested and conflictual ways, the search for cultural sense necessitates an analytical ethnographic investigation into how "cosmopolitanism is formed and reformed in particular locales and everyday spaces" (Binnie et al. 2006, 12). This is what Kendall et al. (2009) call a "reflexive style of cosmopolitanism"—the emic meanings of cosmopolitanism by way of contextualizing them through the experiences and practices of its beholders. In other words, cosmopolitanist nostalgia needs to be substantiated through an ethnographic intervention by cosmopolitans themselves. For that, I will now return to the Rum Polites.

Stories of Cosmopolitan Memories

She was searching as you would search in a deep chest, full, overflowing with clothes, or as you would shuffle through a drawer of small things. In-between buttons, belts, gloves, collars you search, search to discover a piece of lace...

A piece of lace that you don't even remember when you bought it, not even its shape, but you know that it exists. That it would be somewhere there. This way she was digging, whenever she had some time, this way she was shuffling through her memories. Somewhere would that moment be hidden, surely somewhere would it lie buried.

The paragraph above is an excerpt from a novel titled *Mistikes Piyes* (Mysterious Sources) by Tatiana Stavrou (1940, 7). The author was born in Istanbul and in 1924 moved to Athens, where she started her career as a writer, researcher, and novelist. During her century-long life (1890–1990), she was awarded many times for her extensive and impressive collection of works, all of which related to the few decades she spent in her birthplace, in Istanbul.

There are many who, like Stavrou's character above, are searching for the right memories, shuffling through the mystical array of their past experiences. And there are many who, like Stavrou herself, express this search in writing. This section is about those Rum Polites who are searching to remember, who are writing while searching, writing not to forget. It is about the body of work, literary or scholarly, produced in Greece and in Greek by writers who were born and raised in Istanbul. This section is on the Rum Polites literature, and the nostalgic reminiscences it reveals.

Here I am presenting the Rum Polites literature as a source of nostalgia to be juxtaposed in comparison to other nostalgic discourses about Istanbul today. In analyzing this body of writing in order to understand how the Rum Polites write about themselves as Rum Polites, I follow the threads of the ways in which the Rum Polites express themselves, remember their past, relate their experiences to others, articulate their sense of being, and conceptualize their identity through the written word. I focus only on the original works created by Rum Polites in Greek and in Greece so as to take into account the decisive factor of Rum Polites living in Athens, and not in Istanbul anymore, giving rise to a special set of reflections, comparisons of there and here, of now and then, of longings as belongings.[10] This restriction further limits the range of attempted audience, in this case the other Rum Polites and the Greeks, with the aim of investigating the extent to which writers are willing to disclose, project, and represent themselves vis-à-vis their own community of Rum Polites and the other members of the current society they live in, the Greeks of Greece.

In its capacity of being an ethnographic source, this body of writing qualifies as indigenous literature; yet to the extent that it achieves an analytical examination of the Rum Polites culture, it begs to be recognized as another set of ethnographic reflections. The perceived difference between the ethnographer and the native in their attempts at writing culture has recently been called into question, especially in relation to the concern with experimental writing, which brought anthropology and literature closer in pursuit of an effective cultural representation. This suggests that the idea of indigenous literature as ethnography may thus be evaluated as part of a broader spectrum of genres of storytelling.

This debate was also echoed in Greece.[11] Calotychos, for one, noted that "to treat all textual traces as representation and event need not lead to the aestheticization of a whole culture" (2003, 13). Similarly, my ethnographic interjection into the Rum Polites literature is not motivated by an intention to tell a single meta-narrative that will put different stories in place. Instead, it is an effort to bring out their emphasis on multiplicity—multiplicity of the stories themselves and of the ideas expressed in those stories—which forms a challenge to the very establishment of grand narratives. For the local histories written by Rum Polites not only address the missing link in the eternal continuity of the historical and cultural versions of the idea of ethnonational homogeneity, they also upset its validity by questioning fundamental concepts such as purity and unity through their emphasis on plurality and hybridity. They are stories of cosmopolitanism—nostalgic as they may be, they operate at an entirely different level than the historical travelogues or the popular contemporary discourses reigning in the city. When they write about Istanbul, the Rum Polites write from afar, in geography and history, traveling in memory. They write to remember, and to remind others of the city, to make them travel there and then through reading about the city. They write about the City they packed and took with them in their minds when they set out to go. Writing is a way that allows them to travel back home.

One reason to travel back in space and time through writing is to evoke living memory. Introducing *Loxandra*, the biographical novel that is a masterpiece of Rum Polites literature, and arguably one of the major Greek works of the twentieth century, the acclaimed author Maria Iordanidou writes that the old Istanbul she lived in the first years of her life remains marked in her mind, but that the "weed of forgetfulness started to grow over that period. Therefore I sat down to write" (1963, 9).

Others, who are also "far away from the birthplace," start to write because they cannot forget; they carry their memories with them continuously: "Wherever I am, be it inside the church or in front of the TV, my mind focuses on that old atmosphere of my own times in the City" (Simalaridou 1992, 16).

Writing in order to disclose and document memories is one of the main motives for the Rum Polites, but it is not the only one. The Rum Polites write for others who would also remember, perhaps differently, those intricacies of living in Istanbul; but they also write for those who would not know all that needs to be known: the difference, the specificity, the grandiosity, the uniqueness of the City. On the one hand, then, this is transmission of memory, oral tradition, or ethnohistory; on the other hand, it is transfer of cosmopolitan knowledge, documentation for the next generation and the masses, for recognition by others, as well as competition within the community for status and prestige. There is at the same time a sense of mission, of historical responsibility, that emerges as a shared element among the present generation of Rum Polites writers: not only do they write to remember, but as members of an ever-shrinking community, they also write not to be forgotten.

Writing to remember and to avoid being forgotten involves writing with a sense of duty, where writing becomes a mission, and an urgent one at that. As Papastratis recognizes, "the Greekness of Istanbul is experiencing its autumn days," and the Rum Polites are facing the danger of being reduced to a "dictionary entry" in a generation or two (1994, 79). This sense of urgency is coupled with a belief that there is a general level of ignorance about the City, and lack of appreciation of its legacy, which only the few remaining Rum Polites can address. "Who remembers the great benefactors from Istanbul and Asia Minor?" asks Koundouraki. "How many of them do we know here in Greece? Very few perhaps! We don't even know those intellectuals who came from there as writers, academics, Nobel prize winners. We owe them all respect and even some gratitude because they also wrote the golden pages of our recent History!" (2002, 158). The ignorance is not limited to the Greeks of Greece, but can be observed also in Istanbul today, "where the current residents, in this crazy period of change, know almost nothing about the previous residents" (Bozi 2002, ii).

Transmitting cosmopolitan knowledge might be an undertaking that is sometimes aggressively pursued. Aleksiadis-Fanariotis demonstrates this antagonistically in the opening lines of his book *Do You Remember*

Fanari?: "Hey you, indifferent stranger! If you have opened this book only out of curiosity without expecting to enrich your knowledge ... you better close it now. You did not see Fanari" (1956, 13). In the Rum Polites literature experience quickly translates to expertise: having origins in a place appears to be a necessary condition to have knowledge of, and authority to write about, that place.[12] This idea still holds valid today, half a century later, as in the memoirs by Konstantinidou-Kloukina (2003, 14), who argues that it is up to the Rum Polites to talk about Istanbul during "the time of Romiosini," because "only those who lived in a place are in a position to narrate the place," along with the sorrows of diaspora (*xenitia*), of nostalgia, of recollections.

The list of things remembered and written about by the Rum Polites is long, but everything on that list is strongly attached to the place, the City. The idea of the City as home persists among the Rum Polites, perhaps not as a place of destination as much as it is what Armbruster calls "an actual place of lived experience and a metaphorical space of personal attachment and identification" (2002, 120). Istanbul is the reference point centering scattered memories, the location that substantiates the connection between the Rum Polites and their imagined past. In other words, it is a conceptual and discursive space of identification, which also works as a nodal point in concrete social relations (Rapport and Dawson 1998; Stock 2010).

Since Rum Polites are entitled to write about Istanbul, they are just the right ones to glorify its history. This is especially true for certain periods, such as that of the Byzantine Empire. "No writers remain in our day" who have "enough living images to draw on in order to establish a deep and tight connection to the Byzantine throne that is lost and forgotten," states the author of the prologue to Simaralidou's *Vosporina Skitsa* (Sketches of the Bosphorus), a memoir that is claimed to make this task possible because it "enlivens the immortal City of our dreams and our legends" (1994, 6). This, then, is the way in which the book becomes a means of establishing the missing link between today and several centuries ago—not through giving historical information but through remembering the place: sketches of Bosphorus help outline the scope of the act of remembrance as being not only temporal but also, if not more so, spatiotemporal. The far-fetched connection with the Byzantines becomes achievable through sharing the same space; the spatialization of memory enables the recovery of lost centuries beyond legends and dreams.

The spatial attachment to the City, then, provides the Rum Polites writers with an exclusive sense of authority. They tell the readers their *istories*, writing history with their stories, blurring the fine line between the two (Sutton 1998). This way, by bringing into visibility narratives of place that had been written out, or ignored, they engage in what Hayden White (1987) calls the politics of place construction. Recording information about events, eras, and areas that other Istanbulites might not have seen, witnessed, or experienced further strengthens the notion of cosmopolitan knowledge as a matter of distinction for Rum Polites and acts as a reconfirmation of their identification with the City.

Therefore, an important point to be made with regard to the emic meanings of cosmopolitanism for the Rum Polites is their close association with certain times and places. For the Rum Polites, being cosmopolitan is equated to being Constantinopolitan, in a period when they were prevailing and prevalent; it is the city of Istanbul that gives them their cosmopolitan character, and to a large extent, vice versa. As much as it may seem an oxymoron, this is a localized form of cosmopolitanism, a type of cosmopolitanism that is geographically and historically specific. It is this specificity that I address elsewhere (Örs 2018), where I highlight three particular contexts of Istanbulite cosmopolitanism that pertain to the specific neighborhoods of Pera, Fanar, and Tatavla at different historical periods and under dissimilar conditions. Taking into account the spatial and temporal contexts aside from ethnic, religious, and economic factors, the Rum Polites' reflections on Istanbulite cosmopolitanism can be summarized in these three modes of cosmopolitanist nostalgia. The rather popular Pera-style cosmopolitanism marks the closing decades of the nineteenth and the first half of the twentieth century, invoking a sense of the multicultural coexistence of religiously and ethnically diverse and heterogeneous cultural groups which belonged to the upper middle classes and maintained a Western, modern, bourgeois lifestyle that was visible in the common public space. Tatavlan cosmopolitanism, by way of contrast, entailed the spatial separation of an autonomously organized and homogenous cultural community made up of lower income groups. From its eighteenth-century roots until at least its destruction by fire in 1929, Tatavla nevertheless could be viewed as a building component of the wider cosmopolitan composition of Istanbul. A similarly secluded but a much more distinguished society was in place under the reign of Fanariot nobility from mid-sixteenth to mid-nineteenth centuries: Fanar-style cosmopolitanism was a conservative, status quo cosmopolitanism linked to preserving an imperial and patriarchal order that was essentially multicultural. These different contexts of cosmopolitanisms shared similar destinies of dissolution with the onset of nationalism, a destiny with its ideological, institutional, economic, and demographic dimensions, a point that I note as missing in popular nostalgic idealizations of cosmopolitan Istanbul.

Whatever their smaller and larger differences, there are a number of common characteristics in all manifestations of Rum Polites-style cosmopolitanism. The most apparent across these expressions of Rum Istanbulite cosmopolitanism is their strong sense of locality. For the Rum Polites, whether it is a specific neighborhood or the city in general, the references to cosmopolitanism are about being from an intrinsically cosmopolitan part of the city which, paradoxically, is rooted in the uniqueness of the place itself. Istanbul, as the City (*i Polis*), is one of a kind among those unique places, for being able to alter the meaning of cosmopolitan etymologically by shifting the weight back and forth from "cosmos" to "polis." Being the prime City of the world, Istanbul becomes a cosmopolitan center in and of itself; thus, the Rum Polites take their cosmopolitanism from their Istanbul roots, not from their world travels. Cosmopolitanism is such an essential component of their Istanbulite identity that it does not get lost even though they now live in Athens. Thus the fact that they are displaced adds a new dimension to the understanding of the place from afar. The City is romanticized and abstracted in memory and in the Rum Polites literature; the image of a cosmopolitan Istanbul distant in time and space becomes the necessary basis for the perpetuation of a cultural identity in diaspora.

Theorizing Cosmopolitanisms of the City

In whichever context it takes place, nostalgia is inevitably subjective. Yet it is a subjectivity that reveals internalized notions of memory and identity. Juxtaposing multiple meanings of cosmopolitanism taken from public discourses of nostalgia in contemporary Istanbul, with those brought to light from within Rum Polites literature from afar, may contribute to diversifying yet specifying the path toward constructing an emic sense of Istanbulite cosmopolitanism. This, in turn, imbues cosmopolitanist platitudes with substance and concrete references to temporal–spatial cultural contexts. Rum Polites' rooted cosmopolitans, in turn, can serve to compare other localized and historicized understandings of the concept, allowing for an ethnographic opening onto etic discussions regarding cultural and political theories of cosmopolitanism.

An overview of the Rum Polites literature indicates, to use the terminology of Kendall et al. (2009), that the Rum Polites engage in a "reflexive mode" of cosmopolitanism, as opposed to the more common versions of a "sampling style" that is encountered in popular discourses of nostalgia. Even though they lack specificity regarding the who, what, when, and how of cosmopolitanism in an Istanbul past, such nostalgic discourses upheld by a wide range in contemporary society bring various actors conceptually closer to an "immersive" mode, one that invokes an understanding of the reasons for the loss of urban cosmopolitanism and an engagement in revoking the conditions thereof. In this vein, cosmopolitanism is also taken as a political project where its disappearance is attributed to the advent of nationalism. The Rum Polites personify a cosmopolitan identity of Istanbul, where harsh encounters with nationalism led to the decay of both the community and the city. This way, adherence to cosmopolitanism, becomes a critique of established meta-narratives, one that is paralleled in social theory as an advocacy of shifting from a "methodological nationalism" to a "methodological cosmopolitanism" (Beck 2004; Wimmer and Glick-Schiller 2002). With a diversity of grounded and experience-based emic meanings, the Rum Polites offer a valuable contribution to the multisided conceptual debates on cosmopolitanism.

As with any fuzzy and fancy buzzword, cosmopolitanism entails multiple interdisciplinary traditions, meanings, perspectives, and levels of analysis, which have been addressed by the growing scholarship on the concept.[13] The ensuing catch-all airiness of the term, however, may well be attributed to the relative weakness of social theory to locate cosmopolitanism. Warf warns that cosmopolitan writers have too long failed to take space and place seriously, even though the geographical specificity of concrete, empirically manifested "on-the-ground" cosmopolitanism reveals a series of context-dependent practices in which broad notions of civility are tailored to the specifics of individual cities and cultures (2012, v). One way of investigating localized cosmopolitanism would be to unearth those places that possess a cosmopolitan character or express a cosmopolitan sensibility, the characteristics of which may well vary according to urban spaces. Another option would be to follow Lamont and Aksartova (2002) in their operationalization of ordinary cosmopolitanism as cultural repertoires—flexible, even contradictory, discursive, practical resources available to social actors to deal with everyday agendas and issues. These may then be encouraged by "particular contexts, fusions of circumstance and motive, and frames of interpretation" (Fine 2008, 108).

To follow Richard Sennett, cosmopolitanism has a very different cast when one thinks of it in terms, not so much of political theory but of social experience of cities. "Once you actually take an institution like the city, the link between cosmopolitan and cosmopolitanism is obviously a particular one" (2002, 42). Recent scholarship in urban studies attests to this point. Hatziprokopiou shows with the case of London that "certain districts become vibrant examples of the cosmopolitan city where diversity manifests itself in the daily experiences of urban life and coexistence at the local level," such that questions related to the ways in which cosmopolitanism is perceived and lived, how it works on the ground, become central (2009, 27). Other urban centers are shown to be home to divergent cosmopolitanisms (for Cairo, see Singerman and Amar 2006; Raymond 2002), sites for negotiating cosmopolitanism between selective cosmopolitans (for Odessa, see Humphrey and Skvirskaja 2012; Sapritsky 2012), or venues for shifting cosmopolitics among reluctant cosmopolitans (for Berlin, see Mandel 2008), to mention only a few. Cosmopolitanism is particularly and historically grounded in Mediterranean cities, where accounts of place-specific practices come to defy the single reading of cosmopolitanism as an overarching discourse or ideology that equates cosmopolitanism with the global and the Western,[14] thereby proving a fertile ground to approach the multiplicity of local notions of cosmopolitanism (Giaccaria 2012). This comes to show that, contrary to the common understanding of the term, a cosmopolitan is not necessarily a "citizen of the world" or "belonging to all parts of the world" but may well refer to a "citizen of the city," a city that embodies the world—thus, "cosmopolitanism should be employed in this placebound understanding, with cosmopolitan sites seen as sites that tie together flows of people, goods, and capital within the larger world in which they are embedded" (Kolluoğlu and Toksöz 2010, 8).

Such a spatial focus on the city as the source of the culture of identity of the Rum Polites has brought out multiple ways of defining what is cosmopolitan. Whether referencing specific sites, practices, phenomena, relations, lineages, idioms, manners, or memory or instead adhering to more generic representations, stereotypes, knowledge, discourses, nostalgic stories, images, attitudes, or sentiments, the meaning of cosmopolitan is always .diverse and particularly associated with the City. Stories of Rum Polites testify to that.

Notes

1. For various studies of social memory in Turkey, see Özyürek (2007), Navaro-Yashin (2009), Biner (2010), and Turan (2011).
2. Until roughly the early 2010s, the AKP government pursued policies where projects of reconciliation toward distressed minorities and related EU reforms were presented to be high on the list of priorities. Now in 2017, a completely different political landscape dominates in Turkey under another government formed by the same party, where the EU is no longer a part of the agenda amidst an intensification of violent conflicts with the Kurds in Turkey. See also the Epilogue.
3. *Lahmacun* is a dish in Middle Eastern cuisine known in Europe as Turkish pizza.
4. The website of the Istanbul Metropolitan Municipality describes the city in this way: "Istanbul, with mosques, churches, and synagogues existing side by side, has always been a center of tolerance."
5. For a commentary on the changing attitudes among the Islamists in Turkey regarding Ayasofya, see Ahmet Hakan's column titled "Savcı Göreve," in *Hürriyet* (19 September 2005). For a commentary on the demands for permission to pray in Ayasofya by Pope Benedict during his yet unaccomplished visit to Istanbul, see Nuray Mert's column titled "Ayasofya ibadete açılsın mı?" in *Radikal* (13 September 2005). For more scholarly analyses, see Nelson (2004), Tanyeri-Erdemir (2017), and Necipoğlu et al. (1992).
6. Tarlabaşı is a neighborhood in Pera, which is subjected to major projects of urban development and gentrification. See Kuyucu and Ünsal (2010), Saybaşılı (2005), Sylvester (2010), Islam (2010), Aygen (2012), Kabutakapua (2015), and Sakızlıoğlu (2007).
7. Sulukule is an area located inside the Byzantine city walls, which for long centuries housed the Romani/Gypsy populations. Despite major international campaigns, the area was subjected to urban gentrification projects and demolished. See Uysal (2012), Foggo (2007), Somersan and Kırca-Schroeder (2007), and Baykal (2009).
8. Located by the Byzantine city walls, Yedikule is site to one of the oldest continuing practices of urban agriculture and is currently resisting demolishment through gentrification. See Kanbak (2016).
9. A civil environmentalist initiative that was founded initially to protect the forest area in Northern Istanbul, which is being destroyed for mega projects such as the Third Bosphorus Bridge and Third Airport (www.kuzeyormanlari.org).
10. This point has been made in relation to Greek scholars working outside Greece, the so-called diaspora critics, who were aided by the distance from

"home" in engaging a view from afar, a *theoria* of Greekness (Calotychos 2003, 15; also see Herzfeld 1982; Faubion 1993; Leontis 1995; Jusdanis 1991).
11. The debate was introduced in anthropology and textual analysis, notably in Clifford (1988) and Clifford and Marcus (1986), and found wide acclaim across genres and disciplines (Benson 1993). For works on Greece that address the relationship between ethnography and fiction, see Herzfeld (1997a), Panourgia (1995), and Calotychos (2003), among others.
12. On the authority of the author in the case of the ethnographer, see Clifford (1983) and Roth (1989).
13. For some of the recent works on cosmopolitanism, see Appiah (2006), Beck (2006), Archibugi (2008), Cheah (2006), Harvey (2009), Rovisco and Nowicka (2011), Breckenridge (2000), Kendall et al. (2009), Fine (2008), Held (2010), and Vertovec (2007).
14. For accounts of cosmopolitanism in various Mediterranean cities, see Jackson (2012), Ilbert and Yannakakis (1992), Ballinger (2003), Mazower (2005), Fregonese (2012), Prato (2009), Driessen (2005), Keyder et al. (1993), Graham (2004), Mazower (2004), della Dora (2006), Mills (2010), Fahmy (2006), Kolluoğlu and Toksöz (2010), Hanssen et al. (2002).

Bibliography

Akgönül, S. (2013). *The Minority Concept in the Turkish Context: Practices and Perceptions in Turkey, Greece, and France (Muslim Minorities)*. Leiden: Brill.

Akın, N. (1998). *19. Yüzyılın İkinci Yarısında Galata ve Pera*. Beyoğlu, İstanbul: Literatür.

Aktar, C. (2002). Cosmopolist: European Capital of Culture Istanbul. *Istanbul, 41*, 182–190.

Aleksiadis-Fanariotis, G. (1956). *Thimase to Fanari*. Athina.

Angé, O., & Berliner, D. (Eds.). (2015). *Anthropology and Nostalgia*. Oxford: Berghahn.

Appiah, A. (2006). *Cosmopolitanism: Ethics in a World of Strangers*. New York: W.W. Norton.

Archibugi, D. (2008). *The Global Commonwealth of Citizens: Toward Cosmopolitan Democracy*. Princeton: Princeton University Press.

Armbruster, H. (2002). Homes in Crisis: Syrian Christian Orthodox in Turkey and Germany. In N. Al-Ali & K. Koser (Eds.), *New Approaches to Migration? Transnational Communities and the Transformation of Home*. London: Routledge.

Aygen, Z. (2012). *International Heritage and Historic Building Conservation: Saving the World's Past*. London: Routledge.

Bali, R. (1999). *Cumhuriyet Yıllarında Türkiye Yahudileri: Bir Türkleştirme Serüveni, 1923–1945*. Cağaloğlu, İstanbul: İletişim.
Bali, R. (2002). *Tarz-ı Hayat'tan Life Style'a: Yeni SeÇkinler, Yeni Mekânlar, Yeni Yaşamlar*. Cağaloğlu, İstanbul: İletişim.
Balibar, É. (2006). *Strangers as Enemies: Further Reflections on the Aporias of Transnational Citizenship*. Working Papers 06/4, MCRI Globalization and Autonomy. Montreal: McMaster University.
Ballinger, P. (2003). *History in Exile: Memory and Identity at the Borders of the Balkans*. Princeton: Princeton University Press.
Barthes, R. (1981). *Camera Lucida: Reflections on Photography*. New York: Hill and Wang.
Baykal, N. (2009). The Discursive Construction of Ethnic Identity: Sulukule Case, Turkey. *The Lingustics Journal: Special Edition*, 121–154.
Beck, U. (2004). Cosmopolitical Realism: On the Distinction between Cosmopolitanism in Philosophy and the Social Sciences. *Global Networks*, 4(2), 131–156.
Beck, U. (2006). *Power in the Global Age: A New Global Political Economy*. Cambridge: Polity.
Beck, U., & Sznaider, N. (2006). Unpacking Cosmopolitanism for the Social Sciences: A Research Agenda. *The British Journal of Sociology*, 57(1), 1–23.
Benson, P. (Ed.). (1993). *Anthropology and Literature*. Urbana: University of Illinois Press.
Biner, Z. Ö. (2007). Retrieving the Dignity of a Cosmopolitan City: Contested Perspectives on Rights, Culture and Ethnicity in Mardin. *New Perspectives on Turkey*, 37, 31–58.
Biner, Z. Ö. (2010). Acts of Defacement, Memories of Loss: Ghostly Effects of the 'Armenian Crisis' in Mardin, Southeastern Turkey. *History & Memory*, 22(2), 68–94.
Binnie, J., et al. (2006). *Cosmopolitan Urbanism*. London: Routledge.
Bissell, W. C. (2005). Engaging Colonial Nostalgia. *Cultural Anthropology*, 20(2), 215–248.
Boyer, D. (2006). Ostalgie and the Politics of the Future in Eastern Germany. *Public Culture*, 18(2), 361–381.
Boym, S. (2001). *The Future of Nostalgia*. New York: Basic Books.
Boym, S. (2007). Nostalgia and Its Discontents. *The Hedgehog Review*, Institute for Advanced Studies in Culture, University of Virginia.
Bozi, S. (2002). *O Ellinismos tis Konstantinoupolis: Koinotita Stavrodromiou-Peran*. Athens: Ellinika Grammata.
Breckenridge, C. A. (Ed.). (2000). *Cosmopolitanism*. Durham, NC: Society for Transnational Cultural Studies by Duke University Press.

Bryant, R. (2008). Writing the Catastrophe: Nostalgia and Its Histories in Cyprus. *Journal of Modern Greek Studies, 26*(2), 399–422. https://doi.org/10.1353/mgs.0.0029.

Bryant, R. (2016). *Post-Ottoman Coexistence: Sharing Space in the Shadow of Conflict.* New York, NY: Berghahn.

Calotychos, V. (2003). *Modern Greece: A Cultural Poetics.* Oxford: Berg.

Cheah, P. (2006). *Inhuman Conditions: On Cosmopolitanism and Human Rights.* Cambridge, MA: Harvard University Press.

Clifford, J. (1983). On Ethnographic Authority. *Representations, 2,* 118–146.

Clifford, J. (1988). *The Predicament of Culture: Twentieth Century Ethnography, Literature, and Art.* Cambridge: Harvard University Press.

Clifford, J., & Marcus, G. (1986). *Writing Culture: The Poetics and Politics of Ethnography.* Berkeley: University of California Press.

Cohen, A. (1985). *The Symbolic Construction of Community.* London: Routledge.

Coller, I. (2011). *Arab France: Islam and the Making of Modern Europe, 1798–1831.* Berkeley: University of California Press.

Deleon, J. (2004). *Balat ve Çevresi.* İstanbul: Remzi.

Dora, V. D. (2006). The Rhetoric of Nostalgia: Postcolonial Alexandria between Uncanny Memories and Global Geographies. *Cultural Geographies, 13*(2), 207–238.

Driessen, H. (2005). Mediterranean Port Cities: Cosmopolitanism Reconsidered. *History and Anthropology, 16*(1), 129–141. https://doi.org/10.1080/0275720042000316669.

Dufft, C. (2009). *Turkish Literature and Cultural Memory: "Multiculturalism" as a Literary Theme after 1980.* Wiesbaden: Harrassowitz.

Erbil, L. (2000). Trianon Pastanesi. In T. Uyar & S. Köksal (Eds.), *İstanbul'da Zaman* (pp. 9–16). İstanbul: Büke.

Erman, T., & Coşkun-Yıldar, M. (2007). Emergent Local Initiative and the City: The Case of Neighbourhood Associations of the Better-Off Classes in Post-1990 Urban Turkey. *Urban Studies, 44*(13), 2547–2566.

Fahmy, N. (2006). Egypt's Unwavering Path to Democratic Reform. *Mediterranean Quarterly, 17*(3), 1–11. https://doi.org/10.1215/10474552-2006-011.

Faubion, J. (1993). *Modern Greek Lessons: A Primer in Historical Constructivism.* Princeton: Princeton University Press.

Fine, R. (2008). *Cosmopolitanism.* London: Routledge.

Fish, S. (1997). Boutique Multiculturalism, or Why Liberals Are Incapable of Thinking about Hate Speech. *Critical Inquiry, 23*(2), 378–395.

Foggo, H. (2007). The Sulukule Affair: Roma against Expropriation. *Roma Rights Quarterly, 4,* 41–47.

Fregonese, S. (2012). Between a Refuge and a Battleground: Beirut's Discrepant Cosmopolitanisms. *Geographical Review, 102*(3), 316–336.

Freitag, U. (2014). 'Cosmopolitanism' and 'Conviviality'? Some Conceptual Considerations Concerning the Late Ottoman Empire. *European Journal of Cultural Studies, 17*(4), 375–391.
Giaccaria, P. (2012). Cosmopolitanism: The Mediterranean Archives. *Geographical Review, 102*(3), 293–315.
Göktürk, D., Soysal, L., & Tureli, I. (Eds.). (2010). *Orienting Istanbul: Cultural Capital of Europe?* London: Routledge.
Graham, S. (Ed.). (2004). *The Cybercities Reader.* London: Routledge.
Gürsel, D. (2012, November 6). Bir Palimpsest Kent olarak İstanbul. *Arkitera.* Retrieved from http://www.arkitera.com/haber/10667/bir-palimpsest-kent-istanbul
Hage, G. (1998). *White Nation: Fantasies of White Supremacy in a Multicultural Society.* Sydney: Pluto Press.
Hanley, W. (2008). Grieving Cosmopolitanism in Middle East Studies. *History Compass, 6*(5), 1346–1367.
Hannerz, U. (1990). Cosmopolitans and Locals in World Culture. *Theory, Culture & Society, 7*(2), 237–251.
Hanssen, J. (2002). *The Empire in the City: Arab Provincial Capitals in the Late Ottoman Empire.* Ergon-Verlag: Würzburg.
Haraway, D. (1989). *Primate Visions: Gender, Race, and Nature in the World of Modern Science.* New York: Routledge.
Harvey, D. (2009). *Cosmopolitanism and the Geographies of Freedom.* New York: Columbia University Press.
Held, D. (2010). *Cosmopolitanism: Ideals and Realities.* Cambridge: Polity.
Herzfeld, M. (1982). *Ours Once More: Folklore, Ideology, and the Making of Modern Greece.* Austin: University of Texas Press.
Herzfeld, M. (1987). *Anthropology Through the Looking-Glass: Critical Ethnography in the Margins of Europe.* Cambridge: Cambridge University Press.
Herzfeld, M. (1991). *A Place in History: Social and Monumental Time in a Cretan Town.* Princeton, NJ: Princeton University Press.
Herzfeld, M. (1997a). *Portrait of a Greek Imagination: An Ethnographic Biography of Andreas Nenedakis.* Chicago: The University of Chicago Press.
Herzfeld, M. (1997b). *Cultural Intimacy: Social Poetics in the Nation-State.* New York: Routledge.
Humphrey, C., & Skvirskaja, V. (2012). *Post-Cosmopolitan Cities: Explorations of Urban Coexistence.* New York: Berghahn.
Iğsız, A. (2015). Palimpsests of Multiculturalism and Museumization of Culture Greco-Turkish Population Exchange Museum as an Istanbul 2010 European Capital of Culture Project. *Comparative Studies of South Asia, Africa and the Middle East, 35*(2), 324–345.
Ilbert, R., & Yannakakis, I. (1992). *Alexandrie, 1860–1960: Un modèle éphémère de convivialité, communautés et identité cosmopolite.* Paris: Editions Autrement.

Iordanidou, M. (1963). *Loxandra*. Athens: Estia.
İslam, T. (2010). Current Urban Discourse, Urban Transformation and Gentrification in Istanbul. *Architectural Design, 80*(1), 58–63.
Jackson, M. (2012). *Other Shore: Essays on Writers and Writing*. Berkeley: University of California Press.
James, W. (1997). The Names of Fear: Memory, History, and the Ethnography of Feeling among Uduk Refugees. *Journal of Royal Anthropological Institute, 3*, 115–131.
Jusdanis, G. (1991). *Belated Modernity and Aesthetic Culture: İnventing National Literature*. Minneapolis: University of Minnesota Press.
Kabutakapua, N. B. (2015). Community Support in Multicultural Neighborhoods: The Case of Tarlabasi. *Turkish Review, 5*(4), 298.
Kanbak, A. (2016). İstanbul Yedikule Bostanları: Bir Yeniden Üretim Pratiği. *Yaşam Bilimleri Dergisi, 6*(1), 166–180.
Kasbarian, S. (2016). The Istanbul Armenians: Negotiating Co-existence. In R. Bryant (Ed.), *Post-Ottoman Coexistence: Sharing Space in the Shadow of Conflict*. Oxford: Berghahn Press.
Kaya, A. (2013). *Europeanization and Tolerance in Turkey: The Myth of Toleration*. London: Palgrave Macmillan.
Kendall, G., Woodward, I., & Skrbiš, Z. (2009). *The Sociology of Cosmopolitanism: Globalization, Identity, Culture and Government*. Basingstoke: Palgrave Macmillan.
Keyder, Ç. (2000). *İstanbul: Küresel ile yerel arasında*. İstanbul: Metis.
Keyder, Ç., Eyüp Özveren, Y., & Quataert, D. (1993). *Port-Cities of the Eastern Mediterranean 1800–1914*. Binghamton, NY: Binghamton U, Fernand Braudel Center.
Kırca, A. (2000). *Azınlıklar: Kaybolan Renkler*. İstanbul: Sabah.
Kolluoğlu, B., & Toksöz, M. (Eds.). (2010). *Cities of the Mediterranean: From the Ottomans to the Present Day*. London: I.B. Tauris.
Konstantinou-Kloukina, A. (2003). *Opou lipon... mia fora kai enan kairo stin Poli, 1949–1958*. Athens: Ikaros.
Koundouraki, D. (2002). *Min kles yiavri mou*. Athens: Trochalia.
Kuyucu, T., & Ünsal, Ö. (2010). 'Urban Transformation' as State-Led Property Transfer: An Analysis of Two Cases of Urban Renewal in Istanbul. *Urban Studies, 47*(7), 1479–1499.
Lamont, M., & Aksartova, S. (2002). Ordinary Cosmopolitanisms Strategies for Bridging Racial Boundaries among Working-Class Men. *Theory, Culture & Society, 19*(4), 1–25.
Leontis, A. (1995). *Topographies of Hellenism: Mapping a Homeland*. Ithaca: Cornell.
Levi, M. (1999). *İstanbul bir Masaldı*. Istanbul: Remzi.
Mandel, R. (2008). *Cosmopolitan Anxieties: Turkish Challenges to Citizenship and Belonging in Germany*. Durham: Duke University Press.

Margulies, R. (2009, June 17). Seçkinlere Teşekkür Ederim. *Taraf.*
Mazower, M. (2004). The Strange Triumph of Human Rights, 1933–1950. *The Historical Journal, 47*(2), 379–398.
Mazower, M. (2005). *Salonica, City of Ghosts: Christians, Muslims, and Jews, 1430–1950.* New York: Alfred A. Knopf.
Millas, A. (2006). *Pera: The Crossroads of Constantinople.* Athens: Troia/Militos.
Mills, A. (2010). *Streets of Memory: Landscape, Tolerance, and National Identity in Istanbul.* Athens: University of Georgia Press.
Mills, A. (2011). The Ottoman Legacy: Urban Geographies, National Imaginaries, and Global Discourses of Tolerance. *Comparative Studies of South Asia, Africa and the Middle East, 31*(1), 183–195.
Mills, A., Reilly, J. A., & Philliou, C. (2011). The Ottoman Empire from Present to Past: Memory and Ideology in Turkey and the Arab World. *Comparative Studies of South Asia, Africa and the Middle East, 31*(1), 133–136.
Navaro-Yashin, Y. (2009). Affective Spaces, Melancholic Objects: Ruination and the Production of Anthropological Knowledge. *Journal of the Royal Anthropological Institute, 15*(1), 1–18.
Necipoğlu, N., Mark, R., & Çakmak, A. Ş. (Eds.). (1992). *Hagia Sophia from the Age of Justinian to the Present.* Cambridge: Cambridge University Press.
Nelson, K. (2007). *Young Minds in Social Worlds: Experience, Meaning, and Memory.* Cambridge: Harvard University Press.
Neyzi, L. (2009). Eski İstanbul'un şehir kültürünü hatırlamak: Yaşanmışlıklar, bellek ve nostalji. In M. Güvenç (Ed.), *Eski İstanbullular, Yeni İstanbullular.* İstanbul: Osmanlı Bankası Arşivi.
Öncü, A. (1999). Istanbulites and Others: The Cultural Cosmology of 'Middleness' in the Era of Neoliberalism. In Ç. Keyder (Ed.), *Istanbul between the Global and the Local.* New York: St. Martins.
Öncü, A. (2007). The Politics of Istanbul's Ottoman Heritage in the Era of Globalism: Refractions Through the Prism of a Theme Park. In B. Drieskens, F. Mermier, & H. Wimmen (Eds.), *Cities of the South: Citizenship and Exclusion in the 21st Century* (pp. 233–264). London, Beirut: Saqi Books.
Örs, İ. R. (2014). Genie in the Bottle: Gezi Park, Taksim Square, and the Realignment of Democracy and Space in Turkey. *Philosophy & Social Criticism, 40*(4–5), 489–498.
Örs, İ. R. (2018). Introduction. In İ. R. Örs, S. Akgonul, C. Aktar, & E. Macar (Eds.), *1964 Expulsions: A Turning Point in the Homogenization of Turkish Society.* Istanbul: Istanbul Bilgi University Press.
Özyürek, E. (2007). *The Politics of Public Memory in Turkey.* Syracuse, NY: Syracuse University Press.
Panourgia, N. (1995). *Fragments of Death, Fables of Identity: An Athenian Anthropography.* Madison: University of Wisconsin Press.
Papastratis, T. O. (1994). *Stin Poli kai stin Thraki.* Athens: Risos.

Parla, A. (2009). Remembering across the Border: Postsocialist Nostalgia among Turkish Immigrants from Bulgaria. *American Ethnologist, 36*(4), 750–767.

Prato, G. B. (2009). Introduction – Beyond Multiculturalism: Anthropology at the Intersections between the Local, the National and the Global. In G. B. Prato (Ed.), *Beyond Multiculturalism: Views from Anthropology* (pp. 1–19). London: Routledge.

Raymond, A. (2002). *Cairo.* Cambridge: Harvard University Press.

Roth, P. A. (1989). Ethnography without Tears. *Current Anthropology, 30*(5), 555–569.

Rovisco, M., & Nowicka, M. (2011). *The Ashgate Research Companion to Cosmopolitanism.* Farnham: Ashgate.

Sakızlıoğlu, N. B. (2007). *Impacts of Urban Renewal Policies: The Case of Tarlabaşı-Istanbul.* Unpublished Master thesis, METU, Ankara.

Sapritsky, M. (2012). Negotiating Cosmopolitanism: Migration, Religious Education and Shifting Jewish Orientations in Post-Soviet Odessa. In C. Humphrey & V. Skvirskaja (Eds.), *Post-Cosmopolitan Cities: Explorations of Urban Coexistence* (pp. 65–93). New York: Berghahn Books.

Saybaşılı, N. (2005). Tarlabaşı: 'Another World' in the City. In A. Franke (Ed.), *B-Zone: Becoming Europe and Beyond* (pp. 100–109). Berlin and Barcelona: KW Institute for Contemporary Art.

Secor, A. J. (2002). The Veil and Urban Space in Istanbul: Women's Dress, Mobility and Islamic Knowledge. *Gender, Place and Culture: A Journal of Feminist Geography, 9*(1), 5–22.

Secor, A. (2004). "There Is an Istanbul That Belongs to Me": Citizenship, Space, and Identity in the City. *Annals of the Association of American Geographers, 94*(2), 352–368.

Sema, S. (1994/1952). *Eski İstanbul'dan Hatıralar.* İstanbul: İletişim.

Sennett, R. (2002). Cosmopolitanism and the Social Experience of Cities. In S. Vertovec & R. Cohen (Eds.), *Conceiving Cosmopolitanism: Theory, Context, Practice.* Oxford: Oxford University Press.

Shaw, C., & Chase, M. (1989). *The Imagined Past: History and Nostalgia.* Manchester: Manchester University Press.

Simalaridou, A. Z. (1992). *Vimata kai chromata stin Thriliki Eptalofo.* Athens: Sillogos Konstantinoupoliton.

Simaralidou, A. Z. (1994). *Vosporina Skitsa.* Athens.

Singerman, D., & Amar, P. (2006). *Cairo Cosmopolitan: Politics, Culture, and Urban Space in the New Globalized Middle East.* Cairo: American University in Cairo Press.

Somersan, S., & Kırca-Schroeder, S. (2007). Resisting Eviction: Sulukule Roma in Search of Right to Space and Place. *Anthropology of East Europe Review, 25*(2), 96–107.

Stavrou, T. (1940). *Mistikes Piges.* Athens: Nea Estia.

Stewart, K. (1998). Nostalgia – A Polemic. *Cultural Anthropology, 3*(3), 227–241.

Stock, F. (2010). Home and Memory. In K. Knott & S. McLoughlin (Eds.), *Diasporas: Concepts, Intersections, Identities* (pp. 24–28). New York: Zed Books.
Stokes, M. (1992). *The Arabesk Debate: Music and Musicians in Modern Turkey.* New York: Oxford University Press.
Sutton, D. (1998). *Memories Cast in Stone.* Oxford: Berg.
Sylvester, Katherine M. (2010). *Public Participation and Urban Planning in Turkey: The Tarlabaşı Renewal Project.* Unpublished Ph.D. dissertation, University of Cincinnati.
Tanrıverdi, F. A. (2003). *Hoşçakal Prinkipo.* İstanbul: Literatür Arkapencere.
Tanyeri-Erdemir, T. (2017). Remains of the Day: Converted Anatolian Churches. In S. Yalman & I. Jevtic (Eds.), *Spolia Reincarnated: ANAMED 10th Anniversary Symposium.* İstanbul: Koç University Press.
Turan, Z. (2011). Material Memories of the Ottoman Empire. In K. Phillips & G. Mitchell Reyes (Eds.), *Global Memoryscapes: Contesting Remembrance in a Transnational Age.* Tuscaloosa: University of Alabama Press.
Türker, O. (1999). *Mega Revma'dan Arnavutköy'e: Bir Boğaziçi Hikayesi.* İstanbul: Sel Yayıncılık.
Türker, O. (2000). *Galata'dan Karaköy'e: Bir Liman Hikayesi.* İstanbul: Sel Yayıncılık.
Türker, O. (2001). *Fanari'den Fener'e: Bir Haliç Hikayesi.* İstanbul: Sel Yayıncılık.
Türker, O. (2003). *Halki'den Heybeli'ye: Bir Ada Hikayesi.* İstanbul: Sel Yayıncılık.
Türker, O. (2004a). *Nihori'den Yeniköy'e: Bir Boğaz Köyünün Hikayesi.* İstanbul: Sel Yayıncılık.
Türker, O. (2004b). *Prinkipo'dan Büyükada'ya: Bir Prens Adasının Hikayesi.* İstanbul: Sel Yayıncılık.
Türker, O. (2006). *Therapia'dan Tarabya'ya: Boğaz'ın Diplomatlar Köyünün Hikayesi.* İstanbul: Sel Yayıncılık.
Türker, O. (2007). *Antigoni'den Burgaz'a: Küçük Bir Adanın Hikayesi.* İstanbul: Sel Yayıncılık.
Türker, O. (2008). *Halkidona'dan Kadıköy'e: Körler Ülkesinin Hikayesi.* İstanbul: Sel Yayıncılık.
Türker, O. (2010a). *Tatavla: Osmanlı İstanbulu'ndan Bir Köşe.* İstanbul: Sel Yayıncılık.
Türker, O. (2010b). *Psomatia'dan Samatya'ya: Bir Bizans Semtinin Hikayesi.* İstanbul: Sel Yayıncılık.
Türker, O. (2016). *Pera'dan Beyoğlu'na: İstanbul'un Levanten ve Azınlık Semtinin Hikayesi.* İstanbul: Sel Yayıncılık.
Uysal, Ü. E. (2012). An Urban Social Movement Challenging Urban Regeneration: The Case of Sulukule, Istanbul. *Cities, 29*(1), 12–22.
Vaka, D. (2003/1923). *The Unveiled Ladies of Istanbul (Stamboul).* Piscataway: Gorgias Press LLC.

Vertovec, S. (2007). *New Directions in the Anthropology of Migration and Multiculturalism*. Oxford: Routledge.
Warf, B. (2012). Nationalism, Cosmopolitanism, and Geographical Imaginations. *Geographical Review, 102*(3), 271–292.
White, H. V. (1987). *The Content of the Form: Narrative Discourse and Historical Representation*. Baltimore: Johns Hopkins University Press.
Wimmer, A., & Schiller, N. G. (2002). Methodological Nationalism and Beyond: Nation-State Building, Migration and the Social Sciences. *Global Networks, 2*(4), 301–334.
Wohlgemut, E. (2009). *Romantic Cosmopolitanism*. Basingstoke: Palgrave Macmillan.
Yentürk, B. (2001). *Ne Lazım Tatavla'da Bakkal Dükkanı: Kurtuluş, Dolapdere, FerikÖy, Bomonti*. İstanbul: Zvi-Geyik Yayınları.

Epilogue

An Attempt to Update: Prospects for the Community, the City, and Cosmopolitanism

The Story of Hope

I was sitting in the last row, enjoying a good view over the crowd of some 70 people ranged in front of me in the Sismanogleio building of the General Consulate of Greece in Istanbul. The lights on the high ceiling of the seminar room were dimmed for the PowerPoint presentation that was taking place. An Istanbul-born Rum was talking about Kath 'imas Anatoli or Etmelan, the group of Istanbulite researchers and scholars based in Athens. His intention was to present the body of academic work conducted by the members of Etmelan, ranging from journals, books, and exhibits to conferences—all centering on the legacy of the Istanbul Rum community. The audience consisted of members of the community, as well as a few who had returned to Istanbul after having migrated to Athens, and some others from a variety of backgrounds who had received an invitation in their capacity of being "friends" to the Rum. After proceeding through a long list of activities, the speaker turned to the audience while changing his tone from scholarly to emotional: "We are experiencing great difficulties in being able to continue this work. Financial problems, problems finding a place to house our archives and our research associates. We believe it is important to continue to make known ... our history, our culture, to make a lasting contribution. Both in Turkey and in Greece. If you think that you can help in any way ... it is our identity."

This monologue ended the presentation, which was followed by the awarding of a prize for the speaker. During this ceremony, a brief talk was given by one of the leading figures of the Istanbul Rum. He first praised the work that is being conducted by Etmelan and then continued to say:

> The Rum of diaspora, in this case Athens, are our family members, friends. They left Istanbul, they felt that they had to leave, because they were made to feel as strangers in this country. Their minds told them that they should leave. But when they left, they left their hearts behind as well. Now that they live away from their homeland, in a strange land, where their hearts are not to be found, they feel themselves to be strangers again ... It is very important that this kind of work that glorifies the legacy of the City should resume. So, my answer to this appeal is this: Come back to the City. We have lots of empty space, wonderful buildings that remain idle, and many other resources. Rumness (*Romiossini*) is alive and has lots of potential. We would welcome you here, and make sure that your valuable research continues ... and in its very hearth, in the City, in Istanbul.

The event was followed by a cocktail reception, during which I managed to get hold of the community leader who had presented the award. He told me that he was not necessarily talking about the return migration of the same people who had been actually displaced. A small group of them, like the members of Etmelan, have not really left because they are keeping their identity as Istanbulites, and through their activities are constantly traveling back to the City in their minds and hearts. But the matter is beyond the number of people who are coming back or staying behind. What was needed, he said, to use a term that he coined, was a "repatriation of hope" (*epanapatrismo tis elpidas*). He told me not to forget what he had said, and then turned to someone else, leaving me with the strong echo of his words.

This anecdote helps summarize the main points I would like to underline in concluding this work. These concern the changing network dynamics among the Rum Polites, the status of them in Istanbul and their relations with the diaspora worldwide, as well as the internal parameters among the Rum Polites in Athens in the wake of recent economic, political, societal, and other developments that have an effect on the community with regards to their cultural dispositions toward their city, identity, history, and their future.

The event at Sismanogleio was an encounter between the two main parts of the Rum Polites community: those who are living in Istanbul, and those who have settled in Athens after their displacement. A get-together between these two groups is always an interesting occasion for bringing out the ways in which former friends or acquaintances relate to each other. Apart from much gossip during the cocktail session following the presentation, many comments were exchanged that showed the attitude of the Rum of Istanbul toward the Athenians, and vice versa.

The reference to the part of the community living in Athens as diaspora is noteworthy, and much of what is presented in this book contributes to this end. This event at Sismanogleio highlights another intricate dimension, however: the display of compassion or pity shown toward the Athenian counterpart of the Rum community (for being displaced, for living in diaspora, for not having the financial means to continue their research projects, for having left their hearts in Istanbul, and thus for feeling like strangers) couples with the notion of self-pity, giving an ironic twist to the statements made by the community leader. His emotional way of inviting the Rum Polites back to their hearth in Istanbul, where there is a lot of space to conduct their business, turns into a statement of harsh reality when the content is further analyzed: the space that is advertised consists of schools, homes, halls, church gardens, and other property that has been abandoned and is currently deteriorating. Lack of people to make use of this space is a direct result of the measures taken against the Rum Polites that led to their eventual migration. In making reference to there being lots of room for return migration, then, this person hints at the inevitability of migration itself. The availability of empty space, therefore, is only another way of looking at the grim emptiness of the urban space: Istanbul is empty without the Rum Polites. It is here that the previous resentment at the Rum for having left Istanbul for Greece gets mixed up with another emotion: an appreciation of the conditions that forced them to leave. There is a shared understanding of the common fate of displacement, which is held by both sides of the migration process, and which in turn translates to the sharing of a common sentiment, a common cultural disposition, and by extension a common identity. This identity is perceived as being shared among members of a displaced community who have experienced harsh conditions that are recorded in their collective memory.

In this attempt to update the state of the Rum Polites community roughly a decade after most of the fieldwork material was gathered, I focus both on the recent situation incurred by changes in the social and political environment, and on how the Rum Polites perceive these to have affected their present and their future prospects. Rather than speculation or projection about what comes next, my intention here is to underline some of the points raised by my informants about how they see their own future as a community.

When asked about the future, the answers of the Rum Polites range from being carefully optimistic to being recoverably pessimistic in relation to the points made earlier. This pendulum also characterizes the statements made by Alexis Alexandris, a historian and diplomat who served as General Consul of Greece in Istanbul (2003–2008), where he was born and raised. In his farewell speech given to his fellow Rum Polites before his departure, Alexandris (2009) addresses the important question: Given the circumstances at present, what are the prospects for the future of the Rum Polites? Alexandris brings together and balances various positions taken on this question, which are summarized and expanded in the following section.

Stories of Pessimism
An overview of answers given to that question would have to start from the pessimistic end. Rum Polites in Istanbul have every reason to fear their disappearance in the near future: they are a dwindling little community, made up of frightened and conservative elders, with a youth that is forgetting its own language and culture by interacting, even forming families, with people outside the community. It is a community with unresolved issues regarding their most basic human rights, especially their rights to their own property. In the past 80 years or so, the Rum Polites in Istanbul were left to watch their situation worsen as their friends and family left the City. At the level of state politics, Turkey and Greece have failed to agree on fundamental problems despite the mild climate of rapprochement during the last decades. At the level of community problems, international pressure has resulted only in limited acts of goodwill and has not helped to register much progress in resolving the outstanding issues.

There is a resentment about government policies in Turkey, and in particular a disappointment with the governing party AKP. A number of years ago I conducted an interview with an informant whom I had the chance to meet again recently. Back in 2003, he was very hopeful that the new AKP government was going to deal with the problems of minorities for two main reasons. First, because their active policy of making Turkey a candidate for full membership in the European Union (EU) would make them address domestic issues such as minorities within a wider European perspective. Second, and to him more importantly, being Islamists in a "radically secularist" country meant that they had a version of repressed minority status themselves. They would be sympathetic to the problems of other minorities as well, he assumed: "We had to hide our language; they have to hide the way they dress. We cannot become government officials; they cannot go to universities with their headscarves. We don't go to certain parts of the city; they don't go to certain parts of the city. They will understand our issues." The expectation was that the conservative background of Erdoğan would not hamper but enhance the process of further modernization of Turkey. Several people likened Erdoğan to Konstantinos Karamanlis, the late leader of the center-right *Nea Demokratia* party in Greece, who is credited with securing the EU membership and Europeanization of Greece. When I met with the same informant again, I asked him what he thought of Erdoğan now. "*Mangas*," he said. This word is rather difficult to translate, but the meaning falls somewhere between *macho* and *maganda*, indicating an overconfident, rascal-like attitude held by a somewhat undignified person, who is not ashamed of not keeping to his promise. With this, he summarized a major disapproval of the AKP and its performance, as reflected in the status of minorities in Turkey in recent years, which I would like to review in the paragraphs below.

In February 2006, a Turkish teenager shot dead a Catholic priest in Trabzon, and two other Catholic priests were attacked later that year. Three died in an attack on a publishing house, which was said to be involved in missionary activities in Malatya, the hometown of Mehmet Ali Ağca, who shot Pope John Paul II in 1981. This was neither the first nor the last case of atrocities directed at minorities. On the fateful day of 19 January 2007, renown public intellectual Hrant Dink, the founder and the editor-in-chief of the Armenian newspaper *Agos*, was brutally murdered by being shot from the back on a busy street. Although his funeral, attended by some 100,000 people, showed a strong reaction to these killings, the inefficiency of the trial process suggests an unwillingness to deal with the ultranationalist motivations behind these violent acts.

Dink's funeral was a landmark event that indicated heightened sensitivity in public opinion toward minority issues in particular, and in general for a cosmopolitanist, democratic coexistence respectful of human rights and rights to the city. Platforms and organizations supporting such causes became more varied and outspoken than ever, giving rise to a pluralistic civil society that became increasingly active in demanding policy changes (Gellman 2013). Of the many movements of dissidence, the most significant was that of Gezi Events in 2013, which started as a sit-in of environmentalists, grew into the occupation of a central park for three weeks, spread to local forums and worldwide protests, and eventually became one of the most important political movements in the history of Turkey (Örs & Turan 2015; Özkırımlı 2014).

The expectations of democratic hopefuls were to subside rather quickly, however, as the immediate response by government forces to Gezi was more than violent and repressive. Arguably, Gezi served as a pretext to increase political pressure on a large segment of the Turkish public, with an effect of harming the pluralistic civil society and inducing severe polarization. In the years that followed, drastic measures including police, judiciary, and military action were taken against minorities of various ethnic, religious, ideological, or other social backgrounds. The spread of international terrorism in the region, particularly associated with the civil war in Syria, the rise of extremist groups such as ISIS, and the breakdown of negotiations known as the Kurdish Initiative, has only contributed to the complexity of these problems. Casualties of targeted execution, mass murders, shelling, suicide bombers, terrorists, and police or military attacks started to become everyday news. More funerals followed, each of them with less of a sense that this is a landmark event not to be repeated. Repressive responses intensified after the 2015 elections that brought the democratic peoples' party HDP of Kurdish background in the parliament, and most notably the coup attempt in July 2016, when measures taken in the framework of successive periods of Martial Law led to the dismissal, arrest, and other forms of pressure toward public officials, journalists, politicians, and academics, who were suspected to be supporting views in opposition to the government. It became clear that it is not only the Rum Polites, but also not only the Christians, or non-Muslims, whose presence is threatened in Turkey. Unfair treatment, prejudice, as well as violence, has been directed against a number of cultural groups, especially Alevis, Amenians, and Kurds. Minority rights in specific, and human rights in general, remain one of the darkest corners in today's Turkish Republic (MRGI 2016).

The process of Turkey's accession to the EU is another issue of high relevance for the Rum Polites community, but this is increasingly seen to be far from being realized. It is only through becoming an EU member that Turkey could attain the necessary level of political stability and democratic development for the Rum minority "to take a deep breath," to use the words of a civil society activist, who voices that there will always be those who are suspicious of the intentions of the Turkish state. "Unless the EU gets in the picture, of course. Membership means minority rights, and a better future for us," she adds. However, she maintains the widely held concern that this no longer seems to be a viable prospect for Turkey, with both sides pushing it down the list of priorities for the near future.

Another major problem affecting the Rum Polites is the Greek financial crisis raging since 2008. Faced with perhaps the most challenging economic deadlock in its history, Greece is struggling to pay off its loans and to remain in the EU at the same time. With the resulting rise of unemployment and poverty, as well as troubles with illegal migrants and refugees, the far-right ultranationalist party Golden Dawn found representation in parliament, raising concerns about increasing xenophobia in Greek society. Rum Polites in Athens, already disillusioned by the Greek state's minority policies, fear that things may get worse in Greece before they get any better.

Given the broader state of affairs, and in connection with the points made above, many Rum Polites claim that there is hardly any way out of the unpleasant situation at hand. Without hope there is also little interest, among one segment of the Rum community, in exerting political will or in doing something to deal with their own problems. Many give up on the future by saying that the Rum Polites in Istanbul are disappearing even without migrating. In a trend often criticized by the older and more conservative members of the community, current generations of the Rum interact much more with people outside their circles. As it is almost impossible to continue living within the tiny community, they deal much more with others in their everyday lives. Relations with school friends, business partners, customers, or neighbors increasingly lead to romantic relationships between the Rum and non-Rum. There is still some suspicion toward marrying outside the community, however. Direct prohibition by the community, or the family, may no longer be an issue, but an internalized version of group pressure is still being problematized even by the most open-minded. "Let me ask you something personal," started off a long-term informant in his early 30s, who then told me about his serious relationship with a Turkish girl whom he was thinking of marrying. "When do you think I should propose?" he asked, because he was not sure how she would handle the issue of religious conversion. He pondered whether it would be best to introduce her to his close circle as well as the eminent members of the community, so that she feels comfortable being around the Rum, and vice versa. It went without saying that it was a prerequisite for him to have her become a Christian Orthodox, and for her to be accepted by the larger Rum community. In this case, the community was for him an extended family, his kith and kin, whose blessing he sought in order to get married. This indicates that religion remains one of the most important markers of community boundaries, which determine inclusion.

One important criterion to evaluate the extent to which community boundaries are dissolving is language. Much to the resentment of the larger community, the younger generations are not very competent in their mother tongue Romeic or *Rumca*. They simply do not have enough scope to practice outside the school or the church. Even there, however, they have difficulties: the recent migration of the Christian Orthodox from Antakya into Istanbul and their subsequent adoption into the Rum community has contributed to the increasing trend of Turkish becoming the *lingua franca* even among the Rum in Istanbul. The Antiochians are seen as a threat by many: "They may have our religion, but they don't have our language, and certainly not our culture. They're Arabs after all!" one informant put it bluntly, evoking negative stereotypes held in Turkey about the Arabs. Even without prejudicial comments, the fact that many children—whose mother tongue is Arabic and second language is Turkish—start school without speaking any Greek is a factor reducing the quality of Greek classes in Rum schools. This way, not only does their fluency in the local accent get lost, but also their competence in the knowledge of Modern Greek or Ancient Greek language becomes restricted. This point works as a competitive disadvantage for Istanbul Rum among other Greek speakers and is evaluated as a loss of identity of the community who historically considered their high level of education and "high culture" as important elements of their pride and distinction.

I witnessed a public debate between several members of the community, where these matters were placed in the center. "Let us unite among ourselves," said one middle-aged man, "let us accept those who had mixed marriages, as well as their children. Let us also resolve our issues with the Antiochians and start seeing them as equal members of our community." A young girl reacted with a brave comment: "How can we talk about the Christians of Antioch, when we have still not come to terms with our own Rum from Imvros and Tenedos?" While the others were nodding, another man jumped in: "We don't have the luxury to say who we take in and who to exclude at this point." He paused a moment, then said in a trembling voice: "*Teleionomaste*. We are finishing." Others also argued that the Rum community should reach out to take in outsiders, such as Greeks from Greece or Turks from Istanbul, and be much more welcoming toward them. There was a proposition that the Istanbul-based daily newspaper *Apogevmatini* should come out with one page in Turkish so that those who are not fluent in Greek can follow the news of the community. This stirred much argument among those who were present. A man in his 80s jumped from his seat and asked, turning to the young girl who had spoken earlier, what the Rum would have if they did not have their language. "Then we would only be Orthodox. Can you have a culture, a community without language?" Counterarguments followed, citing examples from the strong community of Greek Americans, who do not happen to be fluent Greek speakers. Still, the general tendency was not to allow the Rum newspaper to appear in Turkish, because, as somebody has argued: "Today there may be only one page. Tomorrow, we may have two. Then, maybe three. And one day, four pages. What then?" He was not simply counting. Since *Apogevmatini* appears daily with only four pages anyway, he was saying that a page in Turkish would start the countdown. A countdown, that is, of the disintegration of the Rum Polites.

Stories of Optimism
At the other end of the spectrum, however, some manage to stay carefully optimistic about the future of the Rum community in Istanbul. In a seminar held by that community and entitled *Youth Takes the Floor*, the aim was to let the young Rum people talk about their problems at present and their expectations for the future. The youth who presented their papers represented different segments of the Rum community with respect to their background: two of them were from Imvros/Gökçeada, one was from Antakya/Antioch, one from Antigoni/Burgaz island, and one from Athens. Reciting their stories of how they were treated as outsiders, or in some cases altogether excluded from the Rum community for being villagers (in the case of Gökçeada/Imvros), Arabs (in the case of Antioch/Antakya), or Elladites (Greeks from Greece), they voiced their wish to have a much more integrated, less fragmented community, whose members are in close contact with each other. Even the fact that they could sit around the same table in order to discuss the future of the Rum in Istanbul, they confirmed, was a very positive first step toward building a healthier community.

While far from being irrelevant, it needs to be stated that divisions along ethnic, lingual, sectarian, even religious lines matter less today than they did in the previous generation. Earlier, when the community was large enough, Rum Polites were able to live cosmopolitan yet self-contained lives. Unable to maintain this situation, they may be less independent, but also are increasingly pushed toward being more open. As one eminent member critically put it: "They are not going to be more open-minded about this. But at least they started realizing that there is no way of continuing to be like this—closed, I mean, and in fact, there is no need to. This fearful attitude is hopefully going away."

This is true for a certain segment of the Rum Polites in both Istanbul and Athens, whom I refer to as "active Istanbulites." Embracing their identity of the city and the community, these Rum Polites are participating actively in both societies with their intellectual, artistic, philanthropic, and other cultural capacities. The publishing house *istos* must be mentioned as a leading endeavor in this respect: established in Istanbul by young Rum Polites and their friends from Greece, *istos* publishes a wide range of old and new resources related to Istanbul in several languages. Its counterparts in Athens print even more titles to a larger readership in Greece. Rising popularity of Turkish and Greek topics on respective sides of the Aegean, aided by cosmopolitanist nostalgic discourses and increased cultural diplomacy, as well as intensified tourism and business relations between the two countries give a new central importance and opportunities of engagement to Rum Polites. They may be translators, educators, editors, journalists, writers, musicians, researchers, travel agents, bloggers, or hold any other jobs or professions, engaged in either revitalizing decaying Rum Polites institutions or initiating new organizations. Restored buildings, such as the Sismanogleio, the Greek Consulate in Pera, or the Rum School in Galata, constitute cultural centers for many activities that bring together the active Istanbulites with others from within and outside the community. An ever larger attendance is noted on religious feasts or special days in the Greek Orthodox or Rum Polites calendar, particularly on Easter in Greek Orthodox Churches of Istanbul, and on St. George's Day (*Ayayorgi*) in Prince's Island, which until recently went by without notice on the part of the larger urban society. The conveners may or may not be believers, but they are ardent supporters of the cosmopolitan cultural heritage of Istanbul.

No attempt to update can be complete without mentioning one of the most important changes in interpersonal communications worldwide that was introduced during the last decade, namely social media. While writing up my dissertation at Harvard on a grant I received on 2004, I was certainly not aware that a silent revolution was being birthed in the college houses a few blocks away, where Zuckerberg and his friends were launching the first versions of Facebook. Far from being technologically up-to-date, it took me a while to get on board; I eventually joined in 2013, when with the Gezi events the highly censored mainstream Turkish media lost all reliability as a news resource. To my surprise I discovered there was a brand new world of channels of communication among Rum Polites in Istanbul, Athens, and elsewhere around the globe, as well as former and current Istanbulites from all backgrounds. In that global digital space they were reunited with each other, shared stories, memories, news, photographs, concerns, calls for action, and activities around matters of common concern, including protection and preservation of the architectural, historical, linguistic, cultural, and natural heritage of Istanbul. Such an enhancement of the capacity of individuals to be involved in community affairs through online networks clearly contributed to the Rum Polites' part in the establishment of a virtual diaspora of the City.

This careful optimism of primarily the younger generation about the future of the community is enabled by increased levels of communication and interaction—not only owing to the technological advancements under globalization, but also because of the current political situation. While the general state of affairs in Turkey, coupled with the fading trend of the EU membership agenda, generates a deeply pessimistic atmosphere, some developments may be evaluated as positive for the Rum Polites. For one, there is a continuing period of rapprochement between Greece and Turkey in the 2000s. Having suffered tremendously as a result of past crises in bilateral relations, the Rum Polites see the current *détente* environment as nothing but desirable for their interests. Yet they are rather careful in taking this point too far. They have witnessed earlier phases of rapprochement suddenly end with the onset of major disasters, notably the 6–7 September events that followed the post-NATO years of amicable relations in the 1950s. The issue of refugees and illegal migrants crossing the Aegean and Thracian border has accelerated with the Syrian war and has led to one of the biggest tragedies in modern times. While the situation is beyond the ability and scope of the two countries, the everyday experience of it certainly puts both Greece and Turkey in the forefront, with a potential for political tension amidst humanitarian solidarity from locals on both sides of the Aegean. The convergence of this development with similar cases of involuntary displacement between Turkey and Greece, on the other hand, invites an intriguing research agenda that is starting to gain due scholarly attention (Athanasiadis 2016; Ben-Yehoyada 2015).

EU membership would surely enhance the relations of Turkey with Greece and lead to increased contact and exchange between the two nations. Yet the shrinking possibility of this scenario did not detract from the continuation of a Greek–Turkish interaction and collaboration. In fact, the deteriorating Greek economy resulted in increased tourism and commercial relations, while Turkey started being regarded as a land of opportunity and a more desirable place to live. Hopes for a revived economic status for the Rum Polites rose also with the legal amendments made in 2008 regarding ownership rights of minority foundations, which gave way to the gradual release of some confiscated properties back to the non-Muslim communities.

This is where the possibility of revitalization of the Rum Polites community comes into being. There is already a growing body of Greek businessmen, academics, and students who have recently moved to Turkey, and a similar trend among Turks for investing and living in Greece. Newly married couples made up of a Greek and a Turk are also increasing in number. Perhaps they may not necessarily or immediately get integrated into the Rum Polites community, but they tend to pursue parallel lives, often partaking in similar activities or sharing common life worlds. There is also a rising number of Rum Polites, who go back to Istanbul after living in Athens or elsewhere for a few decades or so. One of them said to me that life was hard anywhere, so they decided that they might as well live in their beautiful hometown (*memleket*). After losing their jobs, they really didn't have many more ties in Athens (*bizi oraya bağlayan pek bir şey yok*). Others are aware that theirs was a risky and courageous step, and their example may not be followed by the masses: "It is difficult to leave your life, school, family, friends, your lifestyle (*düzen*) behind and start anew in another place. Don't forget, we all had to do this at least once before. We left Istanbul, and it was very very hard. Now doing this all over again, even if it is to come back to Istanbul, is something that most would find very difficult," said my informant, who is in his late 60s. With these words, he summarized the basic issue with return migration.

All in all, the fact that there are at least as many people who are carefully optimistic about the future of the Rum Polites as there are recoverably pessimistic ones allows us to see a dim light at the end of the very long and very dark tunnel, in which the Rum Polites lost themselves for too long.

The conditions for emergence are subject to the extent to which they see themselves as fit for the task. Understanding their attitudes toward migration and their community, therefore, would be the first step in recognizing the ways in which displacement is problematized as an issue of identity for the Rum.

In this book, I intended to show that the ideas of the Rum Polites about their cosmopolitan identity are comparable to those they have about displacement from Istanbul to Athens: they are in disconcert with each other (Örs 2014a). I have identified "ambiguity of being out of place" and "exclusive diversity" as the two dimensions framing the cultural disposition of the Rum Polites, and finding theoretical relevance in the term cosmopolitanism. The Rum Polites today—as they have been in the past—are torn between competing understandings of cosmopolitanism. On the one hand, there is increasing interaction with the non-Rum, which is evaluated either as a move toward openness or as a threat of disintegration. On the other hand, there are those who react to this development and become more introverted and self-centered. Critics of this attitude indicate that the Rum community had always been diverse, with changing compositions throughout centuries, and that this was precisely their cosmopolitan character and their strength. Others argue that the situation is now different than it was a century ago, because when the community is in the throes of demographic disappearance, dilution is not something the Rum Polites can afford.

Exemplifying what Werbner states that diasporas can be "both ethnic-parochial *and* cosmopolitan" (2010, 75), the complex nature of the Rum Polites diaspora addresses the challenge of disclosing how the tension between these two tendencies is played out in actual situations. The lines of separation within the community are not only drawn by virtue of having differing attitudes toward cosmopolitanism, but also for considering different definitions of the concept. Ethnographic stories about the Rum Polites highlight an abundance of emic conceptions of cosmopolitanism. There is the notion of everyday experience of cosmopolitanism, with a sense of distinction based on the urban cultural capital of cosmopolitan knowledge. There is a notion of exclusive diversity, one that draws community boundaries not so much along primordial lines but on a sense of commitment to the urban cosmopolitan culture of Istanbul. This is an inclusive dimension of a Constantinopolitan cosmopolitanism, which is at the same time quite restricted in the sense that it distinguishes itself as superior to other forms of cosmopolitan living. It is a highly localized and essentialized notion of cosmopolitanism, which finds multiple internal divisions within its all-encompassing diversity; it entails competing contextualized cosmopolitanisms based on different experiences changing with social standing, time, and space in the city. Accordingly, each locality contributes with its own version of Istanbul cosmopolitanism: be it the conservative, status quo, imperial cosmopolitanism of Fanar or the civil, pluralistic, open, visible sharing of a bourgeois public space by institutionally autonomous and privately separate 'others' in Pera or the delineation of self-contained middle working class cultural existences in Tatavla that code Istanbul as a cosmopolitan city, these neighborhood- and experience-based intricacies give much-needed explicitness to an otherwise non-referential notion of cosmopolitanism.

One of my main objectives in this book has been to bring out the diversity of meanings associated with the concept of cosmopolitanism from the looking glass of communities who define themselves as cosmopolitan, and participate in the cosmopolitan diversity in the societies where they live. In this endeavor, I hope I have contributed to an endless scholarly debate that can be both varied and grounded through an ethnographic focus on the likes of the Rum Polites.

The Never-Ending Story
The stories of the City do not have an end. Just as they subside, they commence again. Every catastrophe leads to the rebirth of the City. The City is born and reborn a thousand and one times, as testified by timeless mythical stories of its foundation, related to us by the likes of Evliya Chelebi, great seventeenth-century storyteller of the Ottomans, and Stephan Yerasimos (1993), great contemporary scholar of the Rum Polites. Here is one of those stories of the City.

Legend has it that there was no Bosphorus then. Once upon a time, when Alexander the Great returned from an expedition, he made a stop in a place known today as Pera. At that spot he had a big hole dug in the ground and had all the witches, giants, sorcerers, and wizards he brought with him from the expedition put inside the ditch. These were released for 40 days and 40 nights each winter to roam free the Black Sea and the Mediterranean in order to protect the city with their spells. When Alexander later decided to open a new channel linking the Black Sea with the Mediterranean, in order to punish a rebellious population by flooding their town, the rising water ended up immersing the shores of Istanbul, reaching to the hills of Pera. The magic of the witches and sorcerers buried there was released; the spell was washed away inside the newly opened strait of sea, the Bosphorus.

Another legend has it that there was no Marmara Sea then. It dates from when Alexander was roaming through the city and stopped to go fishing in a creek. He tried and tried but could not catch any fish. An old man said that fishing was nothing like conquering countries; one had to have the right knowledge to capture it. Upon uttering these wise words, the old man reached into the creek and caught three big fish that he duly handed over to Alexander to cook and eat. Alexander tried and tried but could not fry any fish. The fish jumped back in the creek and swam away. Believing that the old man had tricked him with enchanted fish, the furious Alexander had him beheaded. The gush of blood turned to flood, rapidly flowing after Alexander as he galloped away on his mount. When he stopped in a spot known today as Yalova, he looked back at the body of water which now extended all the way back to Istanbul and would come to be called the Sea of Marmara. He mysteriously heard the old man's voice: "That creek was the holy water of eternal life. You did not know any better; you ruined the mystery. The holy water of eternity now remains buried under the sea."

You cannot fry your fish and eat it too, even if you are Alexander the Great, lest you capture the mystery of the City. You have to know the ways of the City. The City has the water of life under its immortal seas that mingle but do not mix. Those who belong to the City are forever bemused with its mystery; they mingle but do not mix with each other, they disperse but do not forget where they spring from. The City will follow them, and they will never leave their City. Everyone takes a bit of the City with them, the magic of the City, spreading the seeds of its cosmopolitan knowledge to build diasporas of the City. The bewitched City is looted, sieged, conquered, attacked, flooded, burnt, and shaken to the ground. Timeless and eternal, the City survives. There is always hope for the City. Hope shall keep repatriating in the City.

Bibliography

Abu-Lughod, L. (1986). *Veiled Sentiments: Honor and Poetry in a Bedouin Society*. Berkeley: University of California Press.

Akar, R. (1992). *Varlık Vergisi Kanunu: Tek Parti Rejiminde Azınlık Karşıtı Politika Örneği*. İstanbul: Belge Yayinlari.

Akar, R. (2006). *Aşkale Yolcuları: Varlık Vergisi Ve Çalışma Kampları*. İstanbul: Mephisto Yayınları.

Akgönül, S. (2007). *Türkiye Rumları: Ulus-Devlet Çağından Küreselleşme Çağına Bir Azınlığın Yok Oluş Süreci*. İstanbul: İletişim.

Akgönül, S. (2010). Les Turcs et les Grecs Peregrinations entre eris et eros. *Mésogeios, 36*, 41–64.

Akgönül, S. (2013). *The Minority Concept in the Turkish Context: Practices and Perceptions in Turkey, Greece, and France (Muslim Minorities)*. Leiden: Brill.

Akın, N. (1998). *19. Yüzyılın İkinci Yarısında Galata ve Pera*. Beyoğlu, İstanbul: Literatür.

Aktar, A. (1996). Economic Nationalism in Turkey: The Formative Years, 1912–1925. *Boğaziçi Journal, Review of Social and Administrative Studies, 10*(1–2), 263–290.

Aktar, A. (2000). *Varlık Vergisi Ve "Türkleştirme" Politikaları*. İstanbul: İletişim Yayınları.

Aktar, C. (2002). Cosmopolist: European Capital of Culture Istanbul. *Istanbul, 41*, 182–190.

Aktar, A. (2003). Homogenizing the Nation, Turkifying the Economy: The Turkish Experience of Population Exchange Reconsidered. In R. Hirschon

(Ed.), *Crossing the Aegean: An Appraisal of the 1923 Compulsory Population Exchange between Greece and Turkey* (pp. 79–95). Oxford: Berghahn.

Aktar, A., Kızılyürek, N., & Özkırımlı, U. (2010). *Nationalism in the Troubled Triangle: Cyprus, Greece and Turkey.* Basingstoke: Palgrave Macmillan.

Aktar, A., Hacıdimitriadis, Y., & Kandemir, F. (2011). *Yorgo Hacıdimitriadis'in Aşkale-Erzurum Günlüğü, 1943.* İstanbul: İletisim Yayınları.

Alavi, S. (2015). *Muslim Cosmopolitanism in the Age of Empire.* Cambridge: Harvard University Press.

Albera, D., & Couroucli, M. (2012). *Sharing Sacred Spaces in the Mediterranean: Christians, Muslims, and Jews at Shrines and Sanctuaries.* Bloomington, IN: Indiana University Press.

Alcalay, A. (1993). *After Jews and Arabs: Remaking Levantine Culture.* Minneapolis: University of Minnesota Press.

Aleksiadis-Fanariotis, G. (1956). *Thimasai to Fanari.* Athina.

Alevropoulos, F. (1982). *Nora.* Athens.

Alexandris, A. (1983). *The Greek Minority of Istanbul and Greek-Turkish Relations, 1918–1974.* Athens: Center for Asia Minor Studies.

Alexandris, A. (2009). *H Poli tou htes, tou simera kai tou avrio: Prosopikes skepseis enos Konstantinoupolitiki Ellina diplomati.* Istanbul: SAZ.

Alexiou, M. (1974). *The Ritual Lament in Greek Tradition.* Cambridge: Cambridge University Press.

Al-Rasheed, M. (1998a). *Iraqi Assyrian Christians in London: The Construction of Ethnicity.* Lewiston, NY: E. Mellen Press.

Al-Rasheed, M. (1998b). *The Shi'a of Saudi Arabia: A Minority in Search of Cultural Authenticity.* Exeter: British Society for Middle Eastern Studies.

Anagnostopoulou, S. (1997). *Mikra Asia, 19os ai.–1919: Oi ellinoorthodoxes koinotites. Apo to millet ton Romion sto Elliniko ethnos.* Athens: Ellinika Grammata.

Anagnostou, D. (2001). Breaking the Cycle of Nationalism: The EU, Regional Policy and the Minority of Western Thrace, Greece. *South European Society and Politics, 6*(1), 99–124. https://doi.org/10.1080/714004933.

Anastasiadou-Dumont, M., & Dumont, P. (2003). *Une mémoire pour la Ville: La communauté grecque d'Istanbul en 2003.* Istanbul: OUI.

Anastassiadou, M. (2009). Greek Orthodox Immigrants and Modes of Integration within the Urban Society of Istanbul (1850–1923). *Mediterranean Historical Review, 24*(2), 151–167.

Anderson, B. R. (1983). *Imagined Communities: Reflections on the Origin and Spread of Nationalism.* London: Verso.

Andersson, R. (2014). *Illegality, Inc.: Clandestine Migration and the Business of Bordering Europe.* Berkeley: University of California Press.

Angé, O., & Berliner, D. (Eds.). (2015). *Anthropology and Nostalgia.* Oxford: Berghahn.

Apostolidis, N. G. (1996). *Anamniseis apo tin Konstantinoupoli*. Athens: Trochalia.
Appadurai, A. (1981). The Past as a Scarce Resource. *Man, 16*(2), 201.
Appadurai, A. (1996). *Modernity at Large: Cultural Dimensions of Globalization*. Minneapolis: University of Minnesota Press.
Appiah, A. (2006). *Cosmopolitanism: Ethics in a World of Strangers*. New York: W.W. Norton.
Archibugi, D. (Ed.). (2003). *Debating Cosmopolitics*. London: Verso.
Archibugi, D. (2008). *The Global Commonwealth of Citizens: Toward Cosmopolitan Democracy*. Princeton: Princeton University Press.
Aretxaga, B. (1997). *Shattering Silence: Women, Nationalism, and Political Subjectivity in Northern Ireland*. Princeton, NJ: Princeton University Press.
Arizpe, L. (1998). Conviviability: The Role of Civil Society in Development. In A. Bernard, H. Helmich, & P. B. Lehning (Eds.), *Cultural Diversity and Citizenship*. Paris: OECD Publishing.
Armbruster, H. (2002). Homes in Crisis: Syrian Christian Orthodox in Turkey and Germany. In N. Al-Ali & K. Koser (Eds.), *New Approaches to Migration? Transnational Communities and the Transformation of Home*. London: Routledge.
Aslan, S. (2007). 'Citizen, Speak Turkish!': A Nation in the Making. *Nationalism and Ethnic Politics, 13*(2), 245–272.
Athanasiadis, I. (2016). Reviving the Mediterranean's Lost Cosmopolitanism. *Newsdeeply*. Retrieved from https://www.newsdeeply.com/refugees/op-eds/2016/03/29/reviving-the-mediterraneans-lost-cosmopolitanism
Atzemoglou, N. (1990). *Ta Ayiasmata tis Polis*. Athens: Risos.
Augustinos, G. (1992). *The Greeks of Asia Minor: Confession, Community, and Ethnicity in the Nineteenth Century*. Kent: Kent University Press.
Aygen, Z. (2012). *International Heritage and Historic Building Conservation: Saving the World's Past*. London: Routledge.
Azak, U. (2010). *Islam and Secularism in Turkey: Kemalism, Religion and the Nation State*. London: I.B. Tauris.
Babül, E. (2006). Claiming a Place Through Memories of Belonging: Politics of Recognition on the Island of Imbros. *New Perspectives on Turkey, 34*, 47–65.
Bali, R. (1999). *Cumhuriyet Yıllarında Türkiye Yahudileri: Bir Türkleştirme Serüveni, 1923–1945*. Cağaloğlu, İstanbul: İletişim.
Bali, R. (2001). Toplumsal Bellek ve Varlık Vergisi. In E. Özyürek (Ed.), *Türkiye'nin Toplumsal Hafızası: Hatırladıklarıyla Ve Unuttuklarıyla*. İstanbul: İletişim.
Bali, R. (2002). *Tarz-ı Hayat'tan Life Style'a: Yeni SeÇkinler, Yeni Mekânlar, Yeni Yaşamlar*. Cağaloğlu, İstanbul: İletişim.
Bali, R. (2008). *II. Dünya Savaşında Gayrimüslimlerin Askerlik Serüveni: Yirmi Kur'a Nafıa Askerleri*. İstanbul: Kitabevi.
Bali, R. (2010). *6–7 Eylül 1955 Olayları: Tanıklar-hatıralar*. İstanbul: Libra.

Balibar, É. (2006). *Strangers as Enemies: Further Reflections on the Aporias of Transnational Citizenship*. Working Papers 06/4, MCRI Globalization and Autonomy. Montreal: McMaster University.

Ballinger, P. (2003). *History in Exile: Memory and Identity at the Borders of the Balkans*. Princeton: Princeton University Press.

Balta, E. (2010). *Beyond the Language Frontier: Studies on the Karamanlis and the Karamanlidika Printing*. Istanbul: Isis Press.

Bareilles, B. (2003). *İstanbul'un Frenk Ve Leventen Mahalleleri: Pera, Galata, BanliyÖler*. İstanbul: Güncel Yayıncılık.

Barkan, E., & Barkey, K. (2014). *Choreographies of Shared Sacred Sites*. New York: Columbia University Press.

Barkey, K. (2005). Islam and Toleration: Studying the Ottoman Imperial Model. *International Journal of Politics, Culture, and Society, 19*(1–2), 5–19.

Barkey, K. (2008). *Empire of Difference: The Ottomans in Comparative Perspective*. Cambridge: Cambridge University Press.

Barth, F. (1969). *Ethnic Groups and Boundaries*. Boston: Little Brown and Company.

Barthes, R. (1981). *Camera Lucida: Reflections on Photography*. New York: Hill and Wang.

Bartu, A. (2000). Eski Mahallelerin Sahibi Kim? Küresel bir Çağda Tarihi Yeniden Yazmak. In Ç. Keyder (Ed.), *İstanbul: Küresel ile Yerel Arasında*. İstanbul: Metis.

Bartu Candan, A., & Kolluoğlu, B. (2008). Emerging Spaces of Neoliberalism: A Gated Town and a Public Housing Project in İstanbul. *New Perspectives on Turkey, 39*, 5–46.

Bartu Candan, A., & Özbay, C. (Eds.). (2014). *Yeni İstanbul Çalışmaları*. İstanbul: Metis.

Bauböck, R. (2006). Towards a Political Theory of Migrant Transnationalism. *International Migration Review, 37*(3), 700–723.

Baumann, M. (2000). Diaspora: Genealogies of Semantics and Transcultural Comparison. *Numen, 47*(3), 313–337.

Baussant, M. (2002). *Pieds-Noirs: Memoires d'exils*. Paris: Stock.

Bayat, A. (2013). *Post-Islamism the Changing Faces of Political Islam*. Oxford: Oxford UP.

Baykal, N. (2009). The Discursive Construction of Ethnic Identity: Sulukule Case, Turkey. *The Linguistics Journal: Special Edition*, 121–154.

Beck, U. (2000). *What Is Globalization?* Cambridge, UK: Polity.

Beck, U. (2002). The Cosmopolitan Society and Its Enemies. *Lebenszeiten*, 389–406. https://doi.org/10.1007/978-3-663-10626-5_23.

Beck, U. (2003). Toward a New Critical Theory with a Cosmopolitan Intent. *Constellations, 10*(4), 453–468.

Beck, U. (2004). Cosmopolitical Realism: On the Distinction between Cosmopolitanism in Philosophy and the Social Sciences. *Global Networks, 4*(2), 131–156.
Beck, U. (2006). *Power in the Global Age: A New Global Political Economy.* Cambridge: Polity.
Beck, U., & Sznaider, N. (2006). Unpacking Cosmopolitanism for the Social Sciences: A Research Agenda. *The British Journal of Sociology, 57*(1), 1–23.
Behar, B. E. (2003). *İktidar Ve Tarih: Türkiye'de "Resmi Tarih" Tezinin Oluşumu, 1929–1937.* İstanbul: İletişim.
Benlisoy, F. (Ed.). (2012). *İstanbul Rumları: Bugün Ve Yarın.* İstanbul: Zoğrafyon Lisesi Mezunları Derneği.
Benlisoy, F., & Benlisoy, S. (2001). Millet-i Rum'dan Helen Ulusuna 1856–1922. In *Cumhuriyet'e Devreden Düşünce Mirası: Tanzimat ve Meşrutiyet'in Birikimi: I* (pp. 367–376). İstanbul: İletişim.
Benlisoy, Y., & Macar, E. Ç. (1996). *Fener Patrikhanesi.* Kızılay, Ankara: AyraÇ Yayınevi.
Bennett, D. (Ed.). (1998). *Multicultural States.* London: Routledge.
Ben-Rafael, E., et al. (2006). *Building a Diaspora: Russian Jews in Israel, Germany and the USA.* Leiden: Brill.
Benson, P. (Ed.). (1993). *Anthropology and Literature.* Urbana: University of Illinois Press.
Benthall, J. (1997). Speaking of Suffering. *Anthropology Today, 13*(3), 1–2.
Ben-Yehoyada, N. (2015). 'Follow Me, and I Will Make You Fishers of Men': The Moral and Political Scales of Migration in the Central Mediterranean. *Journal of the Royal Anthropological Institute, 22,* 183–202.
Benz, W. (1992). Fremde in der Heimat: Flucht-Vertreibung-Integration. In K. Hage (Ed.), *Deutsche im Ausland-Fremde in Deutschland: Migration in Geschichte und Gegenwart* (pp. 374–386). Munich: C.H. Beck.
Beriss, D., & Sutton, D. E. (2007). *The Restaurants Book: Ethnographies of Where We Eat.* Oxford: Berg.
Bernard, R. H. (2006). *Research Methods in Anthropology: Qualitative and Quantitative Approaches.* Lanham and New York: Altamira Press.
Bestor, T. (2002). Networks, Neighborhoods, and Markets: Fieldwork in Tokyo. In G. Gmelch & W. P. Zenner (Eds.), *Urban Life: Readings in the Anthropology of the City.* Prospect Heights, IL: Waveland Press.
Bhabha, H. (Ed.). (1990). *Nation and Narration.* London: Routledge.
Biner, Z. Ö. (2007). Retrieving the Dignity of a Cosmopolitan City: Contested Perspectives on Rights, Culture and Ethnicity in Mardin. *New Perspectives on Turkey, 37,* 31–58.
Biner, Z. Ö. (2010). Acts of Defacement, Memories of Loss: Ghostly Effects of the 'Armenian Crisis' in Mardin, Southeastern Turkey. *History & Memory, 22*(2), 68–94.

Binnie, J., et al. (2006). *Cosmopolitan Urbanism*. London: Routledge.
Bissell, W. C. (2005). Engaging Colonial Nostalgia. *Cultural Anthropology, 20*(2), 215–248.
Borneman, J., & Hammoudi, A. (2009). *Being There: The Fieldwork Encounter and the Making of Truth*. Berkeley: University of California Press.
Boulmetis, T. (2004). *Politiki Kouzina*. Athens: Ellinika Grammata.
Bourdieu, P. (1984). *Distinction: A Social Critique of the Judgement of Taste*. Cambridge, MA: Harvard University Press.
Boyarin, J. (1992). *The Storm from Paradise: The Politics of Jewish Memory*. Minneapolis: University of Minnesota Press.
Boyarin, J., & Boyarin, D. (2002). *Powers of Diaspora: Two Essays on the Relevance of Jewish Culture*. Minneapolis: University of Minnesota Press.
Boyer, D. (2006). Ostalgie and the Politics of the Future in Eastern Germany. *Public Culture, 18*(2), 361–381.
Boym, S. (2001). *The Future of Nostalgia*. New York: Basic Books.
Boym, S. (2007). Nostalgia and Its Discontents. *The Hedgehog Review*, Institute for Advanced Studies in Culture, University of Virginia.
Bozi, S. (2002). *O Ellinismos tis Konstantinoupolis: Koinotita Stavrodromiou-Peran*. Athens: Ellinika Grammata.
Bozi, S. (2003). *Politiki Kouzina: Paradosi aionon*. Athens: Ellinika Grammata.
Brah, A. (1996). *Cartographies of Diaspora: Contesting Identities*. London: Routledge.
Braude, B., & Lewis, B. (Eds.). (1982). *Christians and Jews in the Ottoman Empire*. New York: Holmes and Meier.
Braziel, J. E. (2008). *Diaspora: An Introduction*. Malden, MA: Blackwell.
Breckenridge, C. A. (Ed.). (2000). *Cosmopolitanism*. Durham, NC: Society for Transnational Cultural Studies by Duke University Press.
Brown, K. (1999). Marginal Narratives and Shifty Natives: İronic Ethnography as Antinationalist Discourse. *Anthropology Today, 15*, 13–16.
Brown, K. S., & Hamilakis, Y. (2003). *The Usable Past: Greek Metahistories*. Lanham, MD: Lexington Books.
Brubaker, R. (1996). *Nationalism Reframed: Nationhood and the National Question in the New Europe*. Cambridge: Cambridge University Press.
Brubaker, R. (2010a). *From Ethnic Insiders to Refugee Outsiders: A Community Level Ethnography of Greek Cypriot Identity: Formation and Transference since Displacement*. Oxford: Refugee Studies Centre.
Brubaker, R. (2010b). Migration, Membership, and the Modern Nation-State: Internal and External Dimensions of the Politics of Belonging. *Journal of Interdisciplinary History, 41*(1), 61–78.
Bryant, R. (2008). Writing the Catastrophe: Nostalgia and Its Histories in Cyprus. *Journal of Modern Greek Studies, 26*(2), 399–422. https://doi.org/10.1353/mgs.0.0029.

Bryant, R. (2010). *The Past in Pieces: Belonging in the New Cyprus.* Philadelphia: University of Pennsylvania Press.
Bryant, R. (2016). *Post-Ottoman Coexistence: Sharing Space in the Shadow of Conflict.* New York, NY: Berghahn.
Bryant, R., & Papadakis, Y. (2012). *Cyprus and the Politics of Memory: History, Community and Conflict.* London: I.B. Tauris.
Burke, K. (1969). *A Grammar of Motives.* Berkeley: University of California Press.
Butler, K. D. (2001). Defining Diaspora, Refining a Discourse. *Diaspora: A Journal of Transnational Studies, 10*(2), 189–219.
Çağaptay, S. (2006). *Islam, Secularism and Nationalism in Modern Turkey: Who Is a Turk?* London: Routledge.
Calhoun, C. (2002). The Class Consciousness of Frequent Travellers: Towards a Critique of Actually Existing Cosmopolitanism. In S. Vertovec & R. Cohen (Eds.), *Conceiving Cosmopolitanism: Theory, Context, Practice* (pp. 86–109). Oxford: Oxford University Press.
Calhoun, C. (2004). Accidental Wisdom. *Book Forum.* Retrieved from http://www.bookforum.com/archive/sum_04/calhoun.html
Calhoun, C. J., & Sennett, R. (2007). *Practicing Culture.* London: Routledge.
Calotychos, V. (2003). *Modern Greece: A Cultural Poetics.* Oxford: Berg.
Cartier, C. (1999). Cosmopolitics and the Maritime World City. *Geographical Review, 89*(2), 278–289.
Cassia, P. S. (2005). *Bodies of Evidence: Burial, Memory and the Recovery of Missing Persons in Cyprus.* New York: Berghahn Books.
Chalkousi, X. (2002). *Mirodies kai yevseis tis Polis … kai stin korfi kanela.* Athens: Tsoukatou.
Chatziioannou, M. C., & Kamouzis, D. (2013). From a Multiethnic Empire to Two National States: The Economic Activities of the Greek Orthodox Population of Istanbul, ca. 1870–1939. In *The Economies of Urban Diversity* (pp. 117–143). New York, NY: Palgrave Macmillan.
Cheah, P. (2006). *Inhuman Conditions: On Cosmopolitanism and Human Rights.* Cambridge, MA: Harvard University Press.
Chernilo, D. (2006). Social Theory's Methodological Nationalism: Myth and Reality. *European Journal of Social Theory, 9*(1), 5–22.
Chock, P. P. (1987). The Irony of Stereotypes: Toward an Anthropology of Ethnicity. *Cultural Anthropology, 2*(3), 347–368.
Christidis, C. (2000). *Ta Septemvriana.* Athens: Kentro Mikrasiastikon Spoudon.
Christou, A. (2006). Deciphering Diaspora, Translating Transnationalism: Family Dynamics, Identity Constructions and the Legacy of 'Home' in Second-Generation Greek-American Return Migration. *Ethnic and Racial Studies, 29*(6), 1040–1056.
Christou, A., & Mavroudi, E. (Eds.). (2015). *Dismantling Diasporas: Rethinking the Geographies of Diasporic Identity, Connection and Development.* London: Routledge.

Clark, B. (2006). *Twice a Stranger: The Mass Expulsions That Forged Modern Greece and Turkey*. Cambridge, MA: Harvard University Press.
Clifford, J. (1983). On Ethnographic Authority. *Representations, 2*, 118–146.
Clifford, J. (1986). Introduction: Partial Truths. In J. Clifford & G. Marcus (Eds.), *Writing Culture: The Poetics and Politics of Ethnography* (pp. 1–26). Berkeley: University of California Press.
Clifford, J. (1988). *The Predicament of Culture: Twentieth Century Ethnography, Literature, and Art*. Cambridge: Harvard University Press.
Clifford, J. (1994). Diasporas. *Cultural Anthropology, 9*(3), 302–338.
Clifford, J. (1997). *Routes: Travel and Translation in the Late Twentieth Century*. Cambridge: Harvard University Press.
Clifford, J., & Marcus, G. (1986). *Writing Culture: The Poetics and Politics of Ethnography*. Berkeley: University of California Press.
Clogg, R. (1973). *The Struggle for Greek Independence; Essays to Mark the 150th Anniversary of the Greek War of Independence*. Hamden, CT: Archon Books.
Clogg, R. (1992). *A Concise History of Modern Greece*. Cambridge: Cambridge University Press.
Clogg, R. (Ed.). (1999). *The Greek Diaspora in the Twentieth Century*. London: Macmillan Press.
Cohen, A. (1985). *The Symbolic Construction of Community*. London: Routledge.
Cohen, R. (1997). *Global Diasporas: An Introduction*. London: UCL Press.
Coller, I. (2011). *Arab France: Islam and the Making of Modern Europe, 1798–1831*. Berkeley: University of California Press.
Collins, B. J. (2010). Animal Mastery in Hittite Art and Texts. In D. B. Counts & B. Arnold (Eds.), *The Master of Animals in Old World Iconography* (pp. 59–74). Budapest: Archaeolingua Foundation.
Comaroff, J., & Comaroff, J. (1992). *Ethnography and the Historical Imagination*. Boulder: Westview Press.
Coutin, S. B. (2006). Cultural Logics of Belonging and Movement: Transnationalism, Naturalization, and US Immigration Politics. In A. Sharma & A. Gupta (Eds.), *The Anthropology of the State: A Reader*. Malden: Blackwell.
Cowan, J. K. (1990). *Dance and the Body Politic in Northern Greece*. Princeton, NJ: Princeton University Press.
Crapanzano, V. (2010). At the Heart of the Discipline: Critical Reflections on Fieldwork. In J. Davies & D. Spencer (Eds.), *Emotions in the Field: The Psychology and the Anthropology of the Fieldwork Experience* (pp. 55–78). Stanford: Stanford University Press.
Dannreuther, R. (1999). Cosmopolitan Citizenship and the Middle East. In K. Hutchings & R. Dannreuther (Eds.), *Cosmopolitan Citizenship* (pp. 143–170). London: Macmillan.
Das, V. (1995). *Critical Events: An Anthropological Perspective on Contemporary India*. Delhi: Oxford University Press.

Davis, S. H., & Konner, M. (2011). *Being There: Learning to Live Cross-Culturally.* Cambridge, MA: Harvard University Press.
De Certeau, M. (1988). *The Practice of Everyday Life.* Berkeley: University of California Press.
Deleon, J. (1995). *The White Russians in Istanbul.* İstanbul: Remzi.
Deleon, J. (2004). *Balat ve Çevresi.* İstanbul: Remzi.
Demetriou, O. (2013). *Capricious Borders: Minority, Population, and Counter-Conduct between Greece and Turkey.* Oxford: Berghahn.
Demir, H., & Akar, R. (1994). *İstanbul'un Son Sürgünleri.* İstanbul: İletişim.
Di Pascale, A. (2010). Migration Control at Sea: The Italian Case. In R. Mitsilegas (Ed.), *Extraterritorial Immigration Control: Legal Challenges* (pp. 274–304). Leiden: Martinus Nijhoff.
Dora, V. D. (2006). The Rhetoric of Nostalgia: Postcolonial Alexandria between Uncanny Memories and Global Geographies. *Cultural Geographies, 13*(2), 207–238.
Douglas, M. (1966). *Purity and Danger: An Analysis of Concepts of Pollution and Taboo.* London: Routledge and Kegan Paul.
Douglas, M. (1987). *Constructive Drinking: Perspectives on Drink from Anthropology.* Cambridge: Cambridge University Press.
Dragonas, T. (2004). Negotiation of Identities: The Muslim Minority in Western Thrace. *New Perspectives on Turkey, 30,* 1–24.
Dragonas, T., Ersanli, B., & Frangoudaki, A. (2005). Greek and Turkish Students' Views on History, the Nation and Democracy. In T. G. Dragonas & F. Birtek (Eds.), *Citizenship and the Nation-State in Greece and Turkey* (pp. 161–189). London: Routledge.
Driessen, H. (1992). *On the Spanish-Moroccan Frontier: A Study in Ritual, Power, and Ethnicity.* New York and Oxford: Berg.
Driessen, H. (2005). Mediterranean Port Cities: Cosmopolitanism Reconsidered. *History and Anthropology, 16*(1), 129–141. https://doi.org/10.1080/02757 20042000316669.
Dubish, J. (1995). *In a Different Place: Pilgrimage, Gender, and Politics of a Greek Island Shrine.* Princeton, NJ: Princeton University Press.
Dufft, C. (2009). *Turkish Literature and Cultural Memory: "Multiculturalism" as a Literary Theme after 1980.* Wiesbaden: Harrassowitz.
Dündar, F. (2000). *Türkiye Nüfus Sayımlarında Azınlıklar.* İstanbul: Çiviyazıları.
Duru, D. N. (2015). From Mosaic to Ebru: Conviviality in Multi-Ethnic, Multi-Faith Burgazadası, Istanbul. *South European Society and Politics, 20*(2), 243–263.
Eldem, E. (1999). *French Trade in Istanbul in the Eighteenth Century.* Leiden: Brill.
Eldem, E., Goffman, D., & Masters, B. (1999). *The Ottoman City between East and West: Aleppo, Izmir, and Istanbul.* New York: Cambridge University Press.

Erbil, L. (2000). Trianon Pastanesi. In T. Uyar & S. Köksal (Eds.), *İstanbul'da Zaman* (pp. 9–16). İstanbul: Büke.
Ergül, F. A. (2012). The Ottoman Identity: Turkish, Muslim or Rum ? *Middle Eastern Studies, 48*(4), 629–645.
Erickson, B. (2011). Utopian Virtues: Muslim Neighbors, Ritual Sociality, and the Politics of Convivencia. *American Ethnologist, 38*(1), 114–131.
Eriksen, E. O. (Ed.). (2007). *Making the European Polity: Reflexive Integration in the EU*. London: Routledge.
Erman, T., & Coşkun-Yıldar, M. (2007). Emergent Local Initiative and the City: The Case of Neighbourhood Associations of the Better-Off Classes in Post-1990 Urban Turkey. *Urban Studies, 44*(13), 2547–2566.
Ersanlı, B. (2003). *İktidar ve Tarih: Türkiye'de Resmi Tarih Tezinin Oluşumu, 1929–1937*. İstanbul: İletişim.
Evelpidis, C. (1976). *Politika*. Athens: Papazisis.
Exertzoglou, H. (1996). *Ethniki Taftotita stin Konstantinoupoli ton 19o aiona*. Athens: Nefeli.
Exertzoglou, H. (1999). The Development of a Greek Ottoman Bourgeoisie: Investment Patterns in the Ottoman Empire, 1850–1914. In D. Gondicas & C. Issawi (Eds.), *Ottoman Greeks in the Age of Nationalism* (pp. 89–114). Princeton: The Darwin Press.
Exertzoglou, H. (2003). The Cultural Uses of Consumption: Negotiating Class, Gender, and Nation in the Ottoman Urban Centers during the 19th Century. *International Journal of Middle East Studies, 35*(1), 77–101.
Fahmy, N. (2006). Egypt's Unwavering Path to Democratic Reform. *Mediterranean Quarterly, 17*(3), 1–11. https://doi.org/10.1215/10474552-2006-011.
Falzon, M.-A. (2004). *Cosmopolitan Connections: The Sindhi Diaspora, 1860–2000*. Leiden: Brill.
Falzon, M.-A. (2009). *Multi-Sited Ethnography: Theory, Praxis and Locality in Contemporary Research*. Farnham: Ashgate.
Faubion, J. (1993). *Modern Greek Lessons: A Primer in Historical Constructivism*. Princeton: Princeton University Press.
Feld, S., & Basso, K. H. (2009). *Senses of Place*. Santa Fe: School of American Research Press.
Fernandez, J., & Hubel, M. T. (2001). *Irony in Action: Anthropology, Practice, and the Moral Imagination*. Chicago: Chicago University Press.
Fine, R. (2008). *Cosmopolitanism*. London: Routledge.
Fine, R., & Chernilo, D. (2004). Between Past and Future: The Equivocations of the New Cosmopolitanism. *Studies in Law Politics and Society, 31*, 25–44.
Fischer, M., & Kokolaki, M. (2013). Comments and Reflections. *Urbanites, 3*(2), 114–117.
Fish, S. (1997). Boutique Multiculturalism, or Why Liberals Are Incapable of Thinking about Hate Speech. *Critical Inquiry, 23*(2), 378–395.

Foggo, H. (2007). The Sulukule Affair: Roma against Expropriation. *Roma Rights Quarterly, 4,* 41–47.
Foner, N. (2002). Transnationalism, Old and New: New York Immigrants. In G. Gmelch & W. P. Zenner (Eds.), *Urban Life: Readings in the Anthropology of the City.* Prospect Heights, IL: Waveland Press.
Fortna, B. C., Katsikas, S., Kamouzis, D., & Konortas, P. (2013). *State-Nationalisms in the Ottoman Empire, Greece and Turkey: Orthodox and Muslims, 1830–1945.* London: Routledge.
Foster, G. M., & Kemper, R. V. (1974). *Anthropologists in Cities.* Boston: Little, Brown.
Fregonese, S. (2012). Between a Refuge and a Battleground: Beirut's Discrepant Cosmopolitanisms. *Geographical Review, 102*(3), 316–336.
Freitag, U. (2014). 'Cosmopolitanism' and 'Conviviality'? Some Conceptual Considerations Concerning the Late Ottoman Empire. *European Journal of Cultural Studies, 17*(4), 375–391.
Freitag, U., & Lafi, N. (Eds.). (2014). *Urban Governance Under the Ottomans: Between Cosmopolitanism and Conflict.* London: Routledge.
Freitag, U., Fuhrmann, M., Lafi, N., & Riedler, F. (Eds.). (2011). *The City in the Ottoman Empire: Migration and the Making of Urban Modernity.* London: Routledge.
Friese, H. (2010). The Limits of Hospitality: Political Philosophy, Undocumented Migration and the Local Arena. *European Journal of Social Theory, 13*(3), 323–341.
Fuhrmann, M., & Kechriotis, V. (2009). The Late Ottoman Port-Cities and Their Inhabitants: Subjectivity, Urbanity, and Conflicting Orders: İn Memory of Faruk Tabak (1953–2008). *Mediterranean Historical Review, 24*(2), 71–78.
Geertz, C. (1988). *Works and Lives: The Anthropologist as Author.* Stanford, CA: Stanford University Press.
Gellman, M. (2013). Remembering Violence: The Role of Apology and Dialogue in Turkey's Democratization Process. *Democratization, 20*(4), 771–794.
Gellner, E. (1983). *Nations and Nationalism.* Ithaca: Cornell University Press.
Ghosh, A. (1992). *In an Antique Land.* London: Granta Books.
Giaccaria, P. (2012). Cosmopolitanism: The Mediterranean Archives. *Geographical Review, 102*(3), 293–315.
Gill, T. (2001). *Men of Uncertainty: The Social Organization of Day Laborers in Contemporary Japan.* Albany: State University of New York Press.
Gilroy, P. (2006). *After Empire: Melancholia or Convivial Culture?* Abingdon: Routledge.
Gilsenan, M. (1992). *Recognizing Islam: Religion and Society in the Modern Middle East.* London: I.B. Tauris.
Giordano, C. (2012). Anthropology Meets History: İnvestigating European Societies. *Anthropological Journal of European Cultures, 21*(2), 20–34.

Glick-Schiller, N. (2005). Transnational Migration and the Re-framing of Normative Values. In F. V. Benda-Beckmann, K. V. Benda-Beckmann, & A. M. O. Griffiths (Eds.), *Mobile People, Mobile Law: Expanding Legal Relations in a Contracting World.* Aldershot: Ashgate.

Glick-Schiller, N., Basch, L., & Blanc-Szanton, C. (1992). Transnationalism: A New Analytic Framework for Understanding Migration. *Annals of the New York Academy of Sciences, 645*(1), 1–24.

Göçek, F. M. (1996). *Rise of the Bourgeoisie, Demise of Empire: Ottoman Westernization and Europe.* New York: Oxford University Press.

Göçek, F. M. (2016). *Denial of Violence: Ottoman Past, Turkish Present, and Collective Violence against the Armenians, 1789–2009.* Oxford: Oxford University Press.

Goitein, S. D. F. (1967–1993). *A Mediterranean Society: The Jewish Communities of the Arab World as Portrayed in the Documents of the Cairo Geniza.* Berkeley: University of California Press.

Göktürk, D., Soysal, L., & Tureli, I. (Eds.). (2010). *Orienting Istanbul: Cultural Capital of Europe?* London: Routledge.

Gondicas, D., & Issawi, C. (1999). *Ottoman Greeks in the Age of Nationalism: Politics, Economy, and Society in the Nineteenth Century.* Princeton, NJ: Darwin Press.

Goonewardena, K. (2005). The Urban Sensorium: Space, Ideology and the Aestheticization of Politics. *Antipode, 37*(1), 46–71.

Gözaydın, İ. (2008). Religion, Politics, and the Politics of Religion in Turkey. In D. Jung & C. Raudvere (Eds.), *Religion, Politics, and Turkey's EU Accession.* New York: Palgrave Macmillan.

Graham, S. (Ed.). (2004). *The Cybercities Reader.* London: Routledge.

Greene, M. (2000). *A Shared World: Christians and Muslims in the Early Modern Mediterranean.* Princeton, NJ: Princeton University Press.

Grigoriadis, I. N. (2008). On the Europeanization of Minority Rights Protection: Comparing the Cases of Greece and Turkey. *Mediterranean Politics, 13*(1), 23–41.

Guarnizo, L. E. (1997). The Emergence of a Transnational Social Formation and the Mirage of Return Migration among Dominican Transmigrants. *Identities: Global Studies in Culture and Power, 4*(2), 281–322.

Guarnizo, L. E. (2003). The Economics of Transnational Living. *International Migration Review, 37*(3), 666–699.

Gunaris, B., Mihailidis, I., & Angelopoulos, G. (Eds.). (1997). *Taftotites stin Makedonia.* Athens: Papazisis.

Gupta, A., & Ferguson, J. (Eds.). (1997). *Culture, Power, Place: Explorations in Critical Anthropology.* Durham: Duke University Press.

Gürsel, D. (2012, November 6). Bir Palimpsest Kent olarak İstanbul. *Arkitera*. Retrieved from http://www.arkitera.com/haber/10667/bir-palimpsest-kent-istanbul
Güven, D. (2005). *Cumhuriyet Dönemi Azınlık Politikaları Bağlamında 6-7 Eylül Olayları*. İstanbul: Tarih Vakfı Yayınları.
Hage, G. (1998). *White Nation: Fantasies of White Supremacy in a Multicultural Society*. Sydney: Pluto Press.
Hall, S. (1990). Cultural Identity and Diaspora. In J. Rutherford (Ed.), *Identity: Community, Culture, Difference* (pp. 222-237). London: Lawrence & Wishart.
Hanley, W. (2008). Grieving Cosmopolitanism in Middle East Studies. *History Compass*, 6(5), 1346-1367.
Hannerz, U. (1990). Cosmopolitans and Locals in World Culture. *Theory, Culture & Society*, 7(2), 237-251.
Hannerz, U. (1996). *Transnational Connections: Culture, People, Places*. London: Routledge.
Hannerz, U. (2003). Being There... and There... and There!: Reflections on Multi-Site Ethnography. *Ethnography*, 4(2), 201-216.
Hanssen, J. (2002). *The Empire in the City: Arab Provincial Capitals in the Late Ottoman Empire*. Ergon-Verlag: Würzburg.
Haraway, D. (1989). *Primate Visions: Gender, Race, and Nature in the World of Modern Science*. New York: Routledge.
Harisiadou, M. (2002). Tourkia einai edo.... *Kinsterna*, 1-2, 84-90.
Harrell-Bond, B. E., & Voutira, E. (1992). Anthropology and the Study of Refugees. *Anthropology Today*, 8(4), 6-10.
Harris, R. (2011). Multiculturalism: Theoretical Challenges from Anthropology. *Urbanities*, 1(1), 70-75.
Harvey, D. (2000). *Spaces of Hope*. Berkeley: University of California Press.
Harvey, D. (2009). *Cosmopolitanism and the Geographies of Freedom*. New York: Columbia University Press.
Hassiotis, I., Katsiardi-Hering, O., & Ampatzi, E. (2006). *Oi Ellines stin Diaspora*. Athens: Vouli ton Ellinon.
Hattox, R. S. (1985). *Coffee and Coffeehouses: The Origins of a Social Beverage in the Medieval Near East*. Seattle: Distributed by University of Washington Press.
Hatziprokopiou, P. (2003). Albanian Immigrants in Thessaloniki, Greece: Processes of Economic and Social Incorporation. *Journal of Ethnic and Migration Studies*, 29(6), 1033-1057.
Hatziprokopiou, P. (2006). *Globalisation, Migration and Socio-Economic Change in Contemporary Greece: Processes of Social Incorporation of Balkan Immigrants in Thessaloniki*. Amsterdam: Amsterdam University Press.
Hatziprokopiou, P., & Evergeti, V. (2014). Negotiating Muslim Identity and Diversity in Greek Urban Spaces. *Social & Cultural Geography*, 15(6), 603-626.
Held, D. (2010). *Cosmopolitanism: Ideals and Realities*. Cambridge: Polity.

Heleniak, T. (1997). Internal Migration in Russia during the Economic Transition. *Post-Soviet Geography and Economics, 38*(2), 81–104.
Heraclides, A. (2003). *H Ellada kai o "ex anatolon kindinos"*. Athens: Polis.
Herzfeld, M. (1982). *Ours Once More: Folklore, Ideology, and the Making of Modern Greece*. Austin: University of Texas Press.
Herzfeld, M. (1985). *The Poetics of Manhood: Contest and Identity in a Cretan Mountain Village*. Princeton, NJ: Princeton University Press.
Herzfeld, M. (1987). *Anthropology Through the Looking-Glass: Critical Ethnography in the Margins of Europe*. Cambridge: Cambridge University Press.
Herzfeld, M. (1991). *A Place in History: Social and Monumental Time in a Cretan Town*. Princeton, NJ: Princeton University Press.
Herzfeld, M. (1992). *The Symbolic Production of Indifference: Exploring the Roots of Western Bureaucracy*. New York: Berg.
Herzfeld, M. (1997a). *Portrait of a Greek Imagination: An Ethnographic Biography of Andreas Nenedakis*. Chicago: The University of Chicago Press.
Herzfeld, M. (1997b). *Cultural Intimacy: Social Poetics in the Nation-State*. New York: Routledge.
Herzfeld, M. (2013). Comments. *Urbanities, 3*(2), 118–120.
Hirschon, R. (1989). *Heirs of the Greek Catastrophe: The Social Life of Asia Minor Refugees in Piraeus*. Oxford: Clarendon Press.
Hirschon, R. (2003). Unmixing Peoples in the Aegean Region. In R. Hirschon (Ed.), *Crossing the Aegean: An Appraisal of the 1923 Compulsory Population Exchange between Greece and Turkey* (pp. 3–12). Oxford: Berghahn.
Ho, E. (2002). Names beyond Nations: The Making of Local Cosmopolitans. *Études Rurales, 163/164*, 215–231.
Ho, E. (2004). Empire Through Diasporic Eyes: A View from the Other Boat. *Comparative Studies in Society and History, 46*, 210–246.
Ho, E. (2006). *The Graves of Tarim: Genealogy and Mobility across the Indian Ocean*. Berkeley: University of California Press.
Hoerder, D., Harzig, C., & Shubert, A. (2003). *The Historical Practice of Diversity: Transcultural Interactions from the Early Modern Mediterranean to the Postcolonial World*. New York: Berghahn Books.
Holland, D. C., & Lave, J. (2001). *History in Person: Enduring Struggles, Contentious Practice, Intimate Identities*. Santa Fe, NM: School of American Research Press.
Holston, J. (1999). *Cities and Citizenship*. Durham: Duke University Press.
Holst-Warhaft, G. (1989). *Road to Rembetika: Music of a Greek Sub-Culture: Songs of Love, Sorrow, and Hashish*. Limni: Harvey & Co.
Hristodulu, M. (2013/1913). *Ta Tatavla kai i Istoria tous/Tatavla Tarihi*. İstanbul: İstos.
Huang, Y. (2002). *Transpacific Displacement: Ethnography, Translation, and Intertextual Travel in Twentieth Century American Literature*. Berkeley: University of California Press.

Humphrey, C., & Skvirskaja, V. (2012). *Post-Cosmopolitan Cities: Explorations of Urban Coexistence*. New York: Berghahn.
Husry, K. S. (1974). The Assyrian Affair of 1933. *International Journal of Middle East Studies*, 5(2), 161–176.
Hutchings, K., & Dannreuther, R. (Eds.). (1999). *Cosmopolitan Citizenship*. New York: St. Martin's Press.
Hyman, S. E. (Ed.). (1964). *Perspectives by Incongruity by Kenneth Burke*. Bloomington: Indiana University Press.
Icduygu, A. (2004). Transborder Crime between Turkey and Greece: Human Smuggling and Its Regional Consequences. *Southeast European and Black Sea Studies*, 4(2), 294–314.
Iğsız, A. (2015). Palimpsests of Multiculturalism and Museumization of Culture Greco-Turkish Population Exchange Museum as an Istanbul 2010 European Capital of Culture Project. *Comparative Studies of South Asia, Africa and the Middle East*, 35(2), 324–345.
Ilbert, R., & Yannakakis, I. (1992). *Alexandrie, 1860–1960: Un modèle éphémère de convivialité, communautés et identité cosmopolite*. Paris: Editions Autrement.
İleri, S. (2006). *İstanbul Hatıralar Kolonyası*. İstanbul: Doğan Kitap.
İnalcık, H. (1991). The Status of the Greek Orthodox Patriarch under the Ottomans. *Turcica: Revue d'Etudes Turques*, 21–23, 407–436.
Iordanidou, M. (1963). *Loxandra*. Athens: Estia.
İslam, T. (2010). Current Urban Discourse, Urban Transformation and Gentrification in Istanbul. *Architectural Design*, 80(1), 58–63.
Jackson, M. (1995). *At Home in the World*. Durham: Duke University Press.
Jackson, M. (2012). *Other Shore: Essays on Writers and Writing*. Berkeley: University of California Press.
Jaffe, R., & de Koning, A. (2016). *Introducing Urban Anthropology*. New York: Routledge.
James, W. (1997). The Names of Fear: Memory, History, and the Ethnography of Feeling among Uduk Refugees. *Journal of Royal Anthropological Institute*, 3, 115–131.
Janos, D. (2005). Panaiotis Nicousios and Alexander Mavrocordatos: The Rise of the Phanariots and the Office of Grand Dragoman in the Ottoman Administration in the Second Half of the Seventeenth Century. *Archivum Ottomanicum*, 23, 177–196.
Jansen, S. (2002). The Violence of Memories: Local Narratives of the Past after Ethnic Cleansing in Croatia. *Rethinking History*, 6(1), 77–93.
Jordi, J.-J. (1995). *1962: L'arrive des Pieds-Noirs*. Paris: Editions Autrement.
Jusdanis, G. (1991). *Belated Modernity and Aesthetic Culture: İnventing National Literature*. Minneapolis: University of Minnesota Press.
Kabutakapua, N. B. (2015). Community Support in Multicultural Neighborhoods: The Case of Tarlabasi. *Turkish Review*, 5(4), 298.

Kafadar, C. (2007). A Rome of One's Own: Reflections on Cultural Geography and Identity in the Lands of Rum. *Muqarnas Online*, *24*(1), 7–25.
Kamarados-Vizantios, G. (1980). *Ta Ellinika Tatavla*. Athens: Kamarados-Vizantiou.
Kamouzis, D. (2013). Elites and the Formation of National Identity: The Case of the Greek Orthodox *Millet* (Mid-Nineteenth Century to 1922). In B. Fortna, S. Katsikas, D. Kamouzis, & P. Konortas (Eds.), *State-Nationalisms in the Ottoman Empire, Greece and Turkey: Orthodox and Muslims, 1830–1945*. London: Routledge.
Kanbak, A. (2016). İstanbul Yedikule Bostanları: Bir Yeniden Üretim Pratiği. *Yaşam Bilimleri Dergisi*, *6*(1), 166–180.
Kasbarian, S. (2016). The Istanbul Armenians: Negotiating Co-existence. In R. Bryant (Ed.), *Post-Ottoman Coexistence: Sharing Space in the Shadow of Conflict*. Oxford: Berghahn Press.
Kaya, A. (2001a). *Constructing Diasporas: Turkish Diasporic Youth in Berlin*. Bielefeld: Transaction Publishers.
Kaya, Ç. (2001b). *Kızım Sen Gavur Musun?* İstanbul: Belge.
Kaya, A. (2004). Political Participation Strategies of the Circassian Diaspora in Turkey. *Mediterranean Politics*, *9*(2), 221–239.
Kaya, A. (2013). *Europeanization and Tolerance in Turkey: The Myth of Toleration*. London: Palgrave Macmillan.
Kearney, M. (1995). The Local and the Global: The Anthropology of Globalization and Transnationalism. *Annual Review of Anthropology*, *24*(1), 547–565.
Kechriotis, V. (2005). *The Greeks of Izmir at the End of the Empire: A Non-Muslim Ottoman Community between Autonomy and Patriotism*. Unpublished Ph.D. dissertation, University of Leiden, Germany.
Kendall, G., Woodward, I., & Skrbiš, Z. (2009). *The Sociology of Cosmopolitanism: Globalization, Identity, Culture and Government*. Basingstoke: Palgrave Macmillan.
Keyder, Ç. (2000). *İstanbul: Küresel ile yerel arasında*. İstanbul: Metis.
Keyder, Ç., Eyüp Özveren, Y., & Quataert, D. (1993). *Port-Cities of the Eastern Mediterranean 1800–1914*. Binghamton, NY: Binghamton U, Fernand Braudel Center.
King, R., Iosifides, T., & Myrivili, L. (1998). A Migrant's Story: From Albania to Athens. *Journal of Ethnic and Migration Studies*, *24*(1), 159–175.
Kırca, A. (2000). *Azınlıklar: Kaybolan Renkler*. İstanbul: Sabah.
Kirişçi, K. (2000). Disaggregating Turkish Citizenship and Immigration Practices. *Middle Eastern Studies*, *36*(3), 1–22.
Kirtsoglou, E., & Sistani, L. (2003). The Other Then, the Other Now, the Other Within: Stereotypical Images and Narrative Captions of the Turk in Northern and Central Greece. *Journal of Mediterranean Studies*, *13*(2), 189–213.

Kirtsoglou, E., & Theodossopoulos, D. (2001). Fading Memories, Flexible Identities: The Rhetoric about the Self and the Other in a Community of 'Christian' Refugees from Anatolia. *Journal of Mediterranean Studies, 11*(2), 395–415.
Kızılyürek, N. (2011). *Paşalar, Papazlar: Kıbrıs Ve Hegemonya.* İstanbul: Kalkedon Yayınları.
Kizos, T., et al. (2011). Survival Strategies of Farm Households and Multifunctional Farms in Greece. *The Geographical Journal, 177*(4), 335–346. https://doi.org/10.1111/j.1475-4959.2011.00403.x.
Kleinman, A., Das, V., & Lock, M. M. (1997). *Social Suffering.* Berkeley: University of California Press.
Kleist, J. O., & Glynn, I. (2012). *History, Memory and Migration: Perceptions of the Past and the Politics of Incorporation.* Houndmills, Basingstoke: Palgrave Macmillan.
Koçoğlu, Y. (2001). *Azınlık Gençleri Anlatıyor.* İstanbul: Metis.
Kokkonis-Lambropoulos, E., & Korres-Zografos, K. (1997). Greek Flags, Arms and Insignia. In E. Kokkonis & G. Tsiveriotis (Eds.), *In Memory of Panos Kokkonis* (pp. 47–51). Athens, Greece: Elias Coconis.
Kokot, W., Giordano, C., & Gandelsman-Trier, M. (2013). *Diaspora as a Resource: Comparative Studies in Strategies, Networks and Urban Space.* Vienna: LIT Verlag.
Koliopoulos, J. S., & Veremis, T. M. (2002). *Greece: A Modern Sequel.* New York: New York University Press.
Kolluoğlu, B., & Toksöz, M. (Eds.). (2010). *Cities of the Mediterranean: From the Ottomans to the Present Day.* London: I.B. Tauris.
Konstantinou-Kloukina, A. (2003). *Opou lipon… mia fora kai enan kairo stin Poli, 1949–1958.* Athens: Ikaros.
Kotzamanis, V. (1997). Athènes, 1848–1995. *Revue de Recherches Sociales, 92–93,* 3–30.
Koundouraki, D. (2002). *Min kles yiavri mou.* Athens: Trochalia.
Kouroupou, M., & Balta, E. (2001). *Ellinorthodoxes koinotites tis Kappadokias.* Athens: Center for Asia Minor Studies.
Kuyucu, T., & Ünsal, Ö. (2010). 'Urban Transformation' as State-Led Property Transfer: An Analysis of Two Cases of Urban Renewal in Istanbul. *Urban Studies, 47*(7), 1479–1499.
Lambek, M., & Antze, P. (1996). *Tense Past: Cultural Essays in Trauma and Memory.* New York: Routledge.
Lamont, M., & Aksartova, S. (2002). Ordinary Cosmopolitanisms Strategies for Bridging Racial Boundaries among Working-Class Men. *Theory, Culture & Society, 19*(4), 1–25.
Landau, J. M. (1981). *Pan-Turkism in Turkey: A Study of Irredentism.* Hamden, CT: Archon Books.

Lazaridis, G. (2000). Filipino and Albanian Women Migrant Workers in Greece: Multiple Layers of Oppression. In F. Anthias & G. Lazaridis (Eds.), *Gender and Migration in Southern Europe: Women on the Move* (pp. 26–34). Oxford: Berg.

Lefebvre, H. (1971). *Everyday Life in the Modern World*. New York: Harper and Row.

Lefebvre, H. (1991a). *Critique of Everyday Life*. London: Verso.

Lefebvre, H. (1991b). *The Production of Space*. Oxford, OX, UK: Blackwell.

Lefebvre, H. (2003). *The Urban Revolution*. Minneapolis: University of Minnesota Press.

Leontis, A. (1995). *Topographies of Hellenism: Mapping a Homeland*. Ithaca: Cornell.

Levi, M. (1999). *İstanbul bir Masaldı*. Istanbul: Remzi.

Liakos, A. (2004). Modern Greek Historiography (1974–2000). The Era of Tradition from Dictatorship to Democracy. In U. Brunnbauer (Ed.), *(Re) Writing History. Historiography in Southeast Europe after Socialism* (pp. 351–378). Münster: LIT Verlag.

Linklater, A. (1999). Cosmopolitan Citizenship. In K. Hutchings & R. Dannreuther (Eds.), *Cosmopolitan Citizenship* (pp. 35–59). New York: St. Martin's Press.

Löfgren, O. (1989). The Nationalization of Culture. *Ethnologia Europaea, 19*(1), 5–24.

Low, S. M. (1996). The Anthropology of Cities: Imagining and Theorizing the City. *Annual Review of Anthropology, 25*, 383–409.

Lowenthal, D. (1985). *The Past Is a Foreign Country*. Cambridge: Cambridge University Press.

Macar, E. (2002). *İstanbul'un Yok Olmuş İki Cemaati: Doğu Ritli Katolik Rumlar ve Bulgarlar*. Istanbul: İletişim.

Mackridge, P., & Yannakis, E. (Eds.). (1997). *Ourselves and Others: The Development of a Greek Macedonian Cultural Identity since 1912*. Oxford: Berg.

Madianou, M. (2005). Contested Communicative Spaces: Rethinking Identities, Boundaries and the Role of the Media among Turkish Speakers in Greece. *Journal of Ethnic and Migration Studies, 31*(3), 521–541.

Malkki, L. H. (1995). Refugees and Exile: From "Refugee Studies" to the National Order of Things. *Annual Review of Anthropology, 24*(1), 495–523.

Mandel, R. (2008). *Cosmopolitan Anxieties: Turkish Challenges to Citizenship and Belonging in Germany*. Durham: Duke University Press.

Mango, C. (1973). The Phanariots and the Byzantine Tradition. In R. Clogg (Ed.), *The Struggle for Greek Independence*. Hamden, CT: Archon Books.

Mann, V. B., Glick, T. F., & Dodds, J. D. (Eds.). (1992). *Convivencia: Jews, Muslims, and Christians in Medieval Spain*. New York: George Braziller.

Marcus, G. (1986). Contemporary Problems of Ethnography in the Modern World System. In J. Clifford & G. Marcus (Eds.), *Writing Culture: The Poetics*

and Politics of Ethnography (pp. 165–193). Berkeley: University of California Press.
Marcus, A. (1989). *The Middle East on the Eve of Modernity: Aleppo in the Eighteenth Century.* New York: Columbia University Press.
Marcus, G., & Fischer, M. M. J. (1986). *Anthropology as Cultural Critique: An Experimental Moment in the Human Sciences.* Chicago: Chicago University Press.
Margulies, R. (2009, June 17). Seçkinlere Teşekkür Ederim. *Taraf.*
Markaris, P. (2002). Introduction. In N. Valasiadis (Ed.), *Kai sta Tatavla Hioni.* Athens: Ekdoseis Gavrilidis.
Marovelli, B. (2014). 'Meat Smells Like Corpses': Sensory Perceptions in a Sicilian Urban Marketplace. *Urbanites, 7*(2), 21–38.
Massey, D. S. (1999). International Migration at the Dawn of the Twenty-First Century: The Role of the State. *Population and Development Review, 25*(2), 303–322.
Mattioli, F. (2012). Conflicting Conviviality: Ethnic Forms of Resistance to Border-Making at the Bottom of the US Embassy of Skopje, Macedonia. *Journal of Borderlands Studies, 27*(2), 185–198.
Maynes, M. J., Pierce, J. L., & Laslett, B. (2008). *Telling Stories: The Use of Personal Narratives in the Social Sciences and History.* Ithaca: Cornell University Press.
Mazower, M. (2004). The Strange Triumph of Human Rights, 1933–1950. *The Historical Journal, 47*(2), 379–398.
Mazower, M. (2005). *Salonica, City of Ghosts: Christians, Muslims, and Jews, 1430–1950.* New York: Alfred A. Knopf.
McCabe, I. B., Harlaftis, G., Minoglou, I. P., & Cohen, R. (2005). *Diaspora Entrepreneurial Networks: Four Centuries of History.* Oxford: Berg.
Mehta, P. B. (2000). Cosmopolitanism and the Circle of Reason. *Political Theory, 28*(5), 619–639.
Meijer, R. (2013). *Cosmopolitanism, Identity and Authenticity in the Middle East.* Surrey: Curzon.
Memişoğlu, F. (2013). The Legacy of the Nation-State Building Process: Minority Politics in Greece and Turkey. In J. D. Iglesias, N. Stojanović, & S. Weinblum (Eds.), *New Nation-States and National Minorities: A Comparative Perspective* (pp. 169–190). Essex: ECPR Press.
Migration Rights Group International (MRGI). (2016). *State of the World's Minorities and Indigenous Peoples 2016.* London: MRGI.
Millas, H. (2000). *Türk Romanı ve Öteki.* İstanbul: Sabancı Üniversitesi Yayınları.
Millas, I. (2001). *Eikones Ellinon Kai Tourkon Scholika Vivlia, Istoriografia, Logotechnia Kai Ethnika Stereotypa.* Athina: Ekdoseis Alexandreia.
Millas, A. (2006). *Pera: The Crossroads of Constantinople.* Athens: Troia/Militos.

Mills, A. (2005). Narratives in City Landscapes: Cultural Identity in Istanbul. *Geographical Review*, 95(3), 441–462. https://doi.org/10.1111/j.1931-0846.2005.tb00375.x.

Mills, A. (2010). *Streets of Memory: Landscape, Tolerance, and National Identity in Istanbul*. Athens: University of Georgia Press.

Mills, A. (2011). The Ottoman Legacy: Urban Geographies, National Imaginaries, and Global Discourses of Tolerance. *Comparative Studies of South Asia, Africa and the Middle East*, 31(1), 183–195.

Mills, A., Reilly, J. A., & Philliou, C. (2011). The Ottoman Empire from Present to Past: Memory and Ideology in Turkey and the Arab World. *Comparative Studies of South Asia, Africa and the Middle East*, 31(1), 133–136.

Mintz, S. W., & Du Bois, C. M. (2002). The Anthropology of Food and Eating. *Annual Review of Anthropology*, 31(1), 99–119.

Moore, S. F. (1987). Explaining the Present: Theoretical Dilemmas in Processual Ethnography. *American Ethnologist*, 14(4), 727–736.

Moskos, C. (1989). *Greek Americans: Struggle and Success*. Brunswick: Transaction.

Münz, R., & Ohliger, R. (1998). Long-Distance Citizens: Ethnic Germans and Their Immigrations to Germany. *European Forum*, European University Institute, Centre for Advanced Studies.

Naficy, H. (1991). Exile Discourse and Televisual Fethishization. *Quarterly Review of Film and Video*, 13(1–3), 85–116.

Navaro-Yashin, Y. (2002). *Faces of the State: Secularism and Public Life in Turkey*. Princeton: Princeton University Press.

Navaro-Yashin, Y. (2009). Affective Spaces, Melancholic Objects: Ruination and the Production of Anthropological Knowledge. *Journal of the Royal Anthropological Institute*, 15(1), 1–18.

Navaro-Yashin, Y. (2012). *The Make-Believe Space: Affective Geography in a Postwar Polity*. Durham, NC: Duke University Press.

Necipoğlu, N., Mark, R., & Çakmak, A. Ş. (Eds.). (1992). *Hagia Sophia from the Age of Justinian to the Present*. Cambridge: Cambridge University Press.

Nelson, K. (2007). *Young Minds in Social Worlds: Experience, Meaning, and Memory*. Cambridge: Harvard University Press.

Neyzi, L. (1999). *İstanbul'da Hatırlamak ve Unutmak: Birey, bellek, aidiyet*. İstanbul: Sabancı Üniversitesi Yayınları.

Neyzi, L. (2009). Eski İstanbul'un şehir kültürünü hatırlamak: Yaşanmışlıklar, bellek ve nostalji. In M. Güvenç (Ed.), *Eski İstanbullular, Yeni İstanbullular*. İstanbul: Osmanlı Bankası Arşivi.

Nowicka, M., & Vertovec, S. (2014). Comparing Convivialities: Dreams and Realities of Living-with-Difference. *European Journal of Cultural Studies*, 17(4), 341–356.

Okely, J., & Callaway, H. (1992). *Anthropology and Autobiography*. London: Routledge.

Ökte, F. (1951). *Varlık Vergisi Faciası*. İstanbul: Nebioğlu Yayınevi.
Öncü, A. (1999). Istanbulites and Others: The Cultural Cosmology of 'Middleness' in the Era of Neoliberalism. In Ç. Keyder (Ed.), *Istanbul between the Global and the Local*. New York: St. Martins.
Öncü, A. (2007). The Politics of Istanbul's Ottoman Heritage in the Era of Globalism: Refractions Through the Prism of a Theme Park. In B. Drieskens, F. Mermier, & H. Wimmen (Eds.), *Cities of the South: Citizenship and Exclusion in the 21st Century* (pp. 233–264). London, Beirut: Saqi Books.
Öncü, A. (2010). Narratives of Istanbul's Ottoman Heritage. In N. Diamandouros, T. Dragonas, & Ç. Keyder (Eds.), *Spatial Conceptions of the Nation: Modernizing Geographies in Greece and Turkey* (pp. 205–228). New York: Tauris.
Ong, A. (1996). Cultural Citizenship as Subject-Making. *Current Anthropology*, *37*(5), 737–762.
Oran, B. (2004). *Türkiye'de Azınlıklar: Kavramlar, Teori, Lozan, IÇ Mevzuat, IÇtihat, Uygulama*. Cağaloğlu, İstanbul: İletişim.
Örs, İ. R. (2002). Coffeehouses, Cosmopolitanism and Pluralizing Modernities in Istanbul. *Journal of Mediterranean Studies*, *12*(1), 119–145.
Örs, I. R. (2006). Beyond the Greek and Turkish Dichotomy: The Rum Polites of Istanbul and Athens. *South European Society and Politics*, *11*(1), 79–94 https://doi.org/10.1080/13608740500470349.
Örs, İ. R. (2014a). Cosmopolitanism, City Identity and Disconcerted Displacement: The Greek Orthodox Rum Polites of Istanbul and Athens. In D. Ş. Sert & D. K. Korfalı (Eds.), *Migration in Turkey: Changing Human Geography* (pp. 223–264). İstanbul: Isis.
Örs, İ. R. (2014b). Genie in the Bottle: Gezi Park, Taksim Square, and the Realignment of Democracy and Space in Turkey. *Philosophy & Social Criticism*, *40*(4–5), 489–498.
Örs, İ. R. (2018a). Cosmopolitan Nostalgia: Geographies, Histories, and Memories of the Greeks of Istanbul (Rum Polites). In N. F. Onar, S. Pearce, & F. Keyman (Eds.), *Istanbul: Living with Difference in a Global City*. (pp. 81–96). New Brunswick: Rutgers University Press.
Örs, İ. R. (2018b). Introduction. In İ. R. Örs, S. Akgonul, C. Aktar, & E. Macar (Eds.), *1964 Expulsions: A Turning Point in the Homogenization of Turkish Society*. Istanbul: Istanbul Bilgi University Press.
Örs, İ. R., & Turan, Ö. (2015). The Manner of Contention: Pluralism at Gezi. *Philosophy & Social Criticism*, *41*(4–5), 453–463.
Ortaylı, İ. (2004). *Ottoman Studies*. İstanbul: Bilgi University Press.
Ortner, S. (1995). Resistance and the Ethnographic Refusal. *Comparative Studies in Society and History*, *37*(1), 173–193.
Orum, A. M., & Chen, X. (2003). *The World of Cities: Places in Comparative and Historical Perspective*. Malden, MA: Blackwell Publishers.

Özil, A. (2016). *Anadolu Rumları: Osmanlı İmparatorluğu'nun Son Döneminde Millet Sistemini Yeniden Düşünmek*. İstanbul: Kitap Yayınevi.
Özkırımlı, U. (Ed.). (2014). *The Making of a Protest Movement in Turkey*. Basingstoke: Palgrave.
Özkırımlı, U., & Sofos, S. A. (2008). *Tormented by History: Nationalism in Greece and Turkey*. New York: Columbia University Press.
Özsüer, E. (2012). Türk-Yunan İlişkilerinde "Biz" ve "Öteki" Önyargılarının Dinamikleri. *Avrasya İncelemeleri Dergisi, I*(2), 269–309.
Özsüer, E. (2015). The "Other" Face of History: Re-comprehending History in the Example of Turkey and Greece. *Turkish History Education Journal, 4*(2), 165–201.
Özyürek, E. (2001). *Türkiye'nin Toplumsal Hafızası: Hatırladıklarıyla Ve Unuttuklarıyla*. Cağaloğlu, İstanbul: İletişim.
Özyürek, E. (2006). *Nostalgia for the Modern: State Secularism and Everyday Politics in Turkey*. Durham, NC: Duke University Press.
Özyürek, E. (2007). *The Politics of Public Memory in Turkey*. Syracuse, NY: Syracuse University Press.
Pamuk, O. (2005). *Istanbul: Memories and the City*. New York: Knopf.
Panourgia, N. (1995). *Fragments of Death, Fables of Identity: An Athenian Anthropography*. Madison: University of Wisconsin Press.
Papadopoulos, T. (1952). *Studies and Documents Relating to the History of the Greek Church and People under Turkish Domination*. Hampshire: Variorum.
Papailias, P. (2005). *Genres of Recollection: Archival Poetics and Modern Greece*. New York: Palgrave Macmillan.
Papastratis, T. O. (1998). *Eptalofou Bosporidos Odoioporia: Ellines, Armenoi, Tourkoi, Evraoi*. Athens: Irodotos.
Papastratis, T. O. (1994). *Stin Poli kai stin Thraki*. Athens: Risos.
Pardo, I. (1996). *Managing Existence in Naples: Morality, Action and Structure*. Cambridge: Cambridge University Press.
Pardo, I. (2011). Italian Rubbish: Elemental Issues of Citizenship and Governance. In I. Pardo & G. Prato (Eds.), *Citizenship and the Legitimacy of Governance: Anthropology in the Mediterranean Region* (pp. 25–46). London: Ashgate Publishers.
Pardo, I., & Prato, G. B. (2011). *Citizenship and the Legitimacy of Governance: Anthropology in the Mediterranean Region*. Burlington, VT: Ashgate.
Pardo, I., & Prato, G. B. (2012). *Anthropology in the City: Methodology and Theory*. Farnham: Ashgate.
Parla, A. (2009). Remembering across the Border: Postsocialist Nostalgia among Turkish Immigrants from Bulgaria. *American Ethnologist, 36*(4), 750–767.
Pentzopoulos, D. (1962). *The Balkan Exchange of Minorities and Its Impact upon Greece*. Paris: Mouton.

Petridou, E. (2001). *Milk Ties: A Commodity Chain Approach to Greek Culture.* Unpublished Ph.D. thesis, University of London.
Petridou, E., West, H. G., Paxson, H., Williams, J., Grasseni, C., & Cleary, S. (2012). Naming Cheese. *Food, Culture & Society, 15*(1), 7–41.
Petronoti, M. (1996). Greece as a Place for Refugees. In R. J. Kirin & M. Povrzanovic (Eds.), *War, Exile, Everyday Life: Cultural Perspectives* (pp. 98–112). Zagreb: Institute of Ethnology and Folklore Research.
Philliou, C. (2008). Communities on the Verge: Unraveling the Phanariot Ascendancy in Ottoman Governance. *Comparative Studies in Society and History, 51*(01), 151.
Philliou, C. (2010). *Biography of an Empire: Governing Ottomans in an Age of Revolution.* Berkeley, CA: University of California Press.
Pieke, F. (2000). Serendipity: Reflections on Fieldwork in China. In P. Dresch, W. James, & D. Parkin (Eds.), *Anthropologists in a Wider World: Essays on Field Research* (pp. 129–150). New York: Berghahn Books.
Pitzipios, I. G. (1858). *L'Orient. Les reformes de l'Empire Byzantin.* Paris: E. Dentu.
Portes, A. (2007). Migration, Development, and Segmented Assimilation: A Conceptual Review of the Evidence. *The Annals of the American Academy of Political and Social Science, 610*(1), 73–97.
Prato, G. B. (2009). Introduction – Beyond Multiculturalism: Anthropology at the Intersections between the Local, the National and the Global. In G. B. Prato (Ed.), *Beyond Multiculturalism: Views from Anthropology* (pp. 1–19). London: Routledge.
Prato, G. B., & Pardo, I. (2013). Urban Anthropology. *Urbanities, 3*(2), 80–110.
Psarakis, T. (1991). *Anthologio tis Konstantinoupolis.* Athens: Nea Synora.
Psimmenos, I. (2000). Making of Periphratic Spaces: The Case of Albanian Undocumented Female Migrants in the Sex Industry of Athens. In F. Anthias & G. Lazaridis (Eds.), *Gender and Migration in Southern Europe: Women on the Move.* Oxford: Berg.
Rabo, A. (2012). Conviviality and Conflict in Contemporary Aleppo. In A. N. Longva & A. Sofie (Eds.), *Religious Minorities in the Middle East: Domination, Self-Empowerment, Accommodation.* Leiden: Brill.
Raymond, A. (2002). *Cairo.* Cambridge: Harvard University Press.
Reed-Danahay, D. (1997). *Auto/Ethnography: Rewriting the Self and the Social.* Oxford: Berg.
Remennick, L. (2012). *Russian Jews on Three Continents: İdentity, Integration, and Conflict.* New Brunswick: Transaction Publishers.
Rivoal, I., & Salazar, N. (2013). Contemporary Ethnographic Practice and the Value of Serendipity. *Social Anthropology, 21*, 178–185.

Rodgers, R. (1993). A Batak Antiquarian Writes His Culture: Print Literacy and Social Thought in an Indonesian Society. In P. Benson (Ed.), *Anthropology and Literature* (pp. 89–106). Urbana: University of Illinois Press.

Rogers, A., & Vertovec, S. (1995). *The Urban Context: Ethnicity, Social Networks and Situational Analysis*. London: Berg.

Römhild, R. (1994). Staying or Leaving? Experiences and Expectations of the German Minority in the Former Soviet Union. *Anthropological Journal on European Cultures, 3*(1), 107–121.

Römhild, R. (1999). Home-Made Cleavages: Ethnonational Discourse, Diasporization, and the Politics of Germanness. *Anthropological Journal on European Cultures, 8*(1), 99–120.

Rosaldo, R. (1980). *Ilongot Headhunting, 1883–1974: A Study in Society and History*. Stanford: Stanford University Press.

Rossman, A., & Rubel, P. G. (Eds.). (2009). *Translating Cultures: Perspectives on Translation and Anthropology*. Oxford: Berg.

Rotenberg, R. (1992). *Time and Order in Metropolitan Vienna: A Seizure of Schedules*. Washington: Smithsonian Institution Press.

Rotenberg, R. (2002). The Metropolis and Everyday Life. In G. Gmelch & W. P. Zenner (Eds.), *Urban Life: Readings in the Anthropology of the City* (pp. 60–81). Chicago: Waveland Press.

Roth, P. A. (1989). Ethnography without Tears. *Current Anthropology, 30*(5), 555–569.

Roudometof, V. (1998). From Rum Millet to Greek Nation: Enlightenment, Secularization, and National Identity in Ottoman Balkan Society, 1453–1821. *Journal of Modern Greek Studies, 16*(1), 11–48.

Rouse, R. (1992). Making Sense of Settlement: Class Transformation, Cultural Struggle, and Transnationalism among Mexican Migrants in the United States. *Annals of the New York Academy of Sciences, 645*(1), 25–52.

Rovisco, M., & Nowicka, M. (2011). *The Ashgate Research Companion to Cosmopolitanism*. Farnham: Ashgate.

Safran, W. (1991). Diasporas in Modern Societies: Myths of Homeland and Return. *Diaspora: A Journal of Transnational Studies, 1*(1), 83–99.

Said, E. (1990). Third World Intellectuals and Metropolitan Culture. *Raritan, 9*(3), 27–50.

Sakızlıoğlu, N. B. (2007). *Impacts of Urban Renewal Policies: The Case of Tarlabaşı-Istanbul*. Unpublished Master thesis, METU, Ankara.

Saloutos, T. (1956). *They Remember America: The Story of the Repatriated Greek-Americans*. Berkeley: University of California Press.

Sanjek, R. (1990). Urban Anthropology in the 1980s: A World View. *Annual Review of Anthropology, 19*, 151–186.

Sapritsky, M. (2012). Negotiating Cosmopolitanism: Migration, Religious Education and Shifting Jewish Orientations in Post-Soviet Odessa. In

C. Humphrey & V. Skvirskaja (Eds.), *Post-Cosmopolitan Cities: Explorations of Urban Coexistence* (pp. 65–93). New York: Berghahn Books.
Sarris, N. (1996). Introduction. In N. G. Apostolidis (Ed.), *Anamniseis apo tin Konstantinoupoli*. Athens: Trochalia.
Sayad, A. (2004). *The Suffering of the Immigrant*. Cambridge, UK: Polity.
Saybaşılı, N. (2005). Tarlabaşı: 'Another World' in the City. In A. Franke (Ed.), *B-Zone: Becoming Europe and Beyond* (pp. 100–109). Berlin and Barcelona: KW Institute for Contemporary Art.
Scognamillo, G. (2009/1990). *Bir Levantenin Beyoğlu Anıları*. İstanbul: Metis Yayınları.
Secor, A. J. (2002). The Veil and Urban Space in Istanbul: Women's Dress, Mobility and Islamic Knowledge. *Gender, Place and Culture: A Journal of Feminist Geography, 9*(1), 5–22.
Secor, A. (2004). "There Is an Istanbul That Belongs to Me": Citizenship, Space, and Identity in the City. *Annals of the Association of American Geographers, 94*(2), 352–368.
Sema, S. (1994/1952). *Eski İstanbul'dan Hatıralar*. İstanbul: İletişim.
Sennett, R. (2002). Cosmopolitanism and the Social Experience of Cities. In S. Vertovec & R. Cohen (Eds.), *Conceiving Cosmopolitanism: Theory, Context, Practice*. Oxford: Oxford University Press.
Seremetakis, N. (1991). *The Last Word: Women, Death, and Divination in Inner Mani*. Chicago: University of Chicago Press.
Shaw, C., & Chase, M. (1989). *The Imagined Past: History and Nostalgia*. Manchester: Manchester University Press.
Sheffer, G. (2003). *Diaspora Politics: At Home Abroad*. Cambridge: Cambridge University Press.
Shryock, A. (1997a). *Off Stage/On Display: Intimacy and Ethnography in the Age of Public Culture*. Stanford: Stanford University Press.
Shryock, A. (1997b). *Nationalism and the Genealogical Imagination: Oral History and Textual Authority in Tribal Jordan*. Berkeley: University of California Press.
Silverman, S. (1975). *Three Bells of Civilization: The Life of an Italian Hill Town*. New York: Columbia University Press.
Silverstein, B. (2011). *Islam and Modernity in Turkey*. New York: Palgrave Macmillan.
Simalaridou, A. Z. (1992). *Vimata kai chromata stin Thriliki Eptalofo*. Athens: Sillogos Konstantinoupoliton.
Simaralidou, A. Z. (1994). *Vosporina Skitsa*. Athens.
Singerman, D., & Amar, P. (2006). *Cairo Cosmopolitan: Politics, Culture, and Urban Space in the New Globalized Middle East*. Cairo: American University in Cairo Press.

Skopotea, E. (1988). *To Prototipo Vasilio kai i Megali Idea: Opseis tou ethnikou problimatos. 1830–1880*. Athens: Polytypo.
Smith, M. P. (1992). Postmodernism, Urban Ethnography, and the New Social Space of Ethnic Identity. *Theory and Society*, 21(4), 493–531.
Smith, A. D. (1994). Ethnic Nationalism and the Plight of Minorities. *Journal of Refugee Studies*, 7(2–3), 186–198.
Smith, A. D. (1999). *Myths and Memories of the Nation*. Oxford: Oxford University Press.
Smith, M. P. (2001). *Transnational Urbanism: Locating Globalization*. Davis: University of California.
Somersan, S., & Kırca-Schroeder, S. (2007). Resisting Eviction: Sulukule Roma in Search of Right to Space and Place. *Anthropology of East Europe Review*, 25(2), 96–107.
Sotiriou, D. (1962). *Matomena Chomata*. Athens: Kedros.
Souliotis-Nikolaidis, A. (1984). *Organosis Konstantinoupoleos*. Athens: Dodoni.
Soysal, Y. N. (1994). *Limits of Citizenship: Migrants and Postnational Membership in Europe*. Chicago: University of Chicago Press.
Sözen, Z. (2000). *Fenerli Beyler: 110 Yılın Öyküsü 1711–1821*. Istanbul: Aybay.
Spataris, H. (2004). *Biz İstanbullular BÖyleyiz!: Fener'den Anılar*. Istanbul: Kitap.
Spyridakis, M. (2016). *The Liminal Worker: An Ethnography of Work, Unemployment and Precariousness in Contemporary Greece*. London and New York: Routledge.
Srinivas, T. (2013). Towards Cultural Translation: Rethinking the Dynamics of Religious Pluralism and Globalisation Through the Sathya Sai Movement. In R. Hefner, J. Hutchinson, S. Mels, & C. Timmermann (Eds.), *Religions in Movement: The Local and the Global in Contemporary Faith Traditions* (pp. 230–245). New York: Routledge.
Stamatopoulos, K. (1996). *H Teleftaia Analampi: H Konstantinoupolitiki Romiossioni sta Chronia 1948–1955*. Athina: Ekdoseis Domos.
Stathi, P. (1999). *19.Yüzyıl İstanbul'unda Gayrimüslimler*. Istanbul: Tarih Vakfı Yayınları.
Stathi, P. (2002). Romii stin ipiresia tis İpsilis Pilis. In *Praktika. 13 January 2001*. Athens: Eteria Meletis tis Kath 'imas Anatolis.
Stavlianos–Telis, T. (1995). *Glossario Konstantinoupolitikon Idiomaton Lekseon*. Athens.
Stavrou, T. (1940). *Mistikes Piges*. Athens: Nea Estia.
Stewart, C. (1991). *Demons and the Devil: Moral Imagination in Modern Greek Culture*. Princeton: Princeton University Press.
Stewart, S. (1993). *On Longing: Narratives of the Miniature, the Gigantic, the Souvenir, the Collection*. London: Duke University Press.
Stewart, K. (1998). Nostalgia – A Polemic. *Cultural Anthropology*, 3(3), 227–241.
Stock, F. (2010). Home and Memory. In K. Knott & S. McLoughlin (Eds.), *Diasporas: Concepts, Intersections, Identities* (pp. 24–28). New York: Zed Books.

Stokes, M. (1992). *The Arabesk Debate: Music and Musicians in Modern Turkey.* New York: Oxford University Press.
Strathern, M. (1991). *Partial Connections.* Savage, MD: Rowman & Littlefield.
Suarez-Navaz, L. (2004). *Rebordering the Nation: Boundaries and Citizenship in Southern Europe.* Oxford: Berghahn.
Susser, I., & Schneider, J. (2003). *Wounded Cities: Destruction and Reconstruction in a Globalized World.* Oxford: Berg.
Sutton, D. (1998). *Memories Cast in Stone.* Oxford: Berg.
Sutton, D. E. (2001). *Remembrance of Repasts: An Anthropology of Food and Memory.* Oxford: Berg.
Svolopoulos, K. (1994). *Konstantinoupoli, 1856–1908: H Akmi tou Ellinismou.* Athens: Ekdoseis Athinon.
Sylvester, Katherine M. (2010). *Public Participation and Urban Planning in Turkey: The Tarlabaşı Renewal Project.* Unpublished Ph.D. dissertation, University of Cincinnati.
Tanrıverdi, F. A. (2003). *Hoşçakal Prinkipo.* İstanbul: Literatür Arkapencere.
Tansuğ, F. (Ed.). (2012). *İmroz Rumları: Gökçeada Üzerine.* Istanbul: Heyamola.
Tanyeri-Erdemir, T. (2017). Remains of the Day: Converted Anatolian Churches. In S. Yalman & I. Jevtic (Eds.), *Spolia Reincarnated: ANAMED 10th Anniversary Symposium.* İstanbul: Koç University Press.
Theodossopoulos, D. (2003). Degrading Others and Honouring Ourselves: Ethnic Stereotypes as Categories and as Explanations. *Journal of Mediterranean Studies, 13*(2), 177–188.
Theodossopoulos, D. (2004). The Turks and Their Nation in the Worldview of Greeks in Patras. *History and Anthropology, 15*(1), 1–28. https://doi.org/10.1080/0275720042000191073.
Theodossopoulos, D. (2006). Introduction: The 'Turks' in the Imagination of the 'Greeks'. *South European Society & Politics, 11*(1), 1–32.
Theotokas, G. (1940). *Leonis.* Athens: Estia.
Todorova, M. (1997). *Imagining the Balkans.* New York: Oxford University Press.
Triandafyllidou, A. (2009). Greek Immigration Policy at the Turn of the 21st Century. Lack of Political Will or Purposeful Mismanagement? *European Journal of Migration and Law, 11*(2), 159–177.
Triandafyllidou, A., & Veikou, M. (2002). The Hierarchy of Greekness Ethnic and National Identity Considerations in Greek Immigration Policy. *Ethnicities, 2*(2), 189–208.
Trichopoulou, A., Costacou, T., Bamia, C., & Trichopoulos, D. (2003). Adherence to a Mediterranean Diet and Survival in a Greek Population. *New England Journal of Medicine, 348*(26), 2599–2608.
Tsilenis, S. (2002). Oramata Panselinou. *Kinsterna, 1–2,* 17.
Tsimouris, G. (2001). Reconstructing "Home" among the "Enemy": The Greeks of Gokseada (Imvros) after Lausanne. *Balkanologie, 5*(1–2), 257–289.

Tsitselikis, K. (2007). The Pending Modernisation of Islam in Greece: From Millet to Minority Status. *Südosteuropa Zeitschrift fir Gegenwartsforschung*, 55(4), 354.
Tsoukatou, E. (1999). *H "nihta ton kristallon" tou Ellinismou tis Polis*. Athens: Tsoukatou.
Turan, Z. (2011). Material Memories of the Ottoman Empire. In K. Phillips & G. Mitchell Reyes (Eds.), *Global Memoryscapes: Contesting Remembrance in a Transnational Age*. Tuscaloosa: University of Alabama Press.
Türker, O. (1999). *Mega Revma'dan Arnavutköy'e: Bir Boğaziçi Hikayesi*. İstanbul: Sel Yayıncılık.
Türker, O. (2000). *Galata'dan Karaköy'e: Bir Liman Hikayesi*. İstanbul: Sel Yayıncılık.
Türker, O. (2001). *Fanari'den Fener'e: Bir Haliç Hikayesi*. İstanbul: Sel Yayıncılık.
Türker, O. (2003). *Halki'den Heybeli'ye: Bir Ada Hikayesi*. İstanbul: Sel Yayıncılık.
Türker, O. (2004a). *Nihori'den Yeniköy'e: Bir Boğaz Köyünün Hikayesi*. İstanbul: Sel Yayıncılık.
Türker, O. (2004b). *Prinkipo'dan Büyükada'ya: Bir Prens Adasının Hikayesi*. İstanbul: Sel Yayıncılık.
Türker, O. (2006). *Therapia'dan Tarabya'ya: Boğaz'ın Diplomatlar Köyünün Hikayesi*. İstanbul: Sel Yayıncılık.
Türker, O. (2007). *Antigoni'den Burgaz'a: Küçük Bir Adanın Hikayesi*. İstanbul: Sel Yayıncılık.
Türker, O. (2008). *Halkidona'dan Kadıköy'e: Körler Ülkesinin Hikayesi*. İstanbul: Sel Yayıncılık.
Türker, O. (2010a). *Tatavla: Osmanlı İstanbulu'ndan Bir Köşe*. İstanbul: Sel Yayıncılık.
Türker, O. (2010b). *Psomatia'dan Samatya'ya: Bir Bizans Semtinin Hikayesi*. İstanbul: Sel Yayıncılık.
Türker, N. (2015). *"Vatanım Yok Memleketim Var" İstanbul Rumları: Mekan-Bellek-Ritüel*. İstanbul: İletişim.
Türker, O. (2016). *Pera'dan Beyoğlu'na: İstanbul'un Levanten ve Azınlık Semtinin Hikayesi*. İstanbul: Sel Yayıncılık.
Tziovas, D. (2009). *Greek Diaspora and Migration since 1700: Society, Politics and Culture*. Farnham: Ashgate.
Uysal, Ü. E. (2012). An Urban Social Movement Challenging Urban Regeneration: The Case of Sulukule, Istanbul. *Cities*, 29(1), 12–22.
Vaios, C. (1998). *Anthologia Konstantinoupoliton poiiton tou eikostou aiona*. Athens: Tsokatou.
Vaios, C. (2000). *H Konstantinoupoli diigetai... (Anthologia tou eikostou aiona)*. Athens: Tsoukatou.
Vaka, D. (2003/1923). *The Unveiled Ladies of Istanbul (Stamboul)*. Piscataway: Gorgias Press LLC.

Valasiadis, N. (2002). *Kai sta Tatavla Hioni*. Athens: Ekdoseis Gavrilidis.
Valášková, N., Uherek, Z., & Brouček, S. (1997). *Aliens or One's Own People: Czech Immigrants from the Ukraine in the Czech Republic*. Prague: Institute of Ethnology.
Van Andel, P. (1994). Anatomy of the Unsought Finding. Serendipity: Origin, History, Domains, Traditions, Appearances, Patterns and Programmability. *The British Journal for the Philosophy of Science, 45*(2), 631–648.
Van Hear, N. (1998). *New Diasporas*. London: UCL Press.
Vertovec, S. (2007). *New Directions in the Anthropology of Migration and Multiculturalism*. Oxford: Routledge.
Vizandios, S. (1850). *Konstantinoupolis*. Istanbul.
Volovonis, N. (1988). *Ithele na Ziso. Tourkoi, 1922–1945: Varvaroi olon ton Epochon*. Athens.
Voutira, E. A. (2006). Post-Soviet Diaspora Politics: The Case of the Soviet Greeks. *Journal of Modern Greek Studies, 24*(2), 379–414.
Warf, B. (2012). Nationalism, Cosmopolitanism, and Geographical Imaginations. *Geographical Review, 102*(3), 271–292.
Watson, C. W. (Ed.). (1999). *Being There: Fieldwork in Anthropology*. London: Pluto Press.
Werbner, P. (2002). The Place Which Is Diaspora: Citizenship, Religion and Gender in the Making of Chaordic Transnationalism. *Journal of Ethnic and Migration Studies, 28*(1), 119–133.
Werbner, P. (2008). *Anthropology and the New Cosmopolitanism: Rooted, Feminist and Vernacular Perspectives*. London: Berg.
Werbner, P. (2010). Complex Diasporas. In K. Knott & S. McLoughlin (Eds.), *Diasporas: Concepts, Intersections, Identities* (pp. 74–78). New York: Zed Books.
White, H. V. (1987). *The Content of the Form: Narrative Discourse and Historical Representation*. Baltimore: Johns Hopkins University Press.
Wimmer, A., & Schiller, N. G. (2002). Methodological Nationalism and Beyond: Nation-State Building, Migration and the Social Sciences. *Global Networks, 2*(4), 301–334.
Wohlgemut, E. (2009). *Romantic Cosmopolitanism*. Basingstoke: Palgrave Macmillan.
Yağcıoğlu, D. (2004). *From Deterioration to Improvement in Western Thrace, Greece: A Political Systems Analysis of a 'Traiadic' Ethnic Conflict*. Unpublished Ph.D. dissertation, George Mason University, Fairfax County.
Yasmeen, G. (2013). Not "From Scratch": Thai Food Systems and "Public Eating". In C. Counihan & P. van Esterik (Eds.), *Food and Culture: A Reader*. London: Routledge.
Yentürk, B. (2001). *Ne Lazım Tatavla'da Bakkal Dükkanı: Kurtuluş, Dolapdere, Feriköy, Bomonti*. İstanbul: Zvi-Geyik Yayınları.

Yerasimos, S. (1993). *Konstantiniyye ve Ayasofya Efsaneleri.* İstanbul: İletişim.
Yerasimos, S. (1996). *İstanbul, 1914–1923: Kaybolup Giden Bir Dünyanın Başkenti Ya Da Yaşlı İmparatorlukların Can Çekişmesi.* İstanbul: İletişim.
Yerasimos, S. (2000). *İstanbul: İmparatorluklar Başkenti.* İstanbul: Türkiye Ekonomik Ve Toplumsal Tarih Vakfı Yurt Yayınları.
Yiakoumaki, V. (2006). Local, Ethnic, and Rural Food: On the Emergence of Cultural Diversity and Its Integration in the European Union. *Journal of Modern Greek Studies, 24*(2), 415–445. https://doi.org/10.1353/mgs.2006.0030.
Yıldız, A. (2001). *Türk ulusal kimliğinin etno-seküler sınırları 1919–1938.* İstanbul: İletişim.
Yıldız, S., & Yücel, H. (2014). İstanbul'da ve İmroz'da Rum Olmak, Atina'da Rum Kalmak. *Alternatif Politika, 6*(2), 148–194.
Yorulmaz, A. (1994). *Ayvalık'ı Gezerken.* Ayvalık: Geylan Kitabevi.
Yücel, H. (Ed.). (2016). *Rum olmak, Rum kalmak.* Karaköy, İstanbul: İstos Yayın.
Zachariadis, N. (2014). *Lexiko tou Konstantinupolitikou Idiomatos.* Athens: Gavrilidis.
Zapheriou, N. (1947). *H Elliniki simea apo tin arheotita os simera.* Athens: Elefteri Skepsis.
Zarifis, G. (2002). *Oi Anamnisis mou: Enas kosmos pou efige.* Athens: Troxalia.
Zmegac, J. (2007). *Strangers Either Way: The Lives of Croatian Refugees in Their New Home.* Oxford: Berghahn.
Zolberg, A. R. (1983). The Formation of New States as a Refugee-Generating Process. *The Annals of the American Academy of Political and Social Science, 467*(1), 24–38.
Zubaida, S. (2000). Contested Nations: Iraq and the Assyrians. *Nations Nationalism, 6*(3), 363–382.
Zubaida, S. (2002). Middle Eastern Experiences of Cosmopolitanism. In S. Vertovec & R. Cohen (Eds.), *Conceiving Cosmopolitanism: Theory, Context, Practice.* Oxford: Oxford University Press.
Zubaida, S. (2010, July 20). Cosmopolitan Citizenship in the Middle East. *Open Democracy.* Retrieved from https://www.opendemocracy.net/sami-zubaida/cosmopolitan-citizenship-in-middle-east
Zürcher, E. J. (1998). *Turkey: A Modern History.* London: I.B. Tauris.

Index[1]

A

Aegean Sea, xiv
Agos, Armenian newspaper, 211
Akar, R., 32n19
Akgönül, S., 33n28, 120n26
AKP, governing party in Turkey, 210
Aksartova, S., 195
Aktar, A., 31n16, 32n19
Aktar, C., 181
Albania, Eastern European country, 99
Aleksiadis-Fanariotis, G., 191
Alevropoulos, F., 56
Alexander the Great, 77, 220, 221
Alexandris, A., 31n12, 31n15, 210
Alexiou, M., 121n35
Al-Rasheed, M., 30n8
Ambassador to Great Britain, x
Anagnostopoulou, S., 31n13, 121n30, 141
Anagnostou, D., 121n30
Anastassiadou, M., 31n13
Anastasiadou-Dumont, M., 33n28
Anatoli, 84, 153
Anatolians (Anadolulu), 2, 8, 143, 184
 See also Mikrasiates
Anatoli, Kath 'imas, Istanbulite researchers, 207
Andersson, R., 99, 117n1
Angé, O., 180, 188
Ankara, xvii
Antigoni/Burgaz, 175
Anti-minority policies, 186
Antiochians, 214
Apogevmatini newspaper, 215
Apostolidis, N. G., 74
Appadurai, A., 61, 120n28, 134
Appiah, A., 198n13
Arabesk, 183
Archibugi, D., 198n13
Armbruster, H., 192
Armenian, resident communities, 8
Armenians, xii, 186
Asia Minor, viii, 4, 45
Asia Minor refugees, in Greece, 99

[1]Note: Page numbers followed by 'n' refer to notes.

Asia Minor Rum, 80
Associations of Constantinopolitans, 111
Athenians, xxii, 8
Athens, xx
  and cosmopolitan knowledge, 41–65
Athlitiki Enosi Konstantinoupoliton (Athletic Union of Istanbulites) (AEK), 9
Atzemoglou, N., 118n11
Augustinos, G., 121n30
Ayasofya, *see* Hagia Sophia (Ayasofya)
Ayazma, *see* Ayiasma
Ayazma and ayiasma, 17, 118n11
  ritual act of purification, 118n11
Ayazpaşa, in Pera, 3
Aygen, Z., 197n6
Ayiasma
  Anatolian Rum (Mikrasiates), 80 (*see also* Anatolians (Anadolulu))
  holy water springs (ayazma), 17
Azak, U., 119n21

B

Babel language, xi
Babil Association, 166n5
Babül, E., 30n7
Baklava, 63n4
Balat, 175
Bali, R., 32n23, 165n3, 179, 181
Balkans, 117n1
Balkans war, xiv
Ballinger, P., 198n14
Baloukli hospital, xii
Balta, E., 29n5, 121n30
Bareilles, B., 32n24
Barkey, K., 31n13
Barth, F., 20
Barthes, R., 178

Beck, U., 198n13
Belle époque, 172
Belonging, 97
Benito, 89
Benlisoy, F., 30n10, 31n13, 33n31
Benlisoy, Y., 31n13
Ben-Yehoyada, N., 99, 117n1
Beriss, D., 33n30
Berliner, D., 180, 188
Bhabha, H., 120n28
Biner, Z. Ö., 197n1
Bir Tutam Baharat/A Touch of Spice, 166n10
  See also Politiki Kouzina
Black Sea, 52, 220
Bolshevik Revolution (1917), 32n25
Bolshohay, 111
Börek, pastry dish, 54
Borneman, J., 34n35
Bosphorus Strait, vii, 33n26, 52, 145, 221
Boulmetis, T., 142, 158
Bourdieu, P., 42
Boutique multiculturalism, 179
Boyer, D., 183
Boym, S., 177, 183
Brah, A., 120n26
Braziel, J. E., 120n27
Breckenridge, C. A., 198n13
British Trade Union (1838), xi
Brown, K. S., 165n1
Brubaker, R., 91
Bryant, R., 117n2
Burke, K., 27
Büyükada, 175
  See also Prinkipo/Büyükada
Byzantine Empire, xx, 29n2, 109, 192
Byzantion, viii
Byzantium, viii, 5

C

Çağaptay, S., 64n11, 119n21
Calothychos, V., 198n11
Calvino, I., 134
Cappadocians, *see*
    Karamanlides/Karamanli
Cassia, P. S., 117n3
Catholic priests, 211
Cavafy, C., 41
Cerrahoğlu, N., 186
Chalkousi, memoirs of, 94
Cheah, P., 198n13
Chelebi, E., 220
Christianity, viii
Christian Orthodox community, 6, 17, 25, 214
Christian Orthodox Roman citizen, ix
Christian Orthodoxy, 28n2, 110
Christidis, C., 141
Christou, A., 120n26, 121n30
Cihangir, 186
"Citizen, speak Turkish!" (*Vatandaş Türkçe konuş!*), 49
The City, 9, 110
Civilization, modern, 181
Civil war, in Syria, 212
Clark, B., 101
Clifford, J., 177, 198n11, 198n12
Clogg, R., 103
Coffee, 173
Cohen, A., 179
Coincidence as a method, 24
Commemoration, 149–152
Constantinople, viii, ix, xi
Constantinopolitan, 193
Constantinopolitan cosmopolitanism, 219
Constantinopolitan Greeks, Rum Polites, 3
Control sampling, 24
Conviviality, 78–79
Cosmopolitan, 196
Cosmopolitanism, 1, 88, 110, 174, 176–182, 184–186, 190, 193, 194
    emic meanings of, 193
    Fanar-style, 193
    immersive style of, 187, 188
    imperial, 185
    Istanbulite, 179, 193, 194
    memoires, stories of, 188–194
    methodological, 195
    Ottoman, 176
    Pera-style, 193
    reflexive style of, 188
    Rum Polites style, 194, 195
    sampling style of, 177
    Tatavlan, 193
    theories of, 194–196
Cosmopolitanist nostalgia, 174
Cosmopolitan knowledge, 9, 11, 42, 112, 163, 184, 191, 193
    everyday life in Athens and, 41–63
Cosmos, 194
Cowan, J. K., 64n12
Cultural citizenship, 95
Cultural identities, 1, 7, 8, 10, 12, 27, 33n29, 62, 97, 108, 110, 114, 116, 163
Cultural intimacy, 113–115
Cypriot Greeks, 70
Cypriot Rum, xviii
Cyprus, 70, 136–138, 140, 142, 148, 163
    civil clashes in, 137, 138
Cyprus events (1974), 7, 32n22
"Cyprus is Turkish" Association, 141, 142

D

Dardanelles Strait, 30n7
De Certeau, M., 11, 41
Deleon, J., 32n25
Demetriou, O., 120n26
Demir, H., 32n20
Depoliticization, xiii
Dhiki mas (our own), 91
Di Pascale, A., 99, 117n1
Diaspora of the City, 12
Diaspora (*xenitia*), 1, 9, 10, 12–14, 19, 83, 91, 98, 102–112, 117n1, 121n29, 164, 165, 192, 194, 197n10
Disemia, 11, 114
Distinction, 28
Do You Remember Fanari? (Aleksiadis-Fanariotis), 191–192
Dolma, 77, 118n7
Dora, V. D., 198n14
Double Memory (*Dipli Mnimi*), 151
Douglassian framework, 115
Dragonas, T., 165n1
Driessen, H., 16, 198n14
Dual citizenship, 92
Dumont, P., 33n28

E

Easter bread, *see* Politiko tsoureki
Ecumenical Federation of Polites, 83
Ecumenical Patriarchate, x, 5, 28n2, 31n16, 110
  See also Patriarchate
Eldem, E., 31n14
Elladites, xx, 8, 86, 154, 160, 165
Ellines tis Polis, 91
Emic, 13
Emigration of repatriating Greeks, 98
Eptalofos, 155
Erbil, L., 175–176

Eski İstanbul'dan Hatıralar (Memories from Old Istanbul), 175
Etereia Meletis tis Kath 'imas Anatolis (Etmelan), *see* Research Association of Our Own East
Ethnarch, x, 6
Ethnicity, 8, 9, 14, 19, 20, 28, 32n23, 73, 78, 79, 88, 92, 95–97, 101–103, 107, 110–112, 120n24, 135, 140–142, 153, 163–165, 172, 179, 193
Ethnographic fieldwork
  anthropological fieldwork, 21
  ethnography, 21
European Union (EU), 181, 182, 197n2, 211, 212
Events of 6–7 September 1955, 136, 137, 139, 149, 151, 153–155, 163, 164, 175, 178
  in Greek, 32n21
Exchange of population, xvi, xvii, 7, 29n5, 29n6, 30n7, 30n8, 99, 199n16
  See also Forced Exchange of Populations; Population exchange
Exclusive diversity, 8, 72, 112, 184
Exertzoglou, H., 31n13, 31n14
Exiles, 98
Expulsions (1964), 7, 32n20, 137, 162, 165n5

F

Fahmy, N., 198n14
Faliro, *see* Paleo Faliro
Fanar/Fanari/Fener, 25, 175, 186, 193
Fanariots, x, 4, 29n4, 31n15, 86, 193
  Fanariot families, 6
Fanar-style cosmopolitanism, 193

INDEX 257

Ferris, K., 105
Fine, R., 198n13
Fish, S., 179
Foggo, H., 197n7
Food, 18
Forced conscription, 165n3
Forced displacement, 98
Forced Exchange of Populations, xvi,
    xvii, 6, 7, 29n5, 29n6, 30n7,
    30n8, 92, 99, 199n16
  See also Exchange of population;
    Population exchange
Fortna, B. C., 120n26, 165n1
Foster, G. M., 33n32
Frappé, 33n34
  Turcophone Christian Orthodox,
    29n5
Fregenose, S., 198n14
Friese, H., 99, 117n1

G
Galata/Karaköy, 175, 186
Gavur, 3, 8, 145, 163
Geertz, C., 34n35
General Consulate of Greece, in
    Istanbul, 207
General Consul of Greece, in Istanbul,
    210
Geneva Convention (1951), 99
Genoans communities, 5
Gentrification, 187, 197n6, 197n8
German Athenian, 67
Gezi, 187
Gezi Protests, 212
Glass-doored *vitrin*, 69
Göçek, F. M., 165n3
Goitein, S. D. F., 109
Golden Dawn party, in Greece, 213
Golden Horn, 6
Gondicas, D., 31n13, 121n30
Goonewardena, K., 61

Graham, S., 198n14
Grand Rue du Pera, 172
The Great Catastrophe, 29n6
Greece
  migration in, 117n1
  citizenship of, 92
Greek communities, in diaspora, 12,
    103
Greek Consulate, in Pera, 216
Greek Cypriots, 104
Greek Easter bread, 64n13
  See also Easter bread; Politiko
    tsoureki
Greek irredentism, see Megali Idea,
    "the capital of dreams"
Greek passport, 93
Greeks, 134, 160
"Greeks outside Greece", 12, 103
Greeks rebellion, x
Greek-speakers, 214
Greek–Turkish relations, 7
  rapprochement, 182
Greene, M., 109
Grekoturkish, 95
Gunaris, B., 120n26
Gurbet, 108
Güven, D., 32n23

H
Hagia Sophia (Ayasofya), viii, 186,
    197n5
Hakan, A., 197n5
Halkidona/Kadıköy, 175
Halki/Heybeli, xii, 175
Hall, S., 120n28
Hamilakis, Y., 165n1
Hammoudi, A., 34n35, 120n28
Hannerz, U., 34n35, 120n27
Hanssen, J., 198n14
Haraway, D., 171
Harrell-Bond, B. E., 98

Harvey, D., 198n13
Hassiotis, I., 121n30
Hatziprokopiou, P., 120n27, 196
Hatzopoulos, V., 84
Held, D., 198n13
Hellenic Union of Istanbul (*Elliniki Enosi Konstantinopoleos*), 137
Hellenism, 142, 180
Herzfeld, M., 11, 113, 116, 118n10, 122n37, 165n1, 180, 198n11
Hoerder, D., 109
Holst-Warhaft, G., 121n30, 121n36
Holy water springs (ayazma), 17
Homeland, 13, 78, 84, 95, 100–102, 104–107, 112, 165, 171
Human smuggling, 99
Husry, K. S., 30n8

I
Identity, 194
Ilbert, R., 198n14
Ileri, S., 174
Illegal immigration, 98
Illegal migrants, 217
Imia/Kardak crisis, of 1996, 2
Immigrants, 67, 98
Immigration, *see* Migrants
Imperial cosmopolitanism, 185
Imvriotes, 4
  encounter interviews, 33n33
Imvriotes, Greek Orthodox residents, 30n7
Imvros (Gökçeada), *see* Imvriotes
Inflation, xiii
İnönü government, 32n20
Insider-outsider distinction, 163, 164
Iordanidou, M., 190
ISIS, extremist groups, 212
Islam, ix

Islamic call for prayer, 79
Islamists, 197n5
Issawi, C., 31n13, 121n30
Istanbul, xii, xiii, 2
Istanbul (journal), 181
Istanbul Biennale, 182
Istanbul Cuisine, *see* Politiki Kouzina
Istanbulistan, xxi
Istanbulite, 72
Istanbulite cosmopolitanism, 179, 193, 194
Istanbul/Konstantinoupoli (Poli), 171–196
  as 2010 European Capital of Culture, 181, 182
Istanbullu, 8
İstanbullu Rum in Turkish, 3
Istanbul: Memories and the City, 174
Istanbul Metropolitan Municipality, 197n4
Istanbul Rum community, 207
İstanbullu Rum, non-Muslim minority of, 91
Istos, publishing house, 216

J
Jackson, M., 198n14
James, W., 152
Janos, D., 31n15
Jewish, resident communities, 8
Jews, xii

K
Kabutakapua, N. B., 197n6
Kamouzis, D., 31n13
Kanbak, A., 197n8
Kapıcı, 166n8
Karamanli/Karamanlica language, 29n5, 80
  See also Karamanlides/Karamanli

Karamanlides/Karamanli, 4, 29n5, 150
Karamanli language, 80
Karamanlidika, 29n5
Kasbarian, S., 185
Kath 'imas Anatoli, 83, 103, 104
Kaymak, thick cream, 54
Kebap, 119n14
Kechriotis, V., 31n13
Kemal, M. (Turkey), xiv
Kemper, R. V., 33n32
Kendall, G., 177, 188, 195, 198n13
Kentsel dönüşüm (urban transformation), 187
See also Gentrification
Keyder, Ç., 198n14
King, R., 120n27, 121n30
Kinsterna, 75, 83, 135
Kırca-Schroder, S., 197n7
Kirişçi, K., 119n20
Kirtsoglou, E., 117n3
Koliou, K., 171
Kolluoğlu, B., 198n14
Konstantinou-Kloukina, A., 143, 192
Konstantinoupoli (Constantinople), *see* Istanbul/Konstantinoupoli (Poli)
Konstantinoupolites, Polites, xx
Rum Polites, 3
Konstantinoupolitiki omoyenia, 91
Koundouraki, D., 191
Kourides, 64n19
Kouroupou, M., 121n30
Kristallnacht, 140
kseni (outsiders, foreigners), 91
Kurdish Initiative, 212
Kurds, 64n19, 89, 120n24, 183, 184, 197n2
Kuyucu, T., 197n6
Kuzey Ormanlari Direnişi, 187

L
Labor camp, xviii
Lahmacun, 197n3
Laiki agora (the open-air farmers' market), 44
Lamont, M., 195
Language (*Chipriaka*), 2, 5, 8, 9, 19, 29n5, 30n8, 30n9, 48, 61, 78, 80, 88, 89, 97, 109, 120n25, 145, 147, 152, 163, 172, 173, 175, 178, 181
Lausanne, Treaty of, xii, 7, 29n6, 31n15, 91, 96, 106, 120n24
Lazaridis, G., 120n27
Lefebvre, H., 61
Leontis, A., 121n30
Levantine, 8, 32n24, 78
Levi, M., 179
Lifestyle (*düzen*), 218
Löfgren, O., 108
Lowenthal, D., 153
Loxandra, 55, 190
Lycee, Z., 165n4

M
Macar, E., 30n10, 30n11
Mackridge, P., 120n26
Maganda, 183
Malkki, L. H., 108
Marcus, G., 26, 198n11
Margulies, R., 179
Markaris, P., 142
Marmara, 52
Marmara Sea, 221
Martial Law, 212
Mass migration, xiii
Mazower, M., 198n14
Mediterranean cuisine, 63n7
Mediterranean Sea, 220
Mega Revma/Arnavutköy, xii, 175

Megali Idea, "the capital of dreams", 110, 121n36
Memişoğlu, F., 120n26
Memory (remembrance), xiv, xx, 1, 7, 12, 14, 16, 18, 33n33, 42, 44, 51, 53, 58, 59, 61, 62, 69–71, 75–77, 81, 88–90, 108, 111, 133–165, 172, 175–178, 189–192, 194, 196, 197n1
Methodological cosmopolitanism, 12
Methodological nationalism, 12
Metropolitan knowledge, 42
Migrants, 11, 183
Migrations, 15, 29n3, 30n7, 63n2, 67, 87, 98–101, 103, 105, 106, 117n1, 120n27, 138, 139, 208, 209
  rural-urban, 181
Mikrasiates, xxii, 4, 8, 29n6, 165
  See also Anatolians (Anadolulu)
Military coup, xiii
Millas, A., 165n1
Millet-i Rum, community, x
Millet, religious group, 96
Mills, A., 198n14
Minorities, 11, 96, 141, 143, 154, 157, 176, 178, 179, 181–186
  legal economic rights of, 186
  politics, 182
  rights, 185, 212
Montagu, Lady, 179
Moore, S. F., 149
Moskos, C., 121n30
Mousouros, S., 31n15
Mübadil, *see* Population exchange
Multicultural, 79
Multicultural coexistence, *see* Multiculturalism
Multiculturalism
  boutique, 179
  minority politics, 182
Multireligiosity, 79

Museumization, 182
Muslim Turk, xiii

N
Name day, 47
  yiorti, 55
National Geographic, 171
Nationalism, 6, 11, 12, 21, 27, 28, 74, 75, 90–95, 97, 104, 105, 109, 112, 114–116, 133, 134, 141, 142, 155, 165n1, 166n14, 182, 183, 185, 194
  methodological, 195
  ultranationalism, 163
Navaro-Yashin, Y., 117n4, 119n21, 197n1
Nea Demokratia party in Greece, 211
Necipoğlu, N., 197n5
Nelson, K., 197n5
Neo-Ottomanism, 185
Neos Kyklos Konstantinoupoliton, 150–151
Nihori/Yeniköy, 175
Nostalgia, 12, 158, 196
  cosmopolitanist, 174
Nostalgic stories
  critiques against, 177–180
  identification of, 180–186
  spatializing, 186–188
Nowicka, M., 198n13

O
O Ellinismos tis Konstantinoupolis (Hellenism of Istanbul), 44
Ökte, F., 32n19
Olive oil, 77
Olympic Games, 182
Omoyenia, 5, 119n17, 142, 166n7
Oran, B., 31n15

Örs, I. R., 31n14
Ortaköy, 186
Ottoman Empire, ix, 5, 6, 79, 96, 97, 185
 cosmopolitanism, 176
Ottoman modernization, 184
Ottoman society, x
Özil, A., 31n13
Özkırımlı-Sofos, 117n3
Özsüer, E., 165n1
Özyürek, E., 119n21, 197n1

P
Paleo Faliro, xxi, 2, 3, 9, 43, 87
Palimpsestation, 182
Pamuk, O., 174
Pangrati, in Central Athens, 24
Panourgia, N., 198n11
Panthessalonikeios Athlitikos Omilos Konstantinoupoliton, United Salonican Athletic Union of Istanbulites (PAOK), 9
Papadakis, Y., 117n3
Papailias, P., 64n8
Pardo. I., 33n32, 198n14
Paskalya çöreği, *see* Politiko tsoureki
Patisserie-café meetings, 18, 172
Patriarch, x, 143
Patriarchate, x, 5, 28n2, 31n16, 110
 Ecumenical, 5
Peace Maneuver, 32n22
Peleponnese, x
Penny-pinchers, 78
Pera/Beyoğlu, xi, xii, 139, 140, 148, 175
Pera-style cosmopolitanism, 193
Periptero (kiosk, newsagent), 24, 85
Petridou, E., 118n9
Philliou, C., 29n4, 31n15
Photiadis, J., 31n15
Polis, 194

Polites, 8
Political community, 16
Politika or *Romeika* language, 5, 146
Politiki Kouzina, 18, 45, 76, 94, 158, 159, 164, 166n10
Politiko tsoureki, 49, 50, 53, 64n13
Pontiacs, 80
Pope Benedict, 197n5
Pope John Paul II, 211
Population exchange, 92
 See also Exchange of population; Forced Exchange of Populations
Post-national citizenship, 108
Prato, G. B., 78, 198n14
Prince's Island (*Prinkipos*), 63n6, 77, 216
Prinkipo/Büyükada, 175
Prinkiponisso, 144
Professions of Minorities, restrictions on, 31n16
Progressivist
 generation of Rum Polites intellectuals, 82
 students (*oi proödheftiki fitites*), 83
Psimmenos, I., 121n27
Psomatia/Samatya, 175

R
Reflexive anthropology, 163
Reflexivity, 26
Refugees, xi, 11, 29n6, 68, 85, 98–100, 102, 117n1, 163, 166n13
Religion, 143, 163, 165
Rembetiko, 105, 121n30
Research Association of Our Own East, 83
Rogers, A., 33n32
Roman, x
Roman Empire, viii, 5, 16, 110

Romania, Eastern European country, 99
Romeika, see Politika or Romeika language
Romeos, x, 4
Romios, ix, 4
Rotenberg, R., 42, 62
Roth, P. A., 198n12
Roudometof, V., 31n13
Rovisco, M., 198n13
Rum, 137, 140, 141, 146, 148, 158, 173, 175, 176, 183, 186
Rum-Armenians, 5
Rum azınlık, 96
Rum communities, xviii, 3
Rum-Jews, 5
Rum-Levantines, 5
Rum millet, 6
Rum Polites, 3, 28n1, 41, 133–139, 141–144, 147–161, 163–165, 175–179, 182, 184, 186, 188–196
    ambiguity of class and status, 88
    cases of migrations, 98–102
    cenus records, 29n3
    class or status dimension, 87
    community affairs, 83–84
    Constantinopolitan Greeks, 91
    cuisine, 17–18
    diasporic developments, 102–108
    Ellines tis Polis, 91
    historians story, 15–18
    İstanbullu Rum, 3
    Konstantinoupolites, 3
    Konstantinoupolitiki omoyenia, 91
    literature, 64n10
    nation-states, categorization of, 90–95
    non-Muslim minority, in Turkish Republic, 5
    political undertaking in Athens, 84
    relations to Turks, 84–86
    religious minority in Turkey, 96–97
    Romeic–Hellenic, 4
    Romios, 4
    Rum Polites identity, 72
    social integration into Athenian society, 68
    socioeconomic standards, 85–86
    style cosmopolitanism, 194, 195
    transnationalism, experiences of, 108–116
Rum Polites community, 209
    Christianity state religion, 5
    history of, 5–7
    residence patterns, 87
    Rum Polites lifestyle (Konstantinoupolitiki zoi), 89–90
Rum Polites in Istanbul, 6
Rum millet (see Rum azınlık)
Rum School, in Galata, 216

S
Sakızlıoğlu, N. B., 197n6
Sampling
    control sampling, 24
Sanjek, R., 33n32
Sarris, N., 105
Sayad, A., 101
Saybaşılı, N., 197n6
Scognamillo, G., 32n24
Sea of Marmara, 47
Sea of Pontus, vii
Sea of Propontida, vii
Sema, S., 175
Sennett, R., 196
Sephardic Jewish, 109
September 1955, 7
    See also Septemvriana; 6–7
    September Events, in 1950s
Septemvriana, 32n21

Septemvriana 1955: The 'Night of Crystals' [Kristallnacht] for the Hellenism of the City, 148
Sheffer, G., 121n29
Shostak, M., 20
Sillogos Konstantinoupoliton, 150, 154
Silverstein, B., 119n21
Simaralidou, A. Z., 192
Sismanogleio, 209
Sismanogleio building, 216
6–7 September Events, in 1950s, 217
6-7 September Events/Septemvriana (1955), 136, 137, 139, 149, 151, 153–155, 163, 164, 175, 178
Smith, A. D., 121n29
Smyrnians, 80
Snowballing method, 23
Somersan, S., 197n7
Souvlaki, 57
Soviet Bloc countries, 98
Sözen, Z., 31n15
Special tax, 135
Srinivas, T., 33n30
St.George's Day (*Ayayorgi*), 216
Stathi, P., 31n13
Stavrou, T., 189
Stewart, K., 180
Stewart, S., 113
Stories of involvement, 162–165
Storytelling, 26
Strathern, M., 18
Student Union of Polites (*Fititiki Enosi Konstantinoupoliton*), 83
See also Progressivist, students (oi proödheftiki fitites)
Suffering, 12, 75, 81, 84, 85, 95, 98, 100, 101, 113, 117n1, 121n30, 133–165, 173, 181
  sharing, 152–158
Sulukule, 187
Süryani Assyrians, 4, 30n8

Sutton, D. E., 16, 33n30
Svolopoulos, Konstantinos, 31n14
Sylvester, K. M., 197n6
Synchrona Themata, 83
Syrian war, 217

T
Taksim Square, 187
Tansuğ, F., 30n7
Tanyeri-Erdemir, T., 197n5
Tarlabaşı, 187, 197n6
Tatavla/Kurtuluş, 144, 151, 175, 193
Tatavlan cosmopolitanism, 193
Taxpayers
  Greek Orthodox to Jewish, Armenian, Other Christian, Dönme, and Muslim, xviii
Tenedos (Bozcaada), 30n7
Theodossopoulos, D., 117n3, 165n1
Therapia/Tarabya, 175
Third Airport, 197n9
Third Bosphorus Bridge, 197n9
Toksöz, M., 198n14
Tolerance, 185
Tourkofilos, 74, 117n4
Tourkokratia, xx
Tourkosporoi, 163
Transborder citizenship, 108
Treaty of Lausanne, see Lausanne, Treaty of
Treaty of Sevres, xiv
Triada, Agia, 151
Tsilenis, S., 135
Tsimouris, G., 30n7
Tsitselikis, K., 119n20
Turan, Ç., 33n28
Turkey–Greece relations, 182
Turkification, 7, 32n23, 181, 182
Turkish Christians, 78
Turkish citizenship, 91–93
Turkish elections, 93

Turkish–Greek Aegean sea border, 99
Turkish Republic, 181
Turkish, resident communities, 8
Turkish troops, xiv
Turkogreek, 95
Turks, 133, 134, 142, 143, 149, 154
Turks 1922–1975. Barbarians of All Times, 148
20 Dolar, 20 Kilo, 165–166n5
Tziovas, D., 120n27, 121n30

U

Ultranationalism, 163
Ünsal, Ö., 197n6
Uprootings, 98
Urban anthropology, 20
Uysal, Ü. E., 197n7
Uzunoglou, N., 86

V

Vaios, C., 64n10
Vaka, D., 175
Valasiadis N., 144
Venetians communities, 5
Vertovec, S., 33n32, 184, 198n13
Violence, 133, 140, 141, 147, 153, 155, 156
Vosporina Skitsa (Sketches of the Bosphorus), 192
Voutira, E., 98
Voyvoda of Moldavia, x

W

Watson, C. W., 34n35
Wealth tax, xviii, 7, 32n19, 135–137
Werbner, P., 121n30, 219
White, H., 193
White Russians, 8, 32n25

White Turks, 184
World War I, xiv, 7, 96
World War II, xviii
Writing culture, 26

X

XE AEK, *see* Athlitiki Enosi Konstantinoupoliton (Athletic Union of Istanbulites) (AEK)
xenitia, *see* Gurbet

Y

Yahudi, *see* Jews
Yannakakis, I., 198n14
Yannakis, E., 120n26
Yasmeen, G., 33n30
Yayıncılık, S., 175
Yedikule, 187, 197n8
Yerasimos, S., 31n12, 31n14
Yerasimos, S., 220
Yiannis Papadakis, 117n4
Yıldız, A., 33n28
Yortu, *see* Name day
Yorulmaz, A., 32n24
Young Turks, xii
Yücel, H., 33n28
Yufka, pastry, 63n5
Yunan, in Greece, xviii
Yunanlılar, 160

Z

Zachariadis, N., 64n9
Zagrafeion, eminent schools, xii
Zappeion, eminent schools, xii
Zografeion High School, in Istanbul, 104
Zubaida, S., 30n8
Zürcher, E. J., 31n14

The manufacturer's authorised representative in the EU is Springer Nature Customer Service Centre GmbH, Europaplatz 3, 69115 Heidelberg, Germany. If you have any concerns regarding our products, please contact ProductSafety@springernature.com

Printed and bound by CPI Group (UK) Ltd, Croydon, CR0 4YY

23/03/2026

02076747-0007